IFIP Advances in Information and Communication Technology 549

Editor-in-Chief

IFIP – The International Federation for Information Processing

IFIP was founded in 1960 under the auspices of UNESCO, following the first World Computer Congress held in Paris the previous year. A federation for societies working in information processing, IFIP's aim is two-fold: to support information processing in the countries of its members and to encourage technology transfer to developing nations. As its mission statement clearly states:

IFIP is the global non-profit federation of societies of ICT professionals that aims at achieving a worldwide professional and socially responsible development and application of information and communication technologies.

IFIP is a non-profit-making organization, run almost solely by 2500 volunteers. It operates through a number of technical committees and working groups, which organize events and publications. IFIP's events range from large international open conferences to working conferences and local seminars.

The flagship event is the IFIP World Computer Congress, at which both invited and contributed papers are presented. Contributed papers are rigorously refereed and the rejection rate is high.

As with the Congress, participation in the open conferences is open to all and papers may be invited or submitted. Again, submitted papers are stringently refereed.

The working conferences are structured differently. They are usually run by a working group and attendance is generally smaller and occasionally by invitation only. Their purpose is to create an atmosphere conducive to innovation and development. Refereeing is also rigorous and papers are subjected to extensive group discussion.

Publications arising from IFIP events vary. The papers presented at the IFIP World Computer Congress and at open conferences are published as conference proceedings, while the results of the working conferences are often published as collections of selected and edited papers.

IFIP distinguishes three types of institutional membership: Country Representative Members, Members at Large, and Associate Members. The type of organization that can apply for membership is a wide variety and includes national or international societies of individual computer scientists/ICT professionals, associations or federations of such societies, government institutions/government related organizations, national or international research institutes or consortia, universities, academies of sciences, companies, national or international associations or federations of companies.

More information about this series at http://www.springer.com/series/6102

Christopher Leslie · Martin Schmitt (Eds.)

Histories of Computing in Eastern Europe

IFIP WG 9.7 International Workshop
on the History of Computing, HC 2018
Held at the 24th IFIP World Computer Congress, WCC 2018
Poznań, Poland, September 19–21, 2018
Revised Selected Papers

 Springer

Editors
Christopher Leslie
South China University of Technology
Guangzhou, China

Martin Schmitt
Leibniz Centre
for Contemporary History
Potsdam, Germany

ISSN 1868-4238   ISSN 1868-422X   (electronic)
IFIP Advances in Information and Communication Technology
ISBN 978-3-030-29159-4   ISBN 978-3-030-29160-0   (eBook)
https://doi.org/10.1007/978-3-030-29160-0

This Springer imprint is published by the registered company Springer Nature Switzerland AG
The registered company address is: Gewerbestrasse 11, 6330 Cham, Switzerland

Preface

Fig. 1. Monument to the Polish cryptographers Rejewski, Różycki, and Zygalski in Poznań.

Working Group 9.7 is proud to present this volume, which expands on and challenges current thinking in the history of computing. The genesis of this volume was our 2016 workshop in New York City. Given the location of the 24th IFIP World Congress in Poznań, Poland, in September 2018, we immediately set upon the idea of a workshop devoted to the history of computing in eastern Europe. After the close of the New York workshop, we collaborated on a call for papers and distributed it among our networks as well as to the listservs of relevant professional associations.

As has been our past practice, we required full papers for consideration, and then sent the papers through a rigorous revision process. Each paper was reviewed anonymously at least three times by our distinguished Program Committee, which consisted of a combination of Working Group members and outside experts. Conflicts among the reviewers were adjudicated by the volume editors.

In addition to these authors, we were joined at the Poznań University of Technology by members of the Polish Information Processing Society. Additionally, IFIP historian and WG 9.7 Roger Johnson organized a live, remote decoding of an Enigma message by the National Museum of Computing in Bletchley Park. This activity honored the work of three Polish cryptographers – Marian Rejewski, Jerzy Różycki, and Henryk Zygalski – toward reading Enigma messages in World War II. Comments from Dermot Turing, the nephew of Alan Turing, and Marek Grajek accompanied the "Enigma Live" session. Following the demonstration, delegates were taken on a tour of the Poznan Supercomputing and Networking Center, next door to the university. During breaks, delegates also had the opportunity to explore Poznań's old town and visit the site of the future cryptography museum and a 2007 monument to the Polish trio (Fig. 1).

The papers we selected reflect academic approaches to history along with the expertise of museum and other public history professionals as well as the experience of computing and information science practitioners. In this way, WG 9.7, along with the whole of Technical Committee 9, upholds our commitment to the synergies that come from bringing academics, technical professionals, curators, and others into a conversation about the history of computing. Revised papers were circulated to workshop participants in advance of the workshop. After presentations at the Poznań University of Technology, delegates provided feedback to authors for their consideration. Final revised papers were submitted for consideration in these proceedings.

The organization of the proceedings roughly follows the agenda of the workshop:

1. *Eastern Europe*. The papers in this section offer new glimpses into the history of computing in Armenia, Czechoslovakia, and Hungary. For instance, Szabo offers a compelling portrait of a computing class conducted with a chalkboard in Hungary.
2. *Poland*. These papers, whose authors did not respond to our original CFP, are included as invited papers because they were part of our collaboration with the Polish Information Processing Society and the Enigma Live event.
3. *Soviet Union*. A highlight of these papers is co-authored by the children of two great names in the USSR: Anatoly Kitov and Victor Glushkov. They challenge the notion that Soviet computer science was a failure because it did not result in an ARPA-style national network. Kitov also details his own work in the first article to discuss Soviet control programs that monitored data transfer between multiple terminals for collaborative work.
4. *CoCom and Comecon*. Sikora and Schmitt offer extended examinations of the permutations of the cold war blockades based on their archival research. My own paper, an outgrowth of my presentation to TC 9 in 2014 for the Turku Human Choice in Computing workshop, rounds out the group.
5. *Analog Computing*. We offer two papers about computing before digital computing. Leipälä, Shilov, and Silantiev also include a translation of the book they found in their appendix.
6. *Public History*. Bodrato, Caruso, and Cignoni demonstrate what insights can be gleaned by their project of collecting and reverse-engineering early hardware. Smolevitskaya offers not just an overview of an archive but has also painstakingly tallied Rameev's inventions, including the iterations of Ural computers.

We owe our thanks to the volunteers for our Program Committee, whose comments greatly improved our work and the world congress organizers, who resolved most of the logistical challenges for this workshop for us.

July 2019   Christopher Leslie

Organization

Workshop Chairs

Christopher Leslie   South China University of Technology, China
Martin Schmitt   Center for Contemporary History, Germany

Program Committee

Janet Abbate   Virginia Tech, USA
Barbara Ainsworth   Monash University, Australia
Gerard Alberts   University of Amsterdam, The Netherlands
Chris Avram   Monash University, Australia
Corrado Bonfanti   Italian Computer Society, Italy
Sandra Braman   Texas A&M University, USA
David Burger   Past Chair IEEE History Committee, Australia
Paul Ceruzzi   Smithsonian Institution, USA
Dean Chen   Ramapo College, USA
Giovanni Cignoni   HMR Project, Italy
Giovanni Cossu   Hyperborea srl, Italy
Helena Durnová   Masaryk University, Czech Republic
Lisa Gitelman   New York University, USA
David Alan Grier   George Washington University, USA
Daryl H. Hepting   University of Regina, Canada
Marek Hołyński   Polish Information Processing Society, Poland
Harold Lawson   Lawson Konsult AB, Sweden
Cezary Mazurek   Poznań University of Technology, Poland
Irina Nikivincze   Georgia Institute of Technology, USA
Petri Paju   University of Turku, Finland
Benjamin Peters   University of Tulsa, USA
Victor Petrov   University of Tennessee, Knoxville
Martin Schmitt   Centre for Contemporary History, Germany
Judy Sheard   Monash University, Australia
Valery Shilov   National Research University Higher School of Economics, Russia
Miroslaw Sikora   Institute of National Remembrance, Poland
Rebecca Slayton   Cornell University, USA
Jaroslav Švelch   Charles University, Czech Republic
Ksenia Tatarchenko   Singapore Management University
Arthur Tatnall   Victoria University, Melbourne, Australia
Janet Toland   Victoria University of Wellington, New Zealand

Contents

Analog Computing

Public History

Eastern Europe

Armenian Computers: First Generations

Sergey B. Oganjanyan[1], Valery V. Shilov[2(✉)],
and Sergey A. Silantiev[2]

[1] Moscow Aviation Institute (National Research University),
Moscow 121552, Russia
sbenog@yandex.ru
[2] National Research University Higher School of Economics,
Moscow 125319, Russia
{vshilov, ssilantiev}@hse.ru

Abstract. Armenia was one of the leading centers of Soviet electronic and computer industry. The first in the USSR semiconductor computer, Razdan-2, was designed and built in Armenia in 1960. Armenian computers of the Nairi series for a decade were one of the main calculating facilities of Soviet scientists and engineers. This article is about the first period of the development of Armenian computer technology.

Keywords: Yerevan Scientific Research Institute Of Mathematical Machines (YerNIIMM) · First generation computer · M-3 computer · Aragats · Razdan · Nairi

1 Introduction

After the end of the Second World War, the Armenian Soviet Socialist Republic began a rapid development of its industry, including electrotechnical branch. Large enterprises began to work in the capital of the Republic – Yerevan and other cities of Armenia. This caused the need of training highly qualified specialists in Armenian universities. Armenia did not have a rich raw material and energy base, so emphasis was made on training specialists in natural sciences. Several well-known Armenian scientists in the mid-1950s proposed to the Central Committee of the Communist Party of Armenia to develop a new scientific and technical direction for the Republic, focusing on electronics and computer technology. The party accepted the proposal and sent it to the Central Committee of the CPSU.

By that time, the Soviet leadership had already understood the important role of the computer technology and realized the necessity to liquidate the backlog in this field from the U.S. [1, 2]. The Armenian SSR became one of several regions of the USSR that were chosen to implement the program for the creation of big plants and scientific institutions for the development of computer technology. On 29 June 1956, Resolution No. 897 of the USSR Council of Ministers was adopted: "On the Organization in the Armenian SSR Research Institutes, R&D Bureaus and Instrument-Making Plants in the Structure of the Ministry of Instrument Making and Automation". In particular, it was prescribed to organize a research institute of mathematical machines in Yerevan and a research institute of automation in Kirovakan (now Vanadzor).

On 14 July 1956, the Yerevan Scientific Research Institute of Mathematical Machines (YerNIIMM) was established. The leading role in YerNIIMM activity was played by young mathematician Sergey Mergelyan (Fig. 1), who was appointed as the first head of the institute, and Bogdan Melik-Shakhnazarov was appointed as the chief engineer. Mergelyan (1928–2008) was an extraordinary person and a great scientist. He was the youngest Ph.D. in the history of the USSR (his degree was awarded at the age of 20), the youngest corresponding member of the USSR Academy of Sciences (since 1953 the title was awarded at the age of 24), and the youngest academician of Armenian Academy of Sciences (since 1956). Mergelyan's theorem, which gives the complete solution of the problem of approximation by polynomials, is recognized as classical. He also played outstanding role in the history of Armenian computing. A detailed story of his life is presented in [3, 4].

Fig. 1. Sergey Mergelyan.

In 1957, the Computing Center of the Armenian Academy of Sciences and the Yerevan State University was established. It was closely related with YerNIIMM. In the "YerNIIMM Statute" the main tasks were determined, including:

- carrying out research, theoretical and design work on the design of mathematical digital machines;
- manufacture of electronic digital computers (EDC);
- identification of the needs of the USSR national economy in EDC [5].

Divisions for the development and implementation of computer technology were organized. There were design department, department of automatic systems design, department of mathematical support and testing, subdivision of system analysis and design, electronic design, laboratory for testing of electronic devices and subdivision for working out technical documentation. In order to develop the electronic devices and computers, a special factory was organized in 1960 as a YerNIIMM subdivision. It produced and tested prototypes and formulated technological requirements before the equipment was transferred to serial production. This organization made it possible to achieve high efficiency, working jointly with many research institutes and factories within the framework of established cooperation. In 1961, the Electron factory was built in Yerevan for industrial assembly of computers.

YerNIIMM's first employees were graduates of the electrotechnical faculty of Yerevan Polytechnic Institute (YerPI), the physical-mathematical faculty of Yerevan State University (YerSU), and invited graduates from universities of Moscow, Leningrad and other cities of the USSR. Also, a group of scientists from YerPI and YerSU with a wide research experience was involved in the work (L. Grigoryan, A. Sagoyan, A. Edigaryan, M. Ayvazyan, R. Kazaryan, etc.).

2   The M-3 Computer: The First Experience

Starting from 1953, the development of the M-3 computer designed for engineering calculations was started under the leadership of Nikolay Matyukhin in Moscow at the Laboratory of electrical systems of the Energy Institute of the USSR Academy of Sciences (director: Isaak Bruk). This work was not included in the national plan and was conducted jointly with the All-Union Scientific Research Institute of Electromechanics (VNIIEM; director: Academician Andronik Iosifyan). For this reason, the project could have remained unrealized. However, Soviet scientists and engineers at that time had an acute shortage of computing facilities. Three organizations – Sergey Korolev's R&D bureau (the leading institution of the Soviet space launchers program), VNIIEM, and the Institute of Mathematics of the Academy of Sciences of the Armenian SSR – decided to produce three M-3 prototypes for their needs. The first prototype was produced in 1956, debugged, and at the end of the same year was presented to the State Commission. According to the memoirs of well-known engineer Boris Kagan, "State Commission… did not want to adopt the computer: they say, it was built illegally. But finally Commission had approved the project. But even in this case it was not possible for two years to solve a problem – to start serial production of M-3 computer".

The small-sized digital vacuum tube M-3 computer was intended for utilization at research institutes and R&D bureaus. The first exemplar was left in VNIIEM (Moscow) for testing, the second one was intended for the Yerevan Mathematical Institute of the Armenian Academy of Sciences, and the third for Sergey Korolev's R&D bureau. However, in 1956 YerNIIMM was founded and it was decided to send one M-3 computer there for test operation (see Fig. 2 for basic parameters of the M-3).

Element base	Semiconductor diodes and 774 vacuum tubes (including 43 tubes in power supplies)
Arithmetic	Signed fixed-point
Number of bits	30
Commands	Three-address
Arithmetic unit	Parallel
Execution of basic arithmetical operations	Addition: 60 μs Subtraction: 75–120 μs Multiplication: 1,900 μs Division: 2,000 μs
Primary storage	Magnetic drum with a parallel selection of 2048 capacity of 30-bit binary numbers
Average performance	30 operations per second (ops)
Power consumption	10 kW
Occupied area	About 3 square meters

Fig. 2. Parameters of the M-3 computer

In 1957–1958 at YerNIIMM under the leadership of B. Melik-Shakhnazarov, V. Rusanevich, and others, and with the participation of the staff of the Institute of Mechanics of the Academy of Sciences of Armenia (G. Ter-Mikaelyan, A. Pipinov, and others), in a very short time, modernization, assembly and adjustment of the M-3 computer was fulfilled. The modernization consisted in the introduction of new RAM on ferrite cores (1024 words). This allowed increasing the speed of the computer from 30 to 3000 ops.

The improved M-3 computer model in 1958 was transferred to the Institute of Power Engineering named after Krzhizhanovsky of the USSR Academy of Sciences for solving problems in the field of energy. This work became the first step of YerNIIMM in computer technology.

The M-3 served as a prototype for two industrial series of computers: Minsk and GOAR (later renamed to "Razdan"). Thus, the creation of the M-3 computer played crucial role in the development and production of electronic computers in Armenia and another Soviet Republic: Belarus. Moreover, the first Hungarian electronic computer (which was also named M-3) and the first Chinese electronic computer 103 were almost entirely made on the basis of Soviet M-3 computer specifications [6].

3   Further Developments

By 1960, the main directions of the YerNIIMM research were defined as following:

- development and implementation of small- and medium-sized computers;
- development of specialized computer systems and automated control systems for unique purposes [5].

Research was also carried out in the fields of electronics, computer architecture design, software and test support, automation, power supply and storage devices, etc.

Already in the years of 1958–1960, several computers of the first generation (on vacuum tubes) were developed in YerNIIMM: Aragats (chief designer: B. Khaikin), Razdan-1 (chief designer: E. Brusilovsky), and Yerevan (chief designer: M. Aivazyan). Several researchers from the programming department of the Institute of Mathematics of the Siberian Branch of the USSR Academy of Sciences (Novosibirsk) were sent to Yerevan to help their Armenian colleagues (team leader: A. Merenkov). Tests were successfully completed in May 1960. Thus, Aragats (Fig. 3), Razdan and Yerevan became the first Armenian computers.

Fig. 3. Aragats computer and disk drive cabinet.

The State Commission highly appreciated this work and recommended the small-scale production of the Aragats computer. A total of four these computers were produced. The main designers were V. Karapetyan, A. Kuchukyan, V. Chiganov, S. Mkrtchyan, L. Asoyan, V. Grechka, R. Arutynyan, V. Arustamyan, V. Meleshchenko, and some others. See Fig. 4 for the basic paramaters of this computer.

It is worthwhile to mention that Aragats computer was the first Soviet computer shipped abroad: one exemplar was delivered to Hungary.

At this stage, the first (vacuum tube) generation of computers, designed and produced in Armenia, was completed.

Arithmetic	Floating point
Numbers	42-bits binary
Commands	58 three-address
Range of represented numbers	$0.25 \times 10^{-28} \div 0.9 \times 10^{19}$
Execution time of basic operations	Addition: 11,800 ops
	Multiplication: 4,400 ops
	Division: 2,600 ops
Average performance	8,000 ops
RAM storage on ferrite cores	1,024 numbers
External storage on magnetic tape	Four blocks of 645,000 numbers each
External storage on a magnetic drum	Two blocks of 1,024 numbers each
Speed of information input from film photo-reading device	36 numbers per second
Output of calculation results to printer	20 numbers per second
Vacuum tubes	3,500
Synchronous power generator	220 V, frequency 50 Hz
Power consumption	30 kW (without cooling system)
Occupied area	40 square meters

Fig. 4. Main parameters of Aragats computer.

4   Razdan-2 and Razdan-3

In 1958–1960 in YerNIIMM was designed the first computer in the USSR, completely assembled on semiconductor devices (chief designer: E. Brusilovsky, Fig. 5). It was the universal small-size computer Razdan-2 (Fig. 6).

Fig. 5. E. Brusilovsky, Yu. Bostanjan, and B. Melik-Shakhnazarov (1959).

Fig. 6. The Razdan-2

The primary storage made on ferrite cores of this computer consisted of 3,777 words 36-bits. Access time was 24 μs. To expand the range of tasks that required more memory, the computer was provided with an external storage device – a magnetic tape drive. The capacity of external storage device was 120,000 numbers; reading speed was 2,000 numbers per second. The data input was from punched tape. I/O devices provided data input to the computer from a photo-reading device on perforated film at a speed of 35 numbers per second and output of the results of calculations to the printer at a speed of 20 numbers per second. Basic parameters of this computer are shown in Fig. 7.

Element base	Semiconductor devices; signed floating point arithmetic
Command structure	17 (basic) two-address commands, each with eight modifications
Number characteristics	36-bits binary Mantissa: 29 bits 5 digits Characteristic sign: 1 digit
Average performance	5,000 ops
Power supply	From a three-phase alternating current network with a voltage of 220/380 V, frequency of 50 Hz
Power consumption	About 3 kW
Temperature regime	From 10 to 25°C
Occupied area	20 square meters

Fig. 7. Main parameters of Razdan-2 computer.

Razdan-2 computers after modernization had been introduced in mass production since 1961, and in 1962 it was with great success exhibited at the Exhibition of Achievements of National Economy in Moscow. On the basis of the Razdan-2, the first mobile computing center for military purpose (1963–1968) was built in the USSR. In official documents the project was called as "Mobile computing center", or the "Platform" object [5].

In 1963, in order to effect the standardization of computer elements for the first time in the Soviet Union, the unified constructive complex "Magnesium" was developed based on the most advanced technologies at that time: semiconductor devices and printed wiring (chief designer: V. Karapetyan). The main ideas, design characteristics and technologies of Magnesium were laid in the basis of the Razdan-3 computer (Fig. 3) and some other computers. The Razdan-3 computer (1965; chief designer: V. Rusanevich) had an average performance of 15,000–20,000 ops and 32 kB of main storage [7]. This computer was recognized as one of the most advanced Soviet computers of the second generation and became one of the first exported Soviet computers. Its production was organized at the experimental YerNIIMM and at the Electron factory.

Fig. 8. The Razdan-3 computer.

Less known are other developments of the YerNIIMM second-generation computers – Araks (1964, Fig. 9), Masis (1965, Fig. 10), [8] and Dvin (1967).

Fig. 9. The Arax computer.

Fig. 10. The Masis computer.

5 Nairi and Nairi-2

Especially it is worthwhile to mention the most known, mass-produced small computers of the Nairi series: Nairi, Nairi-2, Nairi-3, Nairi-3-1, Nairi-3-2, Nairi-3-3. (The name comes from ancient Armenian territory, which the Assyrians in the second millennium BC called the "country of Nairi", that is, a "country of rivers").

The development of the first and second models of the Nairi computer was carried out in 1962–1964. It became the first widely used Soviet small computer. The specific characteristics of Nairi computers, which are very similar to main features of modern PCs, were simple maintenance, reduced dimensions, high reliability, and, most importantly, easy learning for specialists in any field of science and technology.

The designer of these computers was Grachya Ovsepyan (born in 1933) (Fig. 11). In 1946, he and his family immigrated to Armenia from Lebanon. Ovsepyan graduated from Faculty of Physics of the Yerevan State University and then with great difficulty got the position of a laboratory assistant in recently organized classified YerNIIMM institute. He worked at the department of E. Brusilovsky, who developed the Razdan computer (the dramatic fate of G. Ovsepyan is described in [9, 10]).

In 1962 at the International computer exhibition in Moscow, Soviet leaders became acquainted with the French CAB-500 transistor computer. They were so impressed that decided to create a similar computer in the USSR. By this time, Ovsepyan's authority was so great that this work – and in fact development the computer of a new class, the small computer – was assigned to him.

Ovsepyan could not accept the demands of the Ministry of Instrument Making to develop a computer fully similar to French CAB-500. He clearly understood that the existing technologies in the USSR would not allow this. He decided to compensate for the technological deficiencies with the originality of technical solutions. Ovsepyan decided to use the microprogram control principle, and its implementation was completely original. Perhaps the lack of technologies played a certain positive role, forcing the developers of Nairi to go their own way.

Fig. 11. Grachya Ovsepyan (1957).

In the technical specification of his computer, Ovsepyan provided the following princ_ples:

1. The computer must be of parallel operation, i.e., when performing arithmetic operations, all the digits of a number should be read at once (not bitwise reading, as in computers of sequential operation).
2. The microprogram control principle should be used in construction.
3. Programs and microprograms are stored in a permanent memory of a large volume, implemented on removable cassettes.
4. For the arithmetic logic unit (ALU), a unified universal adder register should be used, which is also a buffer register for the main storage and external devices.
5. For the auxiliary registers of ALU and the control device, eight fixed memory cells with direct micro-command access should be used.
6. There should be a micro-program simulation of existing computers software.
7. Additional special microprogram and microcommand means should be developed fcr the implementation of special task algorithms.

Fundamentally new circuit designs and advanced software aimed at solving engineering problems arising in engineering practice allowed Ovsepyan to form the basic architecture of the whole Nairi family of small computers, which was patented in many counries. The Nairi (Fig. 12) has become one of the most widespread small computers in the USSR, which found wide application in industry, research and higher educationa_ institutions. Let us consider some of the patented solutions.

Fig. 12. Nairi computer.

For the first time for small computers in the early 1960s, a 36-bit processor architecture was proposed. It used also an arithmetic unit of a parallel type with through bit carry executed arithmetic and logical operations on numbers and commands. It consisted of one 36-bit universal register-adder. Groups of fixed cells of computer random access memory were used as the additional registers. For each fixed cell, the micro-operations of reading and writing were determined, which ensured independence of entire memory cycle and a great increase in performance. The performance of Nairi for fixed-point numbers addition was 2,000–3,000 ops, for fixed-point numbers multiplication 100 ops, and for operations on floating-point numbers 100 ops [11].

Cassette type long-term memory (8 cassettes with a total capacity of 16,384 words) became a fundamentally new feature of computer architecture. It was used for two purposes: for organization of microprograms memory and for storing the built-in software. The choice of address for reading the necessary information was performed by decoder. The necessary length of micro-commands (72 bits) was provided by simultaneous reading of information from two cassettes. The rest of capacity (14,000, 36-bit words) was allocated for the storage of compilers from Assembler and BASIC languages, software packages for solving differential equations, linear algebra tasks, programs for direct calculation of various arithmetic expressions in interactive mode, programs for control of typewriter and punch tape I/O device, for charts and diagrams plotting. Part of the memory was designated for technological programs for testing all units both during computer manufacturing and operation. The memory cycle time (12 µs) made it possible to realize the entire range of tasks with time characteristics better than foreign small computers where magnetic drums were used as software storage devices.

Starting in 1964, the computer was manufactured at two factories: in Armenia and at Kazan computer factory. More than 600 computers were produced for the period from 1964 to 1970.

The most distinctive features of Nairi were shown at the jubilee International Leipzig Fair in spring of 1965 where small computers of various firms and countries were presented, such as England's ICL, France's Bull, Germany's Zuse, etc. The Nairi was the only microprogram 36-bit computer, which provided high performance and increased accuracy of calculations (other computers were 8 and 16 bits). The Nairi outperformed the competition because software was stored in a long-term storage device while in other computers it was stored in external devices such as a magnetic drum.

There were several varieties of Nairi:

- Nairi-M (1965) differed from the basic model by the set of external units (the punched tape input device FS-1500 was produced in Czechoslovakia and the output punched tape device PL-80 at Kazan typewriter factory);
- Nairi-S (1967) had a "Consul-254" electrified typewriter with a thyristor block developed at Kazan factory;
- Nairi-K (1967) differed from Nairi-S by memory capacity (it was increased up to 4,096 words).

The next model of the Nairi computer family was Nairi-2, developed in 1966. It is essentially a modification of the Nairi computer. The main characteristics of this computer were the increased capacity of RAM, utilization of more productive I/O devices and improved design solutions. It had memory on ferrite cores (10 thousand cores of 2 mm diameter in each block of 20×20 cm dimension). A long-term memory on the magnetic drum was also developed.

The Nairi-2 computer became the last computer of the second generation developed in Armenia. Nairi-3 (1970), realized on hybrid integrated circuits, belonged already to the third generation. This computer together with other computers of third generation, designed by Armenian scientists and engineers, deserves the separate consideration.

6 Conclusion

Armenian computers contributed significantly to the development of electronics and computer technology in the USSR. Along with computers of the Ural and Minsk series, they formed the basis of national computing in 1960–1970s.

The Armenian Soviet Socialist Republic, having passed through all the stages of the world practice in the development of computer technology, became one of the leading centers in the USSR for developing computer hardware and software systems. Armenian computers contributed significantly to the development of electronics and computer technology in the USSR. Along with computers of the Ural and Minsk series, they formed the basis of national computing in 1960–1970s.

In the modern world, the next technological revolution is taking place, the transition from a post-industrial society to an information society. Armenia does not have a rich raw material and energy base and can ensure a deserving position on the international labor market only by participating in the production of certain demanded computer and information technologies. The development of computer technology and radio-electronics in the period from 1956 to 1988 allowed Armenia to achieve significant success in the development of science, education, and industry. Today in the country, there are strong scientific schools in the field of computer technologies, universities still training good specialists. The historical experience of the formation and development of the Armenian computer technology shows that if these factors are present, the country can successfully reach the leading position in the IT industry, which will lead to a general rise of its economy. Thus, it is important to learn such the experience, part of which is presented in this paper.

References

1. Krayneva, I.A., Pivovarov, N.Yu., Shilov, V.V.: Development of Soviet science and technology policy in the field of computer hardware and programming (late 1940s – mid 1950s). Ideas Ideals **3**(29), 118–135 (2016). (in Russian). https://doi.org/10.17212/2075-0862-2016-3.1-118-135
2. Krayneva, I.A., Pivovarov, N.Yu., Shilov, V.V.: Soviet computer engineering in the context of economy, education and ideology (late 1940-s – mid 1950-s). Ideas Ideals **4**(30), 135–155 (2016). (in Russian). https://doi.org/10.17212/2075-0862-2016-4.1-135-155
3. Apoyan, G.G.: Essay on mathematician and not just about him. Boston Independent almanac "Swan", 438, 459, 485, 499 (2005–2006). http://lebed.com. Accessed 12 Nov 2018. (in Russian)
4. Oganjanyan, S.B., Silantiev, S.A.: Sergey Mergelyan: triumph and tragedy. In: 2017 Forth International Conference "Computer Technology in Russia and in the Former Soviet Union" SoRuCom 2017, pp. 8–12. IEEE Computer Society (2017). https://doi.org/10.1109/sorucom.2017.00008
5. Oganjanyan, S.B.: Electronics and informatics development in armenian SSR (1960–1988). In: III International Conference SoRuCom-2014, pp. 40–44. IEEE Computer Society (2014). https://doi.org/10.1109/sorucom.2014.16
6. Kovács, G., Shilov, V.V.: M-3: towards the history of the first generation computer. Inf. Technol. **12**(184), 64–73 (2011). (in Russian)
7. "Razdan-3" universal digital computer. Main technical parameters. Yerevan (1965). (in Russian)
8. "Masis-1" digital computer. Brief technical description. Yerevan (1965). (in Russian)
9. Apoyan, G.G.: Nairi: the triumph and drama. Boston Independent almanac "Swan", 355 (2003). http://lebed.com/2003/art3598.htm. Accessed 12 Nov 2018. (in Russian)
10. Oganjanyan, S.B., Silantiev S.A.: "Nairi" computer series – harbingers of the personal computer. In: 2017 Forth International Conference "Computer Technology in Russia and in the Former Soviet Union" SoRuCom 2017, pp. 44–47. IEEE Computer Society (2017)
11. "Nairi". Brief technical description. Yerevan (1964). (in Russian)

The Emergence of Computing Disciplines in Communist Czechoslovakia: What's in a (Sovietized) Name?

Michal Doležel$^{(\boxtimes)}$ (ID) and Zdeněk Smutný (ID)

Faculty of Informatics and Statistics, University of Economics, Prague,
W. Churchill Sq. 4, 130 67 Prague, Czech Republic
{michal.dolezel,zdenek.smutny}@vse.cz

Abstract. Drawing upon archival evidence from the Czechoslovak government and its ministries from the 1970s, this paper presents a preliminary snapshot of the institutional processes that drove the emergence of computing disciplines separate from the rubric of Soviet cybernetics in Communist Czechoslovakia (nowadays, the Czech Republic and the Slovak Republic). We show that the new disciplines were created by a top-down order of the Czechoslovak government, which, in turn, was motivated by a larger scale initiative in the East Bloc. The disciplines created in the 1970s were as follows: *Numerical Mathematics* for an area of education akin to computer science, *Electronic Computers* for an area of education akin to computer engineering, and *Automated Management/Control Systems* for applied computing education. The evidence suggests that the cybernetics metaphor lost its organizing power in 1973 over the broad field of information processing in Czechoslovakia. This disciplinary shift, albeit not immediate, redistributed power between cybernetics and informatics. Indeed, it appears that even nowadays the distribution of power between the two disciplines in the Czech Republic is still in negotiation; what we term a "residual drift" has continued for almost 50 years as an impressive afterglow of the past fame of cybernetics in the east. In sum, the paper raises awareness of the fact that the emergence of computing disciplines behind the Iron Curtain was very different from the West. It also suggests that while academic research analogous to computer science thrived, other computing disciplines in Czechoslovakia were in more complicated positions. Although this paper focuses on Czechoslovakia, the method is generalizable and the data on enrollments may be compared to other countries. Thus, we provide a framework for the further study of similar disciplinary efforts in the remaining East Bloc countries.

Keywords: Comecon · CMEA · History of computing · History of informatics · Institutionalization · Scientific community · Soviet cybernetics · Sovietization

Juliet.

> *What's in a name? That which we call a rose*
> *By any other name would smell as sweet.*

While obviously paraphrasing Shakespeare, the subtitle of this paper also makes reference to a section title in Coy's seminal paper on the definition of informatics in Germany [1].

Published by Springer Nature Switzerland AG 2019
C. Leslie and M. Schmitt (Eds.): HC 2018, IFIP AICT 549, pp. 16–39, 2019.
https://doi.org/10.1007/978-3-030-29160-0_2

1 Introduction

Academic disciplines in the area of computing are known under various names that reflect their focus, historical development, and regional specifics. For example. the very same topic may be researched in an U.S.-based department of computer science and a Europe-based department of informatics [1]. In applied fields such as information systems, this is even more diverse [2]. Although the development of computing disciplines represents an important aspect of the history of computing, little effort has been put into mapping the disciplinary histories of Central and East European computing so far. Specifically in this geographic region, such histories are intertwined with the histories of Soviet-originated cybernetics [3]. During the 1960s and 1970s, cybernetics – as a powerful "umbrella science"[1] – combined several computing fields in the East Bloc (i.e., the Soviet Union and its satellites), while their disciplinary cousins emerged as partly or completely separate domains in the capitalist west (i.e., the United States and Western Europe). Later, as this paper shows, some computing fields were given a certain level of autonomy in the east.

This paper contributes to a better understanding of the idiosyncrasies connected with the rise [4] and fall of cybernetics in the East Bloc. Driven by the commitment to building a gigantic, automated socio-technical system in the East Bloc countries [3, 5], a significant change in the disciplinary landscape occurred in Czechoslovakia in 1973. The present paper suggests that 1973 can be seen as a turning point when cybernetics lost its monopoly over the problems of control and computing in this country, being regarded as "too broad" and thus unable to cope with upcoming challenges. This resonates with Gerovitch's [3] observation that during the 1970s the popularity of cybernetics was already in decline in the Soviet Union. However, a topic not covered in Gerovitch's work is the role of a broader East Bloc initiative that caused a similar disciplinary shift in the remaining East Bloc countries. Our intention is to connect this initiative with tangible disciplinary changes observable in Czechoslovakia during the 1970s.

Currently, our perspective is limited because this paper reports on an ongoing research effort. Specifically, our aim here is to provide a bird's eye view of the disciplinary landscape of Czechoslovak computing disciplines in the 1960s and 1970s. In our subsequent research, this view will be possibly expanded into a geography-based perspective similar to the one presented in [6]. The underpinning philosophy that drives our current macro view is inspired by the perspective of the sociology of science. In that regard, we propose to view concrete disciplines as "amoebas putting out pseudopods as they move in a multidimensional intellectual space" [7]. In taking such a view, it is imperative to recognize the essential role of institutional structures and forces. However, we admit that only a part of the story can be told here. This is mostly due to the fact that our current research has concentrated primarily on governmental archival sources. Thus, it largely omits the perspective of individual thought leaders and professional organizations (e.g., [8]). Nonetheless, we do not view this as a major

---

[1] Reflecting on cybernetics prominent position, Arbib [4] labelled cybernetics during the 1960s even more expressively – as "the superscience of the Soviet Union".

detriment, given that in Communist regimes, the influence of both groups was often limited. This was due to the fact that state administration structures were frequently at the center of decision-making power, instead of academic disciplines as it was in the west. Such a configuration clearly prioritized the ideology of the ruling Communist party over self-governing professionalism [9].

Conceptually, it is also important to emphasize that while this paper may at first sight appear as a taxonomy exercise focused only on Czechoslovakia, it rather aims to offer definite knowledge that should be generalizable beyond this particular context. By doing so, it lays important grounds for the further study of similar disciplinary efforts in the remaining East Bloc countries. In addition, Sect. 4.5 provides, presumably, a complete picture of then existing computing programs in whole Czechoslovakia, supplemented by the numbers of admitted students. This opens a possibility for other researchers to compare the presented data with different countries.

2   A Broader Context: Education in Communist Czechoslovakia

John Connelly's work *Captive University* [9] provides a broader understanding of the educational systems that communists built in Czechoslovakia, Poland, and East Germany (i.e., the German Democratic Republic) during the post-war period. In general, Connelly argues that university systems in these countries – which had previously had strong ties with the West, and whose university traditions had been commonly linked to Humboldtian ideals – were completely remodelled after the Soviet example. The newly introduced form exhibited little academic autonomy due to the subordination of universities to the state. In Czechoslovakia, a similar process of purging and disciplining universities was introduced soon after 1948 when the Communists took over the government. Notably, the process resulted in both numerous ideologically motivated dismissals from academia and also the creation of an atmosphere of fear. Another salient effect was singling out scientific research as an activity that would only be carried out at the Czechoslovak Academy of Sciences, a research-based institution created according to a Soviet example. The new view of universities was purely utility-based. Simply put, universities were the places where new cadres for the centrally planned needs of the Communist regime were trained. The original, Western ideal of universities – being typically viewed as cathedrals of knowledge and academic freedoms – was gradually removed.

However, universities were not the only affected parts of society. In fact, the above countries were expected to fully duplicate the elements of the political and administrative system that then existed in the Soviet Union. Connelly argues that the

> process of duplication … was unprecedented; within a few years, a once multifarious scenery of cultures and histories between Elbe and Bug resembled a belt of miniature Soviet Unions, each with collectivized agriculture, steel and coal industries, broad alleyways of socialistrealist communal housing, marching columns of uniformed youths, omnipresent banners of little Stalins like Walter Ulbricht, Klement Gottwald, or Boleslaw Bierut. Western observers were stunned at the apparent totality and uniformity of [the] transformation (p. 1).

Interestingly, this process was largely improvised because – despite the Soviets' grandiose visions – concrete steps and guidelines for certain areas were not adequately communicated by the Soviets. While local political leaders in Czechoslovakia, Poland, and East Germany were desperately seeking tangible information about certain problems that had presumably been already solved in the Soviet Union, it was almost impossible to acquire such information for two reasons. First, the real state of the problems' solution in the Soviet Union was far from ideal[2]. Second, the Soviets were afraid of "ideological contamination" from satellite countries; consequently, they provided to them as little information as possible (p. 46). So, while Sovietization worked seemingly well in the areas where mimicking simple cultural artefacts such as red flags and banners with enthusiastic slogans was enough, it was imperfect when dealing with complex ideas and notions. In other words, while the organization of annual May Day parades celebrating work was easily graspable, it was much harder to translate the Soviet educational system beyond its original territory. In such complex areas, the imperfect duplication in turn resulted in variations of the original concepts.

This brings us to an important conceptual problem. From a North American perspective, the process of the *emergence* of new disciplines is largely decentralized and consensus-based (e.g., driven by curricula standardization efforts). In general, a new discipline is considered fully established when the majority of new professors appointed in a certain field come from Ph.D. graduates in the new discipline. These professors are then set to reproduce epistemic patterns of the newly established discipline [7]. A similarly formulated criteria cannot be applied to the problem analyzed in this paper due to the fact that the *creation* of new disciplines in Czechoslovakia was *artificial*. That means, it was centrally decided and administered by the government. Neither diploma programs (i.e., 4–5-year non-structured educational programs leading toward a first university degree) nor programs for "scientific preparation" (i.e., leading towards the Candidatus degree – a PhD equivalent) were under the full control of particular universities. Rather, disciplinary taxonomies were centrally administered by the government and ministries and were updated only irregularly by passing a new implementing regulation (e.g., [10]). Central planning extended even to the number of students admitted to study in each field; universities were then provided with quotas they were obliged to fulfill.

Moreover, comparing some of the historical taxonomies, one can notice significant inconsistencies between the disciplinary landscapes of diploma and "scientific preparation" programs in various areas of computing through time. For example, for a long period, future computing scholars were "prepared" in two broad cybernetics programs [10], while diploma students were already taught in specialized computing programs (see Sect. 3.2). So, when we discuss in this paper the process of the emergence of new computing disciplines, we basically mean the moment when a new undergraduate program appeared due to governmental fiat.

---

[2] See, for example, the story of the Czechoslovak Jiří Pelikán's visit in the Soviet Union [9]. Attending a hastily organized meeting in Moscow, "[h]e had learned the fundamental lesson of Sovietization: that basic ideas on the implementation of Soviet models would have to be formed locally" (p. 21).

3   The Beginnings: The Reign of Cybernetics

This section aims to briefly explain the historical role of cybernetics in the Soviet Union (Sect. 3.1). Then, the realities of cybernetics in Czechoslovakia are presented (Sect. 3.2). Following this, the central concept of management/control in both technology and human-based systems is introduced (Sect. 3.3).

3.1   The Position of Cybernetics in the Soviet Union

The role of cybernetics in the East Bloc in general and in the Soviet Union in particular was crucial. In fact, much of the progress in computing was initially carried out under the label of cybernetics. The importance of cybernetics spurred from the Soviet delimitation of this discipline, which "included almost any form of computing and systems of control, communication, or information" [11], including economic modelling and operations research.

Interestingly, in the early 1950s, the future cybernetics discipline was still associated with ideological labels such as "reactionary" or "bourgeois pseudo-science." Yet, cybernetics was rehabilitated by the late 1950s [3]. Aside from other key protagonists [5, 12], a great effort was put into this rehabilitation (both in the Soviet Union and in Czechoslovakia) by Arnošt Kolman[3] (1892–1979), who daringly argued [13] in 1956 that the

> nihilistic relationship to cybernetics … is just as harmful as a nihilistic relationship to the Theory of Relativity; the use of quantum mechanics in chemistry; the study of heredity on the basis of [knowledge from] physics and chemistry; mathematical logic (p. 38).

While he further stated that "cybernetics is not [yet] an autonomous scientific discipline" (p. 17), efforts to institutionalize cybernetics were accelerated during the late 1950s and the early 1960s. For the Western audience, the key Soviet theses regarding cybernetics were, with a noticeable irony, summarized by Arbib [4] in 1966: (1) "Cybernetics is the science of control, and will help build socialism", (2) "Cybernetics is a science … and must not be considered a philosophy. It cannot compete with material dialectics [dialectical materialism]", (3) "Bourgeois [i.e., Western] cyberneticians gloss over the vital distinctions between man, machine, and society. To understand the brain of man is the task of Pavlovian research on higher nervous activity. To understand society, we need Marxism-Leninism." Interestingly, while visiting the Soviet Union in 1960s, Arbib noticed the overarching popularity of cybernetics:

> [E]verybody I met (including a pianist, a customs official, Intourist guides, and hotel staff) knew of cybernetics, and commented on my luck in working in such a new and exciting field – a change from the blank looks the word "cybernetics" calls forth in the West (p. 198).

By the 1970s, however, the popularity of cybernetics started to decline. This was due to the unfilled promises of cybernetics, but also due to the previous

---

[3] Kolman was a controversial Soviet figure of Czech origin – a mathematician and Marxist philosopher with a problematic reputation [41].

overpopularization of cybernetics and its conceptual misuse [3]. There seemed to be a gap in the intellectual space asking to be filled in. It was soon filled by informatics – a discipline labelled by a term with unclear boundaries in European context. By some, the term "informatics" might be (even nowadays) used as a synonym for computer science. However, a more appropriate usage, at least from the perspective of disciplinary traditions within continental Europe, is to employ the term to refer to the conglomerate of *all computing disciplines* (e.g., computer science, software engineering, information systems, etc.) [14]. In the Soviet Union, however, a crucial complication lied in the fact that the Russian term *informatika* had previously been established to denote a discipline akin to library science [15].

Following Afinogenov [16], we connect the beginning of the East Bloc shift from cybernetics to Western-style informatics primarily with Andrey Petrovych Ershov (1931–1988), who was very active in redefining the latter term in the Soviet Union. The shift became salient especially after 1976, when F.L. Bauer's *Informatik* was translated from German to Russian, supplemented by a foreword by Ershov. However, as Afinogenov shows, cybernetics never entirely disappeared from the Soviet space due to the strong position it used to have during the 1960s (pp. 573–4). This position can be contrasted with the much weaker role of cybernetics in the West, where "[p]eople [either] stayed in their home disciplines" [17] and never associated their scholarly identity with cybernetics *per-se* (e.g., in the USA), or rejected cybernetics entirely due to its image of "babble" science (e.g., in France) [8].

However, the exact nature of the above shift in the Soviet Union remains an open question. In any case, it would be futile to seek an exact date when cybernetics "died." In the Soviet Union as well as other East Bloc countries, cybernetics has, in fact, never entirely disappeared from the mainstream intellectual space due to the remarkable ongoing co-existence of cybernetics with computing[4]. Yet, due to this set-up, the jurisdiction of cybernetics in this geographic region significantly changed several times during the past few decades.

3.2   Cybernetics in Czechoslovakia

In Czechoslovakia, cybernetics was defined as an autonomous scientific field by a directive of the Minister of Education and Culture of 20 January 1965 [18]. This directive codified a formal list of scientific disciplines in which one can acquire a *Candidatus degree* (CSc., an equivalent of a Ph.D.). The directive stated that Cybernetics is divided into *Theoretical Cybernetics* (within the taxonomy of "Physical-Mathematical

---

[4] See, for example, Ershov's statement from 1988: Although informatics has taken the lead, "we [in the Soviet Union] are not attempting to change either the name of the Council on Cybernetics or the traditions of its first chairman, Aksel' Ivanovich Berg" (a third source quoting Ershov as cited in [16]). Also note that it was not before 1990 that the word "informatics" was added to the official title of the scientific societies focused on control and computing in both republics that then formed the Czechoslovak Federation. Even nowadays – in the two now completely independent countries – two scientific societies with almost identical names continue to span the scientific worlds of control and computing: *The Czech Society for Cybernetics and Informatics* (http://www.cski.cz) and *The Slovak Society for Cybernetics and Informatics* (http://www.sski.sk/).

Sciences") and *Technical Cybernetics* (within the taxonomy of "Technical Sciences"). *Applied Cybernetics* was not explicitly mentioned in the directive. However, in a seminal 1960 article authored by Soviet Academician Aksel Ivanovich Berg (1893–1979) and translated to Czech the same year [19], *Applied Cybernetics* was explicitly defined as an application-oriented, cross-disciplinary field. (For an early taxonomy of key research topics in Soviet cybernetics, including namely theory of "electronic computers", see [12].)

Institutional Basis. Two salient professional organizations related to cybernetics were The Czechoslovak Cybernetic Society (CSCS, *Československá kybernetická společnost*) and The Society for Applied Cybernetics (SAC, *Společnost pro aplikovanou kybernetiku*). CSCS emerged from an informal and conspirative "cybernetics circle" that got together thanks to the mathematician Antonín Špaček (1911–1961) in the mid-1950s. This group also included the computing pioneer Antonín Svoboda [20]. CSCS was formally founded in 1966 when cybernetics was already considered politically "purified" in the Soviet Union (see above). The organization had close ties to the Czechoslovak Academy of Science, and was represented by the first CSCS's chair Albert Perez (1920–2003). This researcher was an interesting figure. Born in Greece, he moved to Paris after the war and then to Prague in 1949. As a mathematician with a lot of international contacts, he became a salient representative of the Czechoslovak school of information theory [21]. The imprint of scientific spirit remained with CSCS, a society with selective membership, even in the following decades.

In contrast, SAC was founded by the end of the 1960s with a totally different organizational grounding. Dominated by engineers and having primarily an application-oriented mission, this professional organization fitted well within the structure of engineering societies, i.e., under the wing of the Czechoslovak Science and Technological Society (*Československá vědeckotechnická společnost*). The philosophy of this organization promoted a broad membership base, including also many engineers working in industry. In 1969, SAC was led by Milan Balda (1924–), a professor of mechanical engineering interested in advancing industrial automation. While conceptually imported from the West, in Czechoslovakia the field of systems engineering was organizationally subsumed under applied cybernetics. Having strong overlaps with the disciplines discussed below,[5] its main aim was to integrate all possible disciplines in order to bridge theory and practice focused on large, complex, socio-technical systems, including the systems of control and computing. Institutionally, the field was represented by a special SAC section formed in 1969 by Zdeněk Dráb (1925–). This section became very active in organizing of popular local conferences (e.g. Systems Engineering, Automatics – *Automatika*) attended during the 1970s and 1980s by both academics and industry professionals.

While CSCS maintained international contacts with the International Federation for Information Processing, SAC maintained contacts with other international organizations For example, the latter organized the seventh world congress of AICA (*Association Internationale pour le Calcul analogique*) in Prague in 1973. In a similar vein,

---

[5] This was not only due to the eclectic nature of systems engineering as established in the west. The other reason was the central role of cybernetics and control concepts in the East [3].

the discipline of operations research – and related international contacts with IFORS (International Federation of Operational Research Societies) – also belonged under the auspices of SAC. Interestingly, a SAC section fully dedicated to operational research was only founded in 1984.

Yet, one should not think of SAC as an umbrella for all thinkable applications of cybernetics. As a contradictory example, Czechoslovak medical cybernetics[6] was associated instead with the above mentioned multidisciplinary "cybernetics circle" that became institutionalized as CSCS in 1966. The key figure in this area was Zdeněk Wünsch, MD (1926–), a professor of psychiatry and a cybernetics enthusiast who co-translated Norbert Wiener's famous book into Czech in 1960.

Institutional Constraints. At this point, however, an important matter should be noted. In essence, it would be illusory to regard any of the above Czechoslovak societies as independent professional bodies with little or no dependence on the political establishment. As early as the 1950s, the Communist state and Communist political bureau were directly involved in passing certain reformist laws related to the organization of scientific and technology-intensive activities. These laws commanded an organizational restructuring and merging of some former (i.e., "bourgeois") scientific and professional societies (e.g., the Czech Academy of Sciences and Arts, which was originally founded in 1890). Hence, one should not think about the above societies as having a total autonomy from the Czechoslovak state.

Below, we provide details of the three important areas of cybernetics officially defined in Czechoslovakia in 1965.

Theoretical Cybernetics – An Interdisciplinary Field Anchored in Mathematics. Following the 1965 directive, Theoretical Cybernetics emerged as a specialization in diploma programs at Charles University in Prague in 1969 [22]. Almost in parallel, the Department of Mathematical Logic was founded there. Inspired by the industrial success of applied and numerical mathematics, Theoretical Cybernetics was intended, in essence, as a tool for "mathematization" of disciplines such as biology, medicine, or social sciences. A concrete vehicle to realize this vision was seen in supplying the mentioned disciplines with the conceptual backing of exact thinking and formal methods. A corresponding idea was to send mathematicians to "non-mathematical workplaces", so they could apply "mathematical disciplines, especially mathematical logic, within non-mathematical fields".

Technical Cybernetics – An Engineering Discipline. The origin of this disciplinary title can be traced to a 1954 book entitled *Engineering Cybernetics*. The book was authored by Tsien Hsue Shen and translated in 1960 into Czech as Technical Cybernetics (Technická kybernetika) [23]. While the term "mathematical machines" was slowly dying away, first computer engineering departments in the Czech Socialist Republic were founded in Prague and Brno in 1964 (also see [24] with regard to

---

[6] Note the promise of medical cybernetics in the Eastern Bloc countries, and the "universalism" of key scientific figures active in cybernetics in general. For example, Soviet scientist Anatoly Ivanovich Kitov (1920–2005) spanned several cybernetics fields, including medical cybernetics [5; see also Kitova and Kitov, "Anatoloy Kitov and Victor Glushkov", this volume].

Slovakia). These departments were to carry almost identical names: Department of Computers (Katedra počítačů) and Department of Automatic Computers (Katedra samočinných počítačů). From a disciplinary perspective, however, they were oriented on teaching and research within the realm of Technical Cybernetics programs. Following this constellation, Mathematical Machines survived as a specialization within the "scientific preparation" programs of Technical Cybernetics for a number of years. Also, it was not until 1973 that Electronic Computers became a diploma program in its own right in Czechoslovakia (see Sect. 4).

Other Relevant Disciplines. Although not completely subsumed under cybernetics, there existed several important sister disciplines in the 1960s that should be mentioned to complete the big picture. Currently, however, we have quite a limited understanding of the circumstances under which these disciplines emerged.

First, in 1963, an undergraduate program called *Mechanization of Economic Evidence (Mechanizace národohospodářské evidence)* was transformed into a program called *Mechanization of Administrative Work (Mechanizace řídících prací)*. At the same time, a new program called *Computation in Economics/Mathematics (Ekonomicko-matematické výpočty)* was created. In the Czech Socialistic Republic, both programs were taught only at the *University of Economics, Prague*. Finally, there were another two programs focused on heavy industry automation. Both programs had some interest in the use of computers. One had its disciplinary home in mechanical engineering, the other in chemical engineering. Their names were *Instrument, Automation and Regulation Technology (Přístrojová, řídící a automatizační technika)* and *Processes, Devices and Automation of Chemical Production (Procesy, zařízení a automatizace chemické výroby)* respectively. All the names stated above indicate that all these disciplines were application-oriented.

3.3 The Doctrine of Management/Control

There was a crucial concept that stemmed from the Soviet cybernetics discourse of the 1960s [3]. In Czech, the concept was labeled *řízení* – a direct equivalent of Russian *upravlenie*. Based on their connotation, these terms were used very broadly both in Czech and Russian. Conceptually, the use of these terms typically did not differentiate between people-based systems vs. technology-based systems. Accordingly, there is no one-to-one English equivalent for these terms. As noted in the English-written administration literature already in 1973 [25], "[i]n various contexts ... [the original terms] may be translated [into English] as administration, management, control, regulation, guidance, or government". In this paper, we use for Czech *řízení* the English equivalents "administration" and "management/control", as appropriate.

Having provided this terminological background, it is also imperative to point out that the concept of *řízení (upravlenie)* was essential, as was cybernetics [3]. Extremely open to individual interpretation, the concept of *řízení* was simply overarching: it ranged from the "scientific management of society" [26] to the regulation of technological processes in individual factories (owned by the state). This was fully in line with the philosophy of central planning, which was fundamental for the Socialist regimes. It should thus come as no surprise that the doctrine of management/control (řízení) was later reflected also in the disciplinary titles. On the one hand, Soviet cybernetics itself, as an early prophet of the management/control philosophy in the East Bloc adapted from the West, remained faithful to its international label.[7] On the other hand, a new broad field – Science of Administration (*věda o řízení* in Czech, *nauchnoe upravlenie* in Russian) – was defined as a partly overlapping conceptual science, including also the "Cybernetics School of Administration". This resulted in what Vidmer [27] later called a "'jungle' of competing views"; these views were ideologically dependent on political economy and largely incompatible with Western approaches to management.

In addition, the technology-oriented disciplines that were to transform the conceptually neat theoretical ideas of *řízení* (*upravlenie*) into the messy East Bloc reality acquired their own specific titles (see Sect. 4). Even disciplines recognizable by their titles in the West (e.g., systems engineering) should not be confused with their Soviet/East Bloc equivalents because the latter had quite unique features and unclear boundaries. For example, in Czechoslovakia, *Systems Engineering* de facto conceptually competed with *Technical Cybernetics*, which should also justify the presence of both disciplines in this paper. Interestingly, Czechoslovak *Systems Engineering* also covered many aspects of Western industrial engineering, because the latter never emerged as a distinct discipline in Communist Czechoslovakia.

4   The Emergence of New Computing Disciplines

In this section we provide original findings based on our archival research of previously unexplored archival materials[8]. In line with our goal to focus on the beginnings of autonomous computing disciplines in Czechoslovakia, we have primarily studied two different versions of *The Conception of Higher and Middle Education of Qualified Cadres/Experts in the Area of Computer Technology* (in short "Conception", in original: *Koncepce výchovy kvalifikovaných vysokoškolských a středoškolských kádrů/odborníků v oblasti výpočetních techniky*). We regard the first one [28], stored in the Ministry of Education archival collection (the T-73-7-72 version), as a draft from 1972, while the second one [29], stored in the Government Office archival collection (the 245-12-72 version), as the finalized document presented to the government in January 1973. There are important differences between the documents (e.g., different arguments, different names that were proposed for the emerging disciplines, added phrases

---

[7] Gerovitch citing Berg's statement from 1961: "Many people don't seem to like the word cybernetics. I don't like it either, but we haven't yet come up with a better one. It would be better to use a Russian word. That's why we often speak of a new science of government [upravlenie]." [3] (here "Science of Administration").

[8] The archival collections we benefited from in this research are presently uncatalogued and not freely accessible. The pre-selection of archival documents was carried out by the archivists of the National Archives, Prague. It could happen that the resulting material available for our study did not include all the items essential for getting a complete picture of the presented historical events.

such as "based on foreign [i.e., Soviet?] experience", etc.). Some of them are analyzed below. Unfortunately, we have not yet succeeded in locating the archival documents that would reflect inter-ministerial and other comments, i.e., what was happening with the content of the proposed Conception in the meantime, and why.

To begin with, the key idea underpinning a broader East Bloc initiative was to promote the creation of *four* types of computing disciplines by defining certain common principles shared among the East Bloc countries. As shown further, this proposal was implemented imperfectly in Czechoslovakia – below we explain the creation of *three* concrete disciplines which were adjusted to the Czechoslovak reality.

4.1   The Role of the Council for Mutual Economic Assistance

Following the Soviet example [3], the use of computers for various activities, especially for *řízení,* had become a cardinal topic for most of the Socialist governments in the East Bloc by the end of 1960s. Attempts to eliminate overlapping research and development activities gradually resulted in the centralization of these efforts under the wing of the *Council for Mutual Economic Assistance* (CMEA), also known as *Comecon.*[9] CMEA was an economic organization comprised of East Bloc countries and dominated by the Soviet Union [30]. Czechoslovakia was among its six founding members in 1949. Under the auspices of CMEA, an agreement in the area of computing was signed on 23 December 1969 in Moscow [31]. The agreement was focused on research, development, production, and supplies of computer technology among CMEA members. The signing members were as follows: the Soviet Union, Poland, the German Democratic Republic (East Germany), Hungary, Bulgaria, and Czechoslovakia. Cuba and Romania later joined. Following this agreement, a governing body for these activities was instituted – the *Intergovernmental Commission for Computer Technology* (ICCT, *Mezivládní komise pro výpočetní techniku*). Under the auspices of ICCT, several working groups and sub-commissions were created. Two of them are of particular interest: the *Council of Chief Designers* (*Rada hlavních konstruktérů*) and the *Working Group for Automated Management/Control Systems* (*Pracovní skupina pro automatizované systémy řízení*). Put simply, the former focused on the research and development of third generation computer hardware including peripheries, and the latter on the use of computers for *řízení,* i.e., for controlling the national economy from the top (i.e.,. macro level industry management) to the bottom (i.e., organizational management and technology control within individual enterprises).

The Working Group for Automated Management/Control Systems was further hierarchically organized into temporary sub-working groups called "councils of specialists" (*rady specialistů*). Among these, one such council was designated to deal with specific problems of computing education. The rather complicated formal title of the council was *Council for Educational Matters of the Cadres for Automated Management/Control Systems* (*Rada specialistů pro výchovu kádrů pro automatizované*

---

[9] See Sikora, "Cooperating with Moscow, Stealing in California", this volume.

systémy řízení). This computing education council took the lead role in the curriculum standardization efforts carried out across all the countries involved.

Although the process of unification was reportedly cumbersome, a tangible result emerged. Specifically, a common nomenclature of computing disciplines valid across CMEA countries was defined. However, instead of using the term "computing" as such, the areas proposed by the nomenclature had another common denominator – the concept of Automated Management/Control Systems (AMCS, in Russian: *avtomatizirovannyje sistemy upravlenija*[10]). Arguably, such a focus can be attributed to the previous importance of cybernetics and systems disciplines in the East Bloc, and to the dominance of the Soviet Union where the concept was very popular [3].

The nomenclature defined four specialization areas in computing/automation education. The areas of education for specialists in AMCS were:

- economic/organizational and informational problems
- mathematical/programming problems
- technology-related problems
- applications in industry

The above nomenclature represented the key framework for the subsequent changes in the computing education landscape in Czechoslovakia (and presumably also in the remaining CMEA countries).

A detailed local report explaining the above nomenclature and the aims of the new computing programs was published by Milan Balda (1924–) and Jan Ehleman (1930–2010) in 1973 [32]. In their paper, they also described the existence of the Conception (see below) and highlighted the fact that the working group had already "discussed and approved the structure of the disciplines, the requirements for [related] educational programs and a list of courses for [educating] the first group of specialists".

Meanwhile, following the Soviet paragons and the activities of ICCT at the international level, on 22 December 1971 the government of the Czech Socialist Republic adopted a seminal resolution (No. 306/1971 [33]). It contained one high-level instruction for the Minister of Development and Technology, and one for the Minister of Education. While the first one was an assignment concerning country-wide coordination of the implementation and use of computer technology, the second one gave instructions to *deepen the education in the area of computing at secondary schools and universities*. Also, the task of preparing a conception of the training and education of "expert cadres" in the area of computing by 30 September 1972 was formulated.

Following the events described above, a local commission of experts was appointed to work on the *conception of training and education for computing*. It is highly probable that there was significant overlap in membership in the local commission and the Czechoslovak part of the international computing education council. Specifically, we assume that both M. Balda and J. Ehleman took parts in all these activities. In the following subsections, we examine several basic elements of the Conception.

---

[10] Автоматизированные системы управления.

4.2   The Conception

The Conception was a document aiming to formulate the key principles of future education of computing professionals in the Czech Socialist Republic. As a motivation, the Conception claimed [28] that other countries had been concerned with the "education of experts capable of [applying] systems approaches to solve complex problems of current society, and well-versed in related theoretical and technical tools". The earlier version of the Conception further stated that other countries had already "concentrated such education into new study programs ..., especially informatics [!] and Automated Management/Control Systems". It is debatable what countries were meant by the term "other countries", but presumably the authors of the Conception had in mind Bulgaria, Hungary, East Germany, Poland, and the Soviet Union (see Appendix 3 in [29]). The Conception also mapped the situation in Czechoslovak academic computing at that time. Table 1 provides an overview of computing programs that already existed in 1972. These programs represented the starting point for changes implemented subsequently.

4.3   Learning from the Soviets

Observing the development in the Soviet Union closely, the authors of the final version of the Conception supplied it with several new attachments. Arguably the most interesting one is Appendix No. 3, which summarized some features of computing education in the remaining countries of the East Bloc. On top of that, the Russian-to-Czech translation of a Soviet paper about computing education [34] was included. The paper was authored by Vjacheslav Petrovich Eljutin (1907–1993), the Minister of Higher and Middle Education of the Soviet Union. In his paper, Eljutin described the organization of computing disciplines in the Soviet Union. Referring to the directives of the *24th Congress of the Communist Party of the Soviet Union* in spring 1971, he repeated that Soviet economy had been in need of more specialists on administration, management, planning, economical modelling, and modern computing methods. He also mentioned that several new computing programs had been created in the Soviet Union in 1968, for example *Automated Management/Control Systems* (0646), *Applied Mathematics* (0647), *Design and Production of Electronic Digital Devices* (0648). In addition, an older program had been transformed into *Electronic Computers* (0608). He also highlighted the importance of *Economic Cybernetics* programs.

Not surprisingly, many of the disciplinary titles presented by Eljutin were incorporated into the Czech proposal on the new computing disciplines word-for-word (see below). Nonetheless, two vital questions to be asked here are: To what degree was this duplication accurate in terms of the "inner content" of the disciplines? And was the mimicking process enforced officially from the top, or decided by the authors of the conception themselves, given the political context they lived within? (Regarding the conceptual dilemma of Sovietization vs. "self-Sovietization", refer to Connelly [9]). Unfortunately, this paper does not provide these answers due to the early stage of development of our research project.

Table 1. The starting programs with an overlap to computing as of 1972. Adapted from [29]. The acronyms have the following meaning: CU = Charles University in Prague; UJEP = University of Jan Evangelista Purkyně (today Masaryk University), Brno; CTU = Czech Technical University, Prague; BUT = Brno University of Technology; CMEE = College of Mechanical and Electrical Engineering (today University of West Bohemia), Plzeň; UCT = University of Chemistry and Technology, Prague, Pardubice; UE = University of Economics Prague; TUO = Technical University of Ostrava.

Program	University	Branch
Mathematics (specializations: Numerical Mathematics, Programming and Statistics) [Matematika (zaměření numerická matematika, programování a statistika)]	CU Prague UJEP Brno	Mathematics
Instrument, Automation and Regulation Technology [Přístrojová, automatizační a regulační technika]	CTU Prague	Mechanical Engineering
Technical Cybernetics [Technická kybernetika]	CTU Prague BUT Brno CMEE Plzeň	Electrical Engineering
Processes, Devices and Automation of Chemical Production [Procesy, zařízení a automatizace chemické výroby]	UCT Prague, Pardubice	Chemical Engineering
Computation in Economics/Mathematics [Ekonomicko-matematické výpočty]	UE Prague	Economics/Management
Mechanization and Automation of Administrative Work [Mechanizace a automatizace řídících prací]	UE Prague	Economics/Management
Systems Engineering [Systémové inženýrství]	TU Ostrava	Engineering (General)

4.4   Academic Programs to Be Created

A major contribution of the Conception [29] was the new taxonomy of academic programs and disciplines in the area of computing. This taxonomy was meant to be mappable to the four specialization areas codified as the CMEA nomenclature (see Sect. 4.1). However, such a clear mapping was not provided in the Conception. Nonetheless, the key argument regarding the already existing programs, such as *Technical Cybernetics*, was that currently "the education is carried out within [too] broad study programs, not fully assuring [the required specialization in computer skills] in an adequate extent and quality" (p. 18).

Hence, the newly proposed Czechoslovakian disciplinary taxonomy codified three new study programs at university level. These were as follows (p. 19): *Electronic Computers*, *Numerical Mathematics*, and *Automated Management/Control Systems*. Correspondingly, it was suggested that three new programs for "scientific preparation" should be created. Interestingly, the first one was not to be named "Electronic

Computers", but rather "Computer Technology" (*výpočetní technika*)[11]. The remaining ones were to carry the same name as their diploma siblings.

Aside from that, it was also discussed how non-computing university programs might benefit from the introduction of computing-related knowledge into their curricula. Some changes in secondary school programs were also proposed. Last but not least, the Conception discussed how the universities could be equipped with computers necessary for teaching students in the new programs. In the following, we limit our discussion to the three new university programs created. We briefly delineate these programs and sketch what was meant as the typical job duties and job titles of their graduates.

Numerical Mathematics. Evolving from general mathematics, the *Numerical Mathematics* program was to be created at (classical) universities. The requirements on the graduates of this program were defined as: they should be taught to acquire strong background in "common mathematical terms, methods, and [to strengthen their] ability of conceptual thinking". The studies were thus to focus on mathematical "analysis, functional analysis, algebra, discrete mathematics, numerical and graphical methods in linear algebra, differential calculus, theory of errors etc." [29] (n.p. – Appendix 7). The graduates were to be prepared for work mostly as analysts and system programmers.

Electronic Computers. Stemming from the roots of *Technical Cybernetics*, the *Electronic Computers* program was to be created at technical universities, within their faculties (schools) of electrical engineering. The graduate profile was defined more comprehensively than the previous one. It was further stated that graduates should be fluent in mathematics, physics, and electrical engineering. Interestingly, they should also be able to "design and realize basic software such as operating systems and compilers" [29] (n.p. – Appendix 7). As stated, this program was to make them ready for positions of design engineers, system and operations programmers, analysts, or even computing researchers.

Automated Management/Control Systems. Driven by the doctrine of management/control [3], the AMCS programs were to be created at "some technical universities, [and] The University of Economics [, Prague]" (p. 26). The focus was thus on computer applications in various domains (e.g., mechanical engineering, chemical engineering, electrical engineering, and administration), where computers were seen as ideal vehicles for *řízení* (i.e., technological control, organizational management, industry segment control at the macro level, and state administration). It was stated that graduates should gather background in "natural science disciplines, especially mathematics and physics" [29] (n.p. – Appendix 7). In addition to that, they should understand their specific domain, i.e., they would be well educated in the "main engineering and economical-administrative disciplines of their [engineering or administration core] programs". The studies should focus on "economical/administrative and informational,

---

[11] Comparing both versions of the Conception, we speculate that the authors simply forgot to adjust the name of the "scientific preparation" program to the Soviet example. Alternatively, there might be no example to follow. In any case, the three proposed "scientific preparation" programs were not materialized anytime soon.

mathematical/programming, and technical aspects of AMCS". Moreover, the studies should provide a "broad background, emphasizing system approach for problem solving" (n.p. – Appendix 7).

Taken together, the disciplinary landscape in the area of computing can be visualized as follows (Fig. 1). The central part of the picture (black boxes) represents the new programs proposed by the Conception and confirmed by the government of Czech Socialist Republic on 31st January 1973 [35]. The part above them shows the original programs and specializations of the 1950s and 1960s. The part below the black boxes portrays the future development and unification of these disciplines under the tent of "Informatics", which happened roughly at the end of the Communist period (1989). This progress will be briefly discussed in Sect. 5.

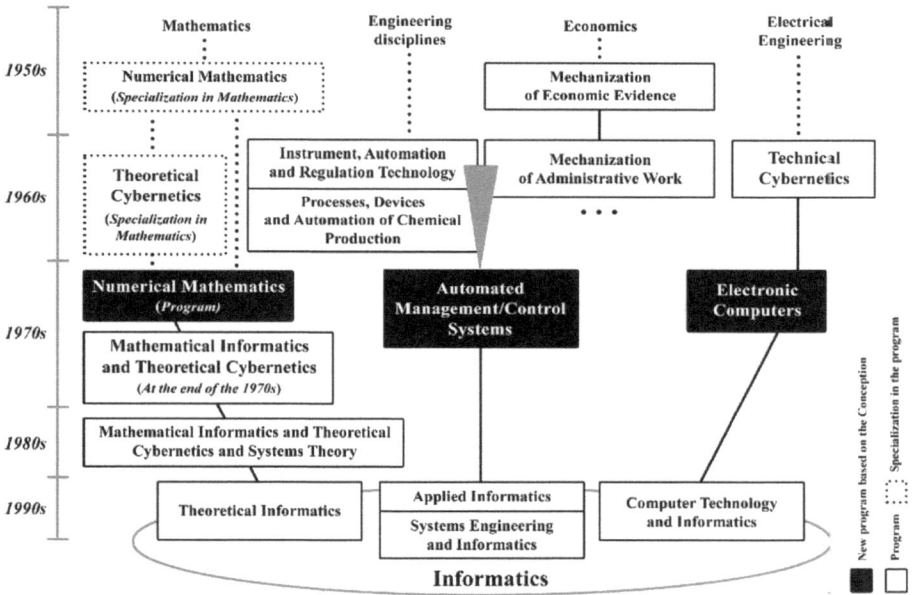

Fig. 1. The genealogy of Informatics in Czechoslovakia (1950s–1990s).

4.5   Results One Year Later

In early 1975, the Czechoslovak Government debated a material that dealt with the use of computer technology and the "implementation of AMCS by all authorities" in Czechoslovakia during 1974 [36]. Part of this material was a discussion of computing education in Czechoslovakia after the taxonomy reforms. Table 2 provides a look at the number of admitted students (in term 1974/75) into respective computing programs in the Czech Socialist Republic (CSR), the Slovak Socialist Republic (SSR), and a sum for Czechoslovakia (CSSR). While the new programs (marked with an asterisk – ours) were clearly gaining attention (especially the AMCS program), it is also interesting to see that junior students were still admitted to the original programs as well, with an exception of Theoretical Cybernetics. Programs marked by us with "O" (for original) were listed in the Conception as those that had already existed prior the reform. Currently, we know little about the emergence of the two remaining programs (i.e., Theoretical Cybernetics and Cybernetics in Transportation and Communications) since they were not explicitly discussed by the Conception. Perhaps, the latter one existed only in Slovak Socialist Republic.

Table 2. Diploma computing programs in Czechoslovakia in 1974/75 (adapted from [36])

Program	Code	Number admitted		
		CSSR	CSR	SSR
Numerical Mathematics (*)	11-70-8	78	78	-
Instrument, Automation and Regulation Technology (O)	23-37-8	224	144	80
Technical Cybernetics (O)	26-15-8	542	330	212
Electronic Computers (*)	26-62-8	160	80	80
Processes, Devices and Automation of Chemical Production (O)	28-28-8	114	80	34
Cybernetics in Transportation and Communications	37-28-8	46	-	46
Automated Management and Control Systems (*)	39-43-8	298	268	30
Theoretical Cybernetics	39-50-8	-	-	-
Computation in Economics/Mathematics (O)	62-36-8	154	56	98
Mechanization and Automation of Administrative Work (O)	62-37-8	87	87	-
Systems Engineering (O)	62-40-8	154	40	114
Total		**1857**	**1163**	**694**

5 Discussion and Epilogue

Although somewhat limited due to space constraints, the material presented in this paper offers some interesting insights. First and foremost, by providing important arch val evidence the paper contributes to the body of knowledge on the specifics of historical developments in computing/informatics in Europe (e.g., [1, 6, 8]). The perspective taken in this paper was motivated by our own earlier struggle to understand the genealogies of Czech computing communities and the unique taxonomy of their titles.

There was truly a diverse, unique disciplinary landscape created in the area of Czechoslovak computing and automation in 1973. In this context, a natural question to ask is: *Were the disciplines really that different from each other?* At this point, we must admit that it is very hard to answer this question without clarifying the detailed content of the particular study programs. Nonetheless, it seems that the creation of the CMEA nomenclature of computing disciplines was intended as a declaration that there *should exist* a significant differentiation and specialization within the studies of computing/ automation in the East Bloc. However, what is missing here is an understanding of how exactly this idea was implemented in different East Bloc countries, including Czechoslovakia, and to what extent the disciplinary content was copied from the Soviets.

To analyse the problem further, it seems appropriate to draw on the already mentioned observation recorded in Connelly's work [9] stating that "basic ideas on the implementation of Soviet models would have to be formed locally". In the case of the emergence of new computing disciplines in Czechoslovakia, there could be a similar pattern. While the new disciplines were administratively created and named according their Soviet siblings, we do not propose that their content was absolutely identical with the Soviet paragons. If it were, there would hardly have been any need to run a later initiative called "the convergence of university study programs in Czechoslovakia and the Soviet Union" (ca. 1980). This later initiative focused on curriculum details, including unification of the syllabi of core courses. However, due to currently missing details about this later initiative, we just make a note about its existence for a future study.

Finally, we propose that while the above disciplines grew up from distinct roots of their reference disciplines (e.g., mathematics or electrical engineering), it would be very hard to draw clear boundaries between various branches of computing/informatics that one can encounter in the Czech Republic nowadays. In fact, we suggest that after 1989 informatics became a *melting pot* in which the original computing disciplines described in this paper have become increasingly interdependent. Below we provide some details about how this happened.

5.1   From Numerical Mathematics to Mathematical Informatics

Few years after the Conception defined the field of *Numerical Mathematics*, the term "mathematical informatics" slowly started to dominate the area of research and education similar to computer science. According to our preliminary findings, this finally brought "informatics" into Czechoslovak academic computing space as an official term. This was roughly the same year when Bauer's *Informatik* was translated from German to Russian (1976, see Sect. 3.1).

However, it was not before 1986 (!) that *Mathematical Informatics* became officially listed among scientific fields in which a Candidatus degree could be obtained [37]. Still, the legacy of cybernetics continued to be salient even after 1986. The full title of the scientific field remained *Mathematical Informatics and Theoretical Cybernetics*, while the diploma program contained the additional addendum *and Systems Theory*.

The reason for the observed conceptual struggles was that in the Soviet Union the term "informatics" had been previously reserved for a field akin to library science [15], and Czechoslovakia closely followed an official taxonomy of scientific disciplines established in the Soviet union [38]. The Soviet understanding was in turn influenced by the dominance of cybernetics [3]. We believe that the development in Czechoslovakia can be contrasted, for example, with development in Poland or East Germany, where the term "informatics", presumably, was part of the official expert discourse much earlier. It is imperative to note, however, that the term had been semi-officially present in the Czechoslovak community since (at least) 1972. That year the international conference *Mathematical Foundations of Computer Science* (MFCS, Matematické základy informatiky) was first held in Jablonna, Poland. The 1973 conference was organized in the High Tatras, Czechoslovakia.

The MFCS conference was a pivotal forum attended also by many reputable Western academics. Based on this observation we are convinced that Czechoslovak *Mathematical Informatics* succeeded in maintaining important knowledge links with outside (i.e., western) computer science communities even during the Communist era. From today's perspective, we consider it fully integrated in relevant global scientific communities.

In Czechoslovakia, the diploma programs in *Mathematical Informatics* have been located at classical universities (a rough equivalent of liberal arts and science colleges in the U.S. system). Presently, these programs might also be labeled as *Theoretical Informatics*, or controversially just as *Informatics*.

5.2 From Electronic Computers to Computer Technology and Informatics

The position of the *Electronic Computers* discipline was more complicated due to its primary focus on hardware aspects of computing. Given the lower maturity of computer technologies in the East Bloc [30], the discipline obviously lagged behind computer engineering in the West. Interestingly, the discipline also encountered significant administrative problems in Czechoslovakia when it was striving for a greater level of autonomy from electrical engineering. For various reasons, this was basically not possible until 1989. Finally, around 1990, the programs were renamed mostly to *Computer Technology and Informatics* (*Výpočetní technika a informatika*[12]). So, one can say that the post-revolution liberalism of the 1990s finally enabled these programs to be accepted into the broad "informatics family".

Nowadays, one can study this area of computing education in engineering programs residing at electrical engineering or information technology faculties (schools) of technical universities (the latter typically split from the former during the 2000s). These days, however, there is a much greater diversity in the computing program titles that can be studied in this academic environment. This diversity indicates that such programs do not closely follow the original focus of the area of education in computer engineering. In fact, the programs repositioned themselves and became wide computing education platforms, including also many areas of applied computing. Considering the broadness of the term "informatics" in Western Europe [39], this development is perhaps not surprising.

5.3 From Automated Management/Control Systems to Applied Informatics

Finally, we think that the discipline *Automated Management/Control Systems* represented a unique phenomenon that deserves further attention. We put this phenomenon in the broader context of Soviet cybernetics, because, in our view, the popularity of

---

[12] Or vice versa – *Informatics and Computer Technology* (*Informatika a výpočetní technika*).

AMCS largely stemmed from the former catchiness of the ideas of cybernetics. These included the desire of the Soviets to scientifically "manage Russia" [40] by using sophisticated technical means. As presented, for example, by scholars in the fields of communications and history of science [11, 41], cybernetics became a technocratic tool promising improved information control at all levels of the Soviet society. Importantly, the mechanism it represented was quite different from the "control by fear" imposed during the previous era of Stalinist totalitarianism. In addition, cybernetics was seen as a means of salvation for the national economy. These were arguably the two most appealing aspects that inspired the passion for cybernetics-driven administration aiming at all levels of the gigantic socio-technical system (i.e. the Soviet economy and society). As time passed, however, not all promises of cybernetics were fulfilled. We suggest that as a result, the AMCS discipline (being at that time a "blank slate") was designated to become a key successor of the stale cybernetics. Building on the ideas of control and backing them up with the support of computers, it *de facto* became a form of "Technical Cybernetics 2.0".

However, it is also important to recognize that the ideas of *řízení* (formalized as *Science of Administration*) were not only about using computers for control. Briefly stated, *řízení* was an over-arching philosophy of the administration of state and society. The use of "automated management/control systems" (i.e., computers) was just one important piece in the controlling puzzle [26]. At the time, this fact was perhaps dismissed by some. It is also worth noting that while the AMCS discipline – keeping the original title – survived for two decades in Czechoslovakia (1973 – ca. 1990), the embodied meaning of the title surely evolved. We are convinced that, as AMCS approached the end of its journey, arguably only very few people remembered much about the original wide cybernetics vision. For those in mechanical engineering, the AMCS discipline became perhaps a form of applied control theory – a purely technical discipline. For those in schools of economics and "business", it morphed into managerial informatics. For others, it simply became a synonym for applied informatics (i.e., applied computing). The overarching aspect of *řízení* (*upravlenie*) – the state administration philosophy ranging from the top to the very bottom by combining society and technology – gradually disappeared.

There is yet another important aspect of AMCS as a discipline. Viewed from a global perspective, the doctrinal constraints related to AMCS had a devastating influence on the level of western-oriented contacts in applied computing fields such as Business Informatics or Management Information Systems. Given that these disciplines as such did not exist in Communist Czechoslovakia[13], only the last decade has seen certain attempts to establish stronger links between the emerging Czech Business Informatics community and the partner communities in the west [42]. It may be thus argued that the applied computing fields in what was then Czechoslovakia, now the Czech Republic and the Slovak Republic, have been clearly among the losers of the former CMEA standardization game dominated by the Soviets.

---

[13] This was partly due to the non-existence of the science of business administration/management in its prevailing international meaning [26].

6 Conclusion

This paper provides an overview of the disciplinary realms related to computing and automation in Communist Czechoslovakia, and more generally, in the East Bloc. First and foremost, the paper points out that while "informatics" has been a common term in Western Europe for a number of decades [1, 8], the Central and East European realities were different. Specifically, we have argued that the term "informatics" was introduced to fill the intellectual vacuum left by emasculated cybernetics in the first half of the 1970s. Interestingly, this happened under the Western influence. Together with Afinogenov we believe that the existence of the informatics discipline in Germany and France significantly influenced a prominent Soviet figure, Andrey Ershov, to argue in favour of informatics in the Soviet Union.

Yet, being a complex social structure, informatics in the Soviet Union did not emerge from nowhere nor was entirely copied from the West. We propose that while the term was adopted from the West, the "cybernetics DNA" of Soviet-style informatics continued to play a major role within the latter discipline. Further, while in 1973 cybernetics was officially considered "too broad" in Czechoslovakia, we believe that the main reason for the disciplinary reform was *de facto* similar as in the Soviet Union – the cybernetics fashion simply passed, as did the catchiness of "cyberspeak" [3]. Expressively and speculatively stated: In 1973, Czechoslovak cybernetics, as a wide conceptual umbrella, was sacrificed, because the key people felt (or were instructed by the Soviets) that the end of the "cybernetics game" [3] is near.

While, as a discipline, cybernetics continued its journey even after the changes implemented by the Conception, it clearly lost part of the previous scope. The next big thing was computers. From 1973 onwards, the technological concept of automated management/control *(automatizované řízení),* which had been rooted in cybernetics [12], was institutionalized within the boundaries of computing (see the full title of the Conception and its prevailing tone). Considering this, one should recall that the title of AMCS came from the Soviet Union where it was introduced into the educational segment ca. 5 years before the Conception was debated in Czechoslovak government [34].

However the Conception resulted in a significant overlap between the concepts of applied computing and automated management/control, it clearly made a huge step towards Western-style informatics. But was the key outcome of the Conception just in renaming some of the disciplines and adding a few new ones? We do not think so. Resulting directly from the import of Western knowledge by boundary spanners like Ershov, in our view the Conception rather initiated a complex transformational process. The full story of this transformation, so as of the disciplinary conflicts the transformation presumably caused in the intellectual space of Czechoslovak universities, is still to be told. Yet, the emergence of the three disciplines described here was arguably the most salient manifestation of the transformational process in Czechoslovakia.

In sum, this paper suggests that 1973 can be seen as a turning point when cybernetics lost its monopoly in the broad field of information processing in Czechoslovakia. The Conception, as put into practice that year, triggered a disciplinary drift which started redistributing power between cybernetics and informatics. Naturally, the drift did not stop anytime soon; it was a rather long, complicated process. In fact, one can argue that the drift still has not ended because it appears that even nowadays the distribution of power between the two disciplines in the Czech Republic is renegotiated from time to time [43]. From our personal perspective, this "residual drift", which has continued for almost 50 years, is probably the most impressive afterglow of the past fame of cybernetics in the East. Viewed from a different perspective, however, the persistence of the drift seems to be quite natural. In the metaphorical terms proposed by sociologists of science [7], both amoebas (i.e., cybernetics and informatics) simply continue to fight for their intellectual living space.

Turning finally to administrative issues discussed in this paper, an interesting feature of computing education in Communist Czechoslovakia was the high level of state involvement in computing education standardization – an initiative primarily driven by CMEA dominated by the Soviets. Naturally, the state effort did not stop with the unification of disciplinary titles. Curricula content and profiles of graduates were also largely standardized (at least across Czechoslovakia). This fact had significant influence on the disciplines that were fighting for greater autonomy from their reference disciplines (e.g. *Electronic Computers* from electrical engineering). In general, all these processes might be of interest to researchers who strive to understand how academic disciplines evolved in Central and Eastern Europe under the Communist reign.

Lastly, elaborating on the above ideas, there are numerous avenues open for future research. In our subsequent research we want to focus on gaining a deeper understanding of the activities of the above mentioned Intergovernmental commission under the wing of CMEA. Specifically, we plan to explore the extent of its international involvement in curricula standardization. It would also be extremely interesting to map the geography of computing disciplines [6] across the former CMEA countries. However, the key challenge is that aside from the Conception, only a very limited number of archival sources have been found in relevant collections of the National Archives, Prague so far. We thus call to action also researchers from the remaining countries that were formerly allied in CMEA, who might want to explore their national landscapes. In parallel, we plan to continue our research in archival collections of the Czech universities mentioned in this paper.

Acknowledgement. We thank archivists of the National Archives, Prague for their helpfulness and the time spent while pre-selecting archival materials in uncatalogued collections of the Ministry of Education and the Governmental Office of the Czech Socialist Republic. We also thank the reviewers for their valuable feedback.

References

1. Coy, W.: Defining discipline. In: Freksa, C., Jantzen, M., Valk, R. (eds.) Foundations of Computer Science. LNCS, vol. 1337, pp. 21–35. Springer, Heidelberg (1997). https://doi.org/10.1007/BFb0052074
2. Avgerou, C., Siemer, J., Bjørn-Andersen, N.: The academic field of information systems in Europe. Eur. J. Inf. Syst. **8**, 136–153 (1999)
3. Gerovitch, S.: From Newspeak to Cyberspeak: A History of Soviet Cybernetics. MIT Press, Cambridge (2002)

4. Arbib, M.A.: A partial survey of cybernetics in Eastern Europe and the Soviet Union. Behav. Sci. **11**, 193–216 (1966)
5. Kitov, V.A., Kitov, V.V., Muzychkin, P.A., Nedelkin, A.A.: The Main Scientific Publications of Anatoly Ivanovich Kitov. Plekhanov Russian University of Economics, Moscow (2018)
6. Mounier-Kuhn, P.: Computer science in French universities: early entrants and latecomers. Inf. Cult. **47**, 414–456 (2012)
7. Abbott, A.: Chaos of Disciplines. University of Chicago, Chicago (2001)
8. Mounier-Kuhn, P.-É., Pégny, M.: AFCAL and the emergence of computer science in France: 1957–1967. In: Beckmann, A., Bienvenu, L., Jonoska, N. (eds.) CiE 2016. LNCS, vol. 9709, pp. 170–181. Springer, Cham (2016). https://doi.org/10.1007/978-3-319-40189-8_18
9. Connelly, J.: Captive university. University of North Carolina Press, Chapel Hill (2001)
10. Vyhláška 53/1977 Sb. o výchově nových vědeckých pracovníků [Czechoslovak Academy of Sciences' regulation 53/1977 Coll. over the education of new scientific workers]
11. Lewis, N.: Peering through the curtain: soviet computing through the eyes of western experts. IEEE Ann. Hist. Comput. **38**, 34–47 (2016)
12. Sobolev, S.L., Kitov, A.I., Lyapunov, A.A.: Osnovnye cherty kibernetiki [The main features of cybernetics]. Vopr. Filos. **IX**, 141–165 (1955)
13. Kolman, A.: Kybernetika [Cybernetics] (translated from Russian). Státní nakladatelství politické literatury, Praha (1957)
14. El-Kadi, A.: Stop that divorce! Commun. ACM **42**, 27–28 (1999)
15. Brookes, B.C.: Lenin: the founder of informatics. J. Inf. Sci. **8**, 221–223 (1984)
16. Afinogenov, G.: Andrei Ershov and the soviet information age. Krit. Explor. Russ. Eurasian Hist. **14**, 561–584 (2013)
17. Umpleby, S.: A brief history of cybernetics in the United States. J. Washingt. Acad. Sci. **91**, 54–66 (2005)
18. Věstník Ministerstva školství a kultury [Bulletin of the Ministry of Education and Culture]. XXI/8 (1965)
19. Berg, A.I.: O některých problémech kybernetiky [On some problems of cybernetics] (translated from Russian). Pokrok. Mat. fyziky a Astron. **5**, 718–728 (1960)
20. Durnova, H.: Sovietization of czechoslovakian computing: the rise and fall of the SAPO project. IEEE Ann. Hist. Comput. **32**, 21–31 (2010)
21. Mareš, M.: RNDr. Albert Perez, DrSc. 8.1.1920–11.12.2003. Kybernetika **39**, 761–762 (2003)
22. Vopěnka, P., Renc, Z.: Studium teoretické kybernetiky na MFF UK [The study of Theoretical Cybernetics at Charles University]. Pokrok. Mat. fyziky a Astron. **16**, 22–25 (1971)
23. Tsien, H.S.: Technická kybernetika [Technical Cybernetics] (translated from English). Státní nakladatelství technické literatury, Praha (1960)
24. Dujnic, J., Fristacky, N., Molnár, L., Plander, I., Rovan, B.: On the history of computer science, computer engineering, and computer technology development in Slovakia. IEEE Ann. Hist. Comput. **21**, 38–48 (1999)
25. Schwartz, D.V.: Recent soviet adaptations of systems theory to administrative theory. J. Comp. Adm. **5**, 233–264 (1973)
26. Afanasjev, V.G.: Vědecké řízení společnosti [Scientific management of society] (translated from Russian). Státní pedagogické nakladatelství, Praha (1977)
27. Vidmer, R.F.: Soviet studies of organization and management: a "jungle" of competing views. Slavic Rev. **40**, 404–422 (1981)

28. Koncepce výchovy kvalifikovaných vysokoškolských a středoškolských kádrů v oblasti výpočetních techniky [The conception of higher and middle education of qualified cadres in the area of computer technology]. National Archives, Prague, collection Ministry of Education [not catalogued] (1972)
29. Koncepce výchovy kvalifikovaných vysokoškolských a středoškolských odborníků v oblasti výpočetních techniky [The conception of higher and middle education of qualified experts in the area of computer technology]. National Archives, Prague, collection Úřad vlády ČSR [not catalogued] (1972)
30. Goodman, S.E.: Socialist technological integration: the case of the east european computer industries. Inf. Soc. **3**, 39–89 (1984)
31. Prokudin, V.A., Říha, L.: Vědeckotechnická revoluce a socialistická integrace [Scientific Revolution and Socialist Integration]. SNTL, Praha (1977)
32. Balda, M., Ehleman, J.: Příprava československého vysokého školství na výchovu odborníků v oblasti automatizovaného systému řízení z hlediska mezinárodní spolupráce [The preparation of Czechoslovak university system for the education of AMCS specialists - an international perspe. Mech. a Autom. Adm. [Mechanization Autom. Adm. **13**, 414–417 (1973)
33. Usnesení vlády České socialistické republiky ze dne 22. prosince 1971 č. 306 [Government Resolution/Czech Socialist Republic No. 306/1971]. National Archives, Prague, collection Úřad vlády ČSR [not catalogued]
34. Eljutin, V.P.: Podgotovka spetsialistov po avtomatizirivannym sistemam upravleniya [The preparation of specialists for automated management/control systems]. In: Zhimerin, D.G. (ed.) Avtomatizirovannyye sistemy upravleniya : Primeneniye vychislit. tekhniki i avtomatizir. sistem upravleniya na predpriyatiyakh i v otraslyakh prom-st. Ekonomika, Moscow (1972)
35. Usnesení vlády České socialistické republiky ze dne 31. ledna 1973 č. 26 [Government Resolution/Czech Socialist Republic No. 26/1973]. National Archives, Prague, collection Úřad vlády ČSR [not catalogued] (1973)
36. Zpráva o stavu a efektivnosti využívání výpočetní techniky v ČSSR za rok 1974 [A status and efficiency report about computers usage in Czechoslovakia]. National Archives, Prague, collection Úřad předsednictva vlády - b.s. [not catalogued] (1975)
37. Vyhláška Československé akademie věd č. 5/1986 o výchově vědeckých pracovníků
38. Smutný, Z., Doležel, M.: Ustavení a historický vývoj informatiky a počítačových disciplín ve vybraných evropských zemích a v USA [The Emergence and Historical Development of Informatics and Computing Disciplines in Selected European Countries and the USA]. Acta Inform. Pragensia **6**, 188–229 (2017)
39. Scime, A.: Globalized computing education: Europe and the United States. Comput. Sci. Educ. **18**, 43–64 (2008)
40. Wren, D.A.: Scientific management in the U.S.S.R., with particular reference to the contribution of walter N. Polakov. Acad. Manag. Rev. **5**, 1–11 (1980)
41. Peters, B.: Normalizing soviet cybernetics. Inf. Cult. A J. Hist. **47**, 145–175 (2012)
42. Smutný, Z., Doležel, M.: From soviet cybernetics to western-oriented design science: a business informatics community in transition. In: 17th European Conference on Research Methodology for Business and Management Studies, pp. 380–388. ACPI, Rome (2018)
43. Šmejkal, L.: Zrušíme obor kybernetika? [Are we going to abolish the discipline of cybernetics?]. Automa. 8 (2015)

László Kalmár and the First University-Level Programming and Computer Science Training in Hungary

Máté Szabó[1,2(✉)]

[1] Archives Henri-Poincaré, UMR 7117, Université de Lorraine, Nancy, France
mate.szabo@univ-lorraine.fr
[2] IHPST, UMR 8590, Université Paris 1 Panthéon-Sorbonne, Paris, France

Abstract. The aim of this case study is to provide a detailed description of the first university-level programming and computer science training in Hungary, which started in 1957 at the University of Szeged. The program began due to the strenuous efforts of Professor László Kalmár, who is considered to be "the father of computer science in Hungary". The aim of this study is to add to the literature on Kalmár's work, focusing on his activities in the field of computer science education, and at the same time, to add a detailed study from the Eastern Bloc to the history of computer science education.

Keywords: Eastern Bloc · History of computer science education ·
History of computing · Hungary · Kalmár, László

1 Introduction

This case study provides a detailed description of the first university-level programming and computer science training in Hungary, which started in 1957 at the University of Szeged[1] due to the strenuous efforts of Professor László Kalmár. The aim of this study is twofold: to add to the literature on Kalmár's work, focusing on his activities in the field of computer science education, and, at the same time, to add a detailed study from the Eastern Bloc to the research on the history of computer science education.

Kalmár is recognized internationally more for his work in mathematical logic through the 1930s to the 1950s than for his contributions to computer science, even though his achievements in the field were (posthumously) recognized by IEEE with the Computer Pioneer Award in 1996. Within Hungary, he is often referred to as "the father of computer science in Hungary" or "the pioneer of Hungarian computer science" [1, 2]. Kalmár earned such epithets due to his tremendous impact on the field of computer science in Hungary. He devoted the last two decades of his life to computer science and contributed to every aspect of it, including theoretical computer science, computer design, philosophy of cybernetics, organization of the field in Hungary, and

---

[1] Between 1962 and 1999, the university adopted the name of the Hungarian poet Attila József and was called József Attila Tudományegyetem, JATE. Throughout this paper, I will refer consistently to the university as University of Szeged to avoid confusion.

© IFIP International Federation for Information Processing 2019
Published by Springer Nature Switzerland AG 2019
C. Leslie and M. Schmitt (Eds.): HC 2018, IFIP AICT 549, pp. 40–68, 2019.
https://doi.org/10.1007/978-3-030-29160-0_3

its education. Thus, it is impossible to understand the history of computing in Hungary without Kalmár's contributions. Still, the only source in English devoted solely to his work in the field is Makay's short [3], and some sections of survey papers, e.g.. Kovács [4, Sect. 7], while the Hungarian sources that discuss his work in the field [5, 1, 2] touch upon his educational activities only briefly. This paper addresses this gap in the literature concerning Kalmár's educational work in computer science and its impact on the early generations of programmers in Hungary.

The other goal of this case study is to contribute to the history of computer science education. Just as in the case of the history of computing in general, the history of computer science education has only a few sources in English from the Eastern Bloc. In the case of Hungary, only Raffai [6, Sect. 3] and Sántáné-Tóth [7] are available in English besides some scattered remarks in survey papers discussing the history of computing of the country as a whole. Although this paper focuses narrowly on Hungary, it displays some more general challenges such a program had to face in the Eastern Bloc as well.

When the training started in 1957, there was no running computer in the country yet, and there was no computer at Szeged until 1965. Thus, it had to function without a computer in place for several years while being the only training for programmers at the university-level in the country. This led to some serious problems in the beginning, as well as rather unique solutions, as discussed in detail in the sections *Lack of Internships* and *Programming Without Computers*. Although this case might be extreme even within the Eastern Bloc, it shows rather well that some of these countries faced quite different challenges that those of the West. Besides the scarcity of computers, many of these countries lacked nationwide strategic plans and funding for years to come, unlike for example in the UK [8, 9] and France [10]. Hence, this study not merely augments the sources in English on the history of computer science education in Hungary, but also serves as an addition to a broader Eastern European picture as well. In order to be a useful source for further research, quite a lot of detail is provided, especially in the appendices, about early enrollments, curricula and faculty, etc.

This case study is based on the following archival sources besides the already available literature on Kalmár's work in English and Hungarian. The Kalmár Nachlass in the Klebelsberg Library at the University of Szeged holds several relevant documents. Most importantly, the folder 'Lev-12' contains about 100 pages of Kalmár's official correspondence related to the different programming and computer science training and majors from 1957 to 1974 [11]. The section *The Fast Track to the First Programming and Computer Science Training* and many details in the appendices are based on this folder. Besides this folder, I used Kalmár's personal correspondence and some of his unpublished manuscripts, for example [12]. The use of these archival materials is indicated throughout the text below. Another source for this paper that has to be mentioned here is Sántáné-Tóth [13], which is an indispensable source on the history of computer science in Hungarian higher education. The book contains information about 30 universities and colleges and was the product of a collaboration coordinated under the umbrella of the Forum of Information Technology History at the John von Neumann Computer Society. A shorter, informative English summary of the research is provided in [7].

The structure of the paper is as follows. First, I provide some context about the level of computerization and the system of higher education in Hungary. This is followed by a short description of Kalmár's work on computer science and his creation of a community of researchers and educators in this field. Then, the administrative road to the first programming and computer science training is presented in detail. Next, in the sections *Lack of Internships* and *Programming without Computers*, I discuss the two biggest problems the lack of computers in Szeged posed for the training. This is followed by an overview of other early programming and computer science training in Hungary, the later growth of the training in Szeged, and Kalmár's writings related to computers and education. The *Appendices* include the curricula of the first three classes and the titles of the Master's Theses written by the students in those classes, as well as "Kalmár's fictional machines", and a description of their use as a teaching material in an unpublished abstract of Kalmár's.

2 Computers and Education in Late 1950s Hungary

To provide context for the programming and computer science training at Szeged, I quickly describe the level of computerization in Hungary and the relevant features of its university education system.

It is well known that the computerization of the Eastern Bloc lagged behind the US and Western Europe, see for example [14–16]. However, the computerization of Hungary started out relatively slowly even within the Eastern Bloc, not only in comparison to the Soviet Union but to Poland and Czechoslovakia as well [16, 17].

The first vacuum tube computer in Hungary was running reliably only from early 1959. It was built by the Cybernetics Research Group[2] (founded in early 1956) of the Hungarian Academy of Sciences in Budapest. The group received the blueprints and some of the parts of the Soviet M-3 computer and built the first electronic vacuum tube computer in the country. The M-3 showed its first "signs of life" during 1958 and ran reliably by 1959 [18–20]. By the end of that year, there were three running computers in the country (two Ural-1 computers were installed in other research institutes), all of them in the capital, Budapest. In fact, there was no computer outside of Budapest until 1965!

Hungary caught up with the region by the early 1970s and became a successful member of the Ryad project in the 1970s [21]. For an overview of the history of information technology and computer developments in Hungary, see Szentgyörgyi [22].

In order to understand the beginnings of computer science education, we should consider natural sciences education in Hungary in the 1950s. Those who wanted to study natural sciences had to enroll as high school teachers with two majors (with very few exceptions). Thus, most people who received education in mathematics earned a mathematics-physics or a mathematics-descriptive geometry high school teacher degree. These degrees are considered to be equivalent to a Master's Degree. Their program consisted of four years of coursework including pedagogy and psychology

---

[2] Kibernetikai Kutatócsoport, often referred to as KKCs in papers in Hungarian.

classes. By the late 1950s, these programs were extended to five years to include about a year of teaching practice in a high school at the end and required a thesis to be written and defended in one of the two majors.

The only exception in the case of mathematics was the applied mathematician major offered by Eötvös University in Budapest from 1950. It trained the students to be employed in the industry or at research institutes and did not require coursework in pedagogy and psychology. However, this major accepted fewer than 15 people per year.

3 László Kalmár's Work in Szeged

As we will see below, programming and computer science education in Szeged was started due to Kalmár's one-man mission in 1957. The training that started with only three students gradually became a major with higher enrollments. Of course, this growth required an increase in the number of instructors and in the institutional background. In this section, I briefly discuss Kalmár's career and the institutional changes that accommodated the growing program.

László Kalmár was born in 1905 and worked at the University of Szeged from 1927 until his retirement in 1975. He became an eminent mathematical logician by the end of the 1920s. Although he first learned about mathematical logic and Hilbert's proof theory from von Neumann's [23], meeting Hilbert was decisive for Kalmár's career in choosing mathematical logic as his main focus. In 1928, Kalmár attended Hilbert's address at the International Congress of Mathematicians in Bologna [24] and spent the Summer Term of 1929 in Göttingen. There he attended Hilbert's course on Set Theory, the last third of which was devoted to mathematical logic and proof theory ([25 p. 2, 5, 19]. From the 1930s through the 1950s, he worked on recursion theory, the reduction of the decision problem, incompleteness and undecidability; see [26–28] for examples. The following two facts show Kalmár's acknowledgement of and acceptance by the international community of logicians. First, during the 1940s and 1950s, Kalmár was a member of the editorial board of the *Journal of Symbolic Logic*, the first journal dedicated solely to the topic. Second, when Kalmár applied for a professorship at the University of Szeged in 1946 (which he received in 1947), his letters of recommendation were from John von Neumann [29, p. 226], Alonzo Church [30, pp. 156–157] and Haskell B. Curry.

Besides research, Kalmár was clearly interested in education as well. Together with his lifelong colleague and friend Rózsa Péter, he paved the way for the acceptance of logic in Hungarian mathematics. They presented expository talks and papers both for academic [31, 32] and wider audiences [33], and introduced logic as a subject to university curricula. (On Kalmár and Péter's contributions to mathematics and logic education in Hungary see [34]).

Around the mid 1950s, Kalmár's interest turned toward the applications of logic to computer design and to engineering in general, automata theory, and cybernetics. He devoted most of his time to these subjects until his death in 1976. Kalmár was extremely productive in his last two decades and had a tremendous impact on computer science research and education in Hungary. His work earned him such epithets as "the father of computer science in Hungary" and "the pioneer of Hungarian computer science" [1, 2], and was also recognized by IEEE, receiving their Computer Pioneer Award posthumously in 1996. Because it is almost impossible to list all of Kalmár's achievements in this field, I can only provide a short but hopefully illuminating list of his activities below.

Kalmár knew about the newly founded Cybernetics Research Group in Budapest and the plans to build the M-3 computer. He regularly visited the Group, attended and delivered talks at their meetings and maintained a good relationship with the members of the Group.

Fig. 1. Kalmár and Muszka with the (Szeged) Logical Machine around 1957 [38].

Kalmár started his own seminar at the mathematics department in Szeged in the spring of 1956 to explore his new interests. This seminar led to the founding of the Mathematical Logic and its Applications Research Group with Kalmár as its head in 1957. The activities of the group included the construction of the (Szeged) Logical Machine (Fig. 1) and the Electronic Ladybird, a conditioned reflex model, built by his research assistant Dániel Muszka in cooperation with members of the Pedagogy and Psychology Department in 1957 [35, pp. 48–59]. Kalmár also designed a computer that could be programmed in a mathematical formula language [36]. Although he had several iterations of the plans, the computer was sadly never built in Hungary. However, it had an impact on the MIR computer built between 1963 and 1966 at the Kiev Institute of Cybernetics.[3] In 1963 he founded the *Cybernetics Laboratory*, which grew

---

[3] For a slightly more detailed description of Kalmár's design, see [1, 3, and 37 p. 82]. In terms of its impact on the MIR computer, these sources provide the following short descriptions: "Parts of [Kalmár's] machine plans were utilized in the MIR machine of the Ukrainian Academy of Sciences, built in 1966" [3, p. 12], and "According to an oral communication by Z. L. Rabinovič (Cybernetical Institute of the Ukrainian Academy of Sciences), the first universal formula controlled computer was built in this Institute (1963–1966), on the basis of Kalmár's ideas" [37, p. 82].

rapidly after the arrival of the M-3 computer to Szeged in 1965, and later became the first computer center outside the capital. In 1967, another research group was founded in Szeged to conduct research in mathematical logic and automata theory.

Fig. 2. A picture showing Kalmár and Church, taken by András Ádám at the Colloquium on the Foundations of Mathematics, Mathematical Machines and Their Applications, Tihany, 11–15, September 1962. (picture published with Ádám's approval.)

Besides designing computing devices, Kalmár published extensively in theoretical computer science and even on the philosophical problems of cybernetics. He founded the journal *Acta Cybernetica* in 1969, which is still running today. Kalmár also organized several domestic and international workshops and conferences devoted to these topics. The *Colloquium on the Foundations of Mathematics, Mathematical Machines and Their Applications*, which he organized in 1962 in Tihany, Hungary, was attended by such illustrious scholars as Alonzo Church (Fig. 2), Haskell B. Curry, John McCarthy and Yehoshua Bar-Hillel [39]. In addition, he regularly attended and contributed papers to conferences on computational linguistics [40], and applications of computers and computer science in the fields of medicine [41] and heavy industry [42]. Through these activities, Kalmár had a tremendous impact on the scientific communities in Hungary that did research in computer science.

Kalmár was an active member of the international community as well. In addition to attending multiple international conferences every year, he had an extensive correspondence with scholars from both the "East" and the "West" and visited academic institutions and computer centers around the world. Furthermore, he spent the winter of 1958–1959 in China at the invitation of Fudan University in Shanghai as part of the Hungarian-Chinese cultural treaty. China's first computer, the DJS-1 (or 103) built from 1961, was also based on the Soviet M-3 computer [43 and 44, pp. 151–157]. Over the course of three months, Kalmár delivered lectures about the general problems of programming computers, particular arithmetic operators and algorithms for the M-3 computer, and mathematical logic and computability in Shanghai, Beijing, Wuhan, and Hangzhou [20, p. 2063 and 2065]. During the 1960s, Kalmár represented Hungary and the Hungarian Academy of Sciences in the "Committee of the Scientific Problems of Computer Science and Technology" of the "academies of friendly [socialist] states".

Just as with logic, Kalmár was invested in the education of programming and computer science as well. He regularly delivered expository talks to academic and wider audiences, and he was singlehandedly responsible for starting the university-level training of programmers in Hungary in 1957. To accommodate the growing numbers of programming and computer science students, in 1967 an independent Foundations of Mathematics and Computer Technology Department was created with Kalmár as the head of the department. In 1971, this department morphed into the Computer Science Department, still headed by Kalmár until his retirement in 1975. Through his seminars, research groups, the computer center and independent department, Kalmár created a large community of talented computer science scholars and educators. This community was able to supply instructors for the education of future computer scientists. (See *Appendix* A for the names and biographical information for the instructors of the first couple classes of the training.) The next section discusses the short bureaucratic prehistory of the training, while the later sections provide the details of the first couple classes of the program.

4   The Fast Track to the First Programming and Computer Science Training

According to Varga [1] and Sántáné-Tóth [13] Kalmár wanted to start a major with a focus on programming and computer science, similar to the Applied Mathematician major in Budapest, but with a focus on programming and computer science. However, his requests were denied by the Ministry of Education and Culture.[4]

After all, in 1957 Kalmár was allowed to start the first programming and computer science training at the university-level in Hungary. I use the term "training" here, because the first iteration of this program was neither a major in the sense of mathematics and physics high school teacher double majors, nor in the sense of the applied mathematician major provided by Eötvös University.

This section describes the timeline of the rather quick official process that led to the start of the training. It is based on, and closely follows Kalmár's official letter to Ágoston Budó, Dean of the School of Natural Sciences at the University of Szeged, dated March 25, 1960. The letter can be found in the 'Lev-12' folder [11]. The 9-page letter describes in detail the administrative road to start the training. Kalmár's description appears to be precise, as many of the documents mentioned in the letter can also be found in the folder.

---

[4] Művelődésügyi Minisztérium in Hungarian.

On 15 May 1957, the Ministry of Education and Culture permitted 5% of talented students with double majors to drop one of their majors at the beginning of their third or fourth year in order to gain deeper knowledge and conduct research in their other major.[5] However, the Ministry kept the right to specify the number of such students with mathematics or biology majors on a year by year basis.

On 5 July Kalmár made an application[6] to the Ministry to allow his department to train such talented students, dropping their second, non-mathematics major for the programming of computers ("digital calculators") and their theory. Kalmár argued that there was a need for such training, as the country would need "programming mathematicians" at the Cybernetics and other research groups, as well as at large factories, in order to run the M-3 continuously, and to supply it, and future computer centers, with programs and problems to solve. He suggested that the Ministry communicate with the Cybernetics Research Group and the Planbureau (the government body responsible for economical planning) to determine the number of programming experts needed in the near future. He proposed that after their coursework at Szeged, the students could have an internship, a practical training, on the M-3 computer of the Cybernetics Research Group in Budapest.

As he did not receive any notification about a decision, Kalmár inquired at the Ministry upon returning from an academic trip abroad on 8 or 9 September. He was informed that the Ministry approved the training. However, the students would have to study more traditional applied mathematics classes, e.g., partial differential equations, besides programming and computer science. They would earn the title High School Mathematics Teacher – Applied Mathematician.

On 10 September, Kalmár recognized that the University of Szeged did not yet receive any official approval of the training. In a personal letter he urged the Ministry to send the official documents for him to be able to start preparing the training. Two days later, on 12 September, he received a call from the Ministry informing him that the official approval was on its way to the university and he could begin preparations for the training. On the same day, Kalmár announced the start of the new training to the students on the department bulletin boards and organized an informative meeting about it.

On 16 September, Kalmár was informed by the Dean of the Faculty of Science that the official approval arrived and that the headcount of the training would be limited to 3 students. On the next day, Kalmár announced to the students that they would have to submit a special application to the Dean's Office in order to enroll in the new training.

Students submitted their application to the training two days later, on 19 September. Two students at the beginning of their third year and four students at the beginning of their fourth year applied. The committee, consisting of Kalmár and two other professors of mathematics, accepted third-year student József Jónás and fourth year students Ilona Fidrich and László Leindler. The students were notified on 23 September about the decision.

---

[5] For those students who chose this path at the beginning of their fourth year, the training lasted only one year. This was allowed, as the country needed highly trained experts quickly in many fields.

[6] This letter of Kalmár's can also be found in the 'Lev-12' folder [11].

The curriculum of the training was approved on 21 September by the Dean's Office of the Faculty of Science. The classes began on the 26 September 1957. (The semester began a couple of weeks earlier; thus the other classes were already going on for a while.)

To sum up: during the course of the summer of 1957 the Ministry of Education and Culture approved the University of Szeged to start a programming and computer science training for three students. These students were allowed to drop their second major in order to enroll this training. Though the focus of the training was in programming and computer science, they also had to learn further, "more traditional", topics in applied mathematics. After their fourth year in Szeged they were to go through a practical training internship at the Cybernetics Research Group in Budapest. The location of the internship was a necessity, as computers were to be found only in Budapest at the time. At the end they earned a High School Mathematics Teacher – Applied Mathematician degree. Sometimes they were informally referred to as Calculator Applied Mathematicians. (For the curricula of the first three classes and the titles of the Master's Theses written by the students in those classes, see Appendices A and B.)

This approval process might appear to be extremely quick. However, Kalmár already had a sizable reputation. He was appointed as a professor in 1947 and became a corresponding member of the Hungarian Academy of Sciences in 1949. He also served as the president of the University of Szeged during the 1950–1951 academic year [45, p. 17]. And most importantly, as Kalmár emphasized in his application letter, there was an urgent need for programmers in the foreseeable future.

Let us take a quick look at the international situation for comparison. The training at Szeged started only four years after University of Cambridge's one-year training, called Diploma in Numerical Analysis and Automatic Computing, which was offered from the fall of 1953, and is considered to be the first computer science training ever [46, p. 96]. In the U.S., as Fein reports [47], there were about 150 universities that offered some kind of computer science or computer related course, seminar, lecture series, etc. in the country by 1959. However, "[o]nly a few universities have made a determined effort to select a field of interest, set up a policy and goal, and implement it" (p. 9). The first computer science department in the U.S. was founded at Purdue University in 1962. The newly founded department started Masters and PhD programs already in its first semester, leading to their first graduates in 1964 and 1966 respectively [48, 49]. However, the earliest PhDs awarded in computer science in the U.S. were given in 1965 [50]. In the Soviet Union, according to Ershov and Shura-Bura [51, Sec. 6], the first course on programming was taught by Lyapunov in the 1952–1953 academic year in Moscow, and the first graduate degrees were defended during the mid-1950s. Also in 1952, "several universities started a new specialty [master's equivalent level] in 'computing mathematics' in addition to the existing specialty in mathematics" (p. 178), with courses predominantly in mathematics and numerical methods. It was only in 1969 that a new computational mathematics specialty was started to fulfill the growing needs for programmers in the country (p. 181). Thus, although the computerization of Hungary began relatively late, its computer science and programming education was timely.

5 Lack of Internships

As mentioned above, there was no computer in Szeged (or anywhere outside Budapest) until 1965. Moreover, though the number of computers was growing in the country, only the M-3 computer at the Cybernetics Research Group could be visited by students and faculty of educational institutions. Thus, every student internship had to be completed at the M-3.

The first class of the training consisted of two fourth-year and one third-year student. By the summer of 1958, the two fourth year students, Ilona Fidrich and László Leindler, completed their high school mathematics teacher major and were missing only their internships to complete the applied mathematician component of their degree.

As the prescribed length of the internship was a year and could take place only in Budapest, the students needed a stipend to be able to attend it. Kalmár asked the Mathematical Committee of the Academy of Sciences to provide such stipends in June of 1958. As the stipends were still not approved by the end of July, both fourth year students accepted the high school mathematics teaching jobs they were offered. The third member of the class, József Jónás, had a similar experience one year later upon finishing. Although Kalmár took action already in April of 1959 to secure a stipend for him, it was still not confirmed by the summer. Jónás accepted a high school teaching position without finishing the Applied Mathematician training as well.

After a year of teaching in a high school, Fidrich completed her internship and became the first graduate of the training (See *Appendix* B for Fidrich's short biography). Leindler also left his high school job and became a doctoral candidate, and later, a faculty member at the Mathematics Department at the University of Szeged; however, he never completed his applied mathematician training. Jónás stayed at his high school teaching job and was required by the high school to complete his previously dropped high school physics teacher major through correspondence classes, as every other high school teacher was able to teach two subjects.

According to Kalmár, this uncertainty about internships, and its career implications, led to decreased interest in the new training. Indeed, while in 1957 they witnessed a surplus of applicants, they received too few applications to even fill the officially approved headcount in subsequent years.[7] However, students at the time were not aware of these issues (based on the author's personal correspondence with Edit Sántáné-Tóth, a member of the second class starting in 1958), so it is unlikely that this impacted the number of applications.

The lack of internships was a problem only for the first class. Every student in the later classes had an internship scheduled for them, and from 1963 they were able to do their internships at computer centers at other research institutes or ministries as well. The requirements of the internship changed, too. Members of the second class had to

---

[7] While in 1957 they received 6 applications for 3 positions, in 1958 they received only 4 applications for 6 places, and only 5 for 12 positions in 1960. (Kalmár's programming and computer science training, among many others, was not allowed to start a new class in 1959 as reforms were put in place in higher education, such as extending of the length of the high school teacher programs to five years).

spend only the second semester of their final, fifth year, as an internship. Members of the third class had to attend two additional, shorter internships during the training: a three week internship after their third year and a five week internship after their fourth year.

As this training was one of the very few options to learn programming in the country (see the section *Other Early Programs*), there was a shortage of programmers throughout the 1960s in Hungary. As a consequence, from the second class on, graduating students usually received multiple job offers from the industry, in many cases from the computer centers where they did their internships.

It has to be pointed out that although their degree qualified the graduating students to teach mathematics in high school, they rarely became teachers, as they were immediately acquired upon graduation by the industry. However, it was never even among the intentions of the training to educate high school teachers. At the time there were no computers at high schools in the country and no plan to include the subject in secondary education. The sole purpose was to train programmers. Indeed, Kalmár argued for the creation of the training to satisfy the (future) needs of the industry, computer centers and research groups. And the training was successful at that.

6 Programming Without Computers

The lack of computers in Szeged meant that, for several years, the students had no regular access to computers during their training. They visited the M-3 about once a semester before their internship in Budapest (based on the authors personal correspondence with Edit Sántáné-Tóth).

This situation led, by necessity, to the so-called "chalk programming" method where programs were written on the blackboard with chalk. Then Kalmár and the students "executed" the programs, an activity they referred to as a "dry run". This method clearly had the didactic drawbacks that it deprived the students from the experience of running a program they wrote, the interactions with the program while debugging and running it again, and finally, the feeling of accomplishment once the program was properly functioning.

In his programming classes, Kalmár used several fictional computers instead of a description of one of the few computers in the country. Throughout the years, he defined more and more fictional computers based on the information they were able to gather about different models, and to accommodate new developments in the field. This led to a universal notational system, in which any actual operation of any actual computer can be expressed. The fictional computers, later referred to as "Kalmár's fictional computers", were introduced with or without index registers, while the operations in their assembly languages could have one, two or even three addresses.

It seems that Kalmár introduced his first fictional computers independently from the well-known idealized computers in the literature as his first versions predate the publication of some of those. It is clear, however, that he was interested in and indeed did follow the literature (see *Appendix* D) on them. However, he preferred to use a whole set of his fictional computers for the following reasons. In class, the students were required to solve different problems on different fictional computers, depending on the pedagogical purpose. For example, the set of operations could be rather restricted if the goal was to show that certain operations are expressible in terms of others. This made it impossible to exploit particular "nice" features of the formalism of the idealized computers in the literature. At the same time, it prepared the students to adapt easily to any kind of computer they ended up working with, which was important for two reasons. First, although there were only a few computers in the country at the time, there were many different models. This continued to be a challenge for the successive years as well. For example, by 1969, there were still only 86 computers in Hungary, but this small selection was comprised of thirty different models [52, p. 7]. Second, computers and programming languages were changing quickly at the time, so this method made it easy not only to adapt to the several different models, but to the computers of the foreseeable future as well (Fig. 3).

Fig. 3. Kalmár during a lecture [53].

During recitations, students were taught all computer models whose descriptions the instructors had access to. In these classes, the students first learned the operations of those specific computers in terms of the operations of Kalmár's fictional computers, and then in their own assembly languages.

Kalmár's fictional computers had a long-lasting impact on the education of programmers at Szeged. They were still in use in the 1970s, although by this time the focus had shifted to high-level languages. For example, Kalmár taught ALGOL 60 from the early 1960s. In [54], Kalmár mentions two reasons for this. First, they believed that every programmer should know how to code in assembly languages, and this method successfully achieved that. Second, it was also out of necessity. As Kalmár said, Hungary was "a computer museum" at the time; on their first job, students might end up working with a computer that was installed in the early 1960s.

A simulator of these fictional computers was even made in the early 1970s. It was written for the Minsk-22 computer that Kalmár's department had at the time [55]. For a short survey of these fictional computers, see *Appendix C*. For Kalmár's description of the educational use of his fictional machines, see *Appendix D*.

7   The Training Becomes a Major: The Later Years in Szeged

As mentioned above, Kalmár originally wanted to start a standalone programming and computer science major, similar to the Applied Mathematician major in Budapest, but his requests were denied. By 1960, when the training was established in Szeged, Kalmár continued petitioning the Ministry of Education and Culture to allow him to start a standalone programming and computer science major.

Based on the experiences of the first couple of years of the training, Kalmár argued for a programming and computer science major in the following way. First, he alluded to the trend of growing numbers of computers in the country, and the need for a skillful crew of 10–12 people to run each of them. Kalmár prognosticated that there would be a shortage of computer experts by the mid-1960s in Hungary, unless a new one-major program were started at Szeged with 10–15 students per year, in addition to continuing the ongoing training where students in their third year were allowed to drop their second major. Furthermore, he argued, the Applied Mathematician program in Budapest would have to offer such a major in the near future as well, while steps should be taken to start a similar major at the University of Debrecen[8] in order to satisfy all future needs.

Kalmár also drew attention to the difficulties the current system was generating. According to him, besides taking time away from their special subject, those who finished the programming and computer science training were only qualified to teach mathematics in high school. As a consequence, high schools were not particularly keen to hire them, were they to become teachers, as all other teachers had two majors. In many cases, if they ended up teaching in a high school, they were required to finish their second major through postgraduate correspondence courses.[9]

Enrollment numbers in high school teacher majors were also low. Thus, Kalmár argued, computer experts should not be drawn away from among those people who were preparing already for at least two years to become high school teachers. On the other hand, a standalone major could be appealing to those students who were interested in engineering or natural sciences but not in becoming teachers.

---

[8] Between 1952 and 2000, the university was called Lajos Kossuth University.

[9] Still, Kalmár proposed that if a standalone major would be started in the future, those who enroll in it should be allowed to earn a High School Mathematics Teacher degree in addition, but not to make it mandatory for them.

Fig. 4. Tibor Varga and Ilona Bereczki at the M-3 computer in Szeged, 1967 [38].

The need for a growing number of computer experts and Kalmár's perseverance finally paid off by the 1963–1964 academic year, when a standalone Mathematician major was finally started, with a possible Program Designer[10] specialization. In the first two years, everyone in the major studied a core mathematical curriculum, while the courses of the specialization[11] began in the third year; students in this major did not have to study pedagogy and psychology anymore. The maximum enrollment in the Program Designer specialization grew from 13 in the beginning of the major in 1963 to 25 in 1969 and around 50 in 1970. This major was last offered during the 1981–1982 academic year.

Interestingly, at the beginning of the new major there was still no computer in Szeged! In 1964 the Cybernetics Research Group in Budapest received an Ural-2 computer, which rendered their old M-3 superfluous. They sold the M-3 to the University of Szeged for 1 Hungarian Forint, worth 2 scoops of ice cream at the time. The M-3 was running reliably again by mid-1965, becoming the first computer outside of the capital (Fig. 4). It was operational until 1968 when Kalmár's department received a Minsk-22, which was in use until 1976.

8   Other Early Programs

Although the programming and computer science training that was started at Szeged in the fall of 1957 was the first university-level, degree-granting, multiple-years-long program, it was not an entirely isolated attempt in higher education. In this section,

---

[10] The Hungarian expression of which 'program designer' is a literal translation sounds odd in Hungarian too. 'Programmer' or 'software engineer' would be the closest contemporary expressions, but I kept the literal translation to convey the anachronistic connotation of the Hungarian original.

[11] Further specializations were, for example, Probability and Statistics or Mathematical Physics.

most y based [13], I give a short rundown of the beginnings of programming education on the university-level in Hungary.

The earliest programming related courses were given by the Hungarian Central Statistical Office.[12] They offered punch card machine operator courses from 1953; by the end of the 1950s, they offered courses which included some information about digital computers and programming as well.

The first course on programming digital computers was, naturally, taught by the members of the Cybernetics Research Group during 1958 and 1959. The course was organized by the Treasury Department to train 10–20 programmers. The 37 lectures that constituted the course were devoted to the programming of the M-3 computer. This course was so popular that it had to be repeated 3–4 times shortly thereafter. Many of the 50 or so participants of these courses later became renowned computer experts in Hungary [13, pp. 38–39].

Members of the Cybernetics Research Group taught programming and computer science related courses at other places as well. One of the early uses of the M-3 computer was to provide calculations for the Planbureau as part of the economic planning. Béla Krekó, a young professor from the Karl Marx University of Economics[13] was hired part-time to help with such applications.[14] By the academic year of 1961–1962, Krekó was able to start a new, so-called Plan-Mathematician major at the University of Economics. This 5-year major trained about 15–20 students in modern, formal economics; the name of the major clearly appeals to the "economic planning" jargon of the time. The major included courses on linear and non-linear programming in economics (taught by Krekó), and electrodynamics, mathematical machines, and programming and computer science taught (regularly) by other members of the Cybernetics Research Group [56].

Surprisingly, engineers and mathematicians had access to regular programming and computer science training and majors only much later, as both Eötvös University and the Budapest University of Technology started their majors several years later, by the very end of the 1960s. Although both universities offered special elective courses or extracurricular activities[15] every now and then from the late 1950s, there was general resistance towards the new subject among their leaders.

An anecdote by Kovács illustrates this attitude rather well. In [59], he tells the story of how he ended up teaching programming and computer science courses in the Plan

---

[12] Központi Statisztikai Hivatal in Hungarian, or KSH in short.

[13] Currently Corvinus University of Budapest.

[14] Krekó (1915–1994) was originally trained as a mathematics-physics high school teacher and worked at the Mathematics Department of the University of Economics from 1954.

[15] For example, László Kozma (1902–1983) at the Technical University built the first relay computer, the MESz-1, in Hungary by 1958, solely for educational purposes. Students could use the MESz-1 for extracurricular research purposes. Kozma, an IEEE Computer Pioneer Award recipient, clearly had the knowledge to design a computer science training similar to what Kalmár had. However, as a former political prisoner who was rehabilitated and reinstated in 1954, Kozma refrained from unnecessary engagement with the authorities. For more information about the MESz-1, see Kozma [57] from 1959 and Képes and Álló [35, pp. 44–49], and about Kozma's life and contributions see Kovács [58] and [4, pp. 297–299].

Mathematician major organized by Krekó. In 1960 Kovács visited several universities in Budapest and offered to teach the subject. First, he visited the University of Technology where the president's response was that at this "serious university they only teach serious engineering knowledge". The people running the Applied Mathematician major at Eötvös University responded rather similarly, claiming that "they only teach mathematics, and this is not mathematics". When Kovács showed his syllabi to Krekó, he immediately asked Kovács to join him in starting the Plan Mathematician major. However, they still had to get approval from the leadership of the university. The reaction of the vice president of the University of Economics was more welcoming: "We teach so many silly subjects, an extra one will not make much difference". Thus, programming and computer science became part of the Plan Mathematician major's curriculum.

In the case of the Budapest University of Technology, there were further reasons for this delay beyond general resistance. One reason was the large size of classes in the engineering majors. For example, it would have been impossible to start general computer science education for hundreds of electrical engineers, when the count of digital computers in the country was still in the single digits. Another reason was the Technical University's own internal regulations, in that every major had to have a complete curriculum for its entirety at its beginning. Thus, nothing other than special elective courses was allowed to be inserted into the curriculum of a student once they were enrolled.

For the sake of completeness, we have to mention a unified computer science education initiative from the early 1970s. As part of the initiative Eötvös University, the University of Szeged and the University of Debrecen cooperated in developing a common curriculum based on other contemporary international curricula. This resulted in the design of a 3-year Programming Mathematician major, providing a "college" or "bachelor" equivalent degree. This new major was offered at all three universities from the 1972–1973 academic year.

Kalmár, of course, was involved with the development of this unified initiative. In the beginning he was against the structure of the proposed new majors for various reasons. But once these new majors were approved he fell in line. In addition, the nationwide initiative also instigated the founding of several new computer science departments around the country. Kalmár traveled around those universities that planned to start a new department to share his experience and their curricula in order to provide guidance.[16]

Students enrolled in this program at Szeged could not switch between this major and the other, 5-year major designed by Kalmár. The new major was designed to quickly fulfill the industry's demand for competent programmers, while the 5-year major was to train researchers and leaders of computer centers.

---

[16] He also argued that computer science had to become institutionally independent from mathematics even on the academic level. Indeed, he believed the reason for the low number of software-related PhD dissertations was the fact that dissertation topics in computer science had to be approved by a mathematical committee at the Hungarian Academy of Sciences. For the details of his pragmatic and methodological reasons, see Szabó [60].

The most talented students in this new Programming Mathematician major could then go on to a 2-year extension, providing a "university" or "master's" equivalent degree at the end. This degree was offered by Eötvös University from 1975–1976, at Szeged from 1979–1980 and at Debrecen from 1988–1989 [13, Sect. 8]. [7, pp. 45–47]. The program was called Program Designer Mathematician, exactly the same as the original 5-year major at Szeged. Thus, the two Program Designer Mathematician majors were simultaneously offered at Szeged for 2 years.

9   Kalmár's Writings on Education and Computers

Kalmár was engaged with computer science education until his death. This section summarizes the main points in his writings on the education of computer science.

In his [61] and [54] Kalmár shares the experience of computer science education in Szeged. The [61] describes the history of the program, its development from training into a major, and the challenges for the time. In [54] Kalmár provides a high-level description of his fictional machines (see *Appendix* C for their description) and argues for their continued use. He mentions that high level languages of the time are not always efficient enough. He also describes Hungary as a "computer museum", where several old machines, installed in the early 1960s, were still running. Thus, programmers have to be able to code in assembly languages as well. Most importantly however, he argues that using his fictional machines in education helps programmers develop intuitions independent of machines (and programming languages). See the section *Programming Without Computers*, as well as an unpublished abstract of Kalmár's in *Appendix* D, for a description of how it was achieved.

Kalmár voiced his opinion on computer science education on other levels than at the university. In the previous section it was already mentioned that Kalmár was involved with the unified computer science education initiative in the early 1970s. Folder 'Lev-12' contains a 24-page long letter from 10 April 1971 detailing his comments and recommendations for the initiative. The letter was sent to György Aczél, the secretary for cultural affairs of the Central Committee of the Hungarian Socialist Workers' Party, upon Aczél's request. In this letter Kalmár gives detailed recommendations for computer science education from elementary school, through high school to university, and even to postgraduate courses and trainings.

Kalmár's vision of computer science education went beyond mere computer science courses and training of programmers. Both in this letter as well as in [62] he emphasizes that everyone needs some understanding of computers in what he called the "age of computers". According to Kalmár, everyone should be able to judge what problems in their own field of expertise could be solved efficiently by computers. Furthermore, they should have the knowledge to describe those problems with such precision that mathematicians and programmers could use that description as a starting point for their computerized solution. In order to cultivate such knowledge even for non-programmers, Kalmár not only suggested inclusion of an introductory computer science class in high school curricula, but also argued that students should be shown the possible uses of computers in every subject, not only in mathematics and computer science.

Another issue that came up in [62] is computer-aided education. There, Kalmár argues for the use of computers in instruction and education, but emphasized that computers should never replace educators, only help them to provide a more personalized education. Kalmár mentions the work of Hunya Péterné Ambrus Margit[17] on the use of computers in multiple choice testing and examination. Hunya Péterné began this work, one of the few computer and machine aided education projects in Hungary,[18] in the second half of the 1960s at the Cybernetics Laboratory led by Kalmár. Although this kind of research fit well with the cybernetic trend in the Eastern Bloc, Kalmár's interest in this field was most likely influenced by Patrick Suppes as well. Indeed, between 1963 and 1965, both Kalmár and Suppes served in the governance of the DLMPS,[19] Kalmár as Vice-President and Suppes as Secretary General, and as members of the Committee on the Teaching of Logic and Philosophy of Science from 1964 until 1968 as well.[20] Their correspondence, found in the Kalmár Nachlass, indicates that Suppes informed Kalmár about his research on computer assisted research, especially on teaching elementary school students logic and arithmetic.

10 Conclusion

The programming and computer science training at Szeged, the first degree-granting, multiple-years-long program at the university-level in Hungary, was started due to Kalmár's one-man mission. However, as there were very few computers in the country at the time, the training faced serious difficulties. Students had to learn programming without access to actual computers and, in the beginning, some of them were unable to finish their training due to lack of internships. After the initial complications, the training became a major and Szeged grew into one of the main hubs of computer science education in Hungary. Simultaneously, it created a community of students, educators and scholars, many of whom became renowned members of the computer science community in Hungary.

Beyond providing a detailed description of a particular program in computer science education that started in the late 1950s, hopefully this case study will be a useful source for more overarching studies in the history of the field. First of all, the challenges the program at Szeged faced were quite typical for the Eastern Bloc: the shortage of computers in the country or region, and a state that, while it had strong control over higher education, failed to recognize the quickly growing need for experts in the field and acted only belatedly. Although Kalmár at Szeged might have faced extreme circumstances even for the Eastern Bloc by running a programming training

---

[17] She also appears as Hunyáné Ambrus Margit or H. Ambrus Margit in certain publications.

[18] See Somogyvári [63] for a short overview and Kovács [4, pp. 313–316] on Kovács Mihály's cybernetic and educational machines that he built together with his high school students.

[19] DLMPS (now DLMPST) stands for Division of Logic, Methodology and Philosophy of Science (T stands for Technology), which is a division of the International Union of History and Philosophy of Science (IUHPS).

[20] The other members of the committee were Jean-Louis Destouches, John Kemeny, Paul Lorenzen and Tamás Varga.

without a computer for eight years, it would be interesting to see how other countries in the region responded to their similar challenges. It would also be worthwhile to compare the timeliness of the different Eastern Bloc countries' reactions to the increasing need for programmers.

Once a wider perspective is gained on the history of computer science education in the Eastern Bloc, several cross-country comparisons between the East and the West could be made. It was already mentioned that, in several countries in the Eastern Bloc, states were late in recognizing and trying to fulfill the need for programmers. For example, the first serious, centralized initiative in computer science education came as late as the early 1970s in Hungary. In stark contrast, the government provision of computers to universities began in the mid-1950s in the UK [8, 9]. Another factor to consider is the impact of the level of interconnectedness of research and higher education on the education of computer science. Mounier-Kuhn [10] explains the success and long-lasting impact of certain computer science departments in France by the conjunction of a computer center, computer science education and conducting research at the department (as opposed to not conducting research on sight). This explanation quite plausibly fits several further countries in Western Europe. However, in the Soviet Union "basic research was largely the confines of the Russian Academy of Sciences, forming the elite research institutions devoid of teaching responsibilities. Most universities were focused almost exclusively on teaching and had no authority to conduct research" [64, p. 174]. Hungary adopted a mixed system, where there were several independent research institutes, but departments were allowed (and sometimes required) to conduct research. In addition, there were even research groups that belonged to the Hungarian Academy of Sciences while being located at departments at universities, such as the aforementioned *Mathematical Logic and its Applications Research Group* led by Kalmár at the University of Szeged. It would be important to understand how different academic systems impact the development of new disciplines at universities, especially if they are strongly resource-dependent.

Acknowledgement. I would like to thank Zoltán Czirkos, Kendra Chilson, Edit Sántáné-Tóth and Lajos Somogyvári for their help in writing this paper. I am also indebted to the anonymous reviewers and Chris Leslie for their recommendations and the work they invested in the improvement of this paper.

Appendix A: The Curricula of the First Three Classes

The following list contains the directly relevant courses for the programming and computer science training. It is based on Sántáné-Tóth [13, pp. 53–58]. The numbers in the tables indicate the length of the weekly lecture/recitation times 45 min, e.g., 2 means 90 min. It is interesting to recognize that, in the first couple years, Kalmár taught basically half of the courses in the training. After the list of the courses, biographical information about their instructors is provided.

1957–1958, 1-year training

1957 Fall Semester	Lecture	Recitation	Instructor
Foundations of Mathematics	3	–	Kalmár
Programming of Automatic Calculators I	2	2	Kalmár
Numerical and Graphical Methods I	2	1	Bakos

1958 Spring Semester			
Programming of Automatic Calculators II	2	2	Kalmár
Numerical and Graphical Methods II	2	1	Bakos

1958–1960, 2 year training

Core Courses	Lecture	Recitation	Instructor
Programming of Automatic Calculators I–IV	2	0 for I–II 2 for III–IV	Kalmár and Bereczki
Numerical and Graphical Methods I–III	2	–	Pollák
Set Theory I	2	–	Fodor
Set Theory II	1	–	Fodor
Mathematical Logic I	2	–	Kalmár
Mathematical Logic II	2	–	Kalmár

Electives	Lecture	Recitation	Instructor
Structural Elements of Calculators I	2	–	Muszka
Structural Elements of Calculators II	2	–	Kalmar
Engineering Applications of Electronic Calculators	2	–	Muszka
Engineering Applications of Mathematical Logic	2	–	Kalmar

1960–1962, 2 year training
The curriculum of the third class differed only in that the recitation for the Programming of Automatic Calculators III and IV was increased to 3 h and the electives offered. Here I list only the new courses.

Electives	Lecture	Recitation	Instructor
Graph Theory	2	–	Ádám
Mathematical Laboratory	–	4	Muszka
Mathematical Symbol Systems	2	–	Kalmár

Ádám, András (1934): mathematician working on graph theory and automata theory. A former student of Kalmár.

Bakos, Tibor (1909–1998): educationist, left Szeged during the summer of 1958 to become the editor of the *Mathematical and Physical Journal for Secondary Schools*, which plays an important part in cultivating mathematical talent in Hungary to this day.[21]

Bereczki, Ilona (1927–2004): logician, famously provided an example in her [65] and [66] for a function that is recursive but not an elementary function.[22] She worked closely with Kalmár, participated in education of logic and programming and preparing textbooks.

Fodor, Géza (1927–1977): mathematician who worked in the field of set theory. A lemma about stationary sets, sometimes also called "the pressing down lemma", bears his name after his [67].

Muszka, Dániel (1930–2018): Kalmár's research assistant and close colleague. He was a radio amateur from an early age but was not allowed to enroll as an electrical engineer for political reasons. Met with Kalmár during his studies in the Mathematics-Physics High School Teacher program and became an indispensable member of his research groups, where Muszka was responsible for engineering and assembling artifacts for example the Szeged Logical Machine (Fig. 1).

Pollák, György (1929–2001): mathematician working in the field of semigroups. Student and later colleague of the famous algebraist and semigroup theorist László Rédei [68].

Appendix B: Master's Theses of the First Three Classes

The following list contains the titles of the Master's Theses from the program from 1959, 1961 and 1963. Sadly, most of the theses were destroyed when the library where they were stored was flooded. All of these theses were written in Hungarian; I provide their titles only in translation.

---

[21] On the education of mathematics in Hungary, see Gosztonyi [34].
[22] Elementary functions are also called Kalmár elementary functions after his [27].

Master's Thesis, 1959

Fidrich, Ilona: *Starting Programs on the M-3 Electronic Calculator*

As mentioned above, Ilona Fidrich (1932–1983) was the only one from the first class in Szeged to complete the training.[23] During the 1959–1960 academic year, Fidrich worked as Kalmár's teaching assistant and applied for an aspirantura[24] in computer science. Her application was accepted and the Hungarian Academy of Sciences delegated her to the Moscow State University. Fidrich became the aspirant of professors I. S. Berezin and N. P. Trifonov at the Mathematics Department in the fall of 1960. She completed her qualifying exams in 1962. Her dissertation was advised by professor Lazar Aronovich Lyusternik and provided a simulation of the production of the Dunaújváros Iron and Steel Plant[25] in Hungary. By defending her dissertation in 1964, Fidrich earned one of the earliest "candidate of science" degrees in computer science in Hungary. Upon returning to Hungary, she taught programming in Szeged for a year as Kalmár's assistant. She worked in various computer centers and research groups in Budapest from 1965 until her death in 1983.

Master's Theses, 1961

Gulácsi, Sára: *Thesis is lost, its title is unknown*

Lugosi, Gábor: *Algorithms to Solve the Assignment Problem (The Hungarian Method for the M-3)*

Sánta, Lóránt: *Numerical Solutions of Differential Equations on the M-3 by the Runge-Kutta Method*

Tóth, Edit: *Floating Point and Conversion Subroutines for the Ural Computer*[26]

Master's Theses, 1963

Bánkfalvi, Zsolt: *Simulating the Kalmár Logical Machine – Predicate Calculus*

Havass, Miklós: *Musical Composition with Electronic Calculators*

Kalmár, Ágota: *Computer Proof (Automated Theorem Proving)*

Maizl, József: *Numerical Integration with the Newton–Coates Formula on the Ural-1*

Megyesi, László: *The Realization of Schreier Extension of Groups on Calculators*

---

[23] The first programming and computer science-related Master's Thesis in Hungary was defended by János Szelezsán in 1958 at Eötvös University under the title, *The Programming of Numerical Solutions of Differential Equations*. Szelezsán was enrolled in the Applied Mathematician major and spent an internship at the Cybernetics Research Group in 1957–1958, of which he later became a member. He was one of the lecturers of the first programming training offered by the Research Group in 1958–1959, and also taught in the Plan Mathematician major at the University of Economics and offered programming related courses at Eötvös University. He is also the author of the first book on programming [69] in Hungarian from 1962.

[24] In the Soviet system of scientific degrees one has to complete an aspirantura to become a Candidate of Science, a PhD equivalent rank.

[25] Called Dunai Vasmű at the time.

[26] Edit Tóth married Lóránt Sánta, and since then she writes under the name Sántáné-Tóth Edit.

Appendix C: Kalmár's Fictional Machines

This appendix provides some details of Kalmár's fictional machines. It is based on the few available published sources, namely on Simon [55, Sects. 2–2.2, pp. 264–266] and Varga [1, pp. 22–24]. As a consequence, the description of Kalmár's fictional machines is fragmentary; for example, the complete instructional set is not given in these sources. I am indebted to Zoltán Czirkos for his help in preparing this appendix, which otherwise would have been impossible for me.

The description below closely follows [55, pp. 264–266]:

Instruction set of the fictional machine
Convention for the notation of registers

E: result register
R: multiplyer/divider register
T: overflow register
U: program counter
I_k: k-th index register

One address machine without index register
The general form of a machine command is "Θ a", where Θ is the symbol of the operation (always one letter) and a is the address part. For example

$$A\,a: \quad (E) + (a) \Rightarrow (E)$$
$$B\,b: \quad (a) \Rightarrow (E)$$

Machines with index registers
The machines with index registers have three versions with one, two or three addresses which leads to the following general forms of machine commands respectively

vΘ a, i
vΘ a, i   b, j
vΘ a, i   b, j   c, k

where

    v denotes the version (number, possibly with auxiliary symbols) and
    Θ is the symbol of the operation (one or two letters).

a		a	
b	addresses	ab	address parts
c		abc	

i		
j	index register references	
k		

$v\Theta$ together is the machine code of the command, for example

1A	a, i	:	$(E) + (a + (I_i)) \Rightarrow (E)$
2AT	a b	:	$(a) + (b) \Rightarrow (E), (a)$
1OF	a b c	:	$(a) \Rightarrow (E)$ if $(b) \geq (c)$
1BX	a, i	:	$(a) \Rightarrow (I_i)$

The following properties hold for all three versions of machines with index registers:

1. the width of the index registers is the same as of the addresses
2. the index reference after the address is optional
3. if the index reference is missing, it means that the index register with address 0 is assigned to the address part
4. the index register with address 0 contains zero and it is forbidden to write to it

This concludes Simon's description of the fictional machines.

As an example, let us consider the following arithmetic problem and its solution for a three address machine as it is provided in ([1], pp. 23–24). The task is $(a + b)(c-d)/(a-b)(c + d) \Rightarrow x$ with the following addresses: $a = (301)$, $b = (302)$, $c = (303)$, $d = (304)$, $x = (305)$. In the solution, m1 and m2 are temporary variables while "CONT." and "ADDR." stand for "content" and "address" respectively.

ADDR.	OPCODE	ADDRESS PART I		ADDRESS PART II		ADDRESS PART III		Remark
		CONT.	ADDR.	CONT.	ADDR.	CONT.	ADDR.	Explanation
201	3AT	a	301	b	302	m1	351	$a+b \Rightarrow m1$
202	3ST	c	303	d	304	m2	352	$c-d \Rightarrow m2$
203	3MT	m1	351	m2	352	m1	351	$(a+b)(c-d) \Rightarrow m1$
204	3ST	a	301	b	302	m2	352	$a-b \Rightarrow m2$
205	3AT	c	303	d	304	m3	353	$c+d \Rightarrow m3$
206	3MT	m2	352	m3	353	m2	352	$(a-b)(c+d) \Rightarrow m2$
207	3DT	m1	351	m2	352	x	305	$(a+b)(c-d)/(a-b)(c+d) \Rightarrow x$

Although a complete instruction set is still not available, we can infer that the first letter in AT stands for *addition*, in ST for *subtraction*, in MT for *multiplication*, and in DT for *division*.

Appendix D: Kalmár's Abstract on the "Application of Ad Hoc Instruction Groups in the Education of 'Program Designers'"

Folder 291 of the Kalmár Nachlass contains an abstract from 1972 about the educational use of his fictional machines. The abstract was prepared for the IFIP Working Conference on Programming Teaching Techniques, held in Zakopane in the same year. Although the proceedings [70] lists Kalmár among the attendees on page 227, there are no abstracts in the volume. Kalmár does not have a paper in the volume and was not on the panel discussions either. I include the entire abstract below, as this is the only source in English I know of where Kalmár describes the use of his fictional machines in his own words, and it is previously unpublished. The ideas described in this abstract were already explained above in sections Programming Without Computers and Kalmár's Writings on Education and Computers. I kept the original typesetting and indentation of the abstract but added references in footnotes:

A b s t r a c t of the paper by László KALMÁR /Szeged, Hungary/:

Application of ad hoc instruction groups in the education of "program designers" at the József Attila University in Szeged to be presented at the IFIP Working Conference on Programming Teaching Techniques, Zakopane, 18 to 22 of September, 1972, needing 20 to 30 min for presentation.

We teach programming at József Attila University /Szeged, Hungary/ since 1957. Of course, since that time, both subject-matter and aim of teaching has been changed several times. Now, we give a five years education to "program designers", i.e. to specialists who will be engaged in some computing centre, besides leading a group of /one to two years course educated/routine programmers, with software design and maintenance. In Hungarian computing centres, there is a big demand for program designers, obviously because we have more different types of computers /and less copies of each type/, partly with a poor software, than any other country at least in central Europe.

We have a whole year, two hours a week with four hours a week problem course, for teaching programming in machine code and related languages, which is, of course, very important for those who have to write compilers, operating systems, application program packages etc. Owing to the above situation in Hungary, we have to give them as a machine independent way of looking at a computer as possible. Hence, teaching to program in the machine code of some concrete computer, running actually in Hungarian or not, would be nonsense. According to our experience, instead of teaching how to program on an idealized computer, like FLAPJACK[27] or MIX,[28] definition of many different instruction groups /rather than those belonging to the instruction code of a computer/ and basing machine code-like programming education on them is much more efficient. Among the instructions defined thus, there are one address, two address and three address instructions, the latter in the first line in order to be used as simple macros in one or two address computers. The instruction codes of the most important real computers

---

[27] See Flores [71, 72].

[28] See Knuth [73].

are defined, mostly in the problem courses, in terms of the "defined instructions". either directly, or as macros. For each programming problem, we give in advance the set of the "defined instructions" which are allowed to be used. Thus, our students acquire skill in replacing instructions which are not available by those which are.

Also, according to our experience, our students understand statements of higher programming languages, like ALGOL or FORTRAN or PL/I, on this basis more easily than in the times when we started with such higher languages.

References

1. Varga, A.: Kalmár László, a magyarországi számítástudomány atyja. (László Kalmár, the Father of Computer Science in Hungary). Polygon **7**(1), 2–29 (1997)
2. Szabó, P.G.: Kalmár László. A számítástudomány hazai úttörője. Alkalmazott Matematikai Lapok **32**, 79–94 (2015)
3. Makay, Á.: The activities of László Kalmár in the world of information technology. Acta Cybern. **18**, 9–14 (2007)
4. Kovács, G.: Hungarian scientists in information technology. In: Tatnall, A. (ed.) Reflections on the History of Computing. IAICT, vol. 387, pp. 289–319. Springer, Heidelberg (2012). https://doi.org/10.1007/978-3-642-33899-1_18
5. Ádám, A., Dömösi, P.: Kalmár László. In: Pénzes, I. (ed.) Műszaki nagyjaink, vol. 6, pp. 47–89. Gépipari Tudományos Egyesület, Budapest (1986)
6. Raffai, M.: Computing behind the iron curtain and beyond hungarian national perspective. In: Impagliazzo, J. (ed.) History of Computing and Education 2 (HCE2). IIFIP, vol. 215, pp. 153–165. Springer, Boston, MA (2006). https://doi.org/10.1007/978-0-387-34741-7_11
7. Sántáné-Tóth, E.: Computer oriented higher education in Hungary. Stud. Univ. Babes-Bolyai Digit. **62**(2), 35–62 (2017)
8. Agar, J.: The provision of digital computers to British universities up to the flowers report (1966). Comput. J. **39**(7), 630–642 (1996)
9. Clark, M.: State support for the expansion of UK university computing in the 1950s. IEEE Ann. Hist. Comput. **32**(1), 23–33 (2010)
10. Mounier-Kuhn, P.: Computer science in French universities: early entrants and latecomers. Inf. Cult. **47**(4), 414–456 (2012)
11. Kalmár, L.: Lev-12 Folder; containing Kalmár's correspondence related to the programming major. Kalmár Nachlass, Klebelsberg Library, University of Szeged (1957–1974)
12. Kalmár, L.: Folder 291; Abstract of the paper: Application of ad hoc instruction groups in the education of "program designers" at the József Attila University in Szeged Kalmár Nachlass, Klebelsberg Library, University of Szeged (1972)
13. Sántáné-Tóth, E.: A Számítástechnika Felsőfokú Oktatásának Kezdetei Magyarországon (The Beginnings of Information Technology Education at the Hungarian Universities). Typotex Kiadó (2012)
14. Berenyi, I.: Computers in Eastern Europe. Sci. Am. **223**(4), 102–108 (1970)
15. Wilczynski, J.: Technology in Comecon. Praeger Publishers, New York (1974)
16. Goodman, S.E.: Socialist technological integration: the case of the East European computer industries. Inf. Soc. **3**(1), 39–89 (1984)
17. Blachman, N.M.: The state of digital computer technology in Europe. Commun. ACM **4**(6), 256–265 (1961)
18. Dömölki, B.: The story of the first electronic computer in Hungary. Stud. Univ. Babes-Bolyai Digit. **62**(2), 25–34 (2017)

19. Kovács, G.: 50 years ago we constructed the first hungarian tube computer, the M-3: short stories from the history of the first Hungarian computer (1957–1960). In: Tatnall, A. (ed.) HC 2010. IAICT, vol. 325, pp. 68–79. Springer, Heidelberg (2010). https://doi.org/10.1007/978-3-642-15199-6_8

20. Szabó, M.: The M-3 in budapest and in szeged. Proc. IEEE **104**(10), 2062–2069 (2016)

21. Davis, N.C., Goodman, S.E.: The soviet bloc's unified system of computers. ACM Comput. Surv. **10**(2), 93–122 (1978)

22. Szentgyörgyi, Z.: A short history of computing in Hungary. IEEE Ann. Hist. Comput. **21**(3), 49–57 (1999)

23. von Neumann, J.: Zur Hilbertschen Beweistheorie. Math. Z. **26**, 1–46 (1927)

24. Hilbert, D.: Problems of the grounding of mathematics. In: Mancosu, P. (ed.) From Brouwer to Hilbert, pp. 227–233. Oxford University Press, Oxford (1998). Translated by P. Mancosu. Originally delivered at the International Congress of Mathematicians in Bologna on September 3, 1928. Originally Published as "Probleme der Grundlegung der Mathimatik." In Mathematische Annalen 102, 1–9 (1929). (1929/1998)

25. Szabó, P.G. (ed.): Kalmárium (The Correspondence of László Kalmár with Hungarian Mathematicians). Polygon, Szeged, Szeged (2005)

26. Kalmár, L.: On the reduction of the decision problem, first paper: ackermann prefix, a single binary predicate. J. Symb. Logic **4**(1), 1–9 (1939)

27. Kalmár, L.: Egyszerű példa eldönthetetlen aritmetikai problémára (Simple Example of an Undecidable Arithmetic Problem). Matematikai és Fizikai Lapok **50**(1), 1–23 (1943)

28. Kalmár, L.: Une forme du théorème de Gödel sous des hypothèses minimales. Comptes Rendus Hebdomadaires des Séances de l'Académie des Sciences **229**, 963–965 (1949)

29. Nagy, F. (ed.): Neumann János és a "Magyar titok" (John von Neumann and the "Hungarian Secret"). Országos Műszaki Információs Központ és Könyvtár, Budapest (1987)

30. Szabó, M.: Kalmár's argument against the plausibility of church's thesis. Hist. Philos. Logic **39**(2), 140–157 (2018)

31. Kalmár, L.: A Hilbert-féle bizonyításelmélet célkitűzései, módszerei, eredményei (The Aims, Methods and Results of Hilbertian Proof Theory). Matematikai és Fizikai Lapok **48**, 65–119 (1941)

32. Péter, R.: Az axiomatikus módszer korlátai (The Limitations of the Axiomatic Method). Matematikai és Fizikai Lapok **48**, 120–143 (1941)

33. Péter, R.: Játék a végtelennel. Playing with Infinity. The first Hungarian edition was published in 1945. The English edition was translated by Z. Dienes and first published in 1961 by the G. Bell and Sons Ltd., London (1945/1961)

34. Gosztonyi, K.: Mathematical culture and mathematics education in Hungary in the XXth century. In: Larvor, B. (ed.) Mathematical Cultures. THS, pp. 71–89. Springer, Cham (2016). https://doi.org/10.1007/978-3-319-28582-5_5

35. Képes, G., Álló, G.: A jövő múltja. The Past of the Future. Bilingual. John von Neumann Computer Society, Budapest (2013)

36. Kalmár, L.: On a digital computer which can be programmed in a mathematica formula language. In: The Proceedings of the II. Hungarian Mathematical Congress, Budapest, Abstracts, vol. 5, pp. 3–16 (1960)

37. Péter, R.: Recursive Functions in Computer Theory. Translated by I. Juhász. Published jointly by Ellis Horwood Limited, West Sussex and Akadémiai Kiadó, Budapest (1981)

38. Szabó, P.G.: Robotkatica és kibernetika – Muszka Dániel élete (Electronic Ladybird and Cybernetics – The Life of Dániel Muszka). Érintő, Elektronikus Matematikai Lapok, June 2018.   http://www.ematlap.hu/index.php/interju-portre-2018-06/737-robotkatica-es-kibernetika-muszka-daniel-emlekere

39. Kalmár, L. (ed.) Proceedings of the Colloquium on the Foundations of Mathematics, Mathematical Machines and Their Applications. Akadémiai Kiadó, Budapest (1965)
40. Kalmár, L.: Meaning, synonymy and translation. Comput. Linguist. **6**, 27–39 (1967)
41. Kalmár, L.: Digitális számológépek és célgépek alkalmazása az orvosi diagnosztikában (The Application of Computers and Single-purpose Machines in Medical Diagnostics). Orvos és Technika **7**, 14–18 (1969)
42. Kalmár, L.: Elektronikus matematikai gépek a kohászatban (Electronic Mathematical Machines in Metallurgy). Dunai Vasmű **4**(2), 7–15 (1963)
43. Sun, Q.: The dawn of Chinese computing. Bull. Comput. Conserv. Soc. **18**, 16–21 (1997)
44. Kovács, G.: Válogatott Kalandozásaim Informatikában (My Selected Adventures in Information Technology). GÁMA-GEO Kft., Masszi Kiadó, Budapest (2002)
45. Kalmár, L.: Curriculum Vitae. In Szabó (2003), 16–25 (1976)
46. Ahmed, H.: Cambridge Computing: The First 75 Years. Third Millennium Publishing, London (2013)
47. Fein, L.: The role of the university in computers, data processing, and related fields. Commun. ACM **2**(9), 7–14 (1959)
48. Rosen, S., Rice, J.R.: The origins of computing and computer science at Purdue university. In: Rice, J.R., DeMillo, R.A. (eds.) Studies in Computer Science. Software Science and Engineering, pp. 31–44. Springer, Boston (1994). https://doi.org/10.1007/978-1-46_5-1791-7_5
49. Rice, J.R., Rosen, S.: History of the computer sciences department at Purdue university. In: Rice, J.R., DeMillo, R.A. (eds.) Studies in Computer Science. Software Science and Engineering, pp. 45–72. Springer, Boston (1994). https://doi.org/10.1007/978-1-46_5-1791-7_6
50. London, R.L.: Who Earned First Computer Science Ph.D.? BLOG at the Communications of the ACM (2013). https://cacm.acm.org/blogs/blog-cacm/159591-who-earned-first-computer-science-ph-d/fulltext. Accessed 31 Aug 2018
51. Ershov, A.P., Shura-Bura, M.R.: The early development of programming in the USSR. In: Metropolis, N., Howlett, J., Rota, G. (eds.) A History of Computing in the Twentieth Century, pp. 137–196. Academic Press, New York (1980)
52. Hujber, E., et al. (eds.): Számítástechnikai Évkönyv (Information Technology Yearbook). Statisztikai Kiadó Vállalat, Budapest (1970)
53. Bohus, M., Muszka, D., Szabó, P.G.: A szegedi informatikai gyűjtemény (The Computer Collection in Szeged) (2005). https://www.yumpu.com/hu/document/read/29881933/a-szegedi-informatikai-gyujtemeny-in-memoriam-kalmar-laszlo. Accessed 18 Mar 2019
54. Kalmár, L.: Géptől független szemlélet kialakítása a programtervezők oktatásában (Developing Computer-independent Intuitions During the Education of Programmers). In A Számítástechnikai Oktatás A Hazai Felsőoktatási Intézményekben, Visegrád, pp. _42–146 (1974b)
55. Simon, E.: A Kalmár-féle fiktív elektronikus számítógép szimulátora Minszk-22 gépen (The Simulation of Kalmár's Fictional Electronic Computer on a Minsk-22 Computer). In: The Proceedings of Programozási Rendszerek 1972, Szeged, pp. 263–268. John von Neumann Computer Society (1972)
56. Forgó, F., Komlósi, S.: Krekó Béla szerepe a közgazdászképzés modernizálásában (The Role of Béla Krekó in the Modernization of the Education of Economics) (2015). http://unipub.lib.uni-corvinus.hu/2188/1/Kreko_paper.pdf. Accessed 2 May 2018
57. Kozma, L.: The new digital computer of the polytechnical university budapest. Periodica Polytech. **3**(4), 321–343 (1959)

58. Kovács, G.: Dr. Kozma László elektromérnök, a távbeszélőtechnika és a számítástechnika magyar úttörője (László Kozma, Electrical Engineer and the Hungarian Pioneer of Telephone Technologies and Computer Science). Magyar Tudomány 48(3), 379–388 (2003)

59. Kovács, G.: Inaugural Speech Upon Receiving the Honorary Doctoral Degree of Corvinus University Budapest (2006). http://szamitastechnika.network.hu/blog/szamitastechnika-klub-hirei/kovacs-gyozo-szekszard-1933-februar-27-budapest-2012-december-18-magyar-villamosmernok-szamitastechnikus-informatikus-az-informatikai-kultura-jeles-terjesztoje. Accessed 3 May

60. Szabó, M.: Kalmár's argument for the independence of computer science. In: Manea, F., Martin, B., Paulusma, D., Primiero, G. (eds.) CiE 2019. LNCS, vol. 11558, pp. 265–276. Springer, Cham (2019). https://doi.org/10.1007/978-3-030-22996-2_23

61. Kalmár, L.: A számítástechnikai szakemberképzés problémái a tudományegyetemeken (The Problems of the University-Level Education of Programmers). In: A SZÁMÍTÁSTE-CHNIKAI OKTATÁS A HAZAI FELSŐOKTATÁSI INTÉZMÉNYEKBEN, Visegrád, pp. 25–30 (1974a)

62. Kalmár, L.: A pedagógus a számítógépek korában (The Teacher in the Age of Computers). Köznevelés 30(20), 3–5 (1974)

63. Somogyvári, L.: Tanítógépek Magyarországon a hatvanas években (Educational Machines in Hungary in the Sixties) (2018). https://www.academia.edu/8846084/Tan%C3%ADtógépek_Magyarországon_a_hatvanas_években. Accessed 1 Nov 2018

64. Froumin, I., Leshukov, O.: The soviet flagship university model and its contemporary transition. In: Douglass, J.A. (ed.) The New Flagship University. IDE, pp. 173–189. Palgrave Macmillan US, New York (2016). https://doi.org/10.1057/9781137500496_8

65. Bereczki, I.: Nem elemi rekurzív függvény létezése (The Existence of a Non-Elementary Recursive Function). In: Az Első Magyar Matematikai Kongresszus Közleményei. 1950. augusztus 27. – szeptember 2, pp. 409–417 (1952a)

66. Bereczki, I.: Lösung eines Markovschen Problems betreffs einer Ausdehnung des Begriffes der elementaren Funktion. Acta Mathematica Academiae Scientiarum Hungaricae 3, 197–218 (1952)

67. Fodor, G.: Eine Bemerkung zur Theorie der regressiven Funktionen. Acta Scientiarum Mathematicarum 17, 139–142 (1956)

68. Megyesi, L.: Pollák György (1929–2001). Polygon 11(2), 1–3 (2002)

69. Szelezsán, J.: Elektronikus számológépek programozása (The Programming of Digital Calculators). 500 copies, 150 p. Published by the Cybernetics Research Group, Budapest (1962)

70. Tursk, W.M. (ed.): Programming teaching techniques. In: Proceedings of the IFIP TC-2 Conference on Programming Teaching Techniques, Zakopane, Poland, 18–22 September 1972. North-Holland Publishing Company, Amsterdam (1973)

71. Flores, I.: Computer Software: Programming Systems for Digital Computers. Prentice-Hall, New Jersey (1965)

72. Flores, I.: Computer Programming. Prentice-Hall, New Jersey (1966)

73. Knuth, D.: The Art of Computer Programming, vol. 1: Fundamental Algorithms. Addison-Wesley Publishing, Reading (1968)

Poland

Early Computer Development in Poland

Marek Hołyński[(✉)]

Polish Information Processing Society,
ul. Solec 38 lok. 103, 00-394 Warsaw, Poland
marek.holynski@gmail.com

Abstract. The paper describes the history of early computing in Poland from the establishment of the Mathematical Apparatuses Group in 1948, which later changed into the independent Mathematical Apparatuses Division of the Polish Academy of Sciences and then finally became the Institute of Mathematical Machines, where the ZAM computers were designed and produced. Two other research and development centers, which were most important in the late 1950s and 1960s are also described: the Faculty of Telecommunications of the Warsaw Institute of Technology (UMC machines) and Elwro (Odra series). When the production of RYAD computers started in 1973, the production of these machines had to be dropped.

Keywords: History of computing · Polish computing

1 Introduction

The early development of computers in Poland has been very sparsely documented in English-language publications. English-language articles published in professional periodicals during that period usually detailed specific technical solutions, and seldom gave sufficient historical context. PIPS – the Polish Information Processing Society (Polskie Towarzystwo Informatyczne – PTI) has been trying to collect all of these articles, but currently only has two of them in its archives [1, 2], which might be partially considered historical studies. Both concentrate primarily on the personal achievements of the authors and dedicate less detail to other works carried out in parallel. Moreover, these works focus on the 1940s and '50s, and do not take into account the consequences of these developments in the following decades.

The Polish-language resources are richer [3–14], but even they do not provide a full picture. Some, which are not referenced here, were simply juxtapositions of dates and milestones. Others were limited to very specific computer applications in particular sectors of the economy or overly personalized memories. Often times, attempts at a more comprehensive summary of the subject contradicted prior work or were continuations of long-outdated controversial discussions.

As the anniversary of the 70th birthday of Polish informatics drew near, PIPS was tasked with the coordination of jubilee ventures prepared by various government institutions, universities, associations and companies. We had to organize our historical knowledge to fill existing gaps and develop a comprehensive description of the history of Polish computing. Not only because this story needs to be better known, but also to

© IFIP International Federation for Information Processing 2019
Published by Springer Nature Switzerland AG 2019
C. Leslie and M. Schmitt (Eds.): HC 2018, IFIP AICT 549, pp. 71–86, 2019.
https://doi.org/10.1007/978-3-030-29160-0_4

serve as a reference during the number of presentations for this event. Moreover, such an overview should not be reduced to a dry litany of technical parameters, people, and inventions. Instead, it should serve as a historical narrative that is interesting even to the ordinary reader or listener. This task was originally assigned to me as chairman of the national commemoration committee.

The preliminary material describing the years 1949–73 consisted of 65 pages. Several corrections were made after consultation with the PIPS's historical section and a number of discussions with the Society board of directors. It was then printed in sections to consecutive PIPS's bulletins [15–20], which are regularly distributed in paper and electronically to all members. Their comments and additions have also been taken into account. The following article is a significantly compressed English version of that text.

The initial part of this paper draws partially from two previously cited articles and the missing data is supplemented by information about other parallel achievements. The data presented has been correlated with facts established in the course of my work at the Institute of Mathematical Machines (IMM) from 1970–81. It was then the country's leading R&D institution in this field, and still employed most of the pioneers from early days of Polish computer science. These pioneers were very happy to share their memories of the 1950s and 1960s, and I was equally happy to write them down.

Two other important resources for historical information used in this paper should also be mentioned. In 2008, I became the IMM director, which gave me direct access to the institution's rich archives. In the same year, I was elected as president of the Polish Information Processing Society. Shortly after, we established a historical section in PIPS, which was officially authorized to access collections of state archives. Thus, we began to gather, organize and digitize all available documents and private relations. Most of the material referring to the 1960s and early 1970s comes from these two sources.

2 Mathematical Apparatuses Group

On December 23, 1948, the weather in Warsaw was particularly bad. Wet snow continued to fall as the inhabitants of the ruined city desperately tried to salvage what they could of their holidays with a meager meal for their family. Only a small group of people seemed untroubled by the worries of the upcoming celebrations. These were attendees of a seminar on electronic calculating machines, listening to a talk given by Kazimierz Kuratowski (Fig. 1).

Fig. 1. Kazimierz Kuratowski. Source: Polish Wikipedia

Kuratowski was a renowned topologist and director of the Institute of Mathematics in the Polish Academy of Sciences. He had just returned from a series of lectures in the United States, where he was shown ENIAC, the first electronic general-purpose computer, dubbed in the press as "the giant brain." His excitement about the newly built machine sparked great motivation among the listeners and led them to the immediately form a new research team.

The team, officially named the Mathematical Apparatuses Group, began building their own computer, despite having access to very limited resources. The researchers, who wore leaky boots and were barely surviving on the food parcels from post-WWII international relief agencies, did not have access to the proper equipment, parts, or even premises to pursue their endeavors. Moreover, the new American advancements in relevant fields were not often shared with the public, much less other countries, due to their applications in the military. Even the technical details which were released did not often reach Poland, as a result of the Iron Curtain.

The Mathematical Apparatuses Group was provided three rooms at the Institute and for quite a while their work remained only on paper. Their first attempts to deal with real devices did not bring significant results. For each damaged module they repaired, another one broke down, and the process would repeat.

3   Analog or Digital?

Finally, in 1953, they were able to get something working: an analog machine built with vacuum tubes, which was called the Differential Equations Analyzer (ARR). It was able to solve complex differential equations with very high accuracy and was used for a number of practical applications, including the design of turbines and aircrafts (Fig. 2).

Fig. 2. Differential Equations Analyzer. Source: Archives of the Institute of Mathematical Machines with permission of the Institute's director.

The next machine, the Algebraic Linear Equations Analyzer (ARAL), also proved to be useful. In subsequent versions, ARAL-1, -2 and -3 served to solve systems of equations (in fact, not only linear). Both ARR and ARAL were analog machines designed exclusively for a single task and nothing more. At the time, they seemed like the obvious choice because of the team's considerable experience in analog construction and the low efficiency of vacuum tubes. However, the advent of digital devices had brought about much more versatile machines that could be programmed for various types of calculations and were less susceptible to accumulating errors.

The first attempt to construct a digital machine was made in the years 1953–1955 by the team led by Romuald Marczyński. The Electronic Machine for Automatic Calculations (EMAL) was said to perform 2000 additions or subtractions, 450 multiplications, and 230 divisions per second. The solution which allowed for the "fast" memory of this machine consisted of a number of glass tubes filled with mercury, which could often not be sealed adequately, resulting in a health hazard (Fig. 3).

Fig. 3. Romuald Marczyński (in a white shirt) while working on the Electronic Machine for Automatic Calculations (EMAL) [2].

According to an anecdote passed from one generation of computer scientists to the next, one of the team members was reminded of a commonly used item made of latex that had the perfect dimensions for sealing the glass tubes. While the saleswomen at the pharmacy were not particularly surprised when he requested one hundred pieces, they were taken aback by the request to invoice these highly personal items to the Polish Academy of Sciences.

Unfortunately, this machine was never fully launched – it was too unreliable. The components available at that time in Poland (lamps, connectors, etc.) were of low quality and caused problems too difficult to overcome. It took significant labor to build individual machine modules, which would cease to function in only two or three days. Repairs were often highly complex and seemingly indefinite, constantly requiring new components.

Newspapers at the time which mentioned these projects usually focused on intellectual challenges and conceptual difficulties in creating an "electronic brain," but selcom focused on the real problems with which the researchers were struggling. How could they make a tangle of cables and electronic components (some of which were remains from the German army during occupation) function properly for a reasonable amount of time? Statistics from these years show that, for these devices, downtime for failures and maintenance significantly exceeded the time of effective operation.

4 From ABC to XYZ

In order to consolidate the existing research and design efforts, the Polish Academy of Sciences established the independent Mathematical Apparatuses Division (Zakład Aparatów Matematycznych – ZAM) in 1957. It was there that in the autumn of 1958, the first Polish electronic digital machine was launched with the name XYZ (Fig. 4).

Fig. 4. XYZ digital computer. Source: Archives of the Institute of Mathematical Machines with permission of the Institute's director.

It used 400 tubes and 2000 diodes, flip-flops on one triode, had drum memory and punched cards for input and output. It could perform up to 1000 arithmetic operations per second and had an internal binary language with symbolic addressing.

The head of the team, prof. Leon Łukaszewicz, when asked by journalists why the machine was named XYZ, would answer: "Well, the version we started with was called

Fig. 5. Leon Łukaszewicz

ABC, and then there were others." Łukaszewicz was also the representative of the Polish Academy of Sciences to IFIP from 1961 to 1985 and Vice President of IFIP from 1964 to 1968 (Fig. 5).

XYZ became a real milestone in the development of Polish computers. The presentations to government officials and the general public aroused great interest and attention was drawn to the possibility of wide-spread production and application.

At that time, commercial applications for such an efficient machine had only just begun to emerge. In 1960 the first improved version of XYZ, called ZAM-2, was built. It included 600 kilobits of memory, teletype and a paper tape reader, and was suitable for mass production. The software, especially System of Automatic Coding SAKO (often dubbed a Polish Fortran), was one of the major selling points of this machine. For the next three years a series of twelve units were produced, a number which was quite significant for the time (Fig. 6).

Fig. 6. ZAM-2. Source: Archives of the Institute of Mathematical Machines with permission of the Institute's director.

ZAM-2 was successfully used in various institutions for numerical calculations and data processing both at home and abroad, as evidenced by the email (quoted here literally) sent by a German user in March 2017, requesting permission to use pictures of the ZAM-2 on his personal website:

Dear Mr. Direktor,
More than 50 years ago the ironworks in village Hennigsdorf have acquired a computer ZAM 2 GAMMA of the IMM. 10 years I was responsible for the servicing of the machine. With pleasure I would publish this event on my homepage. In the draught the pictures which come from the education in the IMM are included. If it was right to them, that I the draught sends as a ZIP file to receive her approval for the publication.

Permission, of course, was granted. Clearly, the machine had some fans.

The Mathematical Apparatuses Division, which by 1962 was operating out of its own building (Fig. 7), began its transformation into the Institute of Mathematical Machines (Instytut Maszyn Matematycznych – IMM), as mentioned in the above email. In order to maintain the tradition, the Institute has existed for years under the old name, despite the burden of facing continuous inquiries (especially from younger generations) about what mathematical machines really are.

The word "computer" was only allowed to appear in the Polish language fairly late – in the mid-1970s. Before, it was routinely replaced by the censors' office with the phrase "electronic calculating machine", a compulsory copy of the Russian term for computers.

Fig. 7. Instytut Maszyn Matematycznych. Source: Archives of the Institute of Mathematical Machines with permission of the Institute's director.

5 We Need More Computers

XYZ proved that building such devices was possible in Poland, so other research centers began to find interest in computers. The Warsaw Institute of Technology (WIT) already had some experience with machines dedicated to specialized mathematical calculations. The system PARK [8] developed there in 1956 was already a digital device, albeit built on relays instead of tubes. It had been used to solve combinations of algebraic equations for over fifteen years.

Shortly after, an impressive set of projects was launched at the Faculty of Telecommunications headed by Antoni Kiliński, later the president of WIT. Incidentally, Kiliński and Marczyński are the only Poles among about one hundred people honored with the IEEE Computer Society Pioneer Award, crediting scientists for their contributions in the creation of computers (Fig. 8).

Fig. 8. Antoni Kiliński. Source: Polish Wikipedia

The part of WIT's strategy of was to create computers dedicated for special tasks. The AMC (Administrative Digital Machine) was to be used for data processing; the GEO had a multiprocessor operating system, Fortran translator, several versions of assembler and geodetic programs sets, and revolutionized land measurements in Poland; the ANOPS series was designed to support biomedical research [9], and many of the 150 machines produced worked in medical centers around the world. In fact, the ANOPS was the first Polish computer ordered by the leading American and Canadian research institutions.

The most well-known of the computers created at the Warsaw University of Technology was undoubtedly the UMC series (Universal Digital Machine). The UMC-1 prototype was developed in 1960 (Fig. 9). It was a machine capable of performing 100 operations per second, equipped with a drum memory capacity of 144 kilobits. The construction was so successful that it was chosen for large-scale serial manufacturing. Its blueprints and documentation was handed to Elwro factory, where industrial production began the next year. By 1964, 25 of these machines were made. UMC-1 was a

Fig. 9. UMC-1 at the exhibition in Moscow; drum memory was exposed in the foreground. Source: Polish Wikipedia

vacuum tube machine, but later versions, such as the UMC-10 (which replaced it in 1965) used transistors and magnetic-core memory.

The third major research center was the Nuclear Research Institute of the Polish Academy of Sciences. A computational group was organized there for supporting the design of nuclear reactors, later transformed into the Department of Applied Mathematics. In 1956, development of the EMAL machine was moved there and shortly after, the machine was put to use. Known as the EMAL-2, it was used for a number of years and then transferred to the Computational Center of the Polish Academy of Sciences.

6   ELWRO

The Elwro factory, established in 1959 in the city of Wrocław, was to be the production base of the national electronics industry. However, according to everyone who remembers those times, the real intention from the very beginning was to create a factory producing computers [10, 11].

In addition to producing UMC machines, Elwro also had its own plans. A development group was created there, which presented the prototype of the Odra 1001 (Odra is a river over which Wrocław is located). For the first time in Poland, floating-point operations were implemented in hardware, although they didn't perform reliably enough.

Their next attempt, the Odra 1003, was reasonably efficient and suitable for serial production, which started in 1964. It was also much smaller than the previous iterations (as it can be seen on Fig. 10). After that, another successful version, the Odra 1013, was developed, which was two times faster than the previous one (a hundred of these were produced in Elwro). There was also one more after this – the Odra 1103 [12].

Fig. 10. Launching Odra 1003. Source: Memoirs of Mr. Wojciech Lipko (https://polskiekomputery.pl/mgr-inz-wojciech-lipko-wspomnienia, last accessed 2018/11/02), who is visible in the foreground in a striped shirt.

The next big leap in quality was with the Odra 1204 project. It was already equipped with an operating system, but still, despite the complete Algol translator, with rather modest software. Without a rich set of programs, one could not take full advantage of the potential of even the most capable computer.

In order to create necessary software, Elwro would have to organize a large group of expert programmers and provide them with the necessary time. Instead, the plan was made to use the software of one of the reputable foreign companies and avoid this problem. That is, instead of creating software for an existing machine, build a computer on which existing software would work properly.

First, they had to find a company that would agree to such a deal. IBM, the strongest player in the global market at that time, was not interested. However, others were more willing to consider the offer, as long as their equipment was purchased as part of the package. Ultimately, the British firm ICT (International Computers and Tabulators), which soon became part of ICL (International Computers Limited), was selected.

ICT machines in Poland had already been in use for some time and several programmers and engineers were quite accustomed to them. It was decided that Poland would buy two large ICL 1900 computer. In return, Elwro would receive their documentation and software. In Fig. 11, the "men in black" are shown in front of the ICT headquarters, having just signed the agreement in July 1967. This contract, as well as the government instructions for the Polish delegation, were published in [13]

Fig. 11. Polish delegation in front of the ICT headquarters [13].

The same team that made the Odra 1204 was assigned to this project, and as a result, many of the solutions they used were simply adopted from their experiences with the previous machine. Their task this time was more difficult, because the goal was to achieve a system that was fully compliant with the provided British hardware.

Despite the challenge, the team was ultimately successful. The first prototype of the Odra 1304, produced in early 1970, behaved exactly the same way as the ICL 1904, supporting all the same features: the George operating system (then regarded as one of the best in the world), several programming languages (including Algol, Fortran and Cobol, the most widespread at the time) and a library of over a thousand ready-to-use programs. An extensive set of external devices also functioned as expected (Fig. 12).

Odra 1304 and its successors, Odra 1305 and Odra 1325, had already started being built on an integrated circuit and were considered the best machines in the Eastern Bloc

Fig. 12. ODRA 1304. Source: Polish Wikipedia

at the beginning of the seventies. With rich software and a full range of external devices, they became the perfect tools for computerization of many enterprises and institutions. In total, 587 units of the Odra 1300 series were produced. Through their lifetime, they enabled the computerization of entire industries such as construction and railway, in addition to various institutions and universities. Top-secret military applications, which were classified for many years, were later revealed to also disclose other use these devices. In 1999, an anti-aircraft system using a (then 20-year-old) Odra 1325 detected and shot down a presumably radar-invisible F-117 during its military mission in Serbia.

Elwro's strategy brought the desired results, but their success has been controversial, even to this day. Many questioned if it was worth copying other work, even if the source material was deemed the best available. Some insist that even when operating at a strict disadvantage, it is best to further develop original ideas, for the sake of scientific discovery and exploration. While clearly the agreement with ICT enabled the massive leap in overcoming complicated technological issues, others still suggest that solving them independently would have been fruitful in the long run.

7 RYAD

This dilemma – the choice between replicating proven solutions and own creation – later appeared again on a much larger scale. In January 1967, a committee in the Academy of Sciences of the USSR decided that the efforts of Comecon countries should be consolidated and that all countries should join forces to create a unified system of computers. It was decided to follow the model of the IBM 360, the most widespread machines in the world at that time.

Once this decision was made, it became difficult to do anything else. If a country insisted on following their own designs, they were accepting the possibility of political consequences and economic marginalization. It was therefore recognized by the Polish government that participation in this unified program was in the best interest of the country. This undertaking was officially dubbed the Unified System of Electronic Computers, or RYAD.

In later years, the widely accepted theory for this period is that the Soviets forced Polish authorities into the RYAD project, in the same way Polish industries were forced to sell coal and ships at favorable prices. This would not have been an obvious supposition, because according to some officials, there did not seem to be too interest in about Poland's participation in the program, largely as a result of the contention from the ICL contract.

The distribution of tasks showed the Soviet disregard for Polish participation even more clearly. A medium size machine called the R-30 (EC 1030) was to be designed by the Yerevan institute and built in a factory in Kazan. The IMM was tasked with designing its own version of such a machine. Poland as a whole was also involved in this undertaking, although marginally, as they were only tasked with the production of printers, tape memories and terminals.

Prior to this effort, the IMM had been working on the ZAM machines, and in particular the ZAM-3 and ZAM-21 (launched in 1965). The last of this series, the ZAM-41 (Fig. 13), was not far from the contemporary notion of a computer. It performed

Fig. 13. ZAM-41. Source: Archives of the Institute of Mathematical Machines with permission of the Institute's director.

30,000 fixed-point operations per second, was equipped with a tape memory, line printer, and other peripherals. Its production started in 1966. Once IMM became involved in R-30, it was forced to drop the ZAM line.

The IMM teams traveled back and forth to their counterpart institute in Yerevan, returning with cheaply bought Ararat cognac for their friends. In Warsaw, however, their task was met without much enthusiasm something which had been forced on them. This lack of enthusiasm ultimately led to the initiative being taken over from the IMM by the more dynamic Elwro.

As it turned out, Wrocław did quite well. The version of the R-30 built by the Polish team was smaller (it was located in just one cabinet while the Soviet one occupied three), did not need as much energy, and was more reliable. Yerevan's R-30 could not be launched at the Poznań International Fair in 1972, and the machine which did not work had to be presented.

Above all, the Polish version of the R-30 was significantly faster. At the Brno fair, all the RYAD devices were compared using a test prepared by the Czechoslovak Academy of Sciences, which measured the time it took to calculate a set of one million basic arithmetic operations. The R-20, developed in Bulgaria and Minsk, dealt with this test in 200 s. The R-30 from Yerevan needed 70 s, and the Elwro computer only 7 s. Another surprising result was the German R-40 machine, which was five times bigger, and ran the test in 9 s. [14].

Despite initial allegations of violation of the design rules established for the entire Unified System, the Polish computer received a separate R-32 number and in 1973 and decision was made to manufacture it (Fig. 14). Even so, the Russians never bought a single piece. Instead, the Kazan factory which had produced the Yerevan R-30 began to implement the solutions used in R-32 in their own modernized R-33.

The development of the Unified System was continued in the 80 s by following the more advanced IBM 370 family. As part of this program called RYAD 2 Elwro manufactured R-34 computers until 1987.

Fig. 14. R-32. Source: Polish Wikipedia

8   Conclusions

As mentioned at beginning, this paper is an extremely compressed English-language version of the material prepared for celebrations of the 70th birthday of Polish informatics in 2018. The Polish report was aimed at presenting the most complete description of the achievements in the years 1949–73 by organizing known facts and supplementing them with first-hand accounts and a large selection of archived materials. Like many such comprehensive reviews, it inevitably still has some gaps. However, after considerable discussion of this material at PIPS meetings and feedback from all Society members, there is hopefully not too much missing.

The Polish-language study, however extensive, still doesn't address some important issues of described period. Firstly, it does not mention the important discussion about what the ultimate purpose of computer would be. This debate first began in the late sixties, and ultimately concluded in a clear shift from the use of computers for strictly scientific use to their use for new applications in business and administration. The study also does not discuss potential benefits or losses as a result of technology transfer, the degree of Soviet influence in Poland or even the evident camaraderie between scientists from different counties despite ideological barriers.

Unfortunately, none of the PIPS members are historians by trade. Therefore, we don't feel qualified to discuss the broader historical and political context of this period – something which certainly merits more discussion. This paper is only a preliminary attempt to gather relevant facts and present them in a way allowing experts with a proper methodology of historical documentation, who may further organize and analyze them. One collection of such source materials is also readily available. Four years ago, PIPS invited its members to submit their memories, which resulted in a book, from which three essays have been cited here [12–14].

References

1. Łukaszewicz, L.: On the beginning of computer development in Poland. Ann. Hist. Comput. **12**, 103–107 (1980)
2. Marczyński, R.: The first seven years of polish digital computers. Ann. Hist. Comput. **2**, 37–48 (1980)
3. Madey, J., Sysło, M.: Początki informatyki w Polsce [The beginnings of computer science in Poland]. Informatyka **9**, 10 (2000)
4. Targowski, A.: Informatyka. Modele rozwoju i systemów [Informatics. Models of development and systems]. PWE (1980)
5. Łukaszewicz, L.: O początkach informatyki w Polsce [On the beginnings of computer science in Poland]. In: Materiały konferencji PTI "40 lat informatyki w Polsce" [Proceedings of the PIPS conference "40 years of computer science in Poland"] (1988)
6. Nowakowski, W.: 50 lat polskich komputerów, historia romantyczna. Esej historyczny [50 years of Polish computers, romantic history. Historical essay]. IMM (2008)
7. Miś, B.: To już pół wieku [It's been half a century]. Studio Opinii (2009)

8. Jasicki, Z., Kordylewski, J., Kudelski, G.: Zastosowanie maszyny matematycznej PARK do obliczania stopnia kompensacji mocy biernej w sieciach elektroenergetycznych [The use of the PARK mathematical machine to calculate the degree of reactive power compensation in power grids]. Appl. Math. **6**, 407–418 (1962)
9. Hołyński, M.: Raport w sprawie ANOPS-a [Report on ANOPS]. Polityka 5 (1977)
10. Bilski, E.: Wrocławskie Zakłady Elektroniczne ELWRO [Wroclaw Electronic Factory ELWRO] (2013). https://aresluna.org/attached/computerhistory/articles/odra. Accessed 02 Nov 2018
11. Maćkowiak, B., Myszkier, A., Safader, B.: Polskie komputery rodziły się w ELWRO [Polish computers were born in ELWRO]. Archiwum Państwowe we Wrocławiu [Wroclaw State Archives] (2018)
12. Lesiński, J., Kociatkiewicz, P.: Komputer Odra 1103 [Computer Odra 1103]. In: Noga, M., Nowak, J.S. (eds.) Polska informatyka: wizje i trudne początki [Polish computer science: visions and difficult beginnings], pp. 277–280. PTI (2017)
13. Bilski, E., Kamburelis, T., Piwowar, B.: Wrocławskie Zakłady Elektroniczne. Okres komputerów Odra 1300 [Wroclaw Electronic Factory. Period of computers Odra 1300]. In: Noga, M., Nowak, J.S. (eds.) Polska informatyka: wizje i trudne początki [Polish computer science: visions and difficult beginnings], pp. 13–35. PTI (2017)
14. Kulisiewicz, T.: Własne konstrukcje, licencje, klony [Own constructions, licenses, clones]. In: Noga, M., Nowak, J.S. (eds.) Polska informatyka: wizje i trudne początki [Polish computer science: visions and difficult beginnings], pp. 57–94. PTI (2017)
15. Hołyński, M.: 70-lecie polskiej informatyki [70th anniversary of Polish computer science] (2016). http://biuletyn.pti.org.pl/BiuletynPTI_2016-04.pdf. Accessed 02 Nov 2018
16. Hołyński, M.: Analog czy cyfra? [Analog or digital?] (2017). http://biuletyn.pti.org.pl/BiuletynPTI_2017-01.pdf. Accessed 02 Nov 2018
17. Hołyński, M.: Pierwszy polski komputer [First Polish computer] (2017). http://www.biuletyn.pti.org.pl/BiuletynPTI_2017-02.pdf. Accessed 02 Nov 2018
18. Hołyński, M.: Mamy ZAM-y [We have ZAMs] (2017). http://biuletyn.pti.org.pl/BiuletynPTI_2017-03-04_ewydanie.pdf. Accessed 02 Nov 2018
19. Hołyński, M.: Wczesne lata 60-te: wysyp maszyn [Early 1960s: abundance of machines] (2018). http://www.biuletyn.pti.org.pl/BiuletynPTI_2018-01_ewydanie.pdf. Accessed 02 Nov 2018
20. Hołyński, M.: Naśladować innych, czy rozwijać własne pomysły? [Imitate others or develop your own ideas?] (2018). http://www.biuletyn.pti.org.pl/BiuletynPTI_2018-02_ewydanie.pdf. Accessed 02 Nov 2018

The Long Road Toward the Rejewski-Różycki-Zygalski Cipher Center in Poznań

Marek Grajek[(⊠)]

Freelance Consultant on Cryptology Applications, Warsaw, Poland

Abstract. This paper presents the plans to create a Rejewski-Różycki-Zygalski Cipher Center at Poznań, Poland, where the story of Enigma breaking took its beginnings, covering a long way of the project since the inauguration of the monument *in memoriam* of the three codebreakers in 2007.

Keywords: Polish Cipher Bureau · Enigma codebreaking · Rejewski · Różycki · Zygalski · Cipher Center

1 A Bit of History

1.1 Start of the Story: The Monument

Rumors persist concerning organization in Poznań, Poland, of a new Enigma Museum. In reality, the new institution will be neither an old-fashioned museum, nor will it be dedicated to German ciphering machine Enigma. This paper is hoped to unravel the mystery of the real nature and purpose of the center being organized, as well as to present the long way leading to its inauguration planned for 2020. It all started eleven years ago; in 2007, a monument commemorating Polish codebreakers, Marian Rejewski, Jerzy Różycki and Henryk Zygalski, was inaugurated in front of the Poznań Castle, place most closely linked with the earliest part of their history.

In 1929, Poznan Castle was housing, among other institutions, the mathematical faculty of Poznań University. At that time, the Cipher Bureau of the Polish army was facing the challenge of a new cipher just introduced by the German Reichswehr. The commanding officer of Bureau's German section, Lt. Maksymilian Ciężki, recalled the hot days of the summer 1920, when the help of the three mathematicians, Stanisław Leśniewski, Stefan Mazurkiewicz and Wacław Sierpiński, had helped the Polish army to break the Soviet ciphers and defeat the Soviet army approaching Warsaw. He decided to reach again for the help of the mathematics and the mathematicians, so he organized the training in cryptology designed for a group of young students of mathematics at Poznań University. The best graduates of this course were later initiated into the subtler methods of cryptology working in Cipher Bureau's branch office conveniently arranged in the military building located across the street from their faculty. In 1932, when only three of the initial twenty-odd candidates for the code-breakers were left, they were put on their real challenge – the ciphers of the German Enigma. The idea of reaching for the help of mathematicians paid off very soon; in the

C. Leslie and M. Schmitt (Eds.): HC 2018, IFIP AICT 549, pp. 87–96, 2019.
https://doi.org/10.1007/978-3-030-29160-0_5

last days of 1932, Enigma was broken and cryptology adopted a new, purely mathematical face. It was thus natural to locate the monument commemorating this history in its proper starting place. From among over twenty proposals (Fig. 1) for the monument's design the jury selected the idea most closely related to mathematics: a simple prism covered with numbers, with codebreakers' names on each of its three faces.

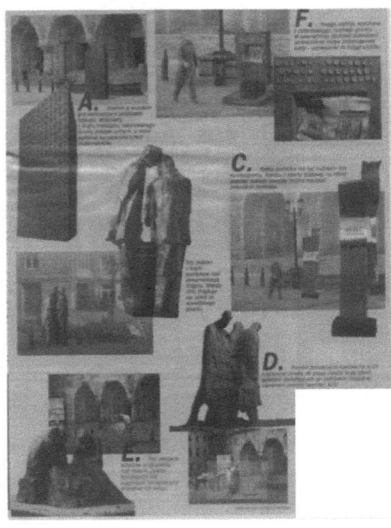

Fig. 1. Some of the proposals in the contest for monument design

Soon thereafter, passers-by were surprised by the view of a group of men pushing around a model of the monument in the search for its best future location (Fig. 2).

Fig. 2. Monty Python episode?

Some of the spectators supposed having watched the filming of the next episode of the "Monty Python's Flying Circus," but their hypothesis was soon disproved when the foundation act and the cornerstone for the future monument were laid and the finally the monument itself was installed (Fig. 3).

Fig. 3. Laying of the foundation act and monument's installation

Finally, on 10 November 2007, the monument was inaugurated (Fig. 4); people who stood behind its erection could start thinking about the next steps. In their common opinion the monument itself should be complemented by a place in its direct neighborhood, where the history of the codebreakers and their achievements could be explained.

Fig. 4. Inauguration of the monument

1.2   Long Road to the Cipher Center

Before the organizers were able to implement that plan, the history started to live its own life. Its heroes, forgotten for over fifty years, were now remembered and honored. In 2008, the ashes of Col. Maksymilian Ciężki were brought back from Par in Cornwall, where he died in 1951 in poverty and solitude, back to his native town of Szamotuły (Fig. 5). It was a triumphal return, the coffin with his ashes being carried by the members of the history reenactment groups wearing the colors of the army of the Greater Poland (1918–1919) uprising and the Polish-German war of 1939, campaigns that Ciężki participated in.

Fig. 5. Lt. Col. Maksymilian Ciężki returns to his native town

Two years later, the remains of Col. Gwido Langer, commanding officer of the Polish Cipher Bureau, were exhumed from the Wellshill cemetery in Perth, where he had been buried after his early death in 1947, and were transferred to his native Cieszyn (Fig. 6).

Fig. 6. Col. Gwido Langer's farewell to his temporary burial place in Scotland

The academic community of Poznań was celebrating the memory of its former members inaugurating in 2008 a series of lectures in mathematics and information science bearing their names. During the last 10 years these lectures were able to gain a prestigious profile and gather leading scholars in both disciplines from all over the world.

Fig. 7. Prof. Clifford Cocks at Rejewski, Różycki & Zygalski lecture in Poznań

The regional government of Poznań province sponsored the exhibition presenting the contribution of the Polish codebreakers towards the Allied victory in the World War II (Fig. 7). Inaugurated in 2010 at the EU Parliament in Brussels, this exhibition exists now in several language versions travelling all over the world and enjoying everywhere a welcome reception (Fig. 8).

Fig. 8. "Enigma. Decipher Victory" exhibition at the European Parliament in Brussels

Younger generations are learning the codebreakers' story participating in the urban games organized initially in Poznań, now spreading every year to new locations in Poland, linked with codebreakers' fates (Fig. 9).

Fig. 9. Winning team at the urban game at Szamotuły

An Internet contest in the codebreaking organized usually one or twice a year represents a natural complement for the urban games (Fig. 10). Addressed mostly to the college students it enjoys an enormous popularity, gathering every time over thousand participants from all over the world, who not only break the ciphers, but also learn about the history of the Polish codebreakers.

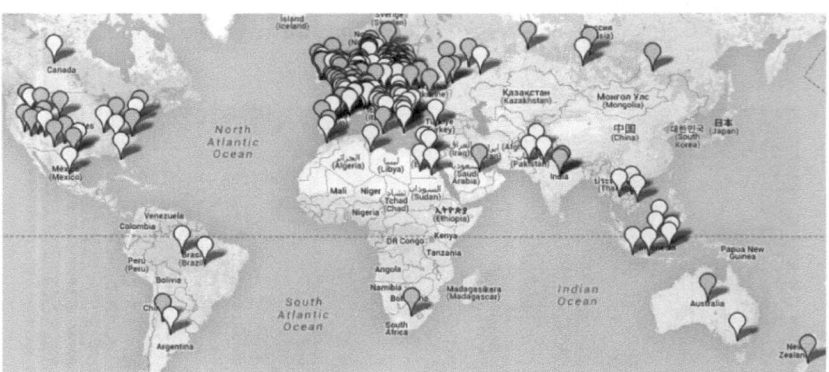

Fig. 10. Participants of the Internet codebreaking contest cobreakers.eu

The importance of the codebreakers' achievements is now being generally recognized. In 2014, the largest professional organization of electric and electronic engineers, IEEE, decided to commemorate their services with one of its Milestone awards

(Fig. 11). A Milestone in electrical engineering and computing dedicated to Rejewski, Różycki and Zygalski was inaugurated in Warsaw, in August 2014.

Fig. 11. IEEE Milestone in Warsaw

The role of the Polish codebreakers in cracking the Enigma cipher is starting to be recognized even in the Great Britain, traditionally favoring the role of its own code-breakers. A new part of the exhibition at Bletchley Park, inaugurated in 2018 in Hut11A, includes the working model of Rejewski bombe provided on the initiative of the Polish embassy in London (Fig. 12).

Fig. 12. Reconstruction of Rejewski's "bomba" at Hut11A, Bletchley Park

1.3   Rejewski, Różycki, Zygalski Cipher Center

It is time to return to place where it all began, Poznań. Two years ago, the regional government of the Poznań province, the mayor of Poznań, and the local university reached an agreement to create an institution commemorating the services of the three codebreakers and illustrating their importance for the history and in the present. The center shall be located in the very particular place, linked most closely to the history of Enigma breaking. The codebreakers used to learn the secrets of their new trade at the building of the local military staff erected at the beginning of the twentieth century (Fig. 13).

Fig. 13. Former building of the Cipher Bureau's branch office in Poznań

The original building was heavily damaged during the heavy fighting in Poznań in February 1945. The new, communist rulers of the country decided to replace it with the new building, designed specially as the location of the local committee of the communist party. In that new role the building was a witness of the violent anti-communist protest in 1956 (Fig. 14).

Fig. 14. Construction of the communist party regional committee (around 1950)

After the collapse of communism in Poland in 1989 the building was donated to the university, which, very appropriately, located therein its historical faculty. However, once the faculty moved out to the new campus, the building was available for other purposes; currently its interiors are being arranged for its new role of the Cipher Center. Although plans for this new institution include some purely historical function, its main purpose will be far from the traditional museums. The experience of the urban games and the internet contests in the codebreaking demonstrated very clearly that cryptography and codebreaking offer a perfect foundation for the adventure addressed to any generation. Therefore, the Rejewski-Różycki-Zygalski Cipher Centre shall represent an adventure park based on the real story of Enigma breaking rather than an old fashioned museum. Its program shall be participatory, assuming spectator's activity during the entire visit (Fig. 15).

Fig. 15. Concept of the future Rejewski, Różycki, Zygalski Cipher Center, fragment

The inauguration of the center is scheduled for 2020, but one may taste its future offer even today. As a teaser for the future center, a so-called crypto container was installed in 2017 in front of the Poznań Castle, right next to the codebreakers' monument (Fig. 16). Arranged externally in the form of the huge Enigma machine the crypto container houses the program presenting an overview of the cryptology development from antiquity to the present times and offers its visitors an opportunity to learn the basic skills of a codebreaker. Popularity of the crypto container among the visitors to Poznań offers good prospects for its permanent successor – the Rejewski, Różycki, Zygalski Cipher Center.

Of course, the existence of the center shall not put an end to activities presented above as the fragments of the way leading to its inauguration. On the contrary, the center and its staff shall offer a permanent and institutional support to numerous activities being structured so far as private or semi-private initiatives, based mostly on the invention and goodwill of their participants.

Fig. 16. Crypto container

Soviet Union

Anatoly Kitov and Victor Glushkov: Pioneers of Russian Digital Economy and Informatics

Olga V. Kitova$^{(\boxtimes)}$ and Vladimir A. Kitov

Plekhanov Russian University of Economics,
Stremyanny per., 36, Moscow, Russia
kitova.ov@rea.ru

Abstract. Recent work in the history of computing published in English might lead scholars to believe that there was little worthwhile research in computers during the cold war in the USSR. This article is devoted to the history of the development of the digital economy and automated information systems for managing the national economy in the Soviet Union. This history shows that the Red Book and OGAS projects were not failures given their impact on the development of the digital economy in Russia. Particular attention is paid to the contribution of two great Soviet scientists, Anatoly Kitov and Victor Glushkov, to the development of the automation of the Soviet economy, as well as the works of computer pioneer V. M. Glushkov in the field of informatics and the information society, artificial intelligence systems, and the creation of computers. The international renown of these scholars and the continuing work of their students to develop their ideas shows that Kitov and Glushkov's basic research had an important and lasting impact.

Keywords: Artificial intelligence systems ·
Automated management information systems ·
Digital automation of computer architecture · Digital economy · Informatics ·
Information society · Red Book ·
State automated management information system for the national economy
(OGAS) · Unified State Network of Computing Centers

1 Introduction

At present, the world is experiencing an active penetration of digital technologies into all spheres of life, the information society and the digital economy developing rapidly. In 2017, Russia approved the federal program "Digital Economy of the Russian Federation", which later became one of the Russian national projects[1]. Also there is the Russian federal program "Information Society" (2011–2020)[2].

The digital economy and the information society in Russia, along with the corresponding models, methods and instruments, did not develop from scratch. They rely on

---

[1] https://strategy24.ru/rf/projects/project/view?slug=natsional-nyy-proyekt-tsifrova-ekonomika&category=communication.

[2] http://fcp.economy.gov.ru/cgi-bin/cis/fcp.cgi/Fcp/ViewFcp/View/2012/369.

© IFIP International Federation for Information Processing 2019
Published by Springer Nature Switzerland AG 2019
C. Leslie and M. Schmitt (Eds.): HC 2018, IFIP AICT 549, pp. 99–117, 2019.
https://doi.org/10.1007/978-3-030-29160-0_6

the achievements of Soviet science and technology, the experience of implementing in the USSR management information systems (MIS, in Russian АСУ - ASU), industry management information systems (IMIS, in Russian ОАСУ - OASU), and the draft State Management Information System (SMIS, or OGAS from the Russian ОГАС).

In this article, we tell about two great Soviet scientists, Anatoly Kitov and Victor Glushkov, and their contribution to the development of the digital economy, informatics, and the information society. The research uses a biographical approach based on an analysis of the scientific papers of Glushkov [1–9] and Kitov [10–14], as well as the works of well-known historians Gerovich [16], Peters [17], Malinowski [18, 19], Kapitonova and Letichevskii [20], Kuteinikov [21], Shilov [22–25], and Prihod'ko [26]. The authors used the materials of the funds in the State Polytechnical Museum of Russia, materials of the Virtual Computer Museum (http://www.computer-museum.ru), archives of the Institute of Cybernetics of the National Academy of Sciences of Ukraine, archives of Plekhanov Russian University of Economics, and the Glushkov and Kitov family archives. Family memories of the present authors also made a certain contribution to the research (V. A. Kitov is the son of A. I. Kitov, and O. V. Kitova is the daughter of V. M. Glushkov).

The names of A. I. Kitov and V. M. Glushkov are inextricably linked with each other. They were not only the founders of and fighters for the automation of the management of the Soviet economy. In their life they were connected by friendship and fruitful scientific cooperation, working on joint projects. In particular, they together created the industry management information system (OASU) of the Ministry of Radio Industry: Glushkov was the scientific leader of this project, and Kitov was the chief designer. This system became a model for the nine defense ministries of the USSR.

This article expands conclusions made in papers [16–27] about the successes of the Soviet school of computer science and about the problems in constructing of a nationwide computer network to drive the Soviet economy, caused by the reluctance of the Soviet bureaucracy to change existing management methods. The non-existence of a Soviet internet, what Gerovich [16] has described the "internyet", has been the focus of other work. Peters [17] also focuses on the uneasy history of the Soviet Internet not paying enough attention to the impact made by Kitov and Glushkov on the development of Russian IT industry and modern Russian projects in the field of digital economy and information society, to their influence on the modern computer science. Malinovsky [18, 19], Kapitonova and Letichevskii [20], Kuteynikov [21], Shilov [22–25], and Prihod'ko [26] also tell about Kitov and Glushkov's research and projects without proper connection with modern research and projects in Russia and worldwide. It is astounding that the obvious application of computing to maintain the Soviet state was not accomplished, and the fact that the project was promoted by two academics with strong research records makes it even more curious. Nevertheless, even if the project had been accomplished, it would not have been similar to CYCLADES, ARPANet, or any other cold war era network. Thus, to dismiss Soviet computing misses the point of basic scientific research and fails to explain how the Russian Federation succeeded in computing after the fall of the USSR. The article reveals the close connection of the Soviet school of computer science with the national scientific mathematical and technical schools, connecting biographical facts with the history of science and the history of the country. First, by understanding the biographies of Kitov and Glushkov, and then by reviewing the wide scope of their research, one comes to appreciate how their work went far beyond what one might say was an effort to "network the nation".

2   Anatoly Ivanovich Kitov

Fig. 1. Colonel Anatoly Ivanovich Kitov (1957).

Pioneer of Russian informatics Anatoly Ivanovich Kitov (1920–2005) spent his school years in Tashkent (now in the Republic of Uzbekistan). At school, he was the best student. In the sixth grade Anatoly chose the brilliant French scientist Blaise Pascal as a model for imitation. It was then that Anatoly told his family that he was going to become a scientist in the future. He regularly compared his actions and achievements with the biography of Pascal, constantly asking himself the question "Did Pascal know this and did he know how to do it when he was at my present age?" (Fig. 1).

In Tashkent, the Kitov family, in which there were five children, lived very poorly. From the age of 13, Anatoly began to earn money by tutoring children of high-ranking Communist officials of Tashkent in various disciplines. Anatoly regularly became the winner of republican and city competitions in mathematics, physics, and a number of other disciplines. Another of Anatoly's passions was sports. He played tennis and volleyball, and also participated in city swimming and chess competitions. He was the champion of Tashkent in gymnastics among schoolchildren. He was engaged in the section of aircraft modeling, and he regularly made hiking or cycling trips to the Chimgan mountains.

In 1939, Kitov graduated with honors from high school and decided to become a nuclear physicist. He enrolled in the Central Asian University, where he studied for only two months, because he was called to the Red Army. Kitov was on the front lines of World War II from June 1941 to May 1945. He moved from anti-aircraft gunner to the commander of an anti-aircraft battery, and he was wounded twice. In the intervals between battles he studied higher mathematics, physics, and other university disciplines. In 1943, twenty-two-year-old senior lieutenant Kitov came up with a new method of shooting enemy aircraft. This was his first scientific work.

After the war in 1945, Kitov entered the Artillery Military Academy and began immediately on the second course. In the academy, in addition to studying, Kitov was actively engaged in scientific work. He was the author of a number of articles on missile ballistics and a patent for the invention of a new type of jet weapon. Kitov participated in the creation of the first Soviet R-1 rocket. Kitov graduated from Artillery Military Academy in February 1950 with a gold medal and was appointed to work as a scientific consultant to the President of the Academy of Artillery Sciences, Chief Marshal N. N. Voronov.

In 1951, after reading Norbert Wiener's book *Cybernetics* in the secret library of the Academy, Kitov immediately appreciated the enormous potential of this science, which at that time communist ideologists officially proclaimed "pseudoscience".[3] He wrote a fundamental article "The Main Features of Cybernetics", the first positive work on cybernetics in the USSR. This article, of which Academician S.L. Sobolev and professor A. A. Lyapunov were co-authors, was published in 1955 in the main ideological journal of the Central Committee of the CPSU, *Questions of Philosophy* [10]. This article was broadly discussed, and it was the beginning of recognition and further development of cybernetics in the USSR. At the same time, the journal *Radio* published another article by A.I. Kitov, "Technical Cybernetics". These publications were preceded by public lectures by Kitov and his associates in Moscow and Leningrad.

In 1952, Kitov was appointed the head of the first department of computers in the USSR created by him in the Academy of Artillery Sciences. In the same year, Kitov defended his Ph.D. thesis on programming called "Programming Problems of External Ballistics for Long-Range Missiles". In 1953, he published pioneer scientific article "The Use of Electronic Computers" (Fig. 2).

In May 1954, Kitov headed the first computer center in the USSR: Computing Center No. 1 of the Ministry of Defense of the USSR. He implemented Strela, one of the first computers, in the center and in some other organizations of the Ministry of Defense of the USSR. In 1954–1960, Computing Center No. 1 provided all the computer calculations necessary for the flights of the Soviet satellites.

In 1956, Kitov published the first in the USSR book on computers and programming, *Electronic Digital Machines* [11]. The final third of the book is devoted to non-arithmetic use of a computer for managing production processes, solving problems of artificial intelligence, machine translation, etc. The book was translated into several foreign languages and was published in the U.S., China, Poland, and Czechoslovakia.

At that time, Kitov developed the basis for building automated information systems for defense purposes and formed a new scientific direction, the development of information retrieval systems. He published a number of articles in the field of military cybernetics and computer science: "The Military Value of Computers", "Mathematics in Military Affairs", "Electronic Computer Science and Its Military Applications", "Cybernetics in Military Affairs", etc.

---

[3] See Doležel and Smutný, "The Emergence of Computing Disciplines in Communist Czechslovakia", this volume.

Fig. 2. A. I. Kitov, pioneer of Soviet cybernetics, head of the Computing Center No. 1 of the Ministry of Defense.

In 1956, Kitov published the co-authored book *Elements of Programming*. In the brochure "Electronic Computers" (1958), he described how to use computers in mathematical calculations, automation of production management, and the solution of economic problems [12]. In this brochure for the first time in the USSR he outlined the prospect of integrated automation of information processing and administrative management processes in the country on the basis of the Unified State Network of Computing Centers (USNCC; in Russian, ЕГСВЦ or EGSVTS). In the same year, in co-authorship with N.A. Krinitsky, he published another book, *Electronic Computers*, which was also published in a number of foreign countries.

In 1959, the State Commission adopted M-100, a specialized computer developed under the leadership of Kitov, working at a speed of 100,000 operations per second, which was at that time the fastest in the Soviet Union and one of the most powerful in the world. In this computer, for the first time, an arithmetic device with conveyor processing of machine instructions was realized, which was patented in the same year. Also in 1959, Kitov, in co-authorship with N.A. Krinitsky, published a classic textbook-monograph *Electronic Digital Machines and Programming*. This was the first textbook in the country on the computers and programming officially admitted by the Ministry of Education of the USSR for training in technical universities. The book was published in many countries of the Central and Eastern Europe. In November of that year at the All-Union Conference on Mathematics and Computer Science, Kitov presented the first in the Soviet Union report on the creation of computer-based management information systems.

In 1967, A. I. Kitov published a monograph "Programming Information-Logical Problems" and in 1970 a book *The Automation System for Programming ALGEM*, written by the team he led. In 1971, he published another fundamental monograph, "Programming of Economic and Managerial Tasks".

Starting in 1971, Kitov began to engage in a new field of activity, the creation of computer information systems for healthcare. From 1976 to 1983, Kitov published monographs "Automation of Information Processing and Management in Healthcare" (1976), "Introduction to Medical Cybernetics" (1977), and "Medical Cybernetics" (1983). From 1980 to 1997, Kitov worked as head of the Informatics Chair and professor at the Moscow Institute of National Economy (now the Plekhanov Russian University of Economics).

Kitov had a reputation that extended beyond the USSR. In the 1970s, he was the official representative of the USSR in authoritative international organizations in the field of medical informatics. He was an official member of Technical Committee 4 of IFIP, which later became the International Federation of Medical Informatics (Med-INFO) . Kitov also represented the USSR in MedINFO. Kitov was one of the seven leaders of the International Medical Informatics Association (IMIA). He participated in the organization of IFIP forums in Sweden (1974), Canada (1977), and Japan (1980). At the forum IFIP-1977 he was the chairman of section T2 (Biomedical Research General). He took an active part in organizing the MEDIS'78 conference (Tokyo-Osaka). He was a member of the MedInfo-1980 program committee.

Overall, Kitov was the author of 12 monographs, which have been translated into nine foreign languages. Over forty of his Russian and foreign students completed their dissertations. He was an outstanding man, full of bold scientific ideas, burning with a high desire to benefit his homeland. Kitov is one of the founders of Russian cybernetics, computer science and programming, the creator of the first computers and management information systems, the author of the first textbooks and monographs on computer technology and programming. Particularly noteworthy is the scholarly and civilian courage of the scientist, who boldly and with risk for his career put forward projects on new approaches to the management of the troops and the national economy of the USSR.

Some books and articles by Kitov are presented below [10–14]. Biography of A. I. Kitov and his scientific achievements are reflected in a number of works [19–24].

3   Victor Mikhailovich Glushkov

Computer pioneer Victor Mikhailovich Glushkov (1923–1982) was born on 24 August 1923 in Rostov-on-Don to the family of a mining engineer. Glushkov graduated with honors from Middle School No. 1 in Shakhty on 21 June 1941. His mother was shot by the Nazis in 1941. After the liberation of the city of Shakhty, Glushkov was mobilized and participated in the restoration of the coal mines of Donbass. He graduated from the Novocherkassk Industrial Institute and in parallel from the Rostov State University in 1948 and moved to Sverdlovsk, where he worked at the Ural Forestry Institute. V. M. Glushkov solved the generalized fifth problem of Hilbert, which was the subject of his doctoral dissertation, "Topological Locally Nilpotent Groups". As is known, in 1900 Hilbert formulated 23 major and complex problems of mathematics, the solution of each of which became a world sensation in science (Fig. 3).

After the successful defense of his doctoral dissertation in 1955, Glushkov received several appointments, among which he chose the sphere connected with computer science. He moved to Kiev, where, starting in 1956, he was the head of the laboratory of Computer Science and Mathematics at the Institute of Mathematics of the Academy of Sciences of Ukraine. Later, the laboratory that he headed turned into the Computing

Fig. 3. Computer pioneer Victor Mikhailovich Glushkov (1964).

Center of the Academy of Sciences of Ukraine, and in December 1962, the Institute of Cybernetics of the Academy of Sciences of Ukraine was established. with Glushkov as it permanent director. Today, it is known as the V. M. Glushkov Institute of Cybernetics of National Academy of Sciences of Ukraine. Under Glushkov's leadership, the Institute became the largest center in the Soviet Union and one of the largest in the world in the field of computer science, cybernetics, computer technology, and management information systems (MIS). More than 5,000 employees worked with him in this center.

The scientific activity of Glushkov in the period 1956–1982 was connected with the theory of informatics, cybernetics, computer technology, programming, and automated management information systems and was based on a powerful foundation of the national mathematical schools.

In 1961, Glushkov published the famous monograph "Synthesis of Digital Automata" [1], later translated into English and published in the United States [2] and other countries. It created the basis for the work on the theory of automata with the use of algebraic methods. In 1964, for a series of works on the theory of automata, Glushkov was awarded the Lenin Prize. The value of these works cannot be overestimated, as the use of the term "machine" as a mathematical abstraction structures and processes inside computers, opened up entirely new possibilities in the technology of computers.

Glushkov built the necessary mathematical tools and showed how the components of a computer can be submitted by algebraic expressions. With the help of this theory, the Kiev Institute of Cybernetics became the leader in the development of computers on a scientific basis. Modern computer-aided design systems of computers use these ideas everywhere. A number of interesting computers were designed in Glushkov's laboratory. From his department came a number of famous scientists (Yu. V. Kapitonova, A. A. Letichevsky, etc.), who became the core of Glushkov's school in the field of digital computers.

Based on Glushkov's theoretical research, a language was developed at the Institute of Cybernetics to describe the algorithms, computer structures and the computer design methodology that were implemented in a number of unique PROJECT systems (CAD systems). With the help of these systems, different computers were developed for both general and special purposes (e.g., military computers) (Fig. 4).

Fig. 4. Glushkov and Kapitonova study a computer block created with the help of the PROJECT system

Glushkov made a great contribution in the development of new architectures of computers and systems. Under his leadership, the computers Dnepr, Kiev, Promin, MIR-1, MIR-2 and MIR-3, ES-2701 and others were created.

In 1974, at the IFIP congress in Sweden, Glushkov made a presentation on a recursive computer. He expressed the opinion that only the development of a fundamentally new non-von-Neumann architecture of computing systems would solve the problem of creating supercomputers whose performance could increase unlimitedly with the build-up of hardware. The idea of constructing a recursive computer, supported by a powerful mathematical apparatus of recursive functions, was ahead of its time and remained unrealized due to the lack of the necessary technical base.

At the end of the 1970s, Glushkov proposed the principle of the macroconveyor architecture of a computer with many command and data streams (MIMD architecture according to the modern classification) as a principle of realization of the non-von-Neumann architecture and received the patent for this invention. The development of a macroconveyor computer was carried out at the Institute of Cybernetics under the leadership of Glushkov by team of scientists. Machines ES-2701 (in 1984) and the computer system EU-1766 (in 1987) became the most powerful computer systems in the USSR with a nominal capacity exceeding the boundary of 1 billion operations per second. They had no peers in the world and were the original development of the ES series of computers in the direction of high-performance systems.

In the field of programming theory and systems of algorithmic algebras, Glushkov made a fundamental contribution in the form of the algebra of regular events. In the framework of the development of this theory, Glushkov anticipated the well-known concept of structural programming proposed by the Dutch scientist Dijkstra in 1968, and proved a fundamental theorem on regularization (reduction to the structured form) of an arbitrary algorithm, in particular a program or microprogram [9].

Glushkov saw ways to improve the technology of program development in the development of algebra of algorithmic languages. In this problem, he invested the general mathematical and even philosophical sense, considering the creation of the algebra of the language of a specific area of knowledge as a necessary stage of its mathematization. Glushkov claimed that the development of common algorithmic languages and the algebra of such languages would lead to the fact that today's computer programs will become as familiar, understandable and convenient as today's analytical expressions. In this case, the difference between analytic and general algorithmic methods will virtually disappear, and the world of computer models will become the main source of development of new modern mathematics, as it is now.

Outside the USSR, Glushkov was recognized as leader in the field of cybernetics. He formed – on the basis of the works of N. Wiener, K. Shannon, A. I. Kitov, S. L. Sobolev, and others – his own understanding of cybernetics as a scientific discipline, its methodology, and structure of research sections. Cybernetics was interpreted by Glushkov broadly as a science on general laws, principles and methods of information processing and management of complex systems. Computer technology was considered as the main technical instrument of cybernetics. This understanding was reflected in the first in the world Encyclopedia of Cybernetics, created on the initiative of V. M. Glushkov and published in 1974 under his editorship [28].

Glushkov was elected academician of the Academy of Sciences of the USSR (1964) and Academy of Sciences of the Ukrainian SSR (1961); he was a member of the Deutsche Akademie der Naturforscher Leopoldina; a foreign member of the Academy of Sciences of Bulgaria, the GDR, and Poland; an honorary doctor of the University of Dresden, and an honorary member of the Polish cybernetic society. From 1962 until the end of his life, he was vice-president of the Academy of Sciences of Ukraine. He was a member of the USSR State Committee for Science and Technology and the Committee on Lenin and State Prizes under the Council of Ministers of the USSR.

In 1963, Glushkov became chair of the Interdepartmental Scientific Council on the introduction of computer technology and economic and mathematical methods in the national economy of the USSR under the State Committee of the Council of Ministers of the USSR on Science and Technology. He was a consultant to the governments of Bulgaria, the GDR, and Czechoslovakia in the field of computer technology, computer science, and automated systems for managing the national economy.

Glushkov was a member of the 8–10 convocations of the Supreme Soviet of the USSR. He had the titles of Hero of Socialist Labor (1969) and Honored Scientist of the USSR (1978). He was winner of the Lenin Prize and two State Prizes of the USSR. He was awarded many government orders and medals, including three Orders of Lenin, the Order of the October Revolution, the Order of the People's Republic of Bulgaria, the Order of the "Banner of Labor" of the GDR, and others.

Glushkov was the author of over 700 works on algebra, computer science, cybernetics, philosophy, the digital economy and the information society, dozens of patents for inventions, the creator of several scientific schools in the field of computer design and artificial intelligence, programming, automated management information systems, under his leadership more than a hundred dissertational works were defended. He was an ideologist and scientific leader of the automated management information systems industry in the USSR and the creator of the project of the State Automated Management Information System for the Soviet economy (in Russian, ОГАС or OGAS).

At the IFIP Congress in 1974 in Stockholm, Glushkov, on the decision of the General Assembly of IFIP, was awarded a Silver Core Award. Thus, the scientist's great contribution to the work of this organization was noted as a member of the Program Committee of the Congresses of 1965 and 1968, and also as Chairman of the Program Committee of the Congress of 1971. Glushkov was an adviser to the UN Secretary-General for Cybernetics.

The international organization IEEE Computer Society in 1996 posthumously awarded Glushkov a Computer Pioneer medal "for digital automation of computer architecture" [29].

Glushkov was an encyclopedically educated person, fluent in English and German, loving poetry and music, and was an excellent orator. He was also a sportsman: a master boxer and a swimmer of long distances. He was devoted to science, was a patriot of his country, and selflessly served it.

Some books and articles by Glushkov are presented below [1–9]. Biography of Glushkov and his scientific achievements are reflected in a number of works of historians and experts in the field of computer science [16–21].

4   The Works of A. I. Kitov on the Use of Computers in the Economy: The Red Book Project

In the second half of the 1950s, Kitov, with his initiatives and scientific publications, strongly insisted on the state necessity of using computers for making calculations when solving problems of economic management and planning the activities of Soviet enterprises. Already in the first positive Soviet article on the cybernetics, "The Main Features of Cybernetics" [10] S. L. Sobolev, A. I. Kitov, and A. A. Lyapunov pointed to the possibility of using computers in various fields of the economy. The last third of Kitov's book *Electronic Digital Machines* [11], which he named "Non-arithmetic Applications of Electronic Digital Computers", was devoted to prospects of using computers in the economy. In his brochure *Electronic Computers* [12], published in the USSR in mass circulation, he outlined the basic directions of using computers in industry and other areas. In this work, Kitov talks about the urgent need to create a number of computing centers in the country for carrying out production, economic, and planning calculations and that in the future it would be expedient to combine these many computing centers into the Unified State Network of Computing Centers (USNCC, EGSVC in Russian).

Being passionate propagandist of new approaches in the economy, Kitov on January 7, 1959 addressed a letter to the head of the USSR, N.S. Khrushchev, in which proposed a radical restructuring of the management system of the entire Soviet economy by moving from the administrative-command style of leadership to a scientific one based on the widespread use of economic and mathematical methods and computers that would be gradually combined in the USNCC. Kitov's proposal for the creation a national computer network on the basis of the USNCC (the prototype of the modern Internet) was the first in the world. Consideration of Kitov's letter to Khrushchev was assigned to L.I. Brezhnev. Brezhnev favorably treated this letter and created for its careful consideration the Governmental Commission chaired by A.I. Berg, well-known specialist in cybernetics. All the proposals of this letter by A.I. Kitov were approved by the leaders of the USSR with the exception of his proposal for the establishment of the USNCC. The historians of Soviet informatics believe that this letter was a catalyst for expanding the production and use of computers in the USSR and played an important role in preparing further decisions of the Government of the USSR on computers [16, 21, 24, 25]. Unfortunately, the main proposal of Kitov on the creation of a nationwide network of computer centers (USNCC) for managing the economy of a large country was not perceived as necessary by the Soviet leadership (Fig. 5).

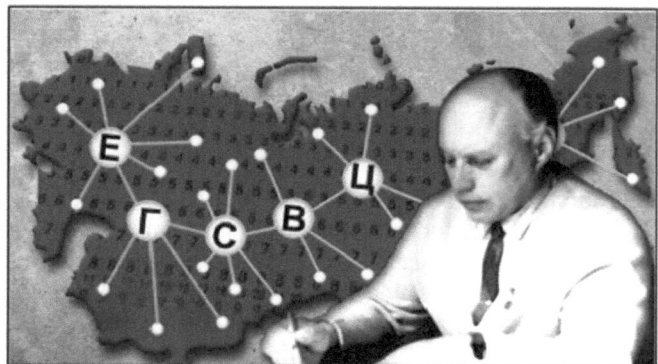

Fig. 5. Kitov and his project of Unified State Network of Computing Centers.

At the same in 1959, Kitov spoke at the All-Union Conference on the use of computers with a report "On the Possibilities of Computerization of the Management of the National Economy". This was the first report on the need to create in the country a statewide automated system for the management and planning of the national economy.

In the fall of 1959, Kitov sent a second letter to Khrushchev, containing the innovative project he developed, which consumed his time for several decades. It was called "The Creation of a National Network of Computer Centers to Improve Governance in the Armed Forces and the National Economy", otherwise known as the Red Book project on the creation throughout the Soviet territory Unified State Network of "dual-purpose" computing centers for managing the economy and the Armed Forces.

The project was rejected, and its author was expelled from the Communist Party and removed from the prestigious position in Computing Center No. 1 of the Ministry of Defense because of the criticism of the existing management system and proposals for its change based on use of scientific methods and digital technologies.

Nevertheless, Kitov continued to fight for the recognition of his ideas of restructuring the Soviet economy management on the basis of the establishment of the USNCC and mathematical methods. In 1961, Kitov published a fundamental article, "Cybernetics and National Economy Management", in which it was proposed to create a large number of regional computing centers in order to collect, process and reallocate economic data for effective planning and management. The unification of all these centers in a nationwide network would, he said, "lead to the creation of a single centralized automated system for managing the national economy of the whole country".

In the 1960s, Kitov was the chief designer of the Industry Automated Management System of the Ministry of Radio Electronics Industry, which was recognized as a model industry automated management system for all defense ministries, he and published the basic scientific articles on management of the country's economy on the basis of computers and economic and mathematical methods. He developed a new method, "associative programming", which was an effective way of solving information-logical problems. He led the creation of a new algorithmic language, ALGEM, for programming the economic and mathematical problems used in hundreds of enterprises of the USSR and countries of Eastern Europe. The results of these works were reflected in Kitov's book *Programming Information-Logical Problems* (1967) and the book *Automation Programming System ALGEM* (1970), written by the team led by him. In 1971, he published another fundamental monograph, *Programming of Economic and Managerial Tasks*.

In addition to military cybernetics, Kitov stood at the origins of Russian medical informatics. He laid the foundations for automation of information processing and management in healthcare and carried out a lot of work on the practical implementation of these systems. The results of this pioneering work were described in his monographs *Automation of Information Processing and Management in Healthcare* (1976), *Introduction to Medical Cybernetics* (1977) and *Medical Cybernetics* (1983), which were recognized in the USSR and abroad.

5   Victor M. Glushkov, a Theorist of the Information Society and the OGAS Project

Beginning in the 1960s, Glushkov was the chief ideologist, scientific leader and one of the main creators of the automated management information systems (AMIS, in Russian ACУ or ASU) industry in the USSR. Glushkov and his school developed a wide range of applications: automated process control systems (APCS), systems for automation of scientific research and testing of complex industrial facilities, automated management information systems (AMIS).

Together with his students and associates, Glushkov made a great contribution to the formation and implementation of the ideas for the creation of an automated process control system, the development of an appropriate theory, mathematical, software and special technical means for managing technological processes in microelectronics, metallurgy, the chemical industry, and shipbuilding. Automation of experimental scientific research in the early 1960s was associated with the automation of measurements and processing of information obtained with the help of the Kiev and Dnepr computers. Computers from Kiev managed steel smelting in the Bessemer converter at a metallurgical plant in Dneprodzerzhinsk and a carbonization column at a soda plant in Slavyansk.

Then, Glushkov proposed to develop automated problem-oriented laboratories, which had to include measurement systems, computers (micro- or minicomputers), and measurement processing programs. He planned five or six such standard laboratories for X-ray analysis, mass spectrography, and other methods of experimental research used in chemistry, physics, and biology. To process the results of complex nuclear experiments, such laboratories were connected to remote computers such as BESM-6 or ES-1060. Because most of the scientific experiments were not limited to the collection and processing of data, but required the exact adjustment of the experimental setup itself, Glushkov set the task of automating the tuning operations of these installations. The specialists of the Institute of Cybernetics automated the tests for mechanical fatigue of materials at the Institute of Strength Problems of the Academy of Sciences of Ukraine, experimental studies at the Institute of Geology and Geophysics, the Institute of Oncology Problems of the Academy of Sciences of Ukraine. Works on automation of testing of complex industrial facilities were carried out for the navy and aviation. For the future, Glushkov saw in this area the prospects for developing algorithms for deductive constructions so that the system not only processed the results of measurements, but also checked hypotheses and built theories on this basis, i.e., acted as an artificial intelligence system in a given domain.

The development of automated management information systems for enterprises (ERP-systems) was started under the leadership of Glushkov in 1963–1964. In 1967, the first automated management information system for the enterprise with a mass character of production "Lviv" was launched at the Lviv television plant "Electron". In 1970, when the system was already successfully exploited, its creators Glushkov, V. I. Skurikhin, A. A. Morozov, V. V. Shkurba and others were awarded the State Prize of Ukraine. After the creation of the "Lviv" system, Glushkov set the task of creating not an individual, but a standard automated management information system for machine-building and instrument-making enterprises. In the early 1970s, work was completed on the *Kuntsevo* system (for the Kuntsevo radio plant), which Glushkov proposed as model for the creation of automated management information systems on enterprises of nine defense ministries.

In 1965, Glushkov developed the concept of a specialized operating system designed for systems with a regular stream of tasks, in contrast to IBM/360 universal computer operating systems that solve random task flows and were good for packet mode of computing centers. Glushkov's monograph "Introduction to Automated Management Information Systems" [4], which was mainly devoted to the systems of organizational management, was published in the second edition in 1974. It systematized the original results he obtained in 1964–1968.

The work on the creation and implementation of the automated management information systems into practice had problems. The reasons for this phenomenon lay in the sphere of the planned socialist economy that was then operating in the USSR, forcing enterprises to "drive the product shaft", not caring about optimizing the technical and economic indicators of production, the quality of manufactured products, and scientific and technological progress.

In the late 1960s, the creation of industrial automated management information systems (IOMIS) became necessary. Glushkov, as the most qualified and authoritative expert in this field, became the scientific adviser and consultant of many large IOMIS projects in the 1970s, in particular in the defense industry. When the Interdepartmental Committee (IAC) of nine defensive ministries was established and the Board of Directors of the main institutes for management, economics and informatics of the defense industries was created, Glushkov became the scientific head of the Committee and of the Board of Directors.

In 1962, on the orders of A. N. Kosygin, at that time the Deputy Chairman of the Council of Ministers of the USSR, Glushkov began to develop a project, which later became the State Automated Management Information System for national economy (SAMIS, in Russian OGAS). Starting to create the OGAS project, Glushkov personally studied the work of more than a thousand objects of the national economy: plants and factories of various industries, mines, railways, airports, and higher management bodies (Gosplan, Gossnab, the Ministry of Finance, etc.). He worked on the application in OGAS of macroeconomic models and instruments to improve the methods of management, which was reflected in his monograph "Macroeconomic Models and Principles of Building OGAS" [5]. Glushkov proposed the concept of OGAS as a unified system for collecting reporting information on the national economy, planning and managing the national economy, and an information base for modeling various options for the development of the national economy.

The Unified State Network of Computing Centers (USNCC) was required to become the technical basis of the OGAS. In the draft design of the USNCC, Glushkov suggested and substantiated the construction of a network of approximately 100 large centers in industrial cities and centers of economic regions, united by broadband communication channels with message switching and connected with 20,000 centers of enterprises and organizations. It was planned to create a distributed data bank and to develop a system of mathematical models of economic management.

Of course, Glushkov understood that with his plan he challenged the Soviet canons in governing the economy. Indeed, the draft of OGAS, submitted to the government in 1964, met with sharp demagogic objections based on creation complexity and high cost from the leadership of the Central Statistical Administration of the USSR (V. N. Starovskiy), then for a long time was processed into the USSR Central Statistical Bureau, the State Planning Committee of the USSR, but it was never implemented. It has often been said that main reasons were the incompetence of the top management of the country, the reluctance of the average bureaucratic unit to work under strict control of computer systems, the unpreparedness of society as a whole, the imperfection of the existing means of computing and communication, the lack of understanding, or even opposition from the scientists-economists. In fact, the concepts of OGAS and USNCC, correctly reflecting in the technical plan the rigidly centralized structure of the Soviet social system, met the resistance of the social system itself. Why was the project of Glushkov threatening? Party leaders – Brezhnev, Kosygin and others – could lose power, because they did not correspond to the new era. However, this points to an additional consideration: to administer the Soviet Union in the digital era it was necessary to admit young technocrats. The structure of the state, formed in the early part of the twentieth century, no longer corresponded to the current processes in the economy. The ideology and political system of the country also needed serious renewal. In addition, the enemies of the USSR organized publications that ridiculed Glushkov and his idea of OGAS. They said he was going to replace the Politburo with a computer, and "the card would control the Kremlin" [21].

Nevertheless, Glushkov did not retreat during the rest of his life. Convinced he was absolutely right, he proposed even more than 40 years ago the task of digitization and computerization of the country. At that time, he could not do anything without large-scale decisions of the government and the Communist Party Central Committee, which became a barrier on this path. In Glushkov's archive, there are copies of many notes to high party and government bodies on questions of the policy of development and use achievements in computer technology and automated systems in the economy, defense capacity, etc. On average, there is one note every two months in the period 1968 to 1980. Reviewing his notes, it is possible to compile a list of cases that could not be carried out within the functioning social system, e.g., using the decision-support system DISPLAN created by Glushkov and his team to manage Soviet economy [9]. This was a tragic component of his life. Like no one else, he understood and told to his relatives that this led to the death the social system and, as further historical events showed, the country as a whole.

Glushkov's academic position was active. His more than 250 publications in popular scientific and public journals and newspapers, as well as the regular cycles of lectures for the top management of the country and the public, testify to this (Fig. 6).

Fig. 6. V.M. Glushkov – pioneer of informatics and information society (1979).

Glushkov was not only the pioneer of digital economy but also a theorist of the information society, the author of works on the philosophy of scientific knowledge and the application of artificial intelligence systems in various fields. He came up and realized new ideas for building artificial intelligence systems such as "eye-hand", natural text reading, and an automation system for mathematical proofs. He worked on computer simulation systems for such intellectual activity processes as decision making in economic, technical, biological and medical fields. The approaches proposed by Glushkov for using natural language tools in information systems have been developed. Glushkov actively promoted a practical approach to the problem of artificial intelligence as a matter objectively evoked to life by the growing power of computers and their penetration into all spheres of human activity.

Even today, students and followers of Glushkov successfully develop his ideas and are engaged in research on structural pattern recognition, methods of analysis of images and speech signals, methods of structural analysis of scenes in the field of view of robots, are engaged in neurocomputer technologies and medical information systems.

Glushkov believed that the consistent accumulation of knowledge and effective ways of processing it, the development of intellectual capabilities of the computer, would provide a breakthrough in the development of civilization and ensure the transition of humanity to the information society. More than 40 years ago, he talked about the digital immortality of a human being. "Fundamentals of Paperless Informatics" is the name of his last monograph, published in 1982 [7]. This book described a mathematical apparatus and a set of ideas related to the problems of digitization of all aspects of life and the transition to the information society. He paid special attention to the digitization of education.

The OGAS concept largely anticipated the ideas of e-government and the digital economy in the world and in Russia. Fundamentally new approaches, methods, models and technical systems developed by Glushkov have made a great contribution to the development of informatics and the information society.

6   Conclusion

The foregoing analysis of the scientific biography of Anatoly Kitov and Victor Glushkov shows the successes of the Soviet school of computer science, which were based on strong connection with national scientific mathematical and technical schools, strong support from the state due to the importance of this field to national defense. Unfortunately, construction of a nationwide computer network to drive the Soviet economy and OGAS project were unsuccessful due to reluctance of the Soviet bureaucracy to change existing management methods and some other reasons mentioned above. Even though national networking was a success in other countries, it is simplistic to dismiss Soviet computing because it did not make a similar accomplishment. The many different developments of Kitov and Glushkov indicate that their work had a different focus. The Red Book and OGAS projects have influenced the creation of the Soviet IT industry, which employed about 700,000 people and the use of automated management information systems in major industries and agriculture. This was the basis for the development of informatics and IT in Russia and the creation of the national project Digital Economy, which is ideologically connected with the works of Glushkov and Kitov. Indeed, the failure to build a nationwide computer network does not reflect a failure of their careers. Their many honors, their international reputations, and the legacy of work that continues into the present day demonstrate the richness of Soviet computing contemporary with networking projects in other countries.

The development of the digital economy and the information society in Russia is based on a powerful foundation laid by a glorious cohort of Soviet scientists, and Kitov and Glushkov are in the first row. Their work in the field of computer theory and practice, programming, mathematical modeling and computer applications in various fields of activity, their great projects of automation of the Soviet economy – the Red Book and OGAS – laid the foundations for the development of the digital economy. Their students continue to work in scientific centers around the world. The Glushkov Institute of Cybernetics of NAS of Ukraine continues its work, as well as created by V. M. Glushkov Department in the Moscow Institute of Physics and Technology, founded with his participation Faculty of Cybernetics in Taras Shevchenko Kiev National University, departments and faculties in other universities in the expanses of the former USSR. Some important ideas of A. I. Kitov and V. M. Glushkov in the field of computer science, artificial intelligence, the development of digital economy and information society are still waiting for implementation.

Acknowledgement. This research was performed in the framework of the basic part of the scientific research state task in the field of scientific activity of the Ministry of Education and Science of the Russian Federation; project name "Intellectual Analysis of Big Textual Data in Finance, Business, and Education by Means of Adaptive Semantic Models"; grant no. 2.9577.2017/8.9.

References

1. Glushkov, V.M.: Sintez cifrovyh avtomatov (Синтез цифровых автоматов), p. 476. GIFML, Moscow (1962)
2. Glushkov, V.M.: Synthesis of Digital Automata. FTD-MT, vol. 64, no. 206. United States Air Force, 467 p. (1965)
3. Glushkov, V.M.: Vvedenie v kibernetiku (Введение в кибернетику). AN USSR (1964)
4. Glushkov, V.M.: Vvedenie v ASU (Введение в АСУ), p. 312. Tekhnika, Kiev (1972)
5. Glushkov, V.M.: Makroekonomicheskie modeli i principy postroeniya OGAS (Макроэкономические модели и принципы построения ОГАС). Statistika, p. 160 (Metody optimal'nyh reshenij), Moscow (1975)
6. Glushkov, V.M., Valah, V.Y.: Chto takoe OGAS? (Что такое ОГАС?), p. 160. Nauka, Moscow (1981)
7. Glushkov, V.M.: Osnovy bezbumazhnoj informatiki (Основы безбумажной информатики), p. 552. Nauka, Moscow (1982)
8. Glushkov, V.M., Cejtlin, G.E., Yushchenko, E.L.: Algebra, yazyki, programmirovanie – 2-e izd., pererab (Алгебра, языки, программирование – 2-е изд., перераб.), p. 318. Naukova dumka, Kiev (1978)

9. Glushkov, V.M.: Kibernetika, vychislitelnaya tekhnika, informatika (Кибернетика, вычислительная техника, информатика. Избранные тр. в трех томах. Т. 1. Математические вопросы кибернетики. Т. 2. ЭВМ — техническая база кибернетики. Т. 3. Кибернетика и ее применение в народном хозяйстве), Naukova dumka, Kiev (1978), p. 318 (1990)

10. Sobolev, S.L., Kitov, A.I., Lyapunov, A.A.: Basic features of cybernetics. Issues of Philosophy, no. 4 (1955). http://www.computer-museum.ru/books/cybernetics.htm

11. Kitov, A.I.: Electronic digital machines. Soviet radio (1956). http://www.computer-museum. ru/books/kitov_ecm.htm

12. Kitov, A.I.: Electronic computers. All-union Society "Znanie." (1958). http://www. computer-museum.ru/books/evm_kitov_1958_2.pdf

13. Berg, A.I., Kitov, A.I., Lyapunov, A.A.: On the possibilities of automating the management of the national economy. In: Presented by A.I. Kitov at the Cybernetics Section of the All-Union Conference on Computational Mathematics and Computer Science, November 1959

14. Kitov, A.I.: Cybernetics and management of the national economy. Cybernetics - for the service of communism. Collection of articles edited by AI Berg, vol. 1. M.-L.: Gosenergoizdat, pp. 203–218 (1961)

15. Bruskin, S.N., et al.: Business performance management models based on the digital corporation's paradigm. Eur. Res. Stud. J. **XX**(4A), 264–274 (2017)

16. Gerovitch, S.: InterNyet: Why the Soviet Union Did Not Build a Nationwide Computer Network. Hist. Technol. **24**, 335–350 (2008)

17. Benjamin, P.: How Not to Network a Nation: The Uneasy History of the Soviet Internet (Information Policy). Massachusets Institute of Technology. MIT Press (2016)

18. Malinovsky, B.: Pioneers of Soviet Computing. Trans. ed. A. Fitzpatrick. Online e-book (2007). http://sovietcomputing.com

19. Malinovsky, B.N.: Istoriya vychislitelnoy tekhniki v litzah (История вычислительной техники в лицах). Kiev: KIT (1995). http://elib.ict.nsc.ru/jspui/bitstream/ICT/545/1/Malinovskiy.pdf

20. Kapitonova, I., Letichevskii, A.: Paradigmy i idei akademika V.M. Glushkova (Парадигмы и идеи академика В.М.Глушкова), 191 p. Naukova Dumka, Kiev (2003)

21. Kuteynikov, A.V.: Na zare computeroy ery: predystoriya razrabotki proekta Obshchego-sudarstvennoy avtomatizirovannoy systemy upravleniya narodnym hozyaystvom SSSR (OGAS) (На заре компьютерной эры: предыстория разработки проекта Общегосударственной автоматизированной системы управления народным хозяйством СССР (ОГАС). Istoriya nauki I tekhniki, no. 2, pp. 46–47 (2010)

22. Kitov, V.A., Shilov, V.V., Silantiev, S.A.: Trente ans ou la vie d'un scientifique. In: IFIP Advances in Information and Communication Technology, vol. 487, pp. 186–202 (2016)

23. Kitov, V.A., Shilov, V.V., Silantiev, S.A.: Anatoly Kitov and ALGEM algorithmic language. In: AISB/IACAP World Congress 2012: Symposium on the History and Philosophy of Programming, Part of Alan Turing Year 2012 (2012)

24. Kitov, V.A., Shilov, V.V.: Anatoly Kitov - pioneer of Russian informatics. In: Tatnall, A. (ed.) HC 2010. IAICT, vol. 325, pp. 80–88. Springer, Heidelberg (2010). https://doi.org/10.1007/978-3-642-15199-6_9

25. Kitov, V.A., Shilov, V.V.: Anatolij Ivanovich Kitov: Lichnost' cherez prizmu dokumentov (Анатолий Иванович Китов: Личность через призму документов). Statistika i Ekonomika, no. 4, pp. 2–7 (2016)

26. Grigor'ev, A.S., Kitov, V.A., Prihod'ko, A.Y., Tugushi, V.A.: Osnovopolozhnik otech-estvennoj voennoj informatiki (Основоположник отечественной военной информатики). Nauchnye trudy Vol'nogo ehkonomicheskogo obshchestva Rossii, vol. 186, pp. 604–610 (2014)

27. Dudnik, M.E., Kitov, V.A., Shcherbakova, D.D.: Istoki ehkonomicheskoj kibernetiki i medicinskoj kibernetiki v SSSR (Истоки экономической кибернетики и медицинской кибернетики в СССР). Nauchnye trudy Vol'nogo ehkonomicheskogo obshchestva Rossii, vol. 186, pp. 611–617 (2014)
28. Glushkov, V.M. (ed.): Entsiklopediya kibernetiki (Энциклопедия кибернетики), vol 1,2. Glavnaya redaktsiya ukrainskoy sovetskoy entsiklopedii. Kiyev (1974)
29. IEEE Computer Society Award Recipient Page Pioneer Victor Glushkov. https://www.computer.org/profiles/victor-glushkov. Accessed 31 Mar 2019

On the History of Gosplan, the Main Computer Center of the State Planning Committee of the USSR

Vladimir A. Kitov[✉]

Plekhanov Russian University of Economics, Stremyanny per., 36,
Moscow, Russia
vladimir.kitov@mail.ru

Abstract. In the 1970s and 1980s, the Main Computer Center (MCC) of the State Planning Committee (Gosplan) of the USSR was one of the largest civilian computer centers in the USSR and in Eastern Europe. Available historical literature contains only the basic facts about this center. In this article, the history of the Main Computer Center of the State Planning Committee of the USSR is supplemented and refined. The article describes the prerequisites for its creation, the transformation of its structure, the chronology of the use of various computers for economic calculations. The author reveals new facts about the Main Computer Center, its leading role in conducting economic calculations on computers, and its coordinating role in organizing the work of the computer centers of the planning committees of the union republics and other socialist countries. This work is based on the works of Soviet computer scientists and historians, on official materials, on the personal memories and archive of the author (who worked as a programmer in the Main Computer Center of the USSR State Planning Committee in the 1970s) and on the memories and personal archives of his former colleagues.

Keywords: ASPR · Calculation of economic planning · EGSVC ·
Main Computer Center of the State Planning Committee of the USSR (Gosplan)

1 Prerequisites for Creation the Main Computing Center of the USSR State Planning Committee

In October 1959, as a result of initiatives and publications of a number of progressive domestic scientists, the Council of Ministers of the USSR issued a decree on the creation of a computer center under the State Planning Committee of the USSR whose main goal would be to ensure calculations on economic plans throughout the country. This computer center, which since 1963 became known as the Main Computing Center (MCC) of the State Planning Committee (Gosplan) of the USSR, existed for more than thirty years until the second half of 1991, when the Soviet Union collapsed.

In the 1950s, before the appearance in the USSR State Planning Committee of its own computing center, there were already computer centers in the USSR, such as the Computer Center No. 1 of the Ministry of Defense, the Computer Center (CC) of the Academy of Sciences, CC of the Moscow State University, CC of the Academy of

© IFIP International Federation for Information Processing 2019
Published by Springer Nature Switzerland AG 2019
C. Leslie and M. Schmitt (Eds.): HC 2018, IFIP AICT 549, pp. 118–126, 2019.
https://doi.org/10.1007/978-3-030-29160-0_7

Sciences of Ukraine, CC at the Institute of applied mathematics, CCs of the nuclear centers Arzamas-16 and Chelyabinsk-70 and for the secret research institute Almaz.

Soviet scientists A. I. Kitov, I. S. Brook, V. S. Nemchinov and A. I. Berg, in the 1950s, wrote letters to the Soviet leaders and other publications [1–5] strongly recommending that leaders of the USSR use computers to solve problems of economic planning and management. Thus, in the article "The Main Features of Cybernetics" (the first positive publication on cybernetics in the Soviet Union, August 1955), S. L. Sobolev, A. I. Kitov and A. A. Lyapunov declared the enormous possibilities of using computers and mathematical methods to solve the problems of the economy. The final part of A. Kitov's monograph *Electronic Digital Machines* (the first book on computers in the USSR, published in February 1956) is devoted to the use of computers for solving economic problems. It is called "Non-Arithmetic Applications of Electronic Digital Computers". In 1956, I. S. Brook at the meeting of the Academy of Sciences made a presentation on a number of problems of using medium-power computers to automate the management of processes in industrial enterprises. 1958 was marked by the publication of A. Kitov's book *Electronic Computers* from the publishing house of the All-Union Society "Knowledge". This book, published in mass circulation, describes the need to create in the USSR many computer centers for making calculations for the needs of planning and production. A. I. Kitov noted that in the future these computer centers should be integrated into a single network with the goal of creating USNCC (United State Network of Computing Centers of the USSR). The proposal of A. Kitov on the need to create the USNCC (EGSVC in Russian) was a prototype of the current Internet project. V. S. Nemchinov, a passionate propagandist of advanced economic approaches, was one of the main organizers in 1958 of All-Union Conference on the use of mathematical methods for solving economic problems.

On 7 January 1959, A. I. Kitov sent a letter to the head of the USSR, N. S. Khrushchev. This letter contained a proposal to restructure the entire system of economic management in the country, moving from an administrative-command style to a scientific one, based on extensive use of computers and mathematical methods. Moreover, in the indicated letter all major computers of the country were proposed in several stages to be linked to the united network, called USNCC. The Secretary of the CPSU Central Committee, Leonid Brezhnev, responsible in those years for scientific and technical issues, mostly approvingly approached Kitov's letter and created for its consideration a governmental commission, headed by A. I. Berg. The members of this commission supported all the statements of this letter from Kitov [9].

Well-known experts in the field of the history of Soviet computer science (V. Gerovich, V. Shilov and A. Kuteinikov) believe that Kitov's letter played a catalytic role in the process of increasing the number of computers produced in the country [7–11]. In particular, this letter contributed to the preparation of the statements of the Plenum of the Central Committee of the Communist Party, held in June 1959. This Plenum considered a set of problems on the creation of computers in the USSR and their use for the needs of the national economy. In the same year, the All-Union Conference on Computational Mathematics and Computer Science was organized, on the cybernetic section of which Kitov made a report "On the Possibilities of

Automating the Management of the National Economy" (co-authors A. I. Berg and A. A. Lyapunov). This report was the first in the country and in the world about the urgent need to implement the nationwide project "State Automated System for Economic Management and Planning". This report was subsequently published as a separate article in the scientific collection of the USSR Academy of Sciences "Problems of Cybernetics". Finally, in October 1959, as a result of these publications and proposals on the urgent need to organize a separate computer center in the country for carrying out routine economic calculations, the deputy chair of the USSR Council of Ministers, Alexei Kosygin, signed a special resolution on this. It was prescribed to create in the State Planning Committee of the USSR (Gosplan of the USSR), a computer center for the purposes of computer planning and economic calculations.

2   The Tasks of the Main Computer Center of the State Planning Committee of the USSR and Its Development

Gosplan of the USSR operated from 1963 to 1991 at the status of a state ministry. Its two main tasks were planning of the development of the national economy and control over the implementation of government plans.

The planning of a centralized socialist economy can be represented in the form of a four-tier hierarchical system:

- The first level was the planning of the socialist economy on the scale of the entire USSR. This was implemented by the State Planning Committee of the USSR.
- The second level was the economic planning for 15 Soviet republics (Russia, Ukraine, Belarus, Moldova, Uzbekistan, Kazakhstan, Kyrgyzstan, Tajikistan, Turkmenistan, Georgia, Armenia, Azerbaijan, Lithuania, Latvia, Estonia). This was done by the State Planning Committees of the republics of the USSR.
- At the third level, economic planning was carried out for the regions of the Soviet republics. This was done by the regional planning commissions.
- At the fourth level, economic planning was carried out for districts and cities that were part of the region. This was done by district and city planning commissions.

In its work, the USSR State Planning Committee was guided by: the CPSU Program, the directives of the Central Committee of the CPSU, and decisions of the Council of Ministers of the USSR.

The main task of the Computing Center of the State Planning Committee was to assist the Gosplan in solving the problems of the first level using computers, i.e., in solving the problems of planning and monitoring the adopted plans throughout the USSR. Among the first computer tasks of the Computer Center were:

- development and practical application of economic-mathematical methods and models in planning and
- demographic forecasting for the USSR and all of its 15 republics.

An important achievement of the Computer Center was the implementation of computer calculations of interbranch balances of production and distribution of the output of the national economy in a natural measure. This was done for the first time in the world. As a basis, the mathematical model of the Nobel Prize winner Wassily Leontief, a scientist with Russian roots, was taken. Before Leontief, the balance was a purely statistical document. Since 1975, the Main Computing Center has fully calculated all state plans on computers.

The attempt to implement ASPR (Automated System for Planned Calculations) was a large-scale project of the Main Computer Center. Its goal was to introduce long-term, medium-term, and short-term economic planning of the national economy of the USSR with the help of computers. This project was not implemented in full.

The first head of the Computer Center of the State Planning Committee of the USSR was M. E. Rakovsky.

In accordance with the decision of the Soviet Government, this center was rapidly growing, primarily due to the involvement of military specialists from the Computer Center No. 1 of the USSR Ministry of Defense. Ten years later, there were already about a thousand people working there, and it became one of the largest civilian computer centers in the USSR and Eastern Europe. It used the accumulated experience of the first in the Soviet Union the Computer Center No. 1 of the USSR Ministry of Defense. This military computer center, created in early May 1954, by 1960 already had a good experience in computer calculations for space missions of rockets and interplanetary stations. Priceless assistance to state planners was provided by military colleagues in the form of highly qualified personnel. In accordance with the decisions of the Soviet government, the positions of deputy heads of the Computer Center of the State Planning Committee in different years were occupied by well-known military scientists from the Computer Center No. 1 of the Ministry of Defense of the USSR: N. A. Krinitskiy, Yu. I. Bezzabotnov, and L. N. Kutsev.

In addition to the transfer of experienced professionals of all levels (from senior management to engineers, analysts and programmers), Computer Center No. 1 of the Ministry of Defense assisted in the deciding of defense planning tasks on computers. These tasks were performed by a large secret department of the Computer Center, to which the entire 10th floor of its building was provided.

The Computer Center of the USSR State Planning Committee also worked closely with several leading research institutes of the Academy of Sciences of the USSR. Among them, it is necessary to single out the Central Economics and Mathematics Institute and the Institute of Economics. In 1963, the Computer Center was named the Main Computer Center of the USSR State Planning Committee (the MCC of Gosplan of the USSR) in accordance with the Resolution of the Central Committee of the CPSU and the Council of Ministers of the USSR No. 564, "On Improving the Management of the Introduction of Computer Technologies and Automated Management Systems in the National Economy", and continued to exist with this name until the end of 1991 (Fig. 1).

Fig. 1. The building of the Main Computer Center of the USSR State Planning Committee in Moscow on the Kirov street (now Myasnitskaya street), 45

The new building of the Main Computer Center was the first building in the country designed specifically for a computer center for civilian purposes. At that time, it was ideal for hosting large computers and specialists.

Approximately 50% of the staff of the Main Computer Center were men (chiefs, engineers, programmers, economists), and 50% were women (operators, perforators, programmers, economists) (Fig. 2).

Fig. 2. 1972. Employees of the information retrieval systems subdepartment of the MCC of Gosplan of the USSR (author is on the left).

The State Planning Committee of the USSR was liquidated in 1991. After several transformations, the Main Computer Center became the Analytical Center under the Government of the Russian Federation in 2005.

3 Periods of Use of Various Computers

The government of the USSR, given the importance of the tasks to be performed at the Main Computer Center, generously allocated money (including currency) for the acquisition of modern computers.

In its early years, the Soviet computers were used in the Computer Center. Two computers, Ural-2 and Ural-4, were used in the first half of the 1960s.

Later, western computers were acquired, such as Emidek-2400 and Elliot-503, as well as the mainframe ICL System 4. The computers Emidek-2400 and Elliot-503 were used in the second half of the 1960s. Two ICL System 4–70 computers were used in the 1970s.

Over its last ten years of work, the Main Computer Center of the USSR State Planning Committee carried out economic calculations on the domestic ES EVM computers. They were used in the 1980s. The first models of ES EVM computers (late 1960s/early 1970s) were clones of IBM System/360 computers. In the 1980s, later ES EVM models were developed by Soviet specialists (Fig. 3).

Fig. 3. The computer Emidek-2400.

ES EVM computers were the last type of computers used in the Main Computer Center of the USSR State Planning Committee until 1991. Work on ES EVM computers for specialists of the Main Computer Center was not a difficult task. There were several reasons for this:

- In the USSR, a large network of training centers was created, providing a variety of educational literature on ES EVM hardware and software.

- Specialists of the Main Computer Center had 10 years of experience working on ICL System 4–70 computers. It was a good preliminary experience for working on ES EVM computers.
- Students of Soviet technical universities carefully studied the hardware and software of IBM System/360 and ES EVM computers for 3–4 years. In addition, they carefully studied various programming languages and technologies.
- Soviet students had good preparation in mathematics.

4   The Main Computer Center's Coordinating Role in the USSR and Socialist Countries

The Main Computer Center of the USSR State Planning Committee fulfilled the important role of intra-union and international coordination of the work of the computer centers of the planning committees of the republics of the USSR, on the one hand, and the computer centers of planning committees of socialist countries, on the other. On a regular basis, a methodical guide was provided for the computer centers of the planning committees of all the Union republics, which for this purpose were equipped with ES EVM computers.

In the late 1970s, a special board of directors of computer centers of planning committees of socialist countries was created. In this organization the Main Computer Center of the USSR State Planning Committee was the actual leader of the activities of its colleagues from the socialist countries. It organized on a regular basis working meetings of its colleagues in the Council for Mutual Economic Assistance (Fig. 4).

Fig. 4. 1972. In the Main Computer Center of the USSR State Planning Committee: leader of Cuba Fidel Castro, Chairman of the State Planning Committee of the USSR N. N. Baibakov, and Head of the Computer Center N. P. Lebedinsky.

5   Conclusion

The article confirms that the Main Computer Center of the State Planning Committee of the USSR was the leading research and production center in the field of solving computer problems in the planning of the national socialist economy. In the USSR, its role was also important as one of the recognized computer centers – pioneers in the practical use of new information and communication technologies and advanced system and application programs. Very important was its coordinating role in organizing the work of the computer centers of the planning committees of the union republics and other socialist countries. Since 2005, the Main Computer Center of the USSR State Planning Committee has been called Analytical Center under the Government of the Russian Federation.

Acknowledgement. The author is grateful to the leading historians of Soviet computer science: Slava Gerovich, Valery Shilov, Nikolai Krotov, Benjamin Peters, and Alexei Kuteinikov. Communication with them was useful for him in his work.

References

1. Sobolev, S.L., Kitov, A.I., Lyapunov, A.A.: The main features of cybernetics. Problems of Philosophy, no. 4 (1955). http://www.computer-museum.ru/books/cybernetics.htm
2. Kitov, A.I.: Electronic Digital Machines. Soviet radio (1956). http://www.computer-museum.ru/books/kitov_ecm.htm
3. Brook, I.S.: Prospects for the use of control machines in automation. Report at the session of the USSR Academy of Sciences on the scientific problems of production automatior (1956). http://www.computer-museum.ru/articles/galglory_ru/278/
4. Kitov, A.I.: Electronic Computers. All-Union Society "Znanie." (1958). http://www.computer-museum.ru/books/evm_kitov_1958_2.pdf
5. Berg, A.I., Kitov, A.I., Lyapunov, A.A.: On the possibilities of automating the management of the national economy. First report in the USSR on the need to establish the National Automated System of Economic Management of the USSR. It was introduced by A. I. Kitov on the cybernetics section of the All-Union Conference on Computational Mathematics and Computer Science in November 1959. In 1961 it was published like special article in the scientific collection of the USSR Academy of Sciences "Problems of Cybernetics". http://www.computer-museum.ru/books/kitov_asu.htm
6. Belik, Y.: Economic Headquarters of the Country (Russian). Sovetskaya Rossiya: newspaper, 25 February 2011
7. Kuteinikov, A.V.: The first projects of automation of the management of the Soviet planned economy in the late 1950s and early 1960s. - "electronic socialism"? (Russian). Econ. Hist. Rev J. **15**, 130, 134–135 (2011). Moscow State University, Moscow
8. Kuteynikov, A.V.: The fate of the original idea of A. I. Kitov, the project to create an automated system for managing the Soviet economy (OGAS). Scientific works of the Free Economic Society of Russia, vol. 143, pp. 132–138 (2010) and on the site "Kitov Anatoly Ivanovich: pioneer of cybernetics, computer science and automated management systems (ASU)". http://www.kitov-anatoly.ru/o-kitove-ai/stati-ob-ai-kitove/kutejnikov

9. Kuteynikov, A.V., Shilov, V.V.: ASU for the USSR: Letter of A.I. Kitov to N.S. Khrushchev (1959). Questions of the History of Natural Science and Technology, no. 3, pp. 45–49 (2011). https://drive.google.com/file/d/0B7DBKVxXzlD_M2M3YjVlMGYtNzlj Ny00MDA5LTlhZDgtMjE4ODZjNDNhYjAy/view
10. Kuteinikov, A.V.: Thesis "The project of the State Management System for the Management of Soviet Economy (OGAS) and the problems of its implementation in the 1960–1980s"
11. Gerovich, S.: From Newspeak to Cyberspeak: Soviet Cybernetics as a Vehicle of Reform and a Bandwagon. Science, Technology and Society Program Colloquium, MIT, April 1999

Main Teleprocessing Monitors for Third-Generation Computers in the USSR

Vladimir A. Kitov[(⊠)]

Plekhanov Russian University of Economics, Stremyanny per., 36,
Moscow, Russia
vladimir.kitov@mail.ru

Abstract. In the 1970s and 1980s, one of the main directions of the development of system software for computers of the third generation was the creation of multi-terminal software complexes that provided interactions of many users of remote terminals with a central computer in the real-time mode. These software complexes (systems) were known under common name teleprocessing monitors (or telemonitors). A teleprocessing monitor (also, transaction processing monitor or TP monitor) is a control program that monitors the transfer of data between multiple local and remote terminals to ensure that the transaction processes complete [1]. This article describes these teleprocessing monitors of the third-generation computers used in the USSR such as OB, PRIMUS, CICS, KAMA and DRIVER. The most popular of these, though, was the original Soviet telemonitor OB (ОБЬ in Russian). OB was created in the secret scientific research institute "Monolith" (Secret Number R-6211) of the Ministry of Defense Industry of the USSR by a group of programmers led by the author of the present article V. A. Kitov. This article is based on the work of computer scientists, the analysis of technical documentation, the personal memories and archive of the author and his colleagues. In the 1970s–1980s, the ES EVM computers were the main computers in the USSR.

The story of this development complicates the notion that the USSR simply borrowed architecture and software from IBM and other IT-companies in the 1970s and 1980s. In fact, adapting these systems for Soviet purposes proved to be frustrating, so innovation resulted. The development of OB shows a high level of Soviet programmers at the end of the cold war. OB was a large software package with over a million lines of code.

Therefore, the history of the creation and use in the USSR of system software telemonitors is an important part of the history of Soviet computers, on the one hand, and important part of the world history of system software telemonitors, on the other hand. How pointed at [14] "CICS generated over $60 billion in new hardware revenue for IBM, and became their most-successful mainframe software product." Soviet programmers created their own original telemonitor OB, which played a similar role as telemonitor CICS. In the Soviet Union more than 40 percent of Soviet ES EVM computers used this telemonitor OB.

The experience of creation and practical use of the telemonitor OB was also important after the end of use of the third-generation computers in the USSR and in the world (in the USSR they were ES EVM computers). In the 1990s, the architectural solutions of the software of telemonitor OB were the basis for creation of the Russian system BAIKONUR for new computers of the next generation: RISC-servers.

© IFIP International Federation for Information Processing 2019
Published by Springer Nature Switzerland AG 2019
C. Leslie and M. Schmitt (Eds.): HC 2018, IFIP AICT 549, pp. 127–135, 2019.
https://doi.org/10.1007/978-3-030-29160-0_8

Keywords: AN2 · BAIKONUR · CICS · ES EVM · IBM System/360 · KAMA · OB · On-line mode · PRIMUS · Real-time software · Teleprocessing monitor · Telemonitor · Time sharing

1 Introduction

The article is devoted to the history of the most popular in the USSR telemonitors for third-generation computers (mainframes IBM/360 and its analogs in the world). Soviet and Western telemonitors such as OB, PRIMUS, CICS, KAMA and DRIVER are considered. Computers of the third generation were the major computers in the world for almost 25 years. An important part of the history of these computers is the history of the creation and use of software teleprocessing monitors, which is not yet well covered. This article is the first to cover the pages of the history of teleprocessing monitors used in the USSR. The creation in the USSR of two own advanced telemonitors OB and PRIMUS refutes the opinion of some historians of science that in the period 1970–1980 there was no original development in the USSR. The article clearly demonstrates the fact that in the USSR in the 1980s, the telemonitor OB was created at the world level of software, which perfectly controlled all huge quantity of types of terminals used in the USSR and provided machine-to-machine exchange between remote computers. It was not yet the Internet, but it was important for concrete data exchange between computers in practice – for example, between the computers of the main computing centers of nine weapon ministries in the USSR.

Initially, users of the first of the third-generation computers handed their sets of punched cards to a special department of operators, where all these sets were combined into a single package of punch cards, which was uploaded by operators for execution on a computer. The resulting data of the user's tasks were printed as a single array of printouts on alphanumeric computer printers. After that, the received printouts were divided by computer operators into separate paper blocks and issued to each user, respectively. The technology of each user's delivery of their set of punched cards to computer operators and getting their printouts from them with the results of their execution on computer had serious drawbacks. First of all, this was a significant slowdown in the overall process of data processing on a computer. The detection of even an insignificant error in the program forced the programmer to give the newly corrected punched cards to the operator's service one more, which led to extremely low speed of obtaining the results. As a result, there was a significant slowdown in making managerial decisions. The batch mode of data processing deprived managers of the possibility of making decisions in real time, i.e., directly in the process of computer data processing.

The realization that the batch processing mode was a strong brake on the effective use of third-generation computers led to the fact that in the developed countries one of the main directions of their improvement was the creation of telemonitors – teleprocessing monitors (also, transaction processing monitors or TPMs).

The teleprocessing monitor was the very important part of the system software of the third generation computer and ensured the work of many remote terminal users with the databases of each computer. Telemonitors made it possible to work with remote terminals in real time in the process of solving the tasks performed by the computer. In the USSR the most popular books about real-time systems were [2, 3] and [4]. The article is based on the author's personal experience in using telemonitors CICS, KAMA, DRIVER, PRIMUS and in creating by him and his team the telemonitor OB, as well as on the memories of his colleagues.

2 Creating and Using the First Telemonitors

At the first stage of creating telemonitors, system software was designed to display ready-made videograms (pre-prepared reference forms). It was the display on the screens of remote terminals of reference information, prepared in advance. The further operation of system telemonitors in management activities became a real factor of significant growth in the efficiency of enterprise management; more informed decisions were made and the quality of each employee's work activity was improved.

The basic functions of telemonitors for third-generation computers were the following: implementation of control and coordination processes of terminals and communication equipment for network interaction of remote computers; control functions of input-output messages from remote terminals and their editing; ensuring parallel processing and transfer of data; identification of errors in transmitted messages and their correction; dispatching queues of transmitted messages. In the third-generation computer, the specified functions for controlling the operation of the terminals were performed by a software complex included in the system software, called a telemonitor.

Starting in 1970, the world's leading computer companies started to develop their own telemonitors in addition to their batch operating systems (OS). In particular, the world giant IBM created a CICS telemonitor for their IBM/360 computers. British ICL corporation for its ICL System 4 computers developed a DRIVER telemonitor. In the Soviet Union, on the first ES EV models of computers on which IBM's borrowed system software was installed, a KAMA telemonitor was used, a copy of the IBM CICS telemonitor [6–10].

Later, two teams of Soviet programmers for Soviet ES EVM computers developed their original OB and PRIMUS telemonitors. Both telemonitors received good reviews from users of the ES EVM computers. The OB telemonitor became very popular and was widely implemented to provide users of thousands of different Soviet information management systems real-time [3–5].

3 System Telemonitors CICS (IBM, USA)
and KAMA (USSR)

In the middle of 1969, the CICS program for the IBM System/360 computers became the world's first industrially used telemonitor. CICS provided an interactive mode of interaction of the computer with users of remote terminals and computers among themselves. For the first ES EVM computers, which were first released in 1969, the system software was illegally taken from IBM. The Soviet telemonitor KAMA for

ES EVM was a direct "copy" of the American CICS. KAMA accurately repeated all the functions of CICS.

Unlike batch mode operation, an abnormal task termination in the KAMA (CICS) memory section resulted, on the one hand, in violation of the normal functioning of the system and in the loss of some of the data entered from the terminals, on the other. To resume the work of this telemonitor, it was necessary to restart it, which was its significant drawback. The working environment of the KAMA telemonitor included terminals, data sets, query queues, application programs and transactions.

Projects with KAMA telemonitors for creating software and technical complexes for data exchange between remote computers demonstrated the need for coordinating data between computer systems. In particular, in the second half of the 1970s in the Ministry of the Merchant Marine of the USSR (MinMorFlot), two such projects were implemented by the team of programmers from the Ministry's computer center under the leadership of V. A. Kitov (the present author). The first project was the creation of a multi-computers complex data exchange between the ES EVM computer (central database computer), the French computer SINTRA (computers switching communications with remote computers and terminals) and ES EVM computers installed in all sixteen shipping companies of the country. In this project, KAMA acted as a telemonitor for the central computer ES EVM. As a result, the delivery of real-time data to the MinMorFlot staff from all the shipping companies of this ministry located in all sea areas of the USSR from Kamchatka to the Baltic republics was achieved.

The same team of programmers developed a second project based on the KAMA telemonitor. It was a software package that provided data processing in the Soviet satellite rescue system for ships and airplanes COSPAS (*КОСПАС* in Russian), which was part of the international rescue complex KOSPAS-SARSAT. In the COSPAS system, the main task of KAMA was to ensure the delivery of operational information to rescue personnel. Every plane and every ship had a radio beacon. This radio beacon began to transmit the coordinates of its location in the event of an accident. As a result, the ministry in Moscow obtained the location (coordinates) of the vessel or aircraft that had suffered the accident. The central ministry computer immediately located the rescue means closest to the accident (for example, other nearby vessels) and informed the rescue personnel who had issued instructions for assistance. This project was created by the USSR, the U.S., Canada, and France.

4   The System Telemonitor DRIVER (ICL, UK)

In 1972, the Main Computer Center of the State Planning Committee of the USSR purchased terminal equipment for two of its powerful computers at that time, ICL System 4–70 s. To enable the use of remote terminals, ICL had created its own telemonitor, called DRIVER. It had the same similar problems like CICS or KAMA. The head of the Main Computer Center ordered the present author, system programmer Vladimir Kitov, to learn DRIVER. The ease of use of the DRIVER telemonitor allowed Kitov to create a simple information system for interactive interaction of users of remote terminals with a computer ICL System 4-70 in just two months. These users were the specialists of data preparation department. Two more months it took Kitov to create, on the basis of the telemonitor DRIVER, the software system TSO: a system for debugging programs in real-time mode.

The British telemonitor DRIVER was successfully used in the five important organizations of the USSR: Computer Center of Vneshtorg, Computer Center of AZLK factory, the Main Computer Center of Gossnab of the USSR, the Main Computer Center of the USSR State Planning Committee, Scientific Institute of Management Problems of AS of the USSR.

5   The System Telemonitor PRIMUS (USSR)

During this time, the architecture and software of the Soviet ES EVM, which had begun as a clone of IBM System/360, increased in complexity. Soviet computer scientists struggled to adapt the American software systems like CICS, CRJE and TSO to the Soviet computers. The moment came when it became clear to the specialists that the Soviet ES EVM computers needed their own telemonitor, one that would take into account all the features of the new models of the ES EVM computers and a very large quantity of types of its terminals. New models of ES EVM computers and new types of Soviet terminal equipment had new standards. And Western software was no longer compatible with these new standards. One of the first national-scale telemonitors of domestic design was the collective access system, called PRIMUS. The main goal of PRIMUS was the remote access of terminal users to databases of the central computer. The first version of the PRIMUS telemonitor appeared in the second half of the 1970s. In the years that followed, this system was gaining increasing popularity in the country for the ES EVM computer. This set the stage for a further development in this area. PRIMUS was a very important step for Soviet informatics because PRIMUS was the first domestic teleprocessing monitor.

6   The System Telemonitor OB (USSR)

In the USSR, the most widespread system telemonitor was the telemonitor OB, the full name of which sounded as the Multi-Terminal System for Distributed Data Processing OB (ОБЬ in Russian). Although development of OB did not start until 1980, by the second half of the 1980s, OB was used on more than 40% of all ES EVM computers of the USSR. At this time, the author of this article worked as head of the real-time data processing software department at the secret Central Scientific Research Institute "Monolith" (secret index R-6211), the main institute of informatics of the Ministry of Defense Industry of the USSR. As a result of the previous eight-year experience in creating interactive software systems, he had a strong opinion that in the Soviet Union an original Russian telemonitor was needed. The new telemonitor would have to satisfy all the requirements for the creation and operation of computer information systems for thousands of enterprises in the country. This was primarily the provision of computer systems that support the simultaneous operation of hundreds remote terminals, the operation of branched network systems of intercomputer interaction, a built-in interactive debugging program, a developed package of service programs, and a well-developed library of standard applied dialog programs. Nevertheless, the creators imagined a distributed computing environment for users who had little expertise in computers but could benefit from the addition of computing power to their work life. OB was a large software package with over a million lines of code.

OB developers did not have a task to create any computer network like NSFNET or others. They had the task to create the program system for managing the multi-terminal networks on each of many enterprises of the USSR.

The creation of the OB was preceded by a period of study of the corresponding theoretical basis and practical use of foreign and Soviet predecessors of OB – tele-monitors CICS, KAMA, DRIVER and PRIMUS. During this time, their shortcomings and inconveniences of use were revealed, so an extensive list of necessary improvements was easy to form. As a result, a team of programmers of the software department of the STD of the Central Research Institute "Monolith" created the original Russian telemonitor OB. The initiator and head of the OB system project was the present author. Leading developers were talented system programmers Vladimir Dyakonov and Igor Kalinchev. The first version of the telemonitor OB appeared at 1981. From the very beginning, OB was created to manage heterogeneous multi-terminal networks and to ensure the functioning of computer networks.

The creators of the telemonitor "OB" (in Russian *ОБЬ*) gave it a name with the Russian letter "Ь," which exists only in the Russian alphabet. This choice stressed the originality of their software. At that time, the Russian character clearly indicated the absence of any foreign analogues in the new software package. It is not a secret that a number of well-known Soviet systems and application programs for the first models of ES EVM were simply borrowed from IBM. Soviet officials did not inform Soviet society about it and the KGB's involvement in this deal. In these borrowed software packages, these allegedly Soviet programs had in their names only those Russian letters that had the same English letters (for example, A, K, M, O, T, etc.). In addition, for the ease of replacing English names in Soviet analogue programs with Russian ones, these programs also had the same number of letters in the title as their American prototypes. For example, Soviet programs KAMA and OKA are the American programs CICS and IMS. KAMA, OKA, and OB (ОБЬ) were three large Soviet software complexes for ES EVM computers. They were named in honor of the three famous rivers of Russia. However, only OB was fully developed in Russia. The telemonitor KAMA was taken from IBM (telemonitor CICS). DBMS OKA is a Soviet adaptation of the American software system IMS.

The telemonitor OB had several important advantages. In addition to its own interface, the OB supported standard telecommunication access methods (protocols) of the BTMD and OTMD of the ES EVM computers and a huge terminal park – several dozen types of terminal devices. As already mentioned, OB was widely distributed in the USSR, where more than forty percent of all ES EVM computers operated under its control, while under IBM CICS, no more than fifteen percent of all ES EVM computers in the country operated. Being significantly less resource-intensive than foreign CICS, the OB had a more user-friendly interface and supported many other types of terminals, including personal computers (PCs). It is logical that some Western telemonitors supported PCs as well. The development of OB demonstrates the high development of computer research in the 1980s in the USSR, which used systems of inter computer data exchange. On the example of the telemonitor OB, it can be seen that in the 1980s, Soviet programmers were at least on same level with Western programmers.

In the creation of the telemonitor OB, the leading role was played by a remarkable team of software developers (first of all, Dr. Vladimir Dyakonov, Dr. Igor Kalinchev, Dr. Igor Zhitenyov and Dr. Vladimir Denisenko) of the department of the real-time software of the Research Institute "Monolith" of the Ministry of Defense Industry of the USSR, headed by Dr. Vladimir Kitov. In the course of eight years of its existence, this department created and successfully used the famous large-program systems at over two hundred enterprises only of the Ministry of Defense Industry of the USSR. These are LISTER, for prompt information management; KDOM, for interactive debugging; the intercomputer data exchange between nine Computer Centers of Defense Ministries of the USSR; two complexes of programs for checking information on disk volumes (PDT) and tape volumes (PLT); FORMATOR, for computer analysis and data preparation for storage in DBMS; TERMES, for viewing and updating information in consecutive files in dialog mode; CONTROL, the dialogue system of execution of instructions and documents; the telemonitor OB, and others. In the middle of 1980s, OB was successfully approved by the State Commission of the USSR and included to the Soviet export fund "Center Program System" (All-Union Fund of Algorithms and Programs) for wide distribution at the enterprises of the USSR and abroad.

7 OB's Second Life

Unlike the vast majority of ES EVM software systems, the OB telemonitor did not come off the stage in the era of personal computers (PCs). In 1996, the telemonitor OB experienced a second birth when the Russian company Epsilon Technologies used the architectural design and functionality of the OB telemonitor as the basis for the new software package BAIKONUR.

BAIKONUR was designed to work on next-generation computers: RISC servers. Then, the company Epsilon Technologies took advantage of the experience of highly qualified programmers from the defense research institute "Monolith" and the Academy of Sciences of the USSR. Thanks to this, based on the ideas and experience of the development of the telemonitor OB, the new software complex mentioned above was born. The most difficult task of the initial stage of its creation, according to Andrey Chesnokov, the head of the BAIKONUR project, was the creation of a well-coordinated team of developers from the old school of system programmers and Borland-style programmers of the new generation. It is the fusion of the programmers of the "old school," brought up in the tradition of multi-tasking and well-structured operating systems of IBM's and ES EVM's mainframes, with developers accustomed to RAD-tools, allowed to combine the convenience of application development and high performance inherent in the BAIKONUR system [11, 12]. Today, the ideas outlined in the creation of large Soviet and Russian software complexes OB and BAIKONUR find further fruitful development in the new projects of the next generation of Russian programmers.

8 Conclusion

In the article for the first time in the historical literature the review of the main system telemonitors used in the USSR for computers of the third generation is done. The leading role of domestic telemonitors is shown. For Soviet computers, the telemonitor OB had significant advantages over similar Western systems. OB was used on forty percent of the total number of ES EVM computers operated in the USSR. By 1990, ES EVM had already ceased to be the main computers in the country. Their positions were replaced by personal computers and next-generation servers. The experience of the creating a purely domestic telemonitor OB was useful even after computers ES EVM leaving the scene. In particular, these were good software architecture ideas and a wealth of programmer experience. The telemonitor OB formed the basis for the next generation software package BAIKONUR (Project Manager Andrey Chesnokov). OB is the typical example of the large software complexes created by the Soviet programmers.

The article uses information from books on data teleprocessing [2, 3], technical documentation on CICS, KAMA, DRIVER, PRIMUS and OB (ОБь) telemonitors [7–11], books and articles by the author and his colleagues [4–6], and works devoted to the systems BAIKONUR [12, 13].

References

1. Teleprocessing monitor. https://en.wikipedia.org/wiki/Teleprocessing_monitor. Accessed 31 Mar 2019
2. Blackman, M.: Projecting of real-time systems. MIR, Moscow, pp. 29–314 (1977)
3. Sipser, R.: Architecture of communication in distributed systems. MIR, Moscow, p. 661 (1981)
4. Dyakonov, V.Yu., Kalinchev, I.A., Kitov, V.A.: Software of data teleprocessing systems. "SCIENCE" Publishing House. (Main edition of physical and mathematical literature. Series "The Library of the Programmer"), Moscow, 165 p. (1992)
5. Dyakonov, V.Yu., Kalinchev, I.A., Kitov, V.A.: The principle of software mobility of multi-terminal distributed data processing systems. Programming, № 2, pp. 46–53 (1984)
6. Dyakonov, V.Yu., Kalinchev, I.A., Kitov, V.A.: Multiterminal system for distributed data processing OB. In: Computer Technology of the Socialist Countries. Finance and Statistics, Moscow, issue 22, pp. 131–136 (1987)
7. Customer Information Control System (CICS) General Information Manual (PDF). White Plains, IBM, New York, December 1972. GH20-1028-3. Accessed 01 Apr 2016
8. Transaction Processing Monitor. http://wiki.c2.com/?TransactionProcessingMonitor
9. IBM Corporation: Customer Information Control System (CICS) Application Programmer's Reference Manual (PDF) (1972). Accessed 4 Jan 2016
10. CICS – An Introduction (PDF). IBM Corporation, 8 July 2004. Accessed 20 Apr 2014

11. Customer Information Control System/Virtual Machine (CICS/VM). IBM, 20 October 1987. Accessed 02 Apr 2016
12. Intel Has Put Baikonur "Very Good" Rating. CRN, # 13 (48) of 17.07 1998. https://www.crn.ru/numbers/reg-numbers/detail.php?ID=3367
13. Baikonur Web Application Server – client-server architecture for Intranet-based access to corporate databases. CIT Forum. http://citforum.ru/programming/application/baiconur.shtml. Accessed 31 Mar 2019
14. CICS. https://en.wikipedia.org/wiki/CICS. Accessed 31 Mar 2019

CoCom and Comecon

Socialist Life of a U.S. Army Computer in the GDR's Financial Sector

Import of Western Information Technology into Eastern Europe in the Early 1960s

Martin Schmitt[(⊠)]

Leibniz Centre for Contemporary History, Potsdam, Germany
schmitt@zzf-potsdam.de

Abstract. This article investigates the role of the first digital computer in GDR's socialist financial system. Why did the GDR's Ministry of Finance import a Univac computer from the U.S. army in 1965, even though the country aimed at computational autarky and was restricted by embargo? The main argument is that the Ministry of Finance imported the computer to kickstart its program for electronic data processing. They succeeded because they not only imported a machine, but also reframed it ideologically. They drew on the notion of the computer as a universal machine and adapted it to local conditions. The process hints to the ambiguity of the later decision of the East Bloc toward copying IBM's system architecture. This article investigates this process by following the traces of an early computer and the ideas surrounding it through the Iron Curtain. It stresses the role of early computer users with the example of GDR's financial system in contrast to better known producer stories. Through the analysis of exclusive material, this is suggesting a different perspective on the import procedures of Eastern European countries in the Cold War. A policy change in the Cold War towards détente becomes visible as early as in 1965.

Keywords: Banking history · Cold War · German Democratic Republic (GDR) · History of computing · Technology transfer

1 Introduction: Why Did the GDR's Ministry of Finance Import a Computer from the U.S. Army?

The first digital computer running in GDR's financial system was a capitalist one. In 1965, the East German Ministry of Finance imported a used midrange computer by Univac from the U.S. Army. This was remarkable for various reasons: it was imported from the ideological enemy, it conflicted with the drive to autarky, it came not from IBM, its import should have been prohibited by external embargos and internal security measures, and its acquisition was carried out by an organization of minor political position in GDR's hierarchy. The main research question resulting out of these contradictory facts is: Why did GDR's Ministry of Finance import a Univac computer from the U.S. army in 1965 even though the country aimed at computational autarky and was restricted by embargo? Why were they able to succeed with their efforts while

© IFIP International Federation for Information Processing 2019
Published by Springer Nature Switzerland AG 2019
C. Leslie and M. Schmitt (Eds.): HC 2018, IFIP AICT 549, pp. 139–164, 2019.
https://doi.org/10.1007/978-3-030-29160-0_9

others failed? My argument is that The Ministry of Finance was able to import the computer to kickstart its distinct program for electronic data processing (EDP) because they not only imported a machine, but also reframed it ideologically. They drew on the notion of the computer as a universal machine and adapted it to local conditions. They benefited from a policy change in the Cold War towards détente already in 1965. The process hints to the ambiguity of the later decision of the East Bloc toward copying IBM's system architecture. This decision was not as clear as it seems in hindsight.

Why was this process so remarkable, as other Eastern European states also imported computers from the west in that year? Firstly, the Ministry of Finance imported a machine of the enemies army. It had been used to fight against socialism, but it ended up in the banking system of a self-proclaimed "peace-loving" socialist country. Secondly, this very procedure conflicted with the approach of the East German government to achieve computational autarky. With its sophisticated "program for the development, implementation and enforcement of electronic data processing" [1], the Socialist Party set the foundation of an East German computer industry in 1964. Importing foreign computers from the ideological enemy did not fit well into that line at first glance.

Thirdly, Western producers were not supposed to deliver computers to their enemies in turn. Especially for the U.S. administration computers were crucial in the global conflict of political systems. The embargo policy of the Coordinating Committee on Multilateral Export Controls (CoCom) should have prevented socialist states from acquiring high-end computer technology [2]. Nevertheless, the Univac Card Tabulator II passed this barrier. Its travel route took it through the heartlands of capitalism: from the United States via the Netherlands, Frankfurt in West-Germany to East Berlin. The UCT II was only one example for how porous the Iron Curtain could be as other states from Eastern Europe also imported similar machines already in 1965 [3]. Fourthly, the Ministry of Finance did not acquire an IBM computer but one from Remington Rand, an early competitor of IBM. So far, historians have often highlighted an early dominance of IBM in the East Bloc [4]. The exemplary fact that officials chose a Remington machine questions the current state of knowledge about imported computers in the Eastern Block. Especially, European producers tried to strengthen their position by expanding into a market not yet dominated by IBM. Fifthly, the banking system in the socialist state had a minor position. Despite its weak power position, its leaders succeeded in importing such an expensive machine earlier than many others (see Table 1).

This article investigates this process by following the traces of an early computer and the ideas surrounding it through the Iron Curtain in three sections. I stress the role of early computer users with the example of GDR's banking system in contrast to better-known producer stories. This provides new insights to technology transfer during the Cold War and into the inner logic of socialist regimes in Eastern Europe. Other institutions and companies in the GDR as well as in countries like Czechoslovakia, Poland and the Soviet Union also began to import computers in 1965. They considered the appropriation of western technology not as a simple takeover, but as the cornerstone on the way towards a socialist information age in its own respect. I am providing evidence through the analysis of so-far unknown documents from German archives and various oral history interviews with key figures of the computer center of the Ministry of Finance. This exclusive material allows me to suggest a different perspective on the import procedures of Eastern European countries in the 1960s [4]. It also deepens our knowledge on recent questions of the history of computing, like computer technology and knowledge transfer [5, 6], early digital technology [7], knowledge acquisition through training [8], communities of practice of programmers [9, 10] and alternative paths to the digital age beyond system borders.

2 Computerization for Socialist Progress: The Electronic Data Processing Program of 1964 as the Basis of an Alternative Information Age

The party leaders of the GDR had high hopes for computer technology [11, p. 35], [12]. Perhaps like no other European country, they tied their fate to the success of computerization. This section shows how they developed their own concepts of a socialist information age [9, p. 4–21] and why it was nevertheless necessary to import western computer and knowledge to do so. In the eyes of the party leaders, computers should build the base for political-organizational reforms and economic growth. The GDR's economic development in the 1950s is known for investments in heavy industry and reconstruction. After having built the Berlin wall in 1961 to stop the exodus of well-trained specialists, the planners felt breathing space for reforms [13]. Party leader Walter Ulbricht and his advisors planned to introduce more market-oriented mechanisms to overcome GDR's lack of productivity in 1963. The 1964 "program for the development, implementation and enforcement of electronic data processing" [1] was ratified as a vital base for these reforms. On the one hand, the party deployed computers as a tool for optimizing the flow of information within the economy. On the other hand, they used them as one tool for control as they were slackening the reins and giving more responsibilities to the corporations. Being in a middle position between East and West, Ulbricht fulfilled Khrushchev's dreams of a nation-wide network of regional computer centers[1] as well as western ideals of price mechanisms having a discipline effect on the economy. He and his advisors imagined computer use for the sake of communism.

Nonetheless, computers and software were a scarce in the GDR. Planners, managers and workers had little knowledge of how to use computers for their sakes or how to integrate them into economic processes. The only "computer" in mass production was an electronic calculator distributed by the optical industry at Zeiss. Zeiss engineers mainly designed the so-called "Zeiss Electronic Calculator 1" (ZRA 1) for scientific calculations in 1956. Employees of the Savings Bank of East Berlin experimented with electronic calculators attached as modules to office machines for book-keeping purposes. Even though, fast input/output capabilities and flexible programmability were missing. Therefore, neither the ZRA 1 nor the modules were useful for mass use in the economy in the long run. The party invested large sums of money in computers between 1964–1971 to change that situation and to base socialism in the digital age. They even rooted digitalization in their first party program:

---

[1] See Kitov, "On the History of Gosplan", this volume. Similar plans were pursued in Poland with ZETO. See Sikora, "Cooperating with Moscow, Stealing in California", this volume.

Mastering and applying the most advanced [...] computer technology and mechanical data processing [...] is of decisive importance for the rationalization of production processes and the highest benefit of labor. The further investigation of economic problems with mathematical methods and the establishment of a network of computer stations and computer centers [...] should therefore be given special attention. (First Program of the Socialist Unity Party of Germany, 1964)

SED party leaders regarded economic autarky as the core of their overall reform program [14, pp. 37–38]. Therefore, they also adapted the computer development program to that line. Their experiences at the beginning of the 1960s fueled the establishment of an autarkic computer and software production. Then, the West-German Government cut exports to the GDR in reaction to SED restrictions of freedom of movement. In many sectors of the GDR economy, this caused grave delays and production problems. In information technology, this should have been prevented by an own production. Based on the manufacturing of own electronic components, often "inspired" by Western design, a vital computer industry was planned. Also, money should be saved by avoiding costly imports. Some planners even hoped to export computer technology and gain foreign currency, as the business machine industry of the GDR succeeded to do since the very beginning of the GDR. The program's main goal was to develop a competitive computer, the Robotron 300. Parallel to establishing hardware production, the party deployed concepts for the implementation of computers in different sectors of state and economy [4], [11, p. 38].

In the early 1960s, cross-national transfer processes were indispensable despite dreams of autarky. The program's preparation as well as its realization were supported by technology and knowhow transfer. Again, the GDR took a middle role between East and West: Technical experts and leading managers of the GDR had a close look especially on West Germany, but also on other socialist countries [11, pp. 37–38]. While they adopted the concept of central, state-run data centers in the region capitals from the Soviet Union [15], they adapted programming methods, process digitalization and usage fields from the West. Since 1962, representatives of the GDR visited data centers in Japan, Switzerland, West Germany, France, Austria, Sweden and the USA in the West, as well as the Soviet Union, Czechoslovakia, Hungary and Poland in the East various times. Delegations of the financial sector participated amongst them. However, the exchange went even further: In order to achieve its goals, the party hired a number of West German experts on electronic data processing in the mid 1960s. Their task was to provide GDR workers the missing expertise of the Digital Age, for example in programming. In addition, the GDR joined the renowned "Diebold research institute for the use of electronic data processing" [16]. They were willing to pay large sums of membership fees in foreign currency for that transfer. The state leadership launched an import offensive of Western and socialist computers to speed up the production of its own computers. The financial institutions of the GDR, mainly the State Bank, played a key role in these efforts. The State Bank[2] was one of the leading forces in the rationalization of mass data processing. They cooperated with national developers of the Robotron 300, participated in user groups, and wrote proposals for an advanced

---

[2] At that time still called "National Central Bank".

computer usage. However, besides electronic calculators running in Berlin, computers were missing in the financial sector.

3   Import vs. Autarchy in a Not-so-Hostile International Landscape

At the end of 1964, the top level of the Ministry of Finance already realized that the deployment of the Robotron 300 would be further delayed. Even though they had a good starting position and were granted early access to the supposedly self-built technology,[3] early access still meant rather 1969–1970 than 1967 [17]. In this section, I analyze how they pursued the import of an U.S. army computer despite the embargo and autarchy because of this delay. Due to these planning uncertainties, many enterprises waited to make organizational changes until computers were finally available. In contrast, the State Bank had prepared a couple of state-of-the-art concepts for computer usage. They aimed at a double, intertwined goal: First of all, a rationalization of mass transaction data processing. Secondly, they wanted to optimize planning with transaction data analysis [18]. The delay in delivering the Robotron 300 endangered the development and implementation of their concepts. Especially the programming part was crucial for a successful deployment: The programs had to be written, tested, debugged, and implemented; the personnel had to be trained; the working routines had to be practiced, and the organizational schemes had to be proofed reliable. However, software testing was not possible without a computer. The banking sector was especially sensitive in terms of security and reliability. Messing up money transfers or savings of the population could possibly lead to discontent and economic disturbances. Party leaders feared that it could produce a decrease in legitimacy of the regime or even cause hard-to-control protests.

3.1   Why Did the Ministry of Finance Decide on an American Computer?

Therefore, the necessity of importing a computer became urgent. The minister of finance, Willy Rumpf, commissioned the Institute for Financial Economics with a study on the ideal type of computer for socialist financial purposes. Their scientists assessed the technical data and the performance of the computer "as well as the necessary accessories for data storage, sorting, input, output and printing [...], the mode of operation and the working rhythm [...] and the level of programming difficulty". Also, the "time of delivery, the price, the assurance of technical maintenance and the supply of spare parts, the expandability and the assurance thereof, the programs and the duration and location of the training of the operating personnel and, to a certain extent, commercial policy aspects" [19] played a vital role in their decision-making process.

---

[3] Many parts of the first Robotron 300 computers were also imported from Western countries because the GDR microelectronics industry was not capable of producing parts of sufficient quality.

Eventually, the Institute's economists put three machines on the shortlist: An ICT 130: from the British manufacturer International Computers and Tabulators, a computer famous for the complicated task of British currency calculations; a Bull Gamma 30 from the French Compagnie des Machines Bull, which was a rebranded RCA 301 in use in several banks all over Western Europe; and finally, an NCR 315 by the U.S. based National Cash Register, known for its sophisticated error-handling and the use of thin film memory as storage.[4] All the machines were competitors of IBMs 1401 in size, speed and price. Therefore, it is more than remarkable that IBM computers did not even get into top three. IBM was strong in the banking and finance sector in Western Europe at that time, especially in the savings banks of Western Germany. Notwithstanding, Remington Rand still was a strong player since the 1950s. In 1965, GDR officials had more specific reasons not buy an IBM machine besides competition: its unwillingness to circumvent export policies.

Finally, Ministry officials took the decision to import the Bull Gamma 30. They had already established good relations with the company in the past. These good experiences and trustworthiness in delivery in times of the CoCom embargo were essential. In contrast, U.S. companies like IBM complied with embargo rules. It is remarkable that IBM, which held advantages from longstanding customer relationships, was ruled out because of missing relationships to the East. The ministers' decision on a machine had to comply GDR's import regulations afterwards. This clearly shows that importing a machine from the West did not run smoothly. Many internal interests of the GDR left their marks on the final decision. Importing a U.S. army computer was not the decision of the Ministry of Finance, but the result of a typical negotiation process in the socialist system. A large number of players were involved in imports and they even changed in between. The decision-making structures in the supposedly centralized, hierarchical GDR state were interwoven and overlapping in terms of electronic data processing. Until 1965, the authority to import computers was primarily in the hands of the State Planning Commission. For a better coordination of the computing approaches of users, they established a commission for "Machine Data Processing" at the end of 1964. Their members issued import recommendations for specific machines and determined rules for evaluating import proposals.

Those import rules were changed between 1964 and 1965 and published in June 1965 [20]. Therefore, the Ministry of Finance had to reformulate their proposal. Every user was obliged to defend their proposal in front of this commission. The recommendations as well as every proposal were assessed from technical experts of the Institute for Data Processing[5] in Dresden. Afterwards, the commission bundled the proposals and decided on their eligibility. Finally, the eligible import proposals went to the highest state offices of the politburo and the council of ministers because they included large sums of foreign currency. After the decision was taken, the foreign trade

---

[4] The State Bank of Poland imported such a machine in 1965. The company producing the Robotron 300 did likewise, which underscores the argument that IBM did not dominate every domain in the early 1960s again.

[5] This institute in turn was part of a bigger association of all manufacturers of information technology in the GDR.

company, "Büromaschinen Export GmbH", was responsible for carrying out the import of the equipment.

During this nested process, the original decision of the Ministry of Finance was changed. The commission members argued that a Univac UCT II computer did fit better for the needs of the Ministry. Officially, their argument was that it was obligatory to have a backup machine. Supposedly, none existed for a Bull Gamma 30. However, a business machine producer from Erfurt issued an import proposal for a UCT II, so the commission allowed only an import of that same computer. This was important for the deciding bodies within the GDR because one user could switch over to similar types of computers in the case of a breakdown. In addition, programs and use cases could be exchanged and maintenance be bundled. Especially, spare parts were a scarce resource and could always fell under the embargo rules, which complicated or prohibited their delivery. Therefore, GDR users of Western computers often ordered the double amount of spare parts and consumable supplies.

Behind the scenes, other interests played a bigger role. Actually, another state institution imported a Bull Gamma 30 at the very same time. That meant that the producer's wish was rated higher in the decision-making process. The company from Erfurt asserted itself against the Ministry of Finance. Furthermore, that the commission members were not aware of that import shows that by no means was the commission the only way to import a computer. Eventually, the price might also have influenced the commission's decision on the UCT II. The Büromaschinen Export GmbH succeeded in getting an offer for a used UCT II computer by the Remington salespeople for a lower price than for a Bull Gamma 30.

The Ministry in turn succumbed under protest, as this machine seemed the only possibility of getting an advanced computer at all. In their second meeting, Deputy Minister of Finance Kaminsky defended the proposal in front of the commission. Afterwards, their members acknowledged the import decision of the UCT II computer. Meanwhile, they denied the import requests of other ministries like that of the Ministry for Trade and Supply [21].

3.2   Reframing the UCT II as a Midrange Universal Vomputer

The UCT II was a special machine. This is important to understand because it explains the decision of the commission and helps historians to keep track of the process. First of all, it bore various names. In the U.S., Australia and other English-speaking parts of the world, Remington marketed the UCT II computer as Solid State II or "SS II" for short. It was obvious that this would not be the best product name in Germany, referring to the Nazi elite soldiers in World War II. Therefore, it was marketed as "Univac Card Tabulator" in Europe.[6] This still refers to the beginnings of an industry and a time in which sale contracts were not based on a standardized portfolio.

---

[6] This name change complicates the task of tracking the path of the computer through the Iron Curtain a lot for the historian. Only with the help of computer journals it was possible for me to assess the imported computer and find its origins.

The UCT II was the successor of the bestselling UCT I that marked a bridge from the punched card world to the digital age. Users could still continue to use their punched card equipment while already enjoying the benefits of digitalization. It was a midrange computer like the IBM 1401 and was especially capable of dealing with many magnet tape units at once. Up to ten units could be connected to one machine, with an addition yet another ten. The UCT II was also able to read from one tape and write on another directly, which gave the computer an advantage in overall speed. Univac engineers wrote specific commands that enabled the machine to sort alpha characters in an optimized way. In finance, this was a huge advantage because it empowered employees to sort customer data not only according to account numbers but by names. For memory, the UCT II used a combination of core and drum memory, which combined the advantages of speed and size. The acceptance of the UCT II by the Ministry of Finance underscores not only the huge importance of magnetic tapes in the digitalization of banking, but also of memory and sorting [22].

The irony of this import is that the UCT II was not only designed for the U.S. Army, but actively used by them. In 1965, IBM delivered the first models of its far-reaching System/360. Supposedly, the U.S. Army upgraded from a leased UCT II to a more versatile IBM 360 and gave back the old one to the producer. Importing a computer used before by military forces of the so-called imperialist aggressor stood in sharp contrast to the GDR's rhetoric of peace. Depicting the GDR as a peace-loving state against an aggressive enemy was one of the main columns of socialist self-understanding. Peace was used as a counter-argument against the Western rhetoric of "freedom".

The official state newspaper *Neues Deutschland* as well as the *Berliner Zeitung* published various articles on the use of computers for the Vietnam War and other violent conflicts between 1961–1969 (ND: 7.4.1966, p. 5; 4.5.1968, p. 8; …). In 1968, an author of the newspaper *Neue Zeit,* reviewing the premier of a French theater play in Leipzig, described the Pentagon even as a computer center and wrote: "They use computers and superweapons to plan the inhumanity of the total war against all of Vietnam" (Neue Zeit, 7.7.1968, p. 4). In contrast, Walter Ulbricht officially declared in a speech that the orientation towards peace "shows that socialism can and will make more fruitful use of cybernetic machines than capitalism has ever been able to" (ND, 27.3.1964, p. 3). Consequently, the computer was understood as a neutral machine and not as a war machine. This interpretative openness made it possible to use the very same computers, but also telling a story of adaptation. In contrast to the current literature [4] the larger import processes were accompanied by a change of language. The perspective on regular computer users and technicians brings that to the front. They adapted English terms like "software" [23, p. 2] or "computer" (exemplary ND: 6.5.1956; 3.1.1965; 10.2.1965; 11.7.1965; 9.1.1966, …) besides official language regulations.

However, adapting the computer to local conditions also meant integrating it into the ideological framing of socialism. In front of employees, the Ministry of Finance supposedly used a legend to cover the belligerent background of the computer: officially, the computer was bought from an Australian department store [16, 24]. This cover story consequently was reproduced in grey literature. It is rather unlikely that this story was true. The first and most convincing point is that with respect to Philipson

(2017), in Australia Remington Rand had a difficult stand with its Univac computers. Philipson cited a substantial list of computers in use in Australia in December 1962. The UCT II appears in this list only at the service bureaus of Univac themselves.[7] Not a single company nor state institution there used Univac computers. There seem to be no sources supporting the thesis of a SS II running in an Australian department store. Even if this would have been the case, it is unlikely that a private company would have given it back after only two or three years of use. Univac introduced the UCT II to the market not earlier than 1962. Regarding that it was necessary and time consuming to adapt all personnel and processes to the machine, it would have produced huge costs to change computers within such a short timeframe. The U.S. military, though, not having such a pressure for profit but for security, were able to upgrade their machines after three years, especially when supporting a national vendor.

The second proof is that GDR technicians told in an interview that they built a module for changing the frequency of electricity from 60 Hz to 50 Hz after the import. This was necessary to adapt the computer to the local conditions. The GDR electricity grid was running on 50 Hz, as the Australian one. However, the frequency of the U.S. electricity grid was 60 Hz. Therefore, it is more likely that the machine ran on 60 Hz in the U.S. and not in Australia before. Otherwise, no module would have had to been built. Also, oral records provide evidence for the U.S. origin of the computer. Three people independently from each other told the story of the U.S. import while only a single person working for the GDR press supported the Australia story [25–27]. Therefore, the Ministry of Finance used the Australian story rather as a cover story that they told to the press and to their employees.

3.3 A Changing International Landscape and the Decision Against a Socialist Machine

By the time the Council of Ministers approved the import request of the Ministry of Finance in 1965, the international political landscape already had begun to change. Both superpowers established communication channels between them after a period of conflict. While the Vietnam War intensified, U.S. president Lyndon B. Johnson used his second term for a more cooperative approach towards the Soviet Union in regards of economic trade and cultural transfer. Looking at the bigger picture, this led to the détente in the years 1969–1975, while on small scale, it made a bunch of sensitive computer imports possible. From the U.S. side, the export was also a two-faced process. The official embargo policy required that if East Bloc producers were able to construct machines by themselves, similar machines were allowed to export. At the same time, the State Department blocked every export request on machines that still were in use in the U.S. Army. Thus, the fact that the UCT II now was dismantled changed the scene for the Ministry of Finance.

---

[7] In Australia, it was marketed as Univac SS II 80. The 80 in the name stood for the use of punch cards with 80 columns instead of 90 columns. This corresponded to the IBM standard, not the standard of Remington Rand.

Furthermore, with the Minsk-22, the East Bloc was in theory able to build a computer more or less similar to the UCT II. It was in the interest of the Western producers to argue that it was more similar than different. Especially, smaller U.S. producers under economic pressure by IBM like Remington Rand and non-U.S. producers like ICT, Bull and later Siemens [28] hoped to conquer the Eastern European market. Their managers wanted to balance IBM's strong position on their respective home markets and to solve their economic problems. While in the years 1963–1964 only a single import proposal was allowed, this situation dramatically changed in 1965: more import requests were issued and suddenly they were approved, as shown in the Appendix. This did not only apply to the GDR, but to many other socialist states like Czechoslovakia, Poland, and even the Soviet Union as well. In addition, the before-mentioned import issued by the Polish National Bank of an NCR 315 in 1965 [29] is another proof for a changing international landscape. In contrast to previous literature, the import of computers to the Eastern Bloc began earlier and did not include IBM machines, even though IBM salesman offered IBM 1400s to socialist officials.

Why did GDR institutions not import computers from the Soviet Union instead of those from the ideological enemy? The so-called "international friendship" with the Soviet Union was an important base for the existence of the socialist state. There are four main reasons for that dismissal: first of all, the Soviet Union leaders decided to reserve their machines for their own institutions. There was a huge demand in the country for computing power. Even though almost 1,000 Minsk-22 were produced between 1965–1970, only a few were exported to the GDR.[8] Furthermore, the production just started in 1965 so that, at first, Soviet institutions were provided with computing power. The second reason was the lower reliability of Soviet computers. As technicians of the Ministry's data center in Berlin affirmed, the quality of the Soviet computers was lower due to missing components and lower standards in mechanical engineering. Thirdly, the high level of maintenance and services that the Western producers promised to deliver attracted Eastern European users. While domestic producers or those from other socialist countries often left their users alone with installation, operation and repair, Western producers regularly sent their own personnel to the users' site. It was part of computing as a service. Moreover, a lot of software already existed for Western computers, ranging from use case scenarios to applications, from system programs to sophisticated solutions to urging problems. This made Western technology even more attractive to socialist users.

3.4   Computer Import Under Embargo Regulations: Adaptation for Security

According to sources in the Ministry of Finance, GDR's foreign trade officials negotiated with the Swiss subsidiary of Remington, a mysterious company called "Mithra". Mysterious, because the company changed its headquarters various times, failed in their research objectives, and experienced a dramatic ending in 1967 [30, pp. 188–190]. In contrast to IBM, Remington had not yet centralized its European sales divisions, but

---

[8] See the paper of Mate Szabo, p. 11.

operated in every country on its own. Until 1967, this did not change. It simplified such deals as the UCT II import despite the embargo. But the GDR side acted not less mysterious, as a letter from Willy Rumpf to the head of the Council of Ministers shows. They knew that the embargo policy prohibited the delivery of a computer to a state institution. Therefore, they ordered the computer in the name of the Central Bank. Unfortunately, the negotiators blabbed out the secret, as Rumpf angrily notes in a letter to the head of state Willi Stoph [31]. Nevertheless, Remington and the Ministry agreed on a contract that included the delivery of the computer and its peripherals.

How did the export computer pass through the Iron Curtain? It is telling that transfer processes were partly reciprocal, as not only technology flowed to the East Bloc but also people and knowledge to the West. The UCT II was delivered by plane via Amsterdam's Schiphol airport. This is not surprising, because more than once, the Netherlands acted as an entry point for computer technology. For example, Amsterdam was an early hub for Arpanet, bringing the TCP/IP protocol suite to Europe [32]. Likewise, the Soviet Union offered their BESM 6 mainframe computer for sale in the Netherlands for the first time in 1965 [2, p. 140]. From Schiphol, the UCT II was then transferred to Frankfurt am Main, West Germany, the location of the European headquarter of Remington. There, Remington engineers overhauled the computer and refurbished it in the beginning of 1966. Meanwhile, the East German Ministry of Finance sent GDR engineers and programmers to Frankfurt for training. All Stasi-approved for travels, they were taught by Remington technicians in usage and programming of the machine. As multipliers, they should afterwards teach GDR workers the basics of the Digital Age [33]. After refurbishment, the computer was then sent to Berlin by truck and crossed the border between capitalism and socialism. After the U.S. military took the computer out of service, it began a new life in East Berlin. According to my thesis, the computer import enabled a total of 30 employees to prepare the introduction of EDP in the financial bodies.

Historians argue about the effect of CoCom restricting computer technology exports [2].[9] The complicated paths of the UCT II suggest, on the one hand, that the export was not a matter of course for GDR's Ministry of Finance. While computer technology producers hoped for high gains in Eastern Europe, the U.S. government especially saw the danger of a computer-armed socialism after the Cold War extended on the battlefield of the economy. Ways to circumvent the embargo existed, especially because of reluctant British and French governments to obey the restrictions [2]. However, serious hurdles complicated the process for import users as well as for export firms. More than once, this restricted an export at all until 1965 (see Table 1). In the course of 1965, spaces for export to Eastern Europe opened up step by step. Notwithstanding, foreign trade officers applied some atrocities to make such deals more difficult. In the case of the UCT II, they allowed the export of the machine and its peripherals. These were the most valuable components, so their export guaranteed high profits to the producers. In contrast to that, officials restricted the export of smaller parts like a processor module to upgrade the speed of the machine or like the 500 magnetic tapes ordered by the Ministry. Despite the low value of these parts, they were

---

[9] See Leslie, "From CoCom to Dot-Com", this volume.

indispensable for the usage of the machine. The GDR was not capable of producing their own magnet tapes yet [34]. Without the magnetic tapes, the UCT II was doomed to idleness and the computer could only be used rudimentary in the first months after its delivery [31]. Only after harsh protests on the GDR side the parts were delivered by Univac. The willful delay of these parts is a good example for the implementation of the CoCom embargo.

Despite the embargo, economic gains were valued higher than possible loss of security by the Western side since 1965. Nevertheless, that did not mean that no security measures were taken. Both sides addressed security issues in this highly sensitive import. Exporting the computer to the GDR, the U.S. side probably added surveillance mechanisms to the computer. GDR technicians who installed the UCT II in Berlin detected irregularities in the computer and bugs. Therefore, it was checked by the State Security Service, who claim to have found several espionage devices in the computer [26]. Stasi officers also briefed every technician and programmer traveling to Frankfurt am Main. For example, they approved only those who were married and politically reliable. The Western side acted likewise. Their State Security Services briefed every technician traveling to the GDR [26] or used them to enforce embargo rules.

The Appendix presents a unique data set of imported computers in the GDR in the 1960s. Based on this data, it is possible to evaluate the regime's import efforts and the flow of foreign computers – not only from IBM, but from many other European companies ranging from Zuse to Bull. Despite strong efforts of IBM to sell 1401 computers to the East Bloc, the GDR officially did not import a single IBM machine until 1968. Only in the background, their engineers conducted research on IBM machines to copy them as well as their operating system. The change towards IBM was made not before 1968, but then full-fledged. Only with the support of GDR programmers, the East got a hand on the operating system of IBM – a reason for the Soviet Union, besides own developments, to choose an IBM architecture for the Unified System of Electronic Computers (ES EVM).

4 Kickstarting the Socialist EDP Program: How GDR's Financial Sector Adapted the Import Computer

It is important to continue analyzing a computerization case after installation. Often, the interesting stories about the impact of computers on users lurk beyond the initial excitement. Stories about first computers describe them more as symbols of modernism and progress than as working machines. This hides the interaction between users and technology. Investigating how the computer actually was used shows a lot about social and economic interaction with information technology. This especially holds true in the case of an import. The foreign machine had to be adapted to local circumstances. Local circumstances had to be adapted to the foreign machine, mainly through software. Therefore, the whole lifecycle of a computer from its design, production, delivery, testing, operation and usage, maintenance, upgrading till scraping and dismantling needs to be addressed [7, pp. 3–7, 207–229]. Afterward, the question of how the computer was or is remembered provides additional insight about the character of former usages [7, p. 259]. After being in use for the U.S. army, the UCT II began a second life in the GDR.

In December 1966, the UCT II finally was delivered. Five months later, in April 1966, East German Minister Willy Rumpf officially opened the first computer center of the Ministry of Finance. After months of preparation, he pushed the button that metaphorically let the computer began to calculate (see Fig. 1). The bulbs of the UCT II happily flashed in rhythm of the processor. This opening ceremony was screened on television at prime time: the most important news broadcast in GDR television called *Aktuelle Kamera* reported a whole minute about the opening of the data center on 26 April [35]. It covered the ceremony, but also the inner life of a computer center.

Fig. 1. Minister of Finance Willy Rumpf at the opening of the computer center, Berlin 1966 [36].

The commentator explained in an easy language the purpose and capabilities of the newly installed computer facility. In long scenes, rotating magnetic tapes, punched card readers and printers were shown. The goal of the screening clearly was to show the future of socialism connected to computers. Not a single word was said on the type of computer nor about its origin. More important for the newsmaker was the fact that the computer center acted as a prototype for the fifteen centers to be built all over the republic. Furthermore, the personnel for these centers should be educated in the Berlin facility, ranging from programmers to data typists. Socialist men and women were shown how they unanimously working on the future of socialism.

In the following paragraphs, I show how the financial sector tried to use the UCT II computer to kickstart its EDP program. Their workers adapted the technology and knowledge transferred from the West to the socialist circumstances. Then, they distributed it through multiplicators like those people shown in TV. Already through this very appearance in the news, the computer was taken out its original context and framed anew in the Socialist State. Looking at the challenges the technicians and programmers had to overcome in this process provides a clearer picture of how technology transfer in the Cold War between East and West worked, as well as an insight into the operation of early digital computers in Eastern European countries in the 1960s.

4.1   Installation of the UCT II: Adapting the Computer to Local Conditions

Installing a computer of that size was something completely different than known before in the Ministry of Finance. The workers of the Ministries Institute for Financial Economics, who were in charge of that task, had gained knowledge on how to build central data gathering offices. However, installing a computer was more like a mix of setting up an assembly line in a factory and a control room of a railway station simultaneously. One of the main goals of the Ministry importing a computer was to acquire expertise in setting it up. Consequently, the months until the computer could be productively used were not as smooth as the television images might suggest. According to my main argument, the Institute's workers adapted the computer to local conditions. First of all, the Institute had to find a building to host the computer. In the GDR's economy of scarcity, space also was scarce. Originally, the Institute intended to set up the computer in a building on the main street Unter den Linden between Brandenburg Gate and the future Berlin TV-tower. Negotiations failed, so they had to find new premises. Finally, they chose an old building on Otto-Nuschke-Straße,[10] just parallel to the newly erected Berlin Wall in the very city center [26] (see Fig. 2). The location chosen for installing the computer underscores the importance it had for the Ministry of Finance. The pulse of electronic calculations of financial transactions beat in the heart of the capital.

In contrast to later computer projects, the Ministry of Finance did not erect a new building that suited the needs of the computer but repurposed an old house where previously a bar was located. Repurposing the rooms to the needs of a computer meant heavy reconstruction: the technicians laid a double floor for taking the cables to the machine room, fortified the ceilings to carry the immense weight of the machine and its peripherals, and installed noise-reducing walls. In addition, the ministry imported air conditioners from Switzerland as well as a power generator to guarantee perfect environmental conditions for the computer. The biggest challenge of adaptation for the technicians posed the fact that the U.S. computer ran on a 60 Hz electricity supply. The

---

[10] Today, Otto-Nuschke-Straße in Berlin is called Jägerstraße.

Fig. 2. UCT II in the computer center of the Ministry of Finance, Berlin 1966 [36].

GDR's electricity frequency was 50 Hz. Therefore, a unique electricity supply with a converter was installed. Separated rooms for reading and archiving of paper tape and of magnetic tape had to be equipped as well as for the personnel.

Workers began repurposing the building months before the delivery. This process already took place in close communication between Univac experts and GDR technicians. While setting up the building, the Ministry did not prioritize security concerns. Instead, they regarded measures that guaranteed a working computer more important. That the ministry acted very differently in later projects shows the kickstarting and learning characteristics of this early installation.

A flow of ideas, data carrier, and people accompanied the physical transfer of electromechanical parts between East and West. They were indispensable for the adaptation. At the end of September 1965, even before the import computer was delivered, Minister Rumpf visited the computing center under construction. Overall, he was satisfied with the progress of work but suggested a number of changes to intensify the preparation. Rumpf clearly noticed that the computer center lacked skilled workers as well as software to integrate the machine to the routines of socialist finance. He did not only demand organizational measures such as an overview of machine utilization but also an active knowledge transfer. Because his staff had already intensively studied the experiences of western savings banks, he set up a lecture devoted explicitly to the question of electronic data processing in savings banks operations. The "programs" of the Savings Banks in Saarbrücken, Vienna and Hamburg were evaluated, adapted to socialist conditions and communicated far beyond savings banks workers. For example, between 1965–1966 two authors from the Ministry of Finance wrote a manual for computer usage in savings banks that was a clear copy of the Saarbrücken manual (original: [37], adaptation: [38]).

Furthermore, the computer center achieved an adaptation of the computer to local conditions by programming. This also was enabled by knowledge transfer. Remington Ranc provided programming support as part of the contract. Therefore, GDR programmers did not only travel to Frankfurt am Main for taking seminars, but Remington consultants also came to the GDR. This was not restricted by CoCom nor by Stasi. It was even supported from the Western side as they could evaluate the civil computer use through their own technicians [2, p. 141]. A Univac instructor travelled to Erfurt and gave courses for people of the computer center for financial services as well as for programmers from Optima in 1966 [27]. Rumpf's inspection and the following consequences are a telling example for the knowledge transfer between East and West.

In the adaptation process, the data center employees connected foreign knowledge with local knowledge entities. For example, the Ministry of Finance pulled off a coup to support the work of their young computer center. Rumpf managed to lure away Wilhelm Pohle from Carl Zeiss Jena, one of the developers of the first mass-produced computer of the GDR. Pohle managed the transition from analog to digital banking at the newly erected computer center. He was one of the people travelling to Frankfurt am Main. Afterward, he trained GDR technicians the maintenance and repair of the UCT II [26]. Wilhelm Pohle is a perfect example for how foreign knowledge was adapted from the West, and how it was integrated with local expertise. Pohle built up the first computer center in the financial sector together with others from the top management of the Institute for Financial Economics. More than once, they relied on their knowledge acquired in West-Germany, combining it with their engineering spirit of the GDR [39].

4.2 Early Use: The UCT II as the Data Processing Power Horse of the Ministry of Finance

In the months following the grand opening, the UCT II became the power horse of data processing at the Ministry of Finance. It was used together with an older Univac 1004 as front-end processor. It calculated everything from transactions to savings, from account numbers to interest. Computing time was seen as a valuable resource, so officials tried to use the machine to the maximum without overloading it. All institutions under the ministry tried to get a hold on the machine. Four main projects were tested or productively run on the machine: a project on settling and clearing giro funds transfer transactions between companies and citizens in Berlin, ranging from the State Bank and the Savings Bank of Berlin to the Agriculture Bank; a project on savings developed together with the Savings Bank of Berlin in 1967; a planning project on the national budged; and a project on pensions. All of the banking projects had experimental status but productive use on a limited scope.

The UCT was imported for programmers to write and test their programs. In the case of the digitalization of the savings project, they sort of fulfilled their task. In this project, the integration of the analog passbook and digital accounting was tested. They aimed to rationalize manual labor, ranging from counter service to interest calculations. It was a reaction on the users' behavior: initially, the Ministry of Finance planned to abandon passbooks as paper technology altogether. However, the customers were reluctant to change and kept their books. Therefore, the Ministry began to use the UCT II for this in early 1968 and ended the test phase in 1969. Based on already existing routines from the giro transaction program, programmers from the computer center wrote thousands of lines of code, preparing working routines and error handling. The tests not only affected the computer center, but also required interaction between them, the Savings Bank of Berlin, the employees and the customers. The results were positive. Minor calculation and organizational errors occurred without affecting compliance. Therefore, the parallel work of manual and automatic processing ceased. The computer alone processed 60,000 accounts from there on. Only because of insufficient capacity, the project was not expanded. At the end of 1969, all the basic testing was finished and the software for the digitalization of banking and finance was created by programmers [40, pp. 23–24].

4.3   Having Done the Job: Transition from UCT II to Robotron 300

In 1969, the Berlin computer center of the Ministry of Finance received their first three Robotron 300 computers. Now, programmers had to convert the projects written for the UCT II to the computers they were once intended for. Scaling programs always is a tricky thing in computer science. The Ministry of Finance and the GDR banks had to learn this the hard way. Since the beginning of that year, they had been working on transferring the programs from the UCT II. There were several reasons the conversion was done: higher cost-effectiveness through the use of self-produced machines, higher compatibility between them, the gain of practical experience with these machines in Berlin, and standardization of preparation and follow-up work. Ultimately, it was also done out of capacity reasons as no further computers would be imported for the financial sector.

In 1970, after the beginning of the transition, more and more production problems emerged. The imported UCT II had already been in operation for four years. Most of the time, it operated steadily. In 1970, it suddenly was working side by side with the R 300. Now, the data production had a much bigger scale which resulted in constant errors. Criticism of the results grew. The banks, savings banks, and financial authorities in Berlin criticized the way projects were processed, from giro payments to the state budget. The savings banks also criticized the quality of analyses carried out by the data center on the UCT II, such as savings statistics. The agricultural bank even preferred to work with programs of third-party stations because they proved more reliable. The general criticism was that the computer center delivered unpunctual and erroneous results. The worker of the computer center often blamed machine failures. When the supervisors checked, though, they realized that most of the time it was not the cause. Due to operating errors, tapes were read twice by mistake, operators used the wrong data, and the quality of digitized data sets were poor. Printing results were hardly legible. Results were sent to the wrong county. Salaries were calculated incorrectly and transferred because after digitization the data was not rechecked. In addition, during the transfer to the R 300, departments were not deleted from the UCT tape, so salaries were transferred twice [41]. What perfectly worked on a small scale on the UCT II caused huge problems on large scale. Without the experiences and software developed on the import machine, the project would have been doomed.

In late 1970, the government of the GDR was about to abandon the whole project because of these huge problems. However, through the personal engagement of banking employees, leaders and support from the highest ranks, the State Bank and the Ministry of Finance managed to find solutions. In their argument they used the UCT II as an example of hope. The computer center operated already in three-shift operation five days a week in 1970. It had a productive runtime of 70%. In September 1970, only 11% of machine time had to be used for repeating wrongly calculated results. Half of them were caused by technical errors, the other half out of operating errors. Robotron 300 stood still 22% of the time while the UCT II experienced only 11% standstill. The director of the Berlin computer center argued in front of the Ministry of Finance that this was due to longer qualification and greater experience of the UCT II shifts [41]. His argument countered the skepticism the new technology faced. The UCT II proved that computers could function in socialist finance. In the end, the state leaders trusted the capacities of the computer center. It would have been too late to change anyway.

4.4   Maintaining a Foreign Computer: How GDR Technicians Kept the UCT II Running

To evaluate the historic impact of technology over time, its maintenance comes into view. Technology should not be taken for granted once it is running [42, p. 4]. These efforts tell a story of how it was actually used, who had interests in it and in general about how computers, software, and people interacted. During its life cycle, the UCT II was maintained by GDR technicians with the support of Univac engineers. They regularly took care of the UCT II, changed parts, cleaned and checked the machine. Univac engineers repaired the machine if errors occurred the GDR technicians could not solve. A former GDR technician remembers: "We had no problems with Univac. They always provided spare parts. They came over to us regularly. That was an incredibly good service" [26]. Maintenance was a tricky business because the party executives demanded high usage rates and production of financial data was time sensitive. Most of the time, maintenance was done in the middle of the night or in the early morning when the banking transactions had not yet come in. Looking at maintenance also brings to the fore the physicality of the foreign machine that was black boxed for customers as well as banking clerks by the party leaders. The highly complex digital computer still was a mechanical thing in many instances. An example for the manual treatment of the machine – not necessarily for a culture clash between Western and Eastern approaches – was a power loss a former GDR technician reported:

> Once, there was no power on the 1004. What did Theo [his head of department] do? He took a hammer and banged it. Then, everything was all right again. The error never occurred again. He said I've done that before. Me and my boss with our diploma stood there amazed. We had measured, we did this and that but the guy just hit it with a hammer and it worked again! [26]

Nevertheless, selling only one old machine was not the business model Univac was aiming at. Rather, they hoped to sell more and newer machines once their socialist customers were locked into their system. The hurdles of the transition from one system to another were already described before. Therefore, Univac technicians often were accompanied by salespeople. They did not only ask for missing spare parts, they were highly interested in further demands of their customers. They always tried to sell more computers in the eastern countries; that was their philosophy.

Meanwhile, Univac delivered the backup UCT II to Optima Erfurt. Berlin technicians had intensive communication with those at the Erfurt center. This second computer was used as a backup only once; most of the time, it served normal productive use. In 1971, just months after the transition to Robotron 300 was completed, a problem in the magnetic tape archive occurred. An operator had accidentally overwritten parts of the primary magnetic tape that contained all the service routines necessary for production. Other parts of the tape had errors. When using the replacement tapes, the responsible personnel realized that all three generations of the magnetic tape had been lost. The first backup tape was handed over to a programmer who overwrote it during test work. The second magnetic tape stored in another building was nowhere to be found. With considerable effort, the magnetic tape was finally restored from the VEB Optima backup system. Until then, production had to be stopped and the results were delivered with a delay of six hours. The conclusions to prevent such an accident were subsequently implemented on the R 300 [43].

4.5   The Process of Aging: Use of the UCT II After It Fulfilled Its Task

With the delivery of the R 300, the UCT II got new neighbors. These were installed in a building specially erected for them, while the UCT II stayed at Otto-Nuschke-Street. The latter was imported to prepare the scene for these computers, but was not out of fashion, yet. Employees wholeheartedly called her "the old lady" [44], as it was now nearly ten years old. Even so, some still perceived it as a better computer than their own R 300. This might be explained by the long experiences gathered with the machine, and also by the personal ties people developed to a machine they worked with so many years. Apparently, serious problems with the UCT II import system occurred for the first time in 1972. The director of the computer center reported that the production goals were difficult to achieve with the machine. Therefore, the Ministry of Finance ordered a separate test of the machine's performance and a comparison with that of VEB Optima. Then it should be decided whether the UCT II was about to be finally replaced or not [45]. Step by step also the smaller programs were transferred to the R 300 computers. Left without cause, the UCT II was mainly used by programmers for testing. However, it still took some years until it was replaced. Finally, it was deconstructed as the new Robotron 4000 was installed in late 1970s. The new machine literally took the place of the UCT II, as it was installed in the very same premises using the infrastructure already in use. The import computer was dismantled and scraped.

5   Conclusion

Following the traces of a computer through the Iron Curtain highlights three important points. First of all, it shows how CoCom embargo was effective in the 1960s, but left spaces of transfer and exchange for ideas as well as for computer technology. GDR engineers and programmers even were sent to West Germany; as well, Univac technicians regularly traveled to the GDR. The countries participating in CoCom did not regard this as breaking the embargo, but rather as a vital part of it enforcing control over exported equipment. However, the import did not necessarily mean a pure take-over of technology. The Ministry of Finances employees adapted the computer through software to their own socialist needs. They kickstarted their distinct EDP program with this Western import. Since 1970, they migrated the developed software to their native Robotron 300s. Then, they widely distributed it to the 15 data centers for financial services in administrative areas. The demand in the East and the interests in profits especially by smaller producers besides IBM fueled a cross-border exchange. That these spaces behind the so-called "Iron Curtain" extended around 1965 points to a policy change in the U.S. as well as to a new openness towards foreign (computer) technology in Moscow and East-Berlin. It is important to note that this change affected all of Eastern Europe and is indicating a broader trend.

Second, I showed how these import processes began already before 1968 and did not only focus on the U.S. This enabled me to establish a different perspective to the existing literature. Especially, banking officials rather looked to West Germany for how to use a computer than to the USA. Furthermore, technical experts and leading managers of the GDR also had a close look on other socialist countries to develop a distinct path to information age. While the computer industries in Eastern Europe might be a special case, computer users in state companies and state institutions not only trusted IBM or Univac, but were inspired by other users' programs, for example of the Savings Bank of Saarbrücken. This also resulted in a change of language, as regular computer users and technicians adapted English terms like "software" or "computer" and continued to use it besides official language regulations.

Third, IBM computers did not even make it into the top three of list of the Ministry of Finance for import. In contrast to the current state of knowledge, this clearly shows that IBM did not dominate the Eastern Europe computing scene until 1968–1969 [4, pp. 34–35].[11] It rather was a competitive situation under CoCom rulings in which all western producers from West Germany, France, Great Britain, the United States and even Japan tried their luck. But it was not a tabula rasa, as the Soviet Union, Czechoslovakia, Poland and the GDR already were developing distinct concepts of a socialist information age [9, 46].

This openness lasted until the beginning of the 1970s when the contract on the "Unified System of Electronic Computers" (ES EVM) was ratified and the combine Robotron was forged. While Cain argues that since the 1970s western computer exports "flooded" Eastern Europe, this thesis needs precise distinctions. While some bigger combines of the GDR longed for faster computers from the West, the financial system of the GDR based their services on self-produced computer technology for decades. Confronted with in an incompatible collage of imported systems resulting of this new openness, officials tightened liberties and centralized all import negotiations in the hands of the so-called "Schalck commission". This commission was subordinated under the Ministry of Foreign Trade but enjoyed close contact to the Ministry of State Security. From 1969 on, their officials forcefully orientated the development towards

---

[11] Doing and other are mentioning various computer imports from Bull, National Elliot, Siemens, Zuse, Univac and others until 1966. Even though, the literature estimated IBM's influence between 1964-1967 much higher so far.

computers from socialist origins. This has to be interpreted in the bigger process of institutions struggling with the results of the first phase of computerization termed "software crisis": the lack of productivity increases through computing, rising incompatibilities, failing software projects and sky-rocketing development and maintenance costs.

The closing remarks of Günther Mittag, Economic Secretary of the Central Committee of the SED, on a conference in Dresden on January 31th 1969 are exemplary for this change. He extensively criticized intellectual orientation toward U.S. solutions in computing. In his opinion, this was an ideological ambiguity dangerous for the GDR. In the following, the party corrected the development program, limited liberties, tried to regulate official language and implemented changes of management personnel [47], [48, p. 17]. This change resulted in a focus on native hardware for the financial institutions of the GDR. Nevertheless, they hold tight contacts especially to West Germany in software development and the possible usages of computers in banking.

Acknowledgement. I am thankful for the valuable feedback on this article by Christopher Neumeier, my three peer-reviewers, and the fruitful discussion at the WCC 2018 in Poznán. Also, I am grateful for Maren Rohleder's grammar and language checks.

Appendix: Computer Imports into the GDR, 1956–1970

Table 1. Computer imports into the GDR, 1956–1970. Overview of selected acquisition and inventory. Source: own compilation.

Year	Organization	Type	Origin	Application
1959	Academy of Science, Berlin	URAL-1	SU	Training and education in EDP; imported from the Soviet Union against the will of the Planning Commission
1962	State Planning Commission	Bull Gamma 3 ET	F	Economic-mathematical modelling of the economy that were not possible with punch card technology
1963	Institute for Applied Mathematics, Berlin	URAL-1	SU	Scientific calculations
1965	VEB Electronic Computing Machines, Karl-Marx-Stadt	NCR 315	USA	Testing of basic programs for the whole economy, especially for the industry. Imported for preparing the introduction of the Robotron 300 computer
-	Ministry of State Security	2x Bull Gamma 10	F	Import request and delivery already in 1964; used for border control

(*continued*)

Table 1. (*continued*)

Year	Organization	Type	Origin	Application
-	Institute for Data Processing, Dresden	National Elliot 503	GB	
-	Ministry of Finance/State Bank	UCT II Univac 1004	USA	Mainly used for payment processing & planning optimization; delivered at the end of December 1965; 3-shift operation
1966	Ministry of Finance	Bull Gamma 10	F	Economic calculations, mainly of prices
-	Ministry of Basic Materials Industry	ZAM 2	PL	Evidence of inventory
-	Ministry of Ore Mining, Metallurgy and Potash	ZAM 2	PL	Evidence of inventory
-	Ministry of Chemical Industry	Zuse Z25 Univac 1004 Elliott Arch 2000	FRG USA GB	Evidence of inventory
-	Ministry of Electronics	NCR 315 Univac 1004 National Elliot 503 Librascope LGP 21	USA USA GB USA	Evidence of inventory
-	Ministry of Transport	Minsk 22	SU	Evidence of inventory
-	Ministry of Trade and Supply:	Siemens 3003	FRG	Evidence of inventory
-	Academy of Science, Berlin	Odra 1003	PL	Evidence of inventory
-	Ministry for Inner German trade	3x Gamma 10/30	F	Evidence of inventory
-	State Head Office for Statistics	7 x Gamma 10	F	Evidence of inventory
-	State Planning Commission	Gamma 10	F	
-	VEB Optima, Erfurt	Univac UCT II	USA	Used as a substitute in the case of damage of the UCT II of the Ministry of Finance
-	VEB Carl Zeiss, Jena	ICT 1900	GB	Import affirmed already in 1964

(*continued*)

Table 1. (*continued*)

Year	Organization	Type	Origin	Application
-	VEB Leuna-Factory "Walter Ulbricht"	CDC 3000er	USA	Included training and education in Frankfurt (Main)
-	Ministry of State Security	Bull GE 100	F/USA	Surveillance, border control
1967	College for Transport, Dresden	Minsk 22	SU	
1968	VEB Maschinelles Rechnen, Dresden	Bull Gamma 10	F	Regional Computer Center working mainly for forestry and other mid-small companies, also used for education and training; 2-shift operation
-	VEB Maschinelles Rechnen, Berlin	Ural-14	SU	Regional Computer Center. also used for education and training
-	Funkwerk, Berlin-Köpenick	Odra 1013	PL	
-	EVW Schwedt	Process Computer		Evidence of inventory
-	Ruhla-Watches	2x Gamma 10	F	Evidence of inventory
1969	VEB Combine for Construction, Berlin	IBM 360/40	USA	Calculations for city planning
-	Mail-Order House, Leipzig	IBM 360/40	USA	Logistics
-	Aluminium factory Rackwitz	Dnepr II		
-	N.N.	2x CDC 3300	USA	Supposedly imported, used by huge combines
-	N.N.	ICL 1905	USA	Supposedly imported, used by huge combines
1970	Institute for High Energy Physics	BESM 6 SIEMENS 4004/26	SU FRG	Combined with a SIEMENS 4004/26 for I/O
-	Ministry of State Security	3x Siemens 4004/45	FRG	Imported in the name of the State Institute for Information and Documentation
-	N.N.	Siemens 4004/45	FRG	Supposedly imported, used by huge combines
-	Computer Center Neubrandenburg	Ural-14	SU	Take-over of a used machine, supposedly from Berlin
-	N.N.	7x IBM 360/40	USA	Supposedly imported, used by huge combines

(*continued*)

Table 1. (*continued*)

Year	Organization	Type	Origin	Application
-	N.N.	2x IBM 360/30	USA	Supposedly imported, used by huge combines
-	N.N.	2x DDP-516	USA	Supposedly imported
-	N.N.	ICL 4/50	GB	Supposedly imported, used by huge combines

References

1. Zentralkomitee der DDR der SED: Programm zur Entwicklung, Einführung und Durchsetzung der maschinellen Datenverarbeitung in der DDR in den Jahren 1964–1970, 23 June 1964. BArch DY30/J IV 2/2–1035
2. Cain, F.: Computers and the cold war: united states restrictions on the export of computers to the soviet union and communist China. J. Contemp. Hist. **40**(1), 131–147 (2005)
3. Ministerium der Finanzen: Niederschrift über die Unterredung des Sekretärs des Ministeriums der Finanzen mit dem Generaldirektor der Büromaschinen-Export GmbH am 20.1.1965, 02 February 1965. BArch DN 1/17445
4. Donig, S.: Appropriating american technology in the 1960s: cold war politics and the GDR computer industry. IEEE Ann. Hist. Comput. **32**, 32–45 (2010)
5. Schlombs, C.: Engineering international expansion: IBM and Remington Rand in European computer markets. IEEE Ann. Hist. Comput. **30**(4), 42–58 (2008)
6. Schlombs, C.: Productivity machines: transatlantic transfers of computing technology and culture in the Cold War. Ph.D., University of Pennsylvania, Ann Arbor (2010)
7. Haigh, T., Priestley, M., Rope, C.: ENIAC in Action: Making and Remaking the Modern Computer. The MIT Press, Cambridge; London 2016
8. Ensmenger, N.: The Computer Boys Take Over: Computers, Programmers, and the Politics of Technical Expertise. The MIT Press, London (2010)
9. Tatarchenko, K.: A House with the Window to the West: The Akademgorodok Computer Center (1958–1993). Princeton University, Princeton (2013)
10. Tatarchenko, K.: "The computer does not believe in tears": soviet programming, professionalization, and the gendering of authority. Kritika: Explor. Russ. Eurasian Hist. **18**(4), 709–739 (2017)
11. Cortada, J.W.: Information technologies in the German Democratic Republic. IEEE Ann. Hist. Comput. **34**(2), 34–48 (2012)
12. Stokes, R.G.: Constructing Socialism: Technology and Change in East Germany 1945–1990. Johns Hopkins University Press, Baltimore (2000)
13. Steiner, A.: The Plans That Failed: An Economic History of the GDR. Berghahn Books, New York (2010)
14. Steiner, A.: Die DDR-Wirtschaftsreform der sechziger Jahre: Konflikt zwischen Effizienz- und Machtkalkül. Akademie Verlag, Berlin (1999)
15. Peters, B.: How Not to Network a Nation: The Uneasy History of the Soviet Internet. MIT Press, Cambridge (2016)
16. Loll, F.: Der Untergang der DDR aus der Sicht ihrer EDV-Berichterstattung. Bastelzwang und Softwareklau. Die ZEIT, Hamburg, 22 September 1995

17. Sobeslavsky, E., Lehmann, N.J.: Zur Geschichte von Rechentechnik und Datenverarbeitung in der DDR 1946-1968. Hannah-Arendt-Institut für Totalitarismusforschung, Dresden (1996)
18. Schmitt, M.: The code of banking. Software as the Digitalization of German Savings Banks. In: Tatnall, A., Leslie, C. (Hgg.): International Communities of Invention and Innovation, New York, pp. 141–164 (2016)
19. Finanzökonomisches Forschungsinstitut beim Ministerium der Finanzen, Sektor Maschinelles Rechnen, 'Vorlage über den Import einer mittleren elektronischen Datenverarbeitungsanlage für das Finanzökonomische Forschungsinstitut beim Ministerium der Finanzen. BArch DN 1/17445 (1964)
20. Staatliche Plankommission: Anordnung über die Ordnung der Verfahrensweise beim Import von elektronischen Rechen- und Datenverarbeitungsanlagen und Lochkartenmaschinen vom 21.06.1965. GBl. II, no. 66, pp. 492–494, June 1965
21. Staatliche Plankommission, Kommission 'Maschinelle Datenverarbeitung', 'Protokoll der 2. Sitzung der Kommission "Maschinelle Datenverarbeitung", 06 January 1965. BArch DN 1/17287
22. Haigh, T.: The chromium-plated tabulator: institutionalizing an electronic revolution, 1954–1958. IEEE Ann. Hist. Comput. **23**(4), 75–104 (2001)
23. Ministerium der Finanzen, Abteilung Datenverarbeitung: Niederschrift über die 8. Sitzung des Beitrates für Datenverarbeitung, 03 October 1968. BArch DN 1/38310
24. Brüll, K.: Eine kleine Zeitreise durch die Geschichte vom VEB Datenverarbeitung der Finanzorgane (2008)
25. Schmitt, M., Hennig, U.: Interview "Projektorganisation und Koordination für die Finanzorgane der DDR", 02 July 2018
26. Schmitt, M., Löwenstein, W., Bartusch, M.: Interview "VEB Datenverarbeitung der Finanzorgane", 12 July 2018
27. Schmitt, M., Wolff, D.: Interview "Programmierung für die Finanzorgane der DDR", 26 June 2018
28. Bergien, R.: Programmieren mit dem Klassenfeind. Die Stasi, Siemens und der Transfer von EDV-Wissen im Kalten Krieg. Vierteljahrshefte für Zeitgeschichte, vol. 67, no. 1, pp. 1–30 (2019)
29. Finanzökonomisches Forschungsinstitut beim Ministerium der Finanzen, Datenverarbeitungszentrum: Bericht zum Erfahrungsaustausch über Fragen der elektronischen Datenverarbeitung mit der Polnischen Nationalbank im Oktober 1965, 30 October 1965. BArch DN 6/3318
30. Bruderer, H.: Erfindung des Computers, Elektronenrechner, Entwicklungen in Deutschland, England und der Schweiz, vol. 2/2. De Gruyter Oldenbourg, Boston (2018)
31. Ministerium der Finanzen, Rumpf, W.: Schreiben Willy Rumpfs an den Ministerpräsidenten Willi Stoph vom 9.2.1966: Durchführung des Beschlusses über die Einführung der elektronischen Datenverarbeitung in der DDR, 09 February 1966. BArch DN 1/13451
32. Paloque-Berges, C., Alberts, G.: Beyond the protocol wars: 1980s user cultures in Dutch internet nodes. Conference talk, Lugano, 14 December 2017
33. Ministerium der Finanzen, Datenverarbeitungszentrum der Finanzorgane: Aktenvermerk: Arbeitsräume, 07 December 1965. BArch DN 1/17439
34. Köhler, K.: Entwicklung und Produktion von Magnetbändern für die elektronische Datenverarbeitung in der DDR. Jenaer Jahrbuch zur Technik- und Industriegeschichte **9**, 209–228 (2006)
35. Aktuelle Kamera: Einweihung von Datenverarbeitungszentrum in Berlin. Aktuelle Kamera, DFF-1, 26 April 1966. DRA ID 325585

36. Re: Finanzorgane erhielten Datenverarbeitungszentrum. Deutsche Finanzwirtschaft, vol. 20, no. 11, p. 23 (1966)

37. Hupp, R., Mohm, W.: Elektronische Datenverarbeitung im Sparkassenbetrieb. Dargestellt und erläutert am Verfahren der Kreissparkasse Saarbrücken, vol. 1/2. Deutscher Sparkassen-verlag, Stuttgart (1964)

38. Jähn, S., Sinnig, K., Weißbach, G.: Elektronische Datenverarbeitung für die Sparkassen der Deutschen Demokratischen Republik, vol. 1/2. Ministerium d. Finanzen, Sektor Sparkassen, Berlin (1967)

39. Augustine, D.L.: Red Prometheus: Engineering and Dictatorship in East Germany, 1945–1990. Massachusetts (2007)

40. Ministerium der Finanzen, Abteilung Rationalisierung und Datenverarbeitung, Magistrat von Groß-Berlin, Abteilung Finanzen: Plan der Einsatzvorbereitung und der Organisation des Übergangs zur elektronischen Datenverarbeitung für die zentralen und örtlichen Finanz- und Bankorgane in der Hauptstadt der DDR, Berlin, 15 July 1969. BArch DN 1/16993-3

41. Ministerium der Finanzen, Abteilung Informationssystem und Datenverarbeitung: Lage im VEB Datenverarbeitungszentrum - zusammengefasste Darstellung, 20 February 1970. BArch DN 1/17439

42. Fidler, B., Russel, A.: Infrastructure and maintenance at the defense communications agency: recasting computer networks in histories of technology (preprint). Technol. Cult. **59** (4) (2018)

43. VEB Datenverarbeitung der Finanzorgane, Inspektion: Vorläufiges Untersuchungsergebnis der Ursachen der Zerstörung aller (3) Generationen des Sammelbandes der Serviceroutine (SEBBA 01), 08 June 1971. BArch DN 1/17439

44. Ministerium der Finanzen: Berichte, Referate, Informationen, Vermerke zu EDV-Problemen für Partei, MR, Minister/Staatssekretär, Finanzrat, Bezirke und Sonstige (1965–1970). BArch DN 1/17437

45. Ministerium der Finanzen, Staatssekretär Kaminsky: Festlegungsprotokoll aus der Beratung am 12. Juli 1972 beim Staatssekretär, Genossen Kaminsky, 17 July 1972. BArch DN 1/17439

46. Paju, P., Durnová, H.: Computing close to the iron curtain: inter/national computing practices in Czechoslovakia and Finland, 1945–1970. Comp. Technol. Transf. Soc. **7**(3), 303–322 (2009)

47. Augustine, D.L.: Innovation and Ideology: Werner Hartmann and the Failure of the East German Electronics Industry. In: The East German Economy, 1945–2010: Falling Behind or Catching Up?, pp. 95–110. Cambridge University Press, New York; Cambridge; The German Historical Institute, Washington, D.C. (2013)

48. Merkel, G.: Institut für Datenverarbeitung. Ein Institut der VVB Datenverarbeitungs- und Büromaschinen. Dresden (2005)

Cooperating with Moscow, Stealing in California: Poland's Legal and Illicit Acquisition of Microelectronics Knowhow from 1960 to 1990

Mirosław Sikora[1,2](✉)

[1] Jagiellonian University, 31-007 Kraków, Poland
miroslaw.sikora@yandex.com
[2] Institute of National Remembrance, Regional Branch,
40-145 Katowice, Poland

Abstract. Electrical calculating machines were designed and manufactured in Poland in small quantities during the 1950s. However, it soon become clear to the government that an autonomous advance in that cutting-edge discipline was simply impossible. Therefore, throughout the 1960s, Polish authorities established various channels of obtaining access to software solutions, transistors and especially integrated circuits that seem to become standard for years to come. The way of adopting IT by communist Poland did not differ much from how it was done in USSR – according to the model described by Mastanduno. It was a smart combination of legal measures like the use of trade agreements, official scientific-technical cooperation and illicit operations run with help of intelligence assets like bribing or blackmailing officials and employees, establishing fake intermediating companies for purchasing embargoed dual-use items. Therefore, medium and large-scale-integration-technology as well as specific types of computers like mainframes, minicomputers and later PCs along with peripheral devices came to the Polish People's Republic through many routes. Moreover, Polish intelligence intensified its cooperation and information sharing with Soviet foreign intelligence service – like its counterparts in GDR, Hungary. etc. As a result, not only ties to the Western world were organized over and under the table, but also relationships with allies in Comecon were arranged in two dimensions. The case of Poland gives an excellent example of how schizophrenic the computer market under Comecon during the 1970s and 1980s was. This paper refers to the research project conducted by the author in the Institute of National Remembrance since 2011 and at the Jagiellonian University since 2018, entitled: "Scientific-technical intelligence of PPR: functions, organization, efficiency." In this contribution the author presents the outcomes of the analysis of the Polish archival sources completing them by foreign archives and secondary sources.

Keywords: CoCom · Cold War · COMECON (CMEA) · Industrial espionage · Poland · Technology transfer

© IFIP International Federation for Information Processing 2019
Published by Springer Nature Switzerland AG 2019
C. Leslie and M. Schmitt (Eds.): HC 2018, IFIP AICT 549, pp. 165–195, 2019.
https://doi.org/10.1007/978-3-030-29160-0_10

1   Introduction

In Poland, electrical calculating machines such as XYZ, EMAL and UMC were designed and constructed in small quantities during the 1950s under the supervision of mathematicians and engineers. Among them were professor Leon Łukaszewicz from the *Polish Academy of Sciences*, Romuald Marczyński from the *Institute of Nuclear Research* and Antoni Kiliński from the *Warsaw University of Technology*. In 1959, the first Polish computer factory Elwro in Wroclaw was established. After a couple of years of experiments with vacuum tube technology, it launched the production of famous "Odra" computers based on the transistor logic [1, 2]. Because of Cold War tensions, Polish scientists and managers did not have any significant access to western knowledge until the late 1950s. When the U.S. government started its so-called differential policy against Poland, they assumed that the thaw under Władysław Gomułka would stepwise bring the Polish state away from the communist camp [3].

Obtaining at least limited access to scientific-technical exchange programs with the USA and other Western countries through foreign scholarship programs like the British Council, DAAD, Humboldt Stiftung, Fort Foundation, Rockefeller Foundation and UN-endorsed international projects, the Polish government started to collect data on the current global development of computer science and engineering [4].

According to detailed analysis delivered by experts working for Polish ministries and think-tank institutes in the 1950s and 1960s, an autonomous advance in that cutting-edge discipline was simply impossible except for superpowers like the U.S. or the Soviet Union [5]. Therefore, throughout the 1960s, Polish authorities came up with various channels of obtaining access to computer technology solutions, especially transistors and integrated circuits that seemed to become standard for years to come. Moreover, embargo restrictions imposed by countries adhering to standards set by the Coordinating Committee for the Multilateral Export Controls (CoCom), on dual-use items,[1] including advanced microelectronics equipment and components that had both civilian and military purposes, did very soon make clear to Polish authorities that any significant progress in computer R&D without taking advantage of illicit measures was impossible. Therefore, already in the turn of 1950s and in the 1960s, the Polish intelligence service was charged with tasks of penetrating West European and American companies as well as smuggling embargoed solutions. The idea of intelligence involvement came from Moscow, where the foreign intelligence service had been used as a tool in the scientific-technical purposes of computer science since the early 1940s [6].

The author's point is to sketch four trajectories (routes) of computer science and equipment transfer that determined the Polish computer market during the Cold War next to the contribution of Polish scientists, engineers and managers. In the future, the author would like to try to determine which of those paths was most efficient, taking into consideration all constraints of that time like the Cold War, planned economy, Polish dependency on USSR, overall technological lag against the West, etc.

---

[1] See Leslie, "From CoCom to Dot-Com," this volume.

2 Methodology

This paper refers to the research project conducted by the author at the Institute of National Remembrance since 2011. After 2018, it has been supported by the National Science Center (NCN) and endorsed by Jagiellonian University, entitled: "Scientific-technical intelligence of PPR: functions, organization, and efficiency." The author analyses Polish, German, Russian and US archival resources and consults Polish specialists on IT who were insiders of PPR's computer industry during the 1970s and 1980s.

The core set of sources regarding the legal transfer of computer know-how and equipment to the Polish People's Republic (PPR) during the Cold War provides the heritage of the Polish Ministry of Machine Industry, since 1981 including metallurgy, responsible for the electronics branch of the industry [7, 8]. Furthermore, the records of the Committee for the Science and Technology [9] and its continuation as the Office for the Scientific-Technical Progress and Implementation [10], available in the Polish Central Archives for the Modern Records (Archiwum Akt Nowych – AAN) in Warsaw, provide insight into the Polish-Soviet high-tech exchange.

The mutual cooperation between Poland, Soviet Union and other states from the Committee for the Mutual Economic Assistance, also known as Comecon or CMEA can be reconstructed by the analysis of extensive reports produced annually by the various Comecon bodies [11]. Probably the best insight into the cooperation in the area of computers deliver documents of the *Permanent Committee for the Radio-technical and Electronics Industry* along with its many sub-committees, occupied with such narrow areas like only integrated circuits [12]. Finally, both the records of Soviet and Polish *Permanent Commissions to the Comecon* seem to be worth an investigation, although the latter are not yet available for the researchers. Comecon documents are stored and accessible in the *Russian State Archive of the Economy (Rossiyskiy Gosudarstvennyy Arkhiv Ekonomiki*, or RGAE).

These sources can be effectively extended by inclusion of domestic documents produced by other Comecon members, though the linguistic obstacle seems to be crucial here. The author was able to investigate only the files produced by GDR, both those documenting official and legal aspects of mutual contacts between Poland and East-Germany in the area of computers [13] and those produced by intelligence services involved in clandestine intelligence share [14].

The hidden, clandestine, illicit dimension of the Polish computer industry and its research and development (R&D) efforts reflects itself in the files, records and cables of Polish foreign intelligence service, in particular, in its branch assigned to the gathering of scientific-technical data in almost every discipline of science. Records available nowadays in the *Archive of the Institute of National Remembrance* (IPN) in Warsaw cover the period of time from early 1950s till the 1990s. Documents are, however, unequally distributed over this time span, in the way that their number is increasing along with the time they are referring to. Hence, insight into the 1980s and 1970s is much better than into the 1960s and 1950s. Such a trend results partly from the procedure of destruction of old documents considered as useless. That was taking place on a regular basis every five or ten years in the intelligence archive.

Unfortunately, such an asymmetry is found just in opposite to the common archival resources in the West, which complicates any attempts of comparative studies. For instance, one can learn a lot from the files stored in the *National Archives and Records Administration/NARA* in College Park, Maryland of such U.S. agencies as the *International Trade Administration* (ITA) linked to the *Department of Trade*. Among them especially from the *Bureau of Foreign Commerce – Office of Economic Affairs* and the *Bureau of East-West Trade – Office of Export Control*, as well as from records of *Department of State*. Nonetheless, the bulk of declassified files originate from the 1950s, 1960s, and to limited extent from the 1970s, while files from the 1980s cannot be accessed by historians as they are still classified.

3   Thesis

According to the author's hypothesis, the Polish state gained remarkable benefits from the outcomes of the scientific-technical intelligence (STI) operations and its cooperation with fraternal services in Comecon. Those "incomes" however – and this is the second part of the hypothesis – did not compensate shortages and failures of the Polish R&D that was forced to work within the constraints of the inefficient planned economy.

Despite of the general incapability to overcome the technological gap in the race with the West, scientific-technical intelligence was able to produce a significant impact on science and R&D in selected areas of microelectronics and IT. Due to the calculations of the powerful Polish intelligence service's chief Mirosław Milewski delivered to the government in the beginning of the 1970s, Polish scientific-technical intelligence had been helping to economize on an average of US$50 million annually and had been about to increase this capacity up to $100 million in 1975 [15]. Furthermore, as we can learn from a report produced in 1989, scientific-technical intelligence services had tried to capture with its clandestine methods solutions for the economy worth some US$300 to 500 million annually in the late 1980s [16]. Approximately half of those savings were in the domain of computing and automatic control systems.

In the course of the project, the author intends also to verify his hypothesis about the quantitative share and significance of both civil and military tasks in the agenda of scientific-technical intelligence related to computers during the examined period of time. According to this hypothesis, Polish scientific-technical intelligence contributed most of all to the civil economy and not to the military complex, as it was the case of the KGB and USSR. A contemporary notion about the *par excellence* military goals of the Polish scientific-technical intelligence is widespread among Polish historians. It derives from the influential works of the former collaborator of the scientific-technical intelligence in the U.S., the famous spy Marian Zacharski and his informant William Bell in Hughes Aircraft Corporation, California [17].

This study is not about how the Polish computer industry developed but where the inspirations, incentives and know-how embedded in components came from. Moreover, the project and this article skips the aspect of the massive legal and illegal transfer of (8-bit) personal computers allowed by CoCom to sell to Comecon during the second half of the 1980s. There are comprehensive studies published in this regard [18, 19].

4   Poland's Starting Position in the Computer Market

In the post-war period, electronic calculating machines were among the super-innovative fields of science and industry. Poland whereas – heavily destroyed during WWII – had to concentrate on the reconstruction and possible expansion of basic branches, such as heavy and chemical industries. Apart from computers, when it came to modern technologies, telecommunication and radio communication were of fundamental importance. One of the most crucial requirements of modernization was the construction of the land communication infrastructure and telephone networks. When considering Poland's position in terms of computerization, it is worth considering the backwardness of its telephone infrastructure in relation to the OECD zone, but also in relation to some Comecon countries. In 1961, the number of telephones per 100 inhabitants in Poland was just a bit over 3, while in Sweden it was 33, in the United Kingdom it was 16 and in East Germany it was 8 [20].

Poland's backwardness in telecommunication was only a part of the great challenge faced by the entire communist block and in particularly USSR, for instance while lunching works on All-State Automated System – so-called OGAS.[2] Regarding the improvement of data transfer and networking both in the societal and economic aspects [21], another challenge for the Polish industry was to supply domestic customers with a sufficient number of radio and land communication equipment operating in the ultra-short wave band, very high frequency. As indicated in an analysis of March 1966, there were about 3,000 mobile radio devices in operation in Poland, while demand in the years 1966–1970 amounted to about 40,000. Just for comparison, in the U.S. in 1965 there were 22 million such devices in operation. In West Germany there were 18,000 of them in 1960, aiming for 200,000 in 1970 [22].

It is difficult to assess today to what extent the authorities of the People's Republic of Poland in the second half of the 1940s were aware of the importance of computers for the country's economy. However, it is not impossible to draw conclusions on this issue. The analysis of the content of popular scientific magazines addressed especially to students, teachers, and engineers gives an idea of which disciplines of science and engineering and the branches of industry have become the subject of interest of journalists. Especially insightful are those entitled *Young Technician, Horizons of Technique* and *Horizons of Technique for the Youth*. Indeed, the 1950s brought a gradual increase in the number of articles on the logic of computers and cybernetics and their design like vacuum tubes and then transistors. The applications of computers in science, medicine, industry, transport and communication, robots including those equipped with artificial intelligence and automation systems were seen more widely [23–25].

Polish specialists were well aware of the economic effects of transistorization in the 1960s. That means the transition from vacuum tube systems to transistors/semiconductors in the manufacture of electronic equipment like radio and television sets, teletransmission equipment. In addition, while improving technical performance and reliability, miniaturization had also dramatically reduced production and operating

---

[2] See Kitov, "On the History of Gosplan," this volume.

costs. Above all, it contributed to reducing electricity usage by several times. In the first half of the 1960s government established specialized authorities (as plenipotentiary for electronic computing technique) to oversee development of young Polish computer industry and prepare long-term plans. In December 1965, the Minister of Heavy Industry, which was then in charge of electronics, instructed the Electronic and Telecommunications Industries Association (UNITRA) to set up a working group to develop a comprehensive transistorization program for electronic equipment in the years 1966–1970 within the entire national economy. Later on, UNITRA was divided into UNITRA and MERA companies. MERA was responsible for computers, automatic control and measurement equipment while UNITRA focused on RTV equipment and electronic components.

An extensive analysis carried out in 1966 by specialists of the electronics and telecommunications team of the Committee of Science and Technology (*Komitet Nauki i Techniki*, or KNiT) concluded that the level of production of semiconductors and electronic components in the PPR was five years behind in comparison to the leading countries. More worrying, however, was the fact that this distance was supposed to increase over the years to come [26].

The state of affairs outlined in the justification for the above resolution was at least disturbing. As estimated in 1965, a total number of about 9,400 computers were in operation in Europe, not including the Comecon countries. Meanwhile, there were barely 76 machines in operation in Poland, roughly the same number as in Ireland at that time. However, there were already 359 in Belgium and 1,610 in France; the highest number of calculating machines, 2,280, was recorded in West Germany [27].

Regarding the development of utilities and programming, Poland had to overcome various paradigms concerning the overall attitude to computers that ruled in USSR. There, computer usage focused on scientific research and military applications, instead of introducing computers into production facilities and in daily life. It is too early to apply Benjamin Peters's concept about the bureaucratic obstacles that impeded the development of computer networks in USSR to the Polish case [21]. The same holds true for Slava Gerovitch's claim of militarization and secretiveness in the Soviet computer program as a major mistake of the Soviet leadership [6]. The reception of cybernetics among Polish mathematicians and engineers in the post war decades never attracted larger attention of historians of technology and therefore still requires basic research.

The tasks set by the government for the Institute of Mathematical Machines in Warsaw and its branches in Krakow and Wroclaw in the mid-60s were quite ambitious. It was intended to design real-time management systems for enterprises and, in addition, to develop calculation methods for partial differential equations in areas such as physics, thermodynamics, flexibility theory, hydrodynamics and aerodynamics, as well as geophysics. The researchers were also asked to study topics such as computer behaviors in development of human psychological and physiological capabilities, programmed teaching, synthesis and analysis of sound in human-machine communication, and translation of foreign languages. Another intriguing problem was the modeling of natural, i.e., biological and atmospheric, and economic processes, i.e., production, investment and consumption plans [28].

At the end of the 1960s, there were also many evidences indicating that Polish authorities were eager to develop computer technology and were ready to look for solutions wherever it would be possible.

5   First Path: Learning and Buying from the West: 1950s–1970s

Since the mid 1950s, the Soviet Union and its satellites wanted to join global markets and were successful in many respects, for example in the export of natural resources and low advanced technologically goods [29]. They failed, however, to overcome the embargo umbrella set up by U.S. administration at the end of 1940s in order to contain Soviet progress in particular concerning atomic energy, the aerospace industry, and calculating machines along with automatic control systems [30].

During the first half of the 1950s, the U.S. and its allies formed CoCom, which launched the first series of restrictions on trade with USSR and its satellites. Over the next decades, other regulations followed limiting dissemination of strategic components, cutting-edge devices and know-how to the communist regimes, including China. However, in the late 1950s if not earlier, military considerations gradually gave way to economic calculations among the CoCom members. Especially, West European governments started to perceive Comecon countries as a promising market for certain – more or less advanced – commodities and technologies, also those of dual-use nature.

The so-called Polish differential in U.S. policy in the area of microelectronics had been launched gradually over the years 1956–1958 along with relaxation of embargo measures toward PPR and increasing willingness of the State Department to grant Poland with "exceptions" for dual-use items. This positive attitude ended abruptly in 1979 with the Export Administration Act, which embodied the end of détente with regard to scientific-technical cross-curtain cooperation.

According to the differential concept, certain solutions should have been shared with Poland as a reward for keeping its distance from the USSR. That approach did not prevent U.S. authorities from scrutinizing Polish requests for embargo "exceptions." The possible military use as well as leakage to USSR was thoroughly examined while checking Polish plants, R&D facilities and universities, submitting for licenses or commodities, especially regarding oscilloscopes and other testing and measurement equipment for the emerging Polish computer industry [31–33]. Sharing technology with Poland, though risky, was also regarded in Washington as a "gateway" leading into the Warsaw Pact; it enabled U.S. authorities to identify technical and further economic needs of PPR and Comecon as a whole.

As détente became a fact in the first half of the 1960s, frictions started to emerge not only in the forum of CoCom but also within individual countries. The U.S. State Department's or International Trade Administration's officials were often discussing whether it made sense to keep outdated solutions away from commerce with Comecon. In addition, British entrepreneurs representing the branch of computing and communication expressed their exasperation after having experienced that electronic items still "controlled" in their countries became meanwhile "decontrolled" in France and sold to Poland [34, 35]. With growing concern and jealousy, U.S. companies were observing the West German Grundig's efforts to build up bridgeheads behind the Iron Curtain [36] During the 1960s, the Polish state annually spent US$1–1.5 million to purchase electronics components for the Polish computer industry abroad and this funding seemed to grow rapidly [26].

It was in this context at the end of 1965, that the Committee for Foreign Trade (KWGzZ) ordered the creation of posts for employees to foster economic and scientific-technical cooperation at Polish diplomatic missions abroad. The tasks assigned to the newly appointed employees included informing KWGzZ:

> about the development trends and achievements of the economy, science and technology of the country of destination, about economic and scientific-technical plans and the way they were implemented, about the economic situation, organizational changes, etc., about economic and scientific-technical cooperation.

Subsequently, these experts were obliged to report to the KWGzZ on specific topics on which Poland could engage in cooperation. The day-to-day duties included reviewing professional periodicals, searching for symposia and congresses, fairs and exhibitions worth visiting by the Polish delegation, as well as supervising the course of internships and the stay of Polish scholarship holders, and exploring the possibility of obtaining scholarships and internships in the country's scientific and industrial centers of interest to the PPR, and finally coordinating the exchange of scientific and technical documentation between the countries [37]. Noteworthy is the list of basic areas of interest for 1967, annexed to the draft guidelines for employees for scientific-technical and economic contacts abroad. It covers 38 items which should be considered key from the point of view of the Polish economy at that time. In total, two major themes can be distinguished: the largest ones were electronics and automation, including production processes in almost every industry branch like energy, steel, chemical and food industries – a total of 10 topics. Furthermore, the chemical and biotechnological industry stood out, a total of 10 topics as well [38].

Taking advantage of scholarship programs, analysis of western press, and journals, as well as economic contacts of Polish embassies in the western countries, Polish think tanks were able to provide the government an extensive overview of trends in the U.S. and worldwide computer market. For instance, Polish engineer and famous computer constructor Jacek Karpiński visited MIT and Harvard University in the early 1960s [39]. Among the most influential computer experts in Poland was Adam Empacher, who worked for the Polish Center for Scientific-Technical and Economic Information (CINTE) in Warsaw. His early works from 1960 and 1965 included a profound analysis of American computer manufacturers and their products. It is, by the way, hard to believe that those works relied only on an analysis of open sources. Intelligence's involvement in providing some information for CINTE is highly likely [40].

Next to the purchase of equipment, Polish officials were inspired by numerous solutions and applications of computers developed in the West. A bold and innovative decision of the Polish government was the establishment of regional electronic computing plants (ZETO), which were to be equipped with computers designed for data processing for the needs of local institutions and state enterprises. The idea referred to the business developed in U.S. already in the 1950s – namely, leasing mainframes to companies or institutions that needed to process large amounts of data. The aim of Polish managers was to save up to 30% of the current expenditure on salaries, to reduce the consumption of raw materials, and to speed up the turnover cycle of funds in enterprises using such services [28] (Fig. 1).

Fig. 1. Polish-French cooperation in the area of automatic control. Prof. Stefan Węgrzyn (who eventually refused to cooperate with Polish intelligence) and Dr. Pierre Vidal in the early 1960s. Source: AIPN Katowice.

The successful introduction of various "Odra" series computers and measurement equipment into mass productions meant tens of computers annually but not hundreds. In the first half of the 1960s, Elwro became a flagship of the Polish computer industry. It was the only company permitted to run trade relationships with western countries by its own involving foreign currencies payments. In the second half of the 1960s, Poland purchased, implemented and even re-exported hardware like 1900 Elliott computers and software like the Operating System George 3 from the British company ICT (later ICL). Later on, Polish officials developed promising contacts with the French company Thomson. The contract with ICL was signed in 1967. It included know-how transfer to the Elwro factory that helped Polish engineers to construct Odra 1304 computers with knowledge of the Elliot ones. The British company did not share technical documents of the computer's manufacturing; nevertheless, technical documents of the Elliott 1904 logic as well as the software user manual passed to Elwro along with memory storage containing operational programs were enough to re-invent ("reverse engineer") and even improve the machine. Engineers translated George 3 into Polish and the resulting Odra turned out to be first computer produced worldwide to be fully compatible with another computer produced by a different company. The Odra 1304 was also a huge jump ahead regarding computer application. It was the first computer in Poland to be extensively used for data processing in various branches of economy, i.e., in factories, transportation and offices and not only in scientific calculations [41].

There were not so many similar achievements resulting from legal know-how transfer with the West. In the late 1960s, Poland signed a contract with French Thomson, obtaining access to the advanced transistor technology. Another example refers to Japan, which was part of CoCom. At the beginning of the 1970s, America Fairchild had been refused by the U.S. government to sell integrated circuits of very high scale of integration to Poland. Therefore, the Polish government immediately addressed the Japanese government with a similar request. This annoyed U.S. diplomats, but it was a quite natural step looking from Warsaw's point of view [42]. Contracts were signed up with companies like Busicom and Ricoh later on. Soon, thousands of calculators of very large-scale integration started to leave assembly lines of Elwro [41].

6 Second Path: Learning from USSR and Cooperation in Comecon: 1960s to 1970s

Up to the late 1950s, there was almost no activity in Warsaw and Moscow regarding the interchange of experiences and knowledge on computers [43].

USSR assistance to the computer industry turned out to be necessary only starting from the moment of transition from the first to the second generation of computers, i.e., transistors, in the late 1950s. Everything seems to indicate that the opening of the Elwro factory was the domestic work of the government of the People's Republic of Poland and Polish engineers. However, with the transition to semiconductor technology, consultations with the Russians have proved necessary. In the years 1960–1964 a number of contracts for the supply of semiconductor products and semiconductor technologies from the USSR to the PPR were signed up on behalf of the PPR by the enterprise PHZ Polimex and on behalf of the USSR by Tiaazhpromexport. In addition to selling materials, the USSR offered advice at the preparatory stage of assembly lines for manufacturing germanium and silicon transistors by Poland [44, 45]. It was the TEWA Semiconductor Factory in Warsaw, the second in importance in Poland after the Elwro plant, that was entrusted with the implementation of semiconductor components. In the first half of the 1960s, the production of germanium diodes and transistors was mastered there, and preparation for the production of silicon diodes and transistors was successfully launched.

Experts were also consulted with respect to the production of raw materials. The factory Aluminum Works in Skawina was producing polycrystalline germanium from germanium dioxide imported from western countries. TEWA itself was producing monocrystalline germanium. On the other hand, work was underway on launching production of high resistance polycrystalline silicon at the nitrogen plant in Tarnów. The targeted production capacity of Tarnów was to reach 5.9 tons per year in 1967. This was even higher than the forecasted demand for this intermediate product until 1970 (Fig. 2).

Fig. 2. In the 1980s, the Polish computer industry was able to export remarkable quantities of minicomputers to Comecon and especially to the Soviet markets, as in case of MERA minicomputers of series 60 manufactured in Silesia. Photo courtesy Piotr Fuglewicz.

Moreover, in the mid-1960s the USSR provided technical assistance in mastering the technology of production of necessary chemical reagents, including hydrochloric acid. nitric acid, hydrofluoric acid or graphite. However, attempts to master modern technologies of semiconductor components production intended to operate on higher frequencies – i.e., epitaxial, planar and epi-planar technology – failed [26].

At the end of August 1964, a Polish delegation conducted extensive consultations with partners from the USSR, especially with the Committee for Electrical Engineering, Committee for International Cooperation, Committee for Black and Color Metallurgy, Committee for the Chemical Industry, etc. They visited the Tomilińsk electronics plant near Moscow and became acquainted with the technology of manufacturing semiconductor diodes. The subject of the visit was also to obtain further assistance from the USSR on the development of the Polish semiconductor industry, together with related branches of the chemical and metallurgical industries, in the years 1964–1968; in the first stage, the supply of equipment, semi-finished products like silicon piles, germanium transistors, silicon diodes, etc. and raw materials necessary to launch production in Poland, was envisaged [46].

In 1965, the heads of the Polish computer industry were invited to visit the leading Soviet scientific and production centers, including the powerful Cybernetics Institute of the Academy of Sciences of the USSR in Kiev. There, 1,700 employees developed, among others, the computers of the Ukraine and Dnieper series. They also visited the equally famous Institute of Mathematical Machines in Yerevan, were 1,200 employees developed, among others, the computers of the Nairi and Razdan series [47]. The visit lasted one month and included also trips to the Central Economic-Mathematical Institute of the Academy of Sciences of the USSR in Moscow, the Computation Centre of Gosplan and to the Computation Centre of the Academy of Sciences of the USSR.[3] The latter worked on the basis of BESM series machines, including a state-of-the-art computer BESM-6, constructed in transistor technology at the Institute of Precision Mechanics and manufactured since 1965 for the next 20 years. In addition, Poles visited the Central Institute of Scientific and Technical Information in Moscow (the so-called WINITI), as well as a huge S. Ordzonikidze Counting Machinery Factory in Minsk, where computers of the Minsk series were produced, and a smaller factory of Counting Machines in Vilnius, origin of the Ruta series computers. The Polish delegation held a conference with the head of the State Committee of Science and Technology of the USSR W. Kirillin, and with the officials of the Ministry of Radio Engineering Industry. However, the solutions applied in the famous Ural computer series computers, manufactured in the computer factory in Penza, were restricted from the Polish delegation.[4]

Poland was particularly interested in obtaining licenses from the USSR to produce line printers, ferrite core memory, magnetic drum (memory) heads, adapters and other components, as well as to purchase analogue computers, laminators and paper perforating machines. It was also planned to arrange cooperation of Elwro with the Counting Machinery Factory in Minsk and with the Institute in Yerevan.

---

[3] See Kitov, "On the History of Gosplan," this volume.

[4] For more information on Ural, see Smolevitskaya, "The Engineering Heritage of Bashir Rameev," this volume.

However, during this visit, the Polish delegation discovered that the USSR lagged far behind the U.S. in terms of computer adaptation in the wider economy:

in the USSR, no electronic data processing system for the needs of business management has yet been set up. This is reflected, among other things, in the fact that mathematical machines are burdened with 90% of technical and scientific calculations on a national scale, and only with 10% of economic calculations.

Such a situation, when one considers the circumstance of the planned economy, which depends on precise forecasts and economic calculations, must have appeared kind of absurd to Poles [47].

There were several visits of Polish delegations in the Soviet factories and institutes following in the second half of the 1960s and the first half of the 1970s [48]. Polish specialists were invited into freshly modernized facilities like the Lviv Elektron television factory. In the early 1970s, the advanced automated control system for streamlining the industrial processes, so-called MISC, was installed and supervised there by the famous Institute of Cybernetics lead by Viktor Glushkov [21].[5]

Eventually, Polish authorities were convinced by the representatives of the Soviet Planning Commission and of the Ministries of radio-technical and electronics industries to join the co called Riad series in December 1969. With much greater effort, Polish experts also made concessions, as it was the case the other remaining members of Comecon.[6] Negotiations lasted for nearly two years prior to this agreement because of the fierce opposition of Elwro. Elwro was so satisfied with the recently obtained ICL architecture, which yet was allowed to be further developed not as a primary but barely as a secondary path (next to the primary IBM 360/370 architecture based Riad 30) Later, Riad 32 and Riad 34 followed in the course of the 1970s. The decision was a great disappointment for the team of Elwro engineers, but finally resulted in quite good products like the third generation Odra 1305/1325 and its military versions. These were acknowledged as very reliable part of radar systems by Czechoslovakia and states which imported their computers from PPR. Therefore, the Riad/IBM series, although being developed simultaneously for Polish and British computers, could be nowadays perceived as an additional positive incentive for Polish computer market that brought IBM standards to Polish scientists and manufacturers – even through the Eastern doors [41]. The Polish computer industry was continuing its cooperation with Soviet institutes over the 1970s and 1980s [49, 50].

7   Third Path: Stealing in the West in the 1970s and 1980s [51]

As historians do not have access to the files of Soviet intelligence, we have to rely on documents produced by states associated in the Warsaw Pact to assess the impact of intelligence operations on Comecon's computerization. In many respects, they reflect

---

[5] See also Kitova and Kitov, "Anatoly Kitov and Victor Glushkov," this volume.

[6] See Schmitt, "Socialist Life," this volume.

Moscow's point of view. The first significant operations of Polish intelligence's branch being addressed to the acquisition of scientific-technical documents and smuggling of embargoed equipment dated back to mid-1950s. After a serious defeat in 1961, when defection of a high-ranking officer escaped to U.S., it gradually recovered throughout the decade. Receiving substantial governmental support, financially and personally, in the early 1970s, it thrived along with Poland's entering global markets and the massive purchase of commodities, licenses and taking out loans. During the 1970s, intelligence proved to be able to bypass CoCom's embargo by bribing not only West European, but also U.S. and Japanese, companies. STI recruited agents with access to devices, especially testing equipment, components like memory disks and documentation, for example of assembly lines. By the end of the 1970s, the Polish computer industry included over a dozen of factories benefiting from covert operations.

The way of assimilating IT by communist Poland did not differ much from the way it was going on in USSR. It was namely a smart combination of legal measures like the use of trade agreements, official scientific-technical cooperation with OECD members, United Nations/UNCTAD/UNESCO programs for technical assistance, scholarships founded by Humboldt and many others and illicit operations. Those latter were run with help of intelligence assets like bribing or blackmailing officials and employees, establishing fake intermediating companies, smuggling devices via private channels, obtaining false end-user certificates, bypassing embargo via neutral and developing countries. Therefore, over many routes MSI- and LSI-technology, as well as specific types of computers along with peripheral devices, came to Poland. This holds true for mainframes, minicomputers, and later PCs.

Electronics and automatic control solutions appeared to be crucial fields of arms race and Cold War rivalry since the very beginning. Therefore, CoCom regulations covered many electric and then electronic items and components at the latest from the late 1950s[7] [30, 52, 53]. With the "National Security Decision Memorandum" no. 247 from 14 March 1974 entitled "US Policy on the Export of Computers to Communist Countries," President Richard Nixon approved new export guidelines. According to them, the USSR was excluded from importing significantly powerful western computers "détente notwithstanding" [54]. Two years later, J. Fred Bucy, executive vice-president of Texas Instruments and chair of a 15-member task force composed of high officials from the Department of Defense and private firms, submitted the so-called Bucy Report. It distinguished between "active" and "passive" technology transfer mechanisms applied by the Soviet Union. "Active" – regarded as the most effective form of intercept – involved close and frequent personal contact between a "donor" and a "receiver"; for example, purchasing turnkey factories, licensing accompanied by an extensive teaching effort and joint ventures. "Passive," far less effective forms, were trade exhibitions, product sales without operating and maintenance information, and commercial literature. The report

---

[7] Electronic measurement equipment and the electronic devices are mentioned at least in the lists from Great Britain in the years 1954, 1958, 1960, 1961, 1962, 1964, 1966, 1969, 1972, 1976, 1980, 1985, (1987 access denied), 1989, 1990, 1991, 1993. Zob. http://evansresearch.org/cocom-lists

distinguished also between "evolutionary" and "revolutionary" advances. The first were improvements made routinely, whereas the latter were "quantum leaps." Therefore, they should be strictly protected "in order to prevent an adversary from making significant gains in a short period of time without having to incur the costs of research and development" [55]. Coming from those considerations, controls were placed on networking and signal processing software, image processing software, artificial intelligence, CAD, and CAM in mid-1984.

Despite that sophisticated legal instrument of restrictions during the five-year plan from 1976 to 1980, the KGB and GRU managed to obtain around 150,000 operational information documents on electronics, informatics, telecommunication, energy, aeronautics and many other branches in Western Europe [56]. It was estimated that the USSR saved 100,000 person-years of scientific research over those 5 years. During the 1970s, the Soviets acquired illegally 2,500 pieces of microelectronics manufacturing equipment and their intelligence services delivered approximately 6,000–10,000 pieces of various hardware and 100,000 documents annually. In order to collect data from open sources, science and technology officers and their agents were visiting conferences, submitting proposals for scholarships and internships, etc. In order to obtain embargoed equipment and components, so called diverters-for-hire were spotted: they were contractors (brokers), who were not disciplined like agents and did not enter into long-term relationships with intelligence but rather came across with KGB/GRU only once in their live for one certain transaction or sometimes a couple of transactions. More regular contractors were working for negotiated fees or were receiving commission, for instance, 10% of equipment purchase price or etc. [57].

Soviet setbacks in computing were at least partly balanced by hyper activity of the intelligence service. Referring to the CIA's assessment on the duality of Soviet industry, Michael Mastanduno claims that "the Soviets had effectively combined legal purchases with illegal acquisition of Western technology and equipment to achieve significant benefits across a wide range of military systems and to save hundreds of millions of dollars in research and development costs" [55].

After the political shift in Poland in the late 1970s, a new administration under Secretary Edward Gierek extended and institutionalized clandestine procedures. Science and Technology Intelligence officers massively purchased necessary microelectronic technology on the "black market": technical documentation and user manuals for mainframes, minicomputers and PCs, as well as software solutions, components, hardware or entire assembly lines. Hundreds of companies had been targeted, predominantly in the U.S., Japan and in Western Europe: RCA, Fairchild, Texas Instruments, CII, ICL, Siemens, AEG-Telefunken. Initially, smuggling commodities as well as money transfers had been conducted over fake companies established in EFTA countries. After tightening of the US-American embargo in the beginning of the 1980s, though, new channels over ASEAN territory were explored.

"Black market" operations were not the sole occupation of Science and Technology Intelligence's Division III (later renamed to VI), responsible for IT. Officers were tracking, assessing and evaluating activity of the leading initiatives, think tanks, producers and users of advanced IT worldwide. During the 1980s, the scope of that surveillance covered, for example, the European Strategic Program on Research in IT, the American Semiconductor Research Corporation, or Japan's famous Ministry of International Trade and Industry and last but not least the Indian National Informatics Center. Polish intelligence officers exploited their covert positions in trade agencies or facilities for Research and Development and attended international computer shows and conferences as "Comdex" or "Logic."

Though numerous vital technologies, intercepted by intelligence, had been applied for instance in automating the assembly lines of the Polish automotive industry or in shipyards, one has to emphasize that the Polish economy with its commercial requirements was not the only beneficiary of the intelligence operations. Selected tasks were performed in favor of the military complex, as for instance in the case of Far Looking Infrared technology used in thermal imaging cameras, sensors and other detecting, targeting and aiming devices. The other important recipient was the Ministry of Internal Affairs itself, which was looking for the system of protection against emanating spurious transmission, i.e., so called Tempest. Probably the most critical incentive for the security service to get access to embargoed hardware and software were requirements of communist government to improve surveillance and data gathering on Polish society (an example makes clandestine acquisition of terminals produced by Honeywell-Bull company, and used for hosting the Polish Common System for Registration of Population – PESEL in the 1970s and then 1980s). Another crucial reason for interest in computers and data processing was maintaining and developing capabilities in both cryptology and cryptanalysis in civil and military special services [58].

There are excellently preserved annual reports of Polish Science and Technology Intelligence accessible in the archive of IPN for researchers, which enable us to get insight into the outcomes of their activity in the domain of computers [59, 60]. In 1970, the Ministry of Internal Affairs established an undercover proxy of intelligence that was operating from within the Ministry for Machine Industry. It was a team of several officers who were officially employees of the machines ministry's Department for Foreign Relations. In fact, they were charged with the task of targeting interesting foreign managers, companies, R&D centers and governmental institutions that came across Polish officials during business negotiations or scientific cooperation.

Summing up the scope of interest of several hundred operations launched by intelligence during 1970–1989, it has to be stressed that Polish Science and Technology Intelligence was able to fulfill almost all types of requirements from Polish industry and Research and Development. The exact number of operations is hard to figure out, but one may assume with high accuracy that it is close to 500, over the mentioned 20 years period of time:

- purchasing embargoed mainframes, minicomputers and later PCs on the black market in small quantities
- purchasing embargoed testing and measurement equipment

- intercepting classified know-how in the form of technical documents, blueprints, patents etc., that enabled reengineering entire assembly lines
- providing big quantities of embargoed components as memory disks, magnetic tapes, and various peripherals, especially printers
- signing up long-term fake contracts, including false invoices and false end-user certificates, that resulted in smuggling of entire assembly lines to Poland for low, medium and finally large scale of integration circuits
- providing follow-up information on western works on "internet." The security service's involvement in the works on "infostrada" – a Polish concept resembling the American ARPANet [61] in the 1970s and 1980s – deserves for sure a separate historical approach [62]
- Other innovative applications of computers, like artificial intelligence, etc.

The major beneficiary of the intelligence operations during those two decades in the area of computers and in a broader sense microelectronics were factories and R&D facilities of Elwro in Wroclaw and CEMI (former TEWA) in Warsaw. The CEMI complex was established in the mid 1960s for manufacturing integrated circuits and was fully operational by the beginning of the 1970s. Technologies of mid-, large- and very-large-scale-integration were obtained unofficially mostly in the U.S., Japan, West Germany and Great Britain from such companies as Kulicke and Soffa, Redac, Kasper, Balzers, Macrodata, ASEA, Electromask, Eberle, Siemens, Philips, Sentinel, Silvar Lisco, Intel or Fairchild-Schlumberger. A large part of intercepted material referred to IBM 370/155, IBM communications processors types 8100/8725, 3705/3725 and was used in the Riad program [63–65].

During the 1970s and 1980s, approximately US$50–100 million were transferred from industry and R&D via secret bank accounts of Science and Technology Intelligence in Poland and abroad to agents and fake companies that sold embargoed goods in the area of microelectronics. However, most of those commodities, although of so called dual-use nature, were ordered not by the Polish military but for the civil economy.

Though the direct financial benefits of illegal acquisition of microelectronics were alluring for Polish government, there were also huge disadvantages. There was no guarantee, so that troubles with illicitly purchased components or devices inevitably involved additional consulting of foreign specialists. They had to be recruited as agents or simply hired only once for money reasons, brought to Poland in a risky operation, and obviously payed high reimbursements. Moreover, as the Soviets experienced many times, the CIA or other American special services were sometimes able to track down clandestine contracts on U.S. or West European soil. They intercepted cargo and damaged it in a very smart way so that the fault became possible to identify only after booting acquired devices or components in the facility of the smuggler, for instance in Poland or the USSR [66].

By enforcing the Export Administration Act by the administration of President Jimmy Carter in 1979 as a response to the Soviet involvement in Afghanistan, U.S.

authorities exacerbated the control of international trade with goods, especially those embedding advanced microelectronics. After General Wojciech Jaruzelski's government introduced martial law in order to crush "*Solidarnosc*" in Poland in late 1981, the Polish People's Republic was additionally punished by Ronald Regan's administration. The U. S. removed the so-called Most Favored Nation status from bilateral trade relations between the two countries. All those political tensions contributed to the shift of proportions between official and clandestine ways of high-tech acquisition by the PPR. In opposite to the 1970s, when legal channels prevailed over smuggling, in the 1980s it was the intelligence activity that was growing rapidly, making official channels usually fruitess and redundant. That phenomenon quickly made the Polish Ministry for Machine Industry, responsible for implementation of computers in domestic economy, entirely addicted to the secret influx of data-processing know-how and equipment. Black market purchases involving IT-goods were consuming on the average several millions of USD annually.

Next to Western Europe, the U.S. and Japan there was a fourth interesting player emerging on the horizon in the early 1980s: China. It was both target and partner, looking from the perspective of PPR's intelligence gathering on computers. That ambiguity resulted from the fact that in the 1980s Beijing was enjoying a U.S. and European differential policy in the area of science and technology similar to the special status granted to Poland and Romania in the 1960s in order to keep those countries away from USSR. Nevertheless, in case of Poland, many crucial technologies remained under restriction to be shared despite of a friendly approach in Washington. Based on its own experience as a privileged communist country, Polish authorities strove for cooperation with China, knowing that it would enable access to very-large-scale-integration technology via the Shenzhen Special Economic Zone. That kind of thinking turned out to be very reasonable. On the eve of the 1990s, Polish intelligence was already negotiating a deal worth US$100 million with the Chinese [51].

Though we do not have many declassified documents confirming the Polish S&T information exchange with other communist countries in the East/South-East Asia region, at least contacts with the Democratic Republic of Vietnam and also with North Korea can be proved. For instance, in 1987, representatives of the Polish computer industry in the UNITRA holding, accompanied by intelligence officers, initiated talks with North Korean companies Undok Group, Korea Jeil Equipment-Export and Import Co. During the meeting in Pyongyang, Koreans proposed intelligence assistance in approaching Japan and U.S. companies. Polish officials were interested in photolithography, ion implementation, and testing equipment with regard to VLSI [67] (Fig. 3).

Секретно

Дополнение к ориентировке
по проблеме № 216
Мини-ЭВМ: аппаратные средства
и программное обеспечение

В настоящее время к классу мини-ЭВМ (*Minicomputers*) при-
нято относить вычислительные машины со следующими параметрами:
а) производительностью от I до I0 (MIPS - *millions instructions per second*)
миллионов инструкций в секунду; б) объемом оперативной памяти
I-I6 мегабайт; в) стоимостью от 20 до 400 тыс. долларов США. Внутри
него обычно различают два подкласса: традиционные и высокопроизводительные мини-ЭВМ (*Traditional and High-End Minicomputers*).
Традиционные мини-ЭВМ могут быть I2,I6,24 разрядными. Они об-
ладают наименьшей производительностью и, как правило, однопоточ-
ной архитектурой (*single bus architecture*); к ним относятся
Micro PDP -II/73, PDP-II/84, *Tempest Pro* -360 фирмы ДЕС
(США) и *System* /36, 5360 *model D* фирмы IBM (США).
Высокопроизводительные машины являются 32 разрядными; сред-
няя производительность ниже,чем у больших ЭВМ, но приближается к
ним по этому показателю. В качестве примера высокопроизводитель-
ных мини-ЭВМ могут быть названы УАХ 8200/8300, УАХ 8600/8650,
УАХ II/750, УАХ II/780, *micro* VAX-II производства фирмы ДЕС и
System -9000 модель 9003 фирмы IBM.
Характерным для рассматриваемого класса машин является воз-
можность их применения в системах автоматизированного проектирования и управления производством (САД/САМ). В последнее время
мини-ЭВМ находят все более широкое применение для организации ло-
кальных сетей рабочих станций в проектных организациях. Это поз-
воляет еще с большей эффективностью использовать автоматизированные системы проектирования. Значителен эффект от применения дан-
ного класса ЭВМ при автоматизации деятельности различного рода
учреждений (*Office Automation*).
Мини-ЭВМ традиционно состоит из таких составных частей, как
логический процессор, оперативная память, постоянное запоминающее
устройство, набор блоков расширения возможностей и периферийные
устройства (клавиатура, дисплей, печатающее устройство, устройства ввода-вывода графической информации, внешние запоминающие ус-

Fig. 3. Example of declassified cables exchanged between Polish and Soviet intelligence
services cooperating in the area of embargoed software. In this analysis the KGB informs Polish
partner about the development of minicomputer market in USA and Western Europe. Source:
AIPN Warsaw

8 Fourth Path: Intelligence Sharing with Warsaw Pact Partners in the 1980s

Next to the operations authorized by the Polish government or party leadership, Polish Science and Technology Intelligence and in effect the entire economy profited from the achievements of spy networks working for the remaining Comecon countries. Intense information exchange started at the latest in the course of the 1960s, though some liaisons between individual STIs existed already in the second half of the 1950s. During the 1970s and in particular the 1980s, Polish Science and Technology Intelligence shared its knowledge with partners. This ranged from KGB's foreign intelligence, the extremely successful Markus Wolf's East German "*Hauptverwaltung Aufklärung*" (HVA), to other intelligence services, especially Czech, Bulgarian and Hungarian. Those ties certainly included reciprocity. A constant stream of western user manuals, blueprints, technical documents, and confidential analysis flowed from Moscow, East Berlin or Prague to Warsaw year by year. However, that interlinked system was not faultless. Contacts on the level of intelligence services implied rivalry, mistrust, and sometimes deception and spitefulness. It occurred that information vital for one country had been hidden by another one in order to impede progress in area that underwent severe competition inside of Comecon [68].

Until the early 1980s, the U.S. government was seemingly unaware of the extent (and sophisticated methodology behind) to which the KGB was penetrating into the Western economies and especially scientific circles, though there were many indications and clues confirming advanced espionage activity. The breakthrough came with French intelligence's recruitment of the high-ranking employee of KGB's Science and Technology Intelligence Vladimir Vetrov, codenamed Farewell. French intelligence handed over documents received earlier from Vetrov to the CIA in the second half of 1981. In 1983, the Soviets learned about the treason and in 1985, the French public and in the world were informed about the affair. "Farewell" disclosed to French and then American intelligence the names of more than 200 staff personal employed in the Soviet Science and Technology Intelligence branch abroad in ten western countries, and approximately 100 sources recruited in favor of line X (as Soviet STI abroad was codenamed). In following months and years, western countries expelled hundreds Soviet diplomats. It was the greatest disaster for KGB and GRU since the beginning of the Cold War. It quickly turned out that line X fulfilled two-thirds to three-fourths of the requirements from Soviet industry and Research and Development [54]. According to a CIA memorandum from 1985: "in recent years, the surrogates among the East European intelligence services possibly have been more successful than Soviet intelligence against priority defense technologies in the United States" [57]. Cases of very successful spies working for Polish intelligence like William Bell and James Harper confirm this notion [69]. East European services had considered success not only in the United States but elsewhere because, in comparison to the Soviets:

> They are generally perceived as a lesser threat than the Soviets; they often may not be perceived as operating in a surrogate role; in some countries, including the United States, they operate under less sever travel restrictions; some, especially the Czechoslovaks and the East Germans, probably find it easier to operate in the West European cultural and commercial climate. [57]

The contribution of communist allies to the joint Science and Technology Intelligence undertakings of Warsaw Pact rose enormously after the Farewell affair. Throughout the 1980s, Polish Science and Technology Intelligence was sharing annually several dozens of computer solutions like batches of technical documentation, user manuals, western think tanks' analysis etc. with its partners in Warsaw Pact Treaty [70]. Reciprocally, the Soviets and GDR and to a lesser extent, other partners, passed on to Poland their achievements in the field of intelligence. One has to emphasize that mutual and unilateral confidence was limited because each intelligence service complied with national interests and domestic computer markets (for statistics, see Appendix). Based on the operation case files covering the last five years of the PPR, one can easily obtain an extensive overview over the scope and content of exchanged material. Altogether, hundreds of secret transfers can be identified.

For instance, during 1984–1985, Polish intelligence received from its East German counterpart various utility programs and operating systems for the mini-computer PDP-11/73 produced by Digital Equipment Corporation. Documents on programs like RSTS/E v. 7.2., DECNET/E v. 2.0./2.1 were delivered in the form of textbooks and recorded tapes. The Polish government – via intelligence – paid several tens of thousands USD. Software was not intended to be used in DEC computers installed in Poland but was considered as vital aid in developing local minicomputers and programs, based on DEC architecture and logic. The long-term objective of the Polish government was to speed up the development of its own hardware and software, and moreover to export in the near future Polish products to the Comecon markets [71]. In 1988–1989, Polish intelligence reciprocated when GDR's *Hauptverwaltung Aufklärung* addressed Poles with request for access to know-how on photolithography of Intel Corporation's processors 80C86, furthermore on microchips. Calculated costs amounted to about US$700,000 (processor) and US$600,000 (RAM). Polish Science and Technology Intelligence exploited its assets in West Germany and Japan and was able to surpass expectations of *Hauptverwaltung Aufklärung* [72].

Among the most relevant objects for the Division VI of the Department I in Polish Ministry of Internal Affairs there were various R&D programs launched by the European Economic Community (EEC) in the mid 1980s. The path was paved already by the European Strategic Program for Research in IT (ESPRIT) launched in 1983. In this program, western companies such as French Thomson or West German Siemens cooperated in order to unify computer systems and build an integrated data transfer network. By exploiting synergies, the full competitiveness of ESPIRIT with the U.S. and Japan was planned to be reached in the first half of the 1990s. The program had a budget of ECU 1.5 billion, which at that time had a rate close to that of today's euro, for its first five years of operation [73].

In March 1985, Mikhail Gorbachev took over the Soviet Union and started his reforms. The so-called Complex Program for the Progress in Science and Technology 2000 (CP 2000) was announced during the extraordinary session of Comecon in Moscow in December 1985 after three years of intensive preparations [74]. It was not the first time that Comecon states tried to coordinate their Research and Development efforts. A similar program, though launched in utterly different circumstances, was initiated in 1971 and failed, according to Comecon's own assessments. The overwhelming bureaucracy was blamed for the setback, while another reason was the demise of détente in the late 1970s [75].

Though there were altogether five areas and 93 sub-projects covered by the CP 2000, one was placed on the top of the list: electronics and automatic control. Those two branches impacted every part of economy much more than chemistry, biotechnology or heavy industry did. Regarding the progress in electronics, Soviet authorities, which presumably contributed to the final version of the program in the greatest degree, distinguished development in following aspects:

1. Supercomputer capable of at least 10 million operations per second, based on artificial intelligence technology
2. Mass production of PCs along with utility programs applied in management, education, computer learning, and for leisure purposes
3. Joint system of digital information transition and significant enlargement of telecommunication infrastructure, the so called TELE JS Riad
4. Fiber optic communication. Indeed, Poland achieved impressing scientific results in fiber optic communication during the 1980s but eventually failed to introduce them into development and production
5. New satellite communication systems and long-range TV transmission
6. Measurement and control equipment
7. Very-large-scale-integration technology.

In the domain of automatic control, there was one major target on the horizon: improving Computerized Numerical Control (CNC) of assembly lines and transforming plants into so-called flexible manufacturing systems. It implied Computer Aided Design and Manufacturing (CAD and CAM) solutions, robots and its components like hydraulic, pneumatic, electronic parts as well as automated loading and unloading equipment etc. [75].

According to West German analyst Henrik Bischof, CP 2000 manifested a third stage of integration efforts within socialist camp: assuming that the first was of economic nature (Comecon), the second of military nature (Warsaw Pact) [74], the third one being of scientific-technical nature. Exactly as the first and the second concept Moscow came up with, also the third endeavor was not inspired from within the communist camp but came as a countermeasure to the western concept of scientific-technical integration. Similarly, Comecon was an alternative to the Marshall Plan in 1949; the Warsaw pact was a counterpart of NATO in 1955. CP 2000 was meant as Comecon's response to European Research Coordination Agency and its massive financial support for R&D initiatives in innovative disciplines of science and fields of technology, especially automated control and electronics [76].

Polish Science and Technology Intelligence was charged with acquisition of know-how for domestic needs and in favor of allies, especially of the USSR. For instance, at the beginning of 1988, the Polish Science and Technology Intelligence's headquarters sent guidelines to selected officers in embassies abroad regarding the scope of interest of EEC countries and companies from beyond the EEC involved in Eureka program. The intelligence proxy in Rome was asked about Eureka's leading projects and sub-topics, R&D centers involved in those projects, especially businessmen, managers and researchers and engineers with ties to Poland [77]. The responses from intelligence officers abroad came usually after several weeks as the example of Vienna proves. The officer there put emphasis on the most promising – according to his assessment – initiatives the Austrian entities were involved in, namely *Flexible Automatisierte Montagesysteme* (FAMOS) coordinated by *Oesterreichisches Forschungszentrum* in Seibersdorf. The officer stressed that seven countries participated in the program, among them West Germany, France, Italy and Great Britain. He described in detail individual research topics carried out in the framework of FAMOS in various companies and research centers, along with providing information about scientists and managers responsible for those topics [78].

Though the focus of information shared in the framework of Comecon intelligence community was put on OECD countries, China's coming out as a user, then producer of American computer technology in the early 1980s shifted KGB's attention as a "trend setter" in the area of intelligence gathering to Southeast Asia. In March 1986, the KGB reported to its Polish counterpart about a semiconductor assembly line in Shanghai where integrated circuits licensed by Japan were going to be manufactured soon. Soviet intelligence passed on to Polish intelligence a complete technical documentation of the assembly line along with sketches of factory buildings [79].

Taking into consideration bad Soviet-China diplomatic relationships dating back to the early 1960s, one can ask whether the KGB was trying to make any use of sometimes much better ties maintained with China by Comecon states in order to intercept scientific-technical intelligence (Fig. 4).

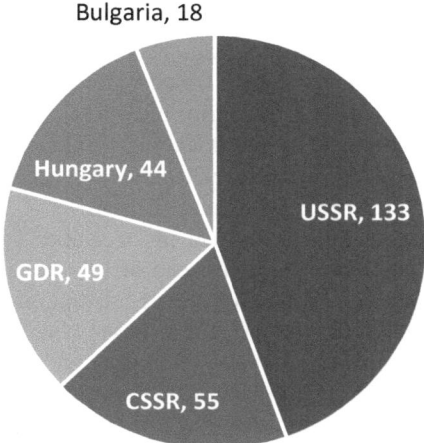

Fig. 4. Solutions received during 1987 from individual intelligence services by Polish STI in the area of microelectronics and software. Source: AIPN Warsaw

9 Conclusion and Further Prospects

Poland attempted to get access to cutting-edge computer technologies through many and various doors. The ones that were legal involved cooperation with senior partners – the USSR and remaining partners from Comecon. CoCom's embargo handicapped, however, the entire Comecon so that every member tried to acquire know-how via illegal channels, usually organized and managed by the individual intelligence services. Poland was also guilty of using those methods, despite a distinct privileged position in commercial relationships with the U.S.

Exactly at the same time when pioneers of the Polish foreign intelligence arrived at Paris, London and Bern, domestic Research and Development programs coordinated either by the Warsaw based Institute of Mathematical Machines or by Wroclaw-based Elwro's experimental unit were initiated. Moreover, a new governmental body called the Committee for Science and Technology sent its representatives to Polish embassies in western countries with the task of tracking local computer markets and setting up contacts with electronics companies prone to cooperate across the Iron Curtain, despite the embargo on dual-use items.

The second channel of know-how transfer was the one set up between Poland and USSR. Both countries signed on to an agreement about scientific-technical cooperation back in 1947, but until the mid-1960s, computer technology was rather beyond the agenda of mutual ties. Know-how exchange followed by trade agreements accelerated only after 1964, partly thanks to the new established Commission for Radio-technique and Electronics in Comecon.

Soviet technical assistance for its communist allies was, however, limited. Moscow was sharing its precious knowledge reluctantly. Perhaps (this is supposition) Soviet authorities was purposefully pushing Poland and other countries into the arms of western sellers. By that occasion Soviet engineers could obtain access to know-how sold by the West to its "satellites states" which otherwise was beyond the range of USSR scientists due to embargo and security measures. Nonetheless, Polish officials and experts failed to persuade the Soviet Planning Commission to take advantage of Poland's positive experience with ICL architecture and use it as a model during the works on a joint Comecon computer standard (Riad).

Eventually, Poland officially joined Riad in December 1969. The entire concept was at that time *in statu nascendi,* but by the end of 1970 it became clear that it would be the architecture of IBM 360 and Small Scale of Integration to make a pattern for the future Comecon computers of various capacities. Elwro chiefs were devastated because Polish industry was not prepared for "reverse engineered" IBM. In order to meet the deadlines scheduled by Soviet authorities for the introduction of R-series in the entire Eastern Bloc and in individual countries, the Polish government decided to pass on some tasks – it was charged within the framework of Comecon community – to its intelligence service.

One has to emphasize that the USSR successfully reverse engineered not only mainframes of IBM series 360/370 as the Riad family in the 1960s or the minicomputers DEC PDP-11/73 in the 70s as Elektronika 60, but also managed to build clones of 8-bit Apple II as Agat-1, 8-bit Intel Corporation processor 8080A as KR5801K80A,

Texas Instruments Integrated circuits 5400/7400 family as Logika-2, 133/155), and even 16-bit IBM-PC with Intel processor 8086 as Iskra 250. Those implementations, based on intelligence data, seem to prove the reliability of STI as a factor in the economy, but only as vehicle for know-how transfer. Communist intelligence – and Polish STI showcases it – cannot replace economic instruments and the entire environment of the western world that includes free market, commercial incentives and competition between enterprises. The planned economy with its all organizational faults and bureaucratic burdens turned out to be too ponderous to take advantage of intelligence operations. Kristie Macrakis made similar observations in regard to GDR's STI [80]. Though the STI was itself efficient, its impact on Polish computer industry was not as significant as legal cooperation with the Soviet partner.

Flashy spy operations together with successful bribery of some leading capitalistic companies or their employees enabled the Polish government a constant updating of the worldwide trends in I.T. However, the intelligence service was incapable of making a decisive impact on the Polish microelectronic industry, with a result that along with the Research and Development sector – constrained by the rules of planned economy – failed to catch up with western producers and inventors.

Moreover, Polish intelligence – like its counterparts in the GDR, Hungary etc. – intensified its cooperation and information sharing with KGB's foreign intelligence service. As a result, not only ties to the Western world were organized twofold on and under the table, but also relationships with allies in Comecon were arranged in two dimensions.

Was the investment in illegal activity worth it? Apart from expenditures on training and employment of tens of intelligence officers working on overt and covert positions in- and outside of the country, there was also the need for financing sophisticated operations abroad. This often included setting up fake companies. Moreover, the intelligence service had to keep up hundreds of secret collaborators, consultants and some other auxiliary staff. Those mentioned experts were responsible for defining requirements for the Polish science and industry. After successfully transfer the technology, they evaluated the documents, patterns, samples and devices obtained by STI. Finally, the "legalization" of intercepted solutions followed by submitting Polish patents and implementing them in the Polish plants. The phenomenon of Science and Technology Intelligence becomes even more fascinating when it comes to payment for Polish agents in the area of I.T. – probably the most money-consuming aspect of black-market operations. It seems that the financing of those purchases was almost entirely covered by the funds earmarked for the Research and Development in the individual ministries that "ordered" a certain solution. It means that sometimes the money invested in STI operations had to be withdrawn from the direct R&D initiatives. The risk emerged in both cases. Domestic R&D works could have ended up with nothing or with outdated solutions, but at the same time clandestine operations could have also failed. For instance, in the 1970s several illegal shipments of cargo from USA had been intercepted by US customs. While the other time black market contractors cheated Polish officers by selling faulty or broken equipment.

On the other hand, there were of course significant benefits generated by the Science and Technology Intelligence – savings resulted from know-how "for free" transmission and so called "reverse engineering" without any licensing costs.

Eventually, the demise of communism in the PPR and subsequently in the USSR, along with the unexpected economic "assault" of U.S. and West European computer manufacturers, the lifting of the embargo and the emergence of free market rules, totally transformed the structure, needs and trajectories of development for microelectronics in now free Poland. For instance, Siemens took over control of Elwro. The case of Poland gives an excellent example of how schizophrenic the computer market in Comecon during the 1970s and 1980s was.

Acknowledgement. Research was funded by National Science Center (NCN), Poland, Project Sonata, Edition 13, No: 2017/26/D/HS3/00250.

Appendix – Statistics on Intelligence Gathering from 1987 to 1989

By **task (operation)**, the undertaking of intelligence officers is meant, officially registered in the intelligence data bases as task; it involves clandestine activity abroad, recruitment of informants, black market purchases, illicit money transfers and trafficking of documents and items; tasks were either company (IBM, DEC, Siemens etc.) or technology orientated (testing equipment, computers, peripherals); were often long-term lasting covering time span from couple of months up to several years.

By "**solution**" is meant: 1. blueprints, patterns, and complete or partial technical documentation allowing "reverse engineering" of: design, layout, construction of electronic device (mainly computers and peripherals) and components (memory tapes and hard disks, CPUs); 2. technological documentation of entire assembly lines (for instance VLSI); 3. software or its elements (assemblers, compilers, translators, utilities, operation systems, libraries), 4. Various automatic control, measurement and testing equipment, drivers, user manuals etc.

The data is selected and juxtaposed by the author. It originated from three extensive reports of STI's Chief covering all STI areas of activity. Some numbers below can be incoherent one to another (Table 1).

Table 1. Efficiency of the Division VI of the Department I in the Ministry for Internal Affairs from 1987–1989. Scope of activity: intelligence gathering in the domains of IT, microelectronics, programming, automatic control systems etc.

	1987	1988	1989
Tasks			
Tasks (operations) accomplished	17	2	14
Tasks (operations) canceled	3	5	16
Tasks (operations) added	7	9	14
Ongoing tasks (operations) by the end of the year	50	52	36
Acquisition			
Solutions received from the informants (agents)	154	293	306
Solutions received from allied intelligence agencies	299	198	?

(*continued*)

Table 1. (*continued*)

	1987	1988	1989
Solutions received from other sources/institutions	23	28	?
Solutions obtained in the framework of tasks (operations) and intel-interchange – total	476	519	?
Dissemination			
Solutions provided to recipients (ministries) in civil domain	265	81	224
Solutions delivered to military and security service (C^3, cryptology)	50	83	13
Solutions shared with partner intelligence agencies	66	167	46
Other recipients	16	16	0
Evaluation			
Solutions evaluated by experts by the end of the year, including solutions delivered in the previous year(s) – total	113	82	132
Evaluated as complete solutions, ready to implement (to manufacture)	4	1	0 (?)
Evaluated as solutions partly ready to be introduced in production	2	1	0 (?)
Evaluated as valuable solutions not ready to be implemented/the need for further R&D	78	50	56
Evaluated as general know-how (informative but superficial)	23	25	75
Evaluated as valueless material	6	5	6

Source: AIPN, Ministerstwo Spraw Wewnętrznych, sign. 001912/5, statistical reports from January 1988, January 1989 and January 1990 for the Internal Intelligence Data Base, status: secret (tajne).

References

1. Frącki, M., et al. (ed.): Zarys historii elektroniki w Polsce. Przedsiębiorstwo Innowacyjne MAJAX (2015)
2. Noga, M., Nowak, J.S. (ed.): Polska Informatyka. Wizje i trudne początki. PTI, Warszawa (2017)
3. Gomułka, W.: The Policy of People's Republic of Poland, "Foreign Affairs", vol. 38, no. 3, April 1960
4. Pleskot, P., Rutkowski, T.P. (eds.) Spętana Akademia. Polska Akademia Nauk w dokumentach władz PRL, vol. 1. Warszawa (2009)
5. Empacher, A.B.: Maszyny liczą same? WP (1960)
6. Gerovitch, S.: From Newspeak to Cyberspeak. The History of Soviet Cybernetics. The MIT Press, Cambridge (2002)
7. AAN, Ministerstwo Przemysłu Maszynowego 1967–1981, Inventory No. 1758
8. AAN, Ministerstwo Hutnictwa i Przemysłu Maszynowego 1981–1987, Inventory No. 1757
9. AAN, Komitet Nauki i Techniki 1963–1972, Inventory No. 787
10. AAN, Urząd Postępu Naukowo-Technicznego i Wdrożeń 1985–1991, Inventory No. 2726
11. RGAE, Sekretariat Soveta Ekonomicheskoy Vzaimopomoshchi 1949–1991 - Fond 561, Postoyannaya Komissiya Po Radiotekhnicheskoy i Elektronnoy Promyshlennosti, Opis No. 14, 14pp, 32s/pp

12. RGAE, Postoyannoye predstavitelstvo SSSR pri Sovete Ekonomicheskoy Vzaimopomoshchi 1949–1988 - Fond 302
13. Federal Archiv (Bundesarchiv) in Berlin-Lichterfelde
14. Stasi Archive (BStU/Behörde des Bundesbeauftragten für die Stasi-Unterlagen) in Berlin
15. Milewski, M.: Rola i Zadania wywiadu MSW (1972). AIPN, sign. 01738/21
16. Sprawozdanie Wiceministra spraw wewnętrznych dla Premiera i in. (projekt), September 1989. AIPN, sign. 02271/21, vol. 23
17. Zacharski, M.: Nazywam się Zacharski. Marian Zacharski. Wbrew regułom. Zysk i S-ka, Poznań (2009)
18. Wasiak, P.: Computing behind the Iron Curtain. Social Impact of Home Computers in the Polish People's Republic. Tensions of Europe. http://www.tensionsofeurope.eu/www/en/files/get/publications/WP_2010_08_Wasiak.pdf. Accessed 28 Sept 2018
19. Kluska, B.: Automaty liczą. Komputery PRL, Gdynia (2013)
20. Kierunki rozwoju przemysłu elektronicznego i teletechnicznego w latach 1966–1970, Warszawa, February 1964. AAN, Ministerstwo Przemysłu Ciężkiego, sign. 37/36
21. Peters, B.: How Not to Network a Nation: The Uneasy History of the Soviet Internet. The MIT Press, Cambridge (2016)
22. Uzasadnienie uchwały Komitetu Ekonomicznego Rady Ministrów (KERM) w sprawie rozwoju radiokomunikacji ruchomej lądowej UKF w latach 1966–1970, 24 March 1966. AAN, KNiT, 787, sign. 10/52
23. "Młody Technik" monthly 1950–1990
24. "Horyzonty Techniki" monthly 1950–1990
25. "Horyzonty Techniki dla Dzieci" monthly 1950–1990
26. Informacja i wnioski w sprawie rozwoju technicznego półprzewodników i podzespołów elektronicznych, Zespół Elektroniki i Telekomunikacji KNiT (1966). AAN, KNiT, 787, sign. 10/52
27. Załącznik nr 10/Tabela nr 1 i 2 - Założenia rozwoju techniki obliczeniowej do 1975 r. AAN, KNiT, 787, sign. 40/247
28. Uzasadnienie projektu Uchwały Rady ministrów w sprawie zadań w zakresie mechanizacji i automatyzacji przetwarzania informacji w gospodarce narodowej w latach 1966–1970 (1966). AAN, KNiT, 787, sign. 10/52
29. Sanchez-Sibony, O.: Red Globalization: The Political Economy of the Soviet Cold War from Stalin to Khrushchev. Cambridge University Press, Cambridge (2014)
30. Cortada, J.W.: The Digital Flood: The Diffusion of Information Technology Across the U.S., Europe, and Asia. Oxford University Press (2012). See also the articles of Chris Leslie and Martin Schmitt in this volume
31. Department of State – Airgram from AmEmbassy Warsaw, Subject: License Application for an Oscilloscope consigned to Institute of Nuclear Science in Swierk, 17 December 1969. NARA, Records Group 59, General Records of the Department of State, Central Foreign Policy Files 1967–1969, Strategic Trade Control, Box 1414
32. Department of State – Telegram from AmEmbassy Warsaw, Subject: US Export to Poland of oscilloscope and spectrum analyzer, 14 February 1972. NARA, RG 59, General Records of the Department of State, Central Foreign Policy Files 1970–1973, Strategic Trade Control, Box 1548
33. Department of State – Airgram from AmEmbassy Warsaw, Subject: Instruments for Polish National Bureau of Measures and Quality Control, 12 January 1967. NARA, RG 59, General Records of the Department of State, Central Foreign Policy Files 1967–1969, Strategic Trade Control, Box 1415

34. Department of State - Telegram from US Mission OECD Paris, Subject: French Transistor Technology to Poland, 8 October 1969. NARA, RG 59, General Records of the Department of State, Central Foreign Policy Files 1967–1969, Strategic Trade Control, Box 1415

35. Memorandum for Mr. Henry A. Kissinger The White House, Subject: French Desire to Sell Transistors Technology to Poland, 23 October 1969. NARA, RG 59, General Records of the Department of State, Central Foreign Policy Files 1967–1969, Strategic Trade Control, Box 1415

36. Department of State – Airgram from AmEmbassy Warsaw, 30 June 1966. NARA, RG 59, General Records of the Department of State, Central Foreign Policy Files 1954–1966, Strategic Trade Control, Box 1441

37. Wyciąg z instrukcji w sprawie zakresu działania, obowiązków i uprawnień pracowników do spraw współpracy gospodarczej i naukowo-technicznej w placówkach zagranicznych PRL oraz zasad ich współdziałania z kierownikiem i poszczególnymi komórkami tych placówek – wprowadzonej Zarządzeniem nr 2 Przewodniczącego Komitetu Współpracy Gospodarczej z Zagranicą przy Radzie Ministrów z dnia 30 grudnia 1965 r. AAN, KNiT, 787, sign. 12/39

38. KNiT – projekt: Wytyczne dla pracowników do spraw współpracy gospodarczej i naukowo-technicznej w placówkach zagranicznych PRL w zakresie współdziałania z Komitetem Nauki i Techniki PRL, 15 December 1966. AAN, KNiT, 787, sign. 12/39

39. Lipiński, P.: Geniusz i świnie. Rzecz o Jacku Karpińskim, JanKa (2014)

40. Empacher, A.B.: Wzrost ilościowy cyfrowych maszyn matematycznych w niektórych krajach (stan dotychczasowy i perspektywy rozwojowe), Warszawa (1965)

41. Maćkowiak, B., Myszkier, A., Safader, B.: Polskie komputery rodziły się w ELWRO we Wrocławiu. Rola Wrocławskich Zakładów Elektronicznych ELWRO w rozwoju informatyki w Polsce. Ed. by G. Trzaskowska. Wrocław (2017)

42. Department of State – Telegram from AmEmbassy Warsaw, Subject: Fairchild sale of integrated circuits technology to Poland, 27 June 1973. NARA, RG 59, General Records of the Department of State, Central Foreign Policy Files 1970–1973, Strategic Trade Control, Box 1548

43. Sikora, M., Pivovarov, N.J.: Formirovaniye sovetsko-polskogo ekonomicheskogo sotrudnichestva v oblasti elektronnoy promyshlennosti v kontse 1950–1960-ye gody. In: XXII Godichnoy nauchnoy mezhdunarodnoy konferentsii Instituta istorii yestestvoznaniya i tekhniki im. S.I. Vavilova RAN 28 marta – 1 aprelya 2016 g., Moscow (2016)

44. Dopolneniye 2 - k kontraktu 7204/3 ot 3 marta 1960 goda na vypolneniye proyektnykh rabot dla stroitelstva proizvodstv poluprovodnikovykh materialov (monokristallicheskogo germaniya i kremniya) v Polskoi Narodnoy Respublike (1961). AAN, KNiT, 787, sign. 40/245

45. Posolstvo Polskoy Narodnoy Respubliki - Byuro torgovogo sovetnika do tov. NIKITINU A. E. Predsedatel Vsesoyuznogo Obedineniya "Tyaazhpromeksport", Moskwa, 30 March 1961. AAN, KNiT, 787, sign. 40/245

46. Sprawozdanie z pobytu delegacji PRL w ZSRR w dniach 29 sierpnia – 6 września (1964). AAN, KNiT, 787, sign. 40/245

47. Sprawozdanie z delegacji służbowej do ZSRR w sprawie Elektronicznej Techniki Obliczeniowej 3 października – 31 października 1965, Warszawa, December 1965. AAN, KNiT, 787, sign. 40/120

48. RGAE, Ministerstvo Radiopromyshlennosti SSSR - Fond 23, Opis 1, Delo 1054, 1381 (60s)

49. RGAE, Gosudarstvennyy Komitet po Nauke i Tekhnike - Fond 9480, Opis 12, Delo 962

50. RGAE, Gosudarstvennyy Komitet SSSR po vychislitelnoy tekhnike i informatike - Fond 680, Opis 1, Delo 71, 72, 75, 189

51. Sikora, M.: Clandestine Acquisition of Microelectronics and Information Technology by the Scientific-Technical Intelligence of Polish People's Republic in 1970–1990. In: Krayneva, I., Tomilin, A. (eds.) 2017 Forth International Conference "Computer Technology in Russia

and in the Former Soviet Union" SoRuCom 2017, Zelenograd, Russia, 3–5 October 2017. IEEE (2017)

52. Cain, F.: Computers and the Cold War: United States restrictions on the export of computers to the Soviet Union and Communist China. J Contemp. Hist. **40**(1), 131–147 (2005)

53. Zatlin, J.R.: Out of the sight: industrial espionage, ocular authority and East German communism, 1965–1989. Contemp. Eur. Hist. **17**(1), 45–71 (2008)

54. Weiss, G.W.: Duping the Soviets. The farewell Dossier. Stud. Intell. **39**(5) (1996)

55. Mastanduno, M.: Economic Containment. CoCom and the Politics of East-West Trade. Cornell University Press, Ithaca (1992)

56. Merlen, É., Ploquin, F.: Carnets intimes de la DST. 30 ans au coeur du contre–espionnage français. Fayard (2003)

57. Soviet Acquisition of Militarily Significant Western Technology: An Update, Office of the Undersecretary of Defense, Memorandum for Administration Defense Technical Information Center, September 1985

58. Bury, J.: Polska Informatyka: Informatyka w służbach specjalnych PRL. Analiza kryminalistyczna. PTI, Warszawa (2017)

59. AIPN, sign. 01789/211 (years 1971–1983)

60. AIPN, sign. 02320/419, vol. 1–2 (years 1984–1987)

61. Schmitt, M.: Internet im Kalten Krieg. Eine Vorgeschichte des globalen Kommunikationsnetzes, transcript Verlag, Bielefeld (2016)

62. Targowski, A.: Historia, teraźniejszość, przyszłość informatyki. Wydawnictwo Politechniki Łódzkiej, Łódź (2013)

63. AIPN, sign. 01789/211

64. AIPN, sign. 0211/963 (jacket)

65. AIPN, sign. 001912/5

66. Cpravka ob usilenii so storony Zapada nad eksportoi v SSSR i deyatelnosti spetssluzhb protivnika na etoi napravlenii v usloviyakh perestroyki sovetskoy ekonomiki, OCH-011727/P/89, 23 November 1989. AIPN, sign. 0449/26, vol. 25

67. KRLD - Notatka Nr 9226/PRL, Warszawa, 6 April 1987. AIPN 02271/21, vol. 7

68. Sikora, M.: Intelligence-interchange in the area of Science and Technology between Poland and Soviet Union, 1986–1990. In: Helerea, E., Cionca, M., Ivănoiu, M. (eds.) Technology in Times of Transition. 41 ICOHTEC Symposium 2014. Transylvania University of Brasov (2014)

69. Lindsey, R.: Some Losers in Silicon Valley said to find wealth in spying. Special to New York Times, 23 October 1983

70. AIPN, sign. 02271/21, Vol. 3, 19, 21 (unilateral meetings, debriefings and data transfer), Vol. 10, 32 (Exchange Poland-Bulgaria), Vol. 14, 26, 36 (exchange Poland – Czechoslovakia), Vol. 11,12, 28 (exchange Poland-GDR), Vol. 13, 24 (exchange Poland-Hungary), Vol. 5–6, 16–18, 20–22, 27, 30–31, 37 (exchange Poland-USSR)

71. AIPN, sign. 01592/474, operation codename "Dekus"

72. AIPN, sign. 02110/51, Vol. 1–2, operation codename "Deram"

73. Raport dot. Założenie PRO krypt. "Archimedes" dla Naczelnika Wydziału VI Dep. I MSW, Warszawa, 16 December 1987. AIPN, sign. 02320/609

74. Bischof, H.: Das "Eureka" - Projekt Osteuropas. Zur Entwicklung der Schlüsseltechnologien in den RGW-Staaten. Studie der Abteilung Aussenpolitik- und DDR-Forschung im Forschungsinstitut der Friedrich-Ebert-Stiftung, Bonn (1986)

75. Monkiewicz, G., Monkiewicz, J., Ruszkiewicz, J.: Zagraniczna Polityka Naukowo-Techniczna Polski. Diagnoza, uwarunkowania, kierunki. Wydawnictwo PAN – Zakład Narodowy im. Ossolińskich (1989)

76. Sandholtz, W.: High-Tech Europe. The Politics of International Cooperation. University of California Press Los Angeles, Berkley (1992)
77. Instrukcja operacyjna Nr 1/0/88 z dnia 1988.01.18 "DIS" Rzym. AIPN, sign. 02320/609
78. Notatka informacyjna dot. udziału Austrii w pracach "Eureka" i nowego programu badawczego FAMOS. "Dan", Wiedeń, 18 February 1988. AIPN, sign. 02320/609
79. KBP ZSRR - Notatka nr 8923/PRL. Warszawa, 26 March 1986. AIPN, sign. 02271/21, vol. 37
80. Macrakis, K.: Does Effective Espionage Lead to Success in Science and Technology? Lessons from the East German Ministry for State Security. "Intelligence and National Security", vol. 19, s. 71 (2004)

From CoCom to Dot-Com: Technological Determinisms in Computing Blockades, 1949 to 1994

Christopher Leslie[(⊠)]

South China University of Technology, Guangzhou, China
chrisleslienyc@hotmail.com

Abstract. The well-known restrictions on exports of computing equipment to the USSR and its allies at the end of the cold war had a curious history. Although the legacy of CoCom is that it seems natural to restrict technology from potential belligerents, it is difficult to determine the policy's efficacy. Started as a corollary to the plan to rebuild Europe after World War II, CoCom originally had nothing to do with computers. High-profile failures brought the usefulness of the economic blockade into question at the same time a new academic definition of technology became popular: technology is not just a material device, but it is also a means of getting something done. Computers were at the center of the quandary: does a device provide an inevitable strategic advantage, or is it the innovation culture that surrounds the device what needs protection? What is more, protecting the institutionalized knowledge from antagonists would require reducing the openness of the academic and scientific institutions that had provided innovation in the first place. When the personal computing revolution was underway, the computing embargo was at the fore-front of CoCom, even though PCs had not been prominent at its inception. With the fall of the Berlin Wall and the dissolution of the USSR, it might seem as if CoCom had been successful, yet contemporary critics and practitioners think otherwise. The determinism that underwrote CoCom then operated in reverse: policies granting access to computing networks were imagined to inevitably bring about cultural and political changes. The failure of CoCom to achieve a meaningful hindrance to technology and the unintended consequences of its implementation failed to make an impact in the political arena, but the lessons about technology transfer grained from the evaluation of the embargo deserve greater attention to guide policy today.

Keywords: CoCom · Comecon · CMEA · Chincom · Technology transfer · Policy · Determinism

1 Introduction

In the past two years, high-profile cases involving transfer of U.S. technology to adversarial countries were in the news. In 2018, the investigation of the Chinese company ZTE for selling phones with U.S. components to consumers in North Korea was one of the most visible episodes. An ex-employee of Apple apprehended on the

© IFIP International Federation for Information Processing 2019
Published by Springer Nature Switzerland AG 2019
C. Leslie and M. Schmitt (Eds.): HC 2018, IFIP AICT 549, pp. 196–225, 2019.
https://doi.org/10.1007/978-3-030-29160-0_11

way to China with sensitive corporate information was another. In 2019, Huawei's prominence in trade negotiations seemed puzzling. Although corporate espionage is nothing new, one might reasonably wonder how it became a concern for international politics. Today, though, almost seventy years of public policy make it seem natural that international relations should be leveraged to provide technological advances to allies and block or forestall technology transfer to other countries.

The cold war blockade is referred to as CoCom because of the name of the committee established by participating countries, the Multilateral Coordinating Committee for Export Controls. It is sometimes deemed to have been a success due to the lower development status of communist countries after the dissolution of the USSR in 1991. However, at the time there was sufficient evidence that demonstrated the impact of the blockade on technology development was limited at best. Nevertheless, the belief that CoCom helped win the cold war makes it harder to see a different point of view: differences in innovation cultures, economic systems, and ideologies were the hindrances to technological advance in the East Bloc.

In spite of the belief that CoCom was successful, its origins were in post–World War II economic recovery policy, a policy concerned with manufacturing equipment and raw materials that had nothing to do with information technology. In headquarters connected to the U.S. embassy in Paris, CoCom started with seven founding nations and came to have seventeen members, mostly overlapping with NATO (without Iceland but including Japan and Australia) [1]. Regardless of the overlap, no treaty ever defined CoCom. Members acceded to the decisions made by the committee only to the extent that national laws could be brought into accord. CoCom monitored the transfer of products to the East Bloc and other countries antagonistic to the alliance for forty-five years, obligating exporters to obtain licenses for a list of restricted products. Disbanded in 1994, the organization solidified the determinist notion that technology provides an inevitable and uniform effect on society.

Placing CoCom into the context of the history of computing serves to underscore how the policy was not the reason for the lack of technological development in the East Bloc. At the same time, this context helps to emphasize the opportunity cost caused by the moratorium on collaboration in the scientific and technology community. While it is possible for some scholars to consider CoCom a success because of the strong message it sent, from the perspective of technology policy to support innovation, CoCom was a failure and a dangerous precedent. Through the history of computing, one can see how CoCom had a greater cost than seen in political circles and why technology blockades in fact threaten the innovative community they purport to protect.

1.1   International Relations Frameworks

Gauging the effectiveness of CoCom in a political context is trickier than it might seem. Even if the blockade did not limit technological development in the East Bloc, some might deem the policy a success in other ways. The debate between two dominant strands of international relations theory, constructivism and structural realism, can be seen in the debate over whether CoCom was effective.

In international relations scholarship, a *constructivist* position is one that suggests that security imperatives like CoCom are intentionally exaggerated positions based on ideological constraints. Once the Cold War was established, a scholar like Wendt [2] say countries' identities as antagonists shaped their further actions and reconstituted the Cold War at each juncture. It was not until the 1980s, Wendt says, that the Soviet Union recognized the wastefulness of this "shared belief" and sought a different self-expression, bringing an end to the Cold War (p. 76). The theory that the west's economic blockade caused deprivation and brought about the Wende does not explain the timing of this choice nor the other times the USSR had instead intensified its position. Wendt reminds us that culture shapes our expectations of events. If I am driving a car in a culture where a red light means *go*, I will fail to anticipate the actions of other drivers when we come to a traffic light and get into an accident – and I may begin to question the efficacy of traffic lights. Once we are all in agreement, though, we will act in ways that reinforce the system. He applies this to the Cold War:

> Once the cultural formation known as the "Cold War" was in place, the U.S. and Soviets had a shared belief that they were enemies which helped constitute their identities and interests in any given situation, which they in turn acted upon in ways that confirmed to the Other that they were a threat, reproducing the Cold War. In each case socially shared knowledge plays a key role in making interaction relatively predictable over time, generating homeostatic tendencies that stabilize social order. (p. 187)

As a result, one might say that the U.S. and Soviet militaries had a "common interest" in continuing the cold war (p. 275). Changing policy and learning to cooperate, Wendt says, means that states must rethink their own identities as much as they must win against their adversaries. A constructivist point of view then can see a policy like CoCom as something that created not only a sense of the USSR as a communist opponent but also embodied an identity for the capitalist west. This construct was dependent upon a vision of technology as an independent, nationalistic actor that is not in accord with the history of technology.

This constructivist view, which Wendt articulated at the end of the cold war, was a response to *structural realism*. In this school of thinking, one assumes that in the international realm, nations act only according to their own self-interest because there is no authority figure. Starting from this point of view, it is best to take threats seriously. Baldwin [3], for instance, states that the economic blockade functioned better as a "symbolic moral condemnation of communism" than an effective drag on the Soviet economic system, which "had little chance of success." Although symbolic, it is not as if the policy had no consequences; the U.S. needed to convince the rest of the world that communism was a threat, which it could not do if it were engaged in friendly trade relations with its purported enemy (p. 241). For this reason, Baldwin says the symbolic nature of embargo has been underappreciated. Even if the blockade fell short of achieving its stated goals, a structural realist could say that it was successful because it helped the U.S. to effectively communicate its intentions and positions. Certainly, Baldwin notes, the USSR did not increase its territory while the embargo was in place and one cannot prove that the USSR's economic growth would have been different had there been no embargo. Looking back on the legacy of these debates, scholars like Blackwill and Harris [4] have recently suggested that the blockade became a way for the U.S. to express its moral superiority over the communist system, even if within the first ten years of its life the blockade did not seem to be accomplishing its stated aims.

The realist position makes evaluating the blockade troublesome. A structural realist position would say that the blockade was successful even if it did not hamper the development of technology in the East Bloc. The policy allowed the U.S. and its allies to communicate its pleasure of displeasure in events in a way less costly than war [3]. Technology blockades remain popular after CoCom, but their effectiveness is in the context of structural realism. In this context, the well-documented ability to circumvent the barrier, the reluctance of practitioners before and after 1991 to credit the embargo for the lack of innovation, and the lost economic opportunity do not mean the blockade was a failure. These costs, in fact, help to make the blockade a more effective symbol.

That the East Bloc failed to match the success of the capitalist west in innovation, particularly in the realm of computers, can combine with the assessment from those who hold a structural realist position to provide legitimacy for implementing controls like CoCom in the future. However, one could just as easily point to internal factors that dampened the development of technology.[1] What is more, the realist position fails to account for the international character of scientific and technical innovation. The cold war frame constructed by CoCom was of an insular, innovative nation that bestows the benefits of its progress only an elite group of allies – which is counter to the essential characteristics of international collaboration that foster innovation.

1.2   Science and Technology Studies Frameworks

A context provided by science and technology studies (STS) supports the notion that this policy would fail to meet its overt goal of hindering technological development in the East Bloc. The design of CoCom relied on the notion of technological determinism, what STS scholars label as a fallacy, presuming that technological devices are innovated in isolation from historical, cultural, or ideological constraints. As a result, determinism leads to the conclusion that a technological device can be easily uprooted and used in other circumstances with divergent histories, cultures, or ideologies, impacting the recipient in an unequivocal and uniform way. A device that gives a strategic advantage to the United States or England can, according to the determinism of CoCom, be easily used in different circumstances.

The determinism implicit in CoCom can be seen in STS studies contemporary with its creation. One notorious example is Wittfogel's 1957 *Oriental Despotism* [5]. In this study, Wittfogel attempts to explain why China's early technical superiority did not lead to a free society. He suggests that the achievement was actually China's downfall: the organization of labor needed to produce large scale irrigation in the pre-modern period led to despotic forms of government. What he calls the "hydraulic state" makes it difficult for contemporary China to embrace the wider swath of authorities needed to "counterbalance and control the political machine" (p. 49). Wittfogel's suggestion that technologies require specific forms of organization that lead inevitably toward only one

---

[1] See Kitova and Kitov's assertion that it was the unwillingness of the Party leaders in the USSR to accommodate new thinkers in "Anatoloy Kitov and Victor Glushkov," this volume.

cultural outcome reflects the same kind of deterministic attitude toward the interaction between technology and society that supported the CoCom embargo.

As the cold war waged on, though, scholars would shy away from inevitable cause-and-effect interpretations. Mumford [6], for instance, suggested in 1964 that the west's lust for nuclear weapons, rockets, and computers puts it in danger of succumbing to totalitarian ideals of the "pyramid builders." Whereas Wittfogel claimed technologies produce inevitable cultural outcomes, Mumford wrote about the danger of totalitarian ideologies in the way that technology was used. That same year, Ellul [7] wrote that technology was not so much as a device but the constellation of methods and techniques used in many human endeavors. In the following years, STS scholars would effect a more nuanced description of the interaction between technology and society. Winner [8] in 1977 proposed a terminology shift: what most people call technologies are really apparatus, so he proposes that we instead study technique, a word he notes comes from the Greek word τέχνη in an effort to think about the behaviors that surround a device and make that device a part of a coherent cultural system.

This developing understanding of technology to a certain extent lessened the concern that the East Bloc would obtain capitalist devices because their ill fit with economic systems and management styles behind the iron curtain would render them less effective. At the same time the formulations of Ellul, Mumford, and Winner blossomed into the modern field of STS, questions about the efficacy of CoCom caused new implementations of the technological blockade, particularly in 1979. In 1990, historian Pacey [9] would coin the phrase "technological dialogue" to describe the innovation that occurs when devices are passed between cultures and adapted to fit new circumstances. Additionally, Pacey points out an unintended opportunity cost of isolation: lost potential innovation. Throughout the history of technology, Pacey shows how the effort to transfer technology from one set of cultural, political, or economic circumstances to another sparks innovation. One example he provides is the printing press, which he describes as the result of interaction among cultural groups. Paper and movable type were invented in the east, but writing in Europe was made on vellum. Writing on calf skin required sharper implements that would destroy Chinese paper, Pacey notes, so when paper was brought to the West, it needed to be strengthened. This more durable paper then supported the development of printing with metal type. As an alternative to the supremacy of one nation's technical system over the other, Pacey's concept of technological dialogue shows how key innovations derived from the community of nations.

This transformation of STS theory neatly follows the development of CoCom. The goal of isolating the East Bloc from materiel that could (uniformly and unequivocally) provide a tactical advantage transformed into a concern for exposing the bloc's engineers and scientists to the organizations and methods for developing technology. Even as the scholarly work in STS and economics came to suggest that withholding devices and threatening international exchange would not accomplish policy aims, the determinism that lies behind a technological blockade remained politically compelling. The reliance on this policy had negative effects. As will be seen below, the embargo led to economic loss and strained diplomatic relations. More importantly, an effective policy to stop transfer of knowledge and experience would have had to be effected in universities, which were loath to sacrifice academic freedom not just because it was a cherished principle but also because of their assumption that a robust international exchange of ideas best fostered innovation. The history of computing technology offers an excellent window onto these debates and transformations because during this period computing devices were, at the time CoCom was first organized, thought of as business machinery, and thus exempt from the blockade, then later increasingly as devices with military applications that should be withheld from the East Bloc and finally as agents of information exchange that could serve as a framework for innovation.

Accordingly, this paper takes up the various iterations of CoCom with an aim of rethinking the received wisdom of these policies. It starts with a history of the iterations of CoCom and the related Comecon and Chincom organizations, providing relevant examples from the history of computing to make the argument that the overt economic goals were not served by the economic embargo. In the subsequent iterations of the policy, it becomes clearer that the technological blockade counters the aims it purports to accomplish.

2   Establishment of the Economic Blockade Concept

CoCom was established in 1949 in The Hague by members of the Atlantic Alliance who agreed to limit exports to the Soviet Union and its allies. Thus, the policy that would be so influential in the diffusion of computers was developed when electronic, programmable computers were in their nascent stages of development.

The notion of an economic blockade had been tested in other contexts. The U.S. 1917 Trading with the Enemy Act and the 1946 Atomic Energy Control Act were important antecedents to the idea that supplies and information should not be given to belligerents [10]. A U.S. report after World War II noted that U.S. technological devices had "significantly assisted" the Japanese air force, and a growing fear was that the same could happen with the Soviet Union [11, p. 131]. In 1948 and 1949, an economic embargo was enforced by a licensing system for goods headed to Europe out of pretext that material was in short supply for U.S. domestic needs. The policy that would come to be well-known for its involvement in hindering the diffusion of computing had little to do with technology at all.

2.1   Enforcing U.S. Policy Beyond Its Borders

Export controls came to be enforced outside the U.S. as a corollary to the Marshall Plan to provide US$12 billion in aid to sixteen European countries to rebuild after the war. When Secretary of State George C. Marshall described his plan to assist European rebuilding at a 5 June 1947 commencement address, he did not mention the embargo. According to Libbey [12], though, in addition to restarting the European economy, a "less public" rationale was to contain communism (p. 137–8). A preliminary meeting in Paris at the end of the month between the U.S., Britain, France, and the USSR demonstrated the awareness of this goal. Soviet Foreign Minister V. M. Molotov declared his opposition on July 2, claiming that the plan would divide Europe and subordinate smaller countries. Thus, before the Marshall plan was codified, there was a recognition that the aid was not entirely altruism.

After Molotov walked out of the meeting, the USSR announced a conference to plan an alternative path to recovery. The USSR would propose facilitating trade among its allies with centrally planned economies through the Council for Mutual Economic Assistance (CMEA, sometimes referred to as Comecon) with Bulgaria, Czechoslovakia, Hungary, Poland, and Romania. As a practical matter, this would mean the USSR and member countries would not be eligible for U.S. financial assistance. This decision "proved painful" for Czechoslovakia and Poland, which had planned to receive U.S. aid [12, p. 135, 138]. The sides were set for a trade war.

Policy makers in the U.S. considered the Soviet rejection of aid to be a "threat to world peace" that justified export controls [13, p. 130]. The same month Molotov walked out, the U.S. Congress passed the first export licensing requirements. Three tiers of exports were delineated. War materiel was embargoed unconditionally, while anything that could enhance war potential and bolster the Soviet economy was subject to limits in quantity (lead, copper, zinc; trucks, steel rails, freight cars) [14]. Businesses seeking to export metals, fuels, and foods – categories that amounted to about twenty percent of U.S. exports – were to obtain prior licenses in an effort to prevent domestic scarcity [12, p. 144]. Although this policy was ostensibly not aimed at the USSR, context makes the intent clear.

Prompted by the Czech coup and the Berlin blockade, the U.S. in March 1948 expanded the embargo to include all goods headed to Europe in anticipation of disbursing Marshall Plan aid. The U.S. Department of Commerce drafted lists of prohibited articles [11]. The embargo lists were completed by August 1948 while the Berlin airlift was well underway. From their offices in Paris, the Economic Cooperation Administration demanded compliance with the lists as a condition of the first year of Marshall Plan funding. Thus, the implicit intention of this policy was revealed to be "political considerations rather than economic necessity" [12, p. 145] and aid was formulated in part as pressure to regulate trade of strategic goods with the Soviet bloc [15, p. 23]. The blockade led to a retaliatory Soviet ban on exports of manganese and platinum to the U.S., metals needed for communication equipment and munitions, at the end of 1948. It was in this context that the U.S. Congress passed the Export Control Act in February 1949, a stringent embargo that included the licensing policy. It would govern trade policy for twenty years.

The first meeting of CoCom in November 1949 came at the end of a tense year. The Berlin airlift had ended in late spring 1949, but in the fall, dreams of unifying the Germanies faded when the Federal Republic of Germany and the German Democratic Republic (GDR) were established. Events in the Chinese civil war also came to a head: Mao Zedong proclaimed the communist People's Republic of China in October, the nationalist opponents fleeing to the island of Taiwan. The early Soviet explosion of an atomic bomb on 29 August 1949, years ahead of U.S. intelligence predictions, was blamed on illicit access to this research. The idea of an economic blockade fit into a larger policy of containment.

The formation of CoCom – a consultative group with at first seven members (see Table 1) – was a diplomatic success on the part of the U.S., but it came with dissensus [13, p. 139]. It would have an immediate economic impact: U.S. exports to the Soviet

Table 1. Members of CoCom. Significant suppliers of technology, such as Sweden, Switzerland, South Korea, and Taiwan, never became part of CoCom. The CoCom export lists were always secret, but one can say that in the mid-1980s the embargoed countries included much more than the East Bloc: Afghanistan, Albania, Bulgaria, Cambodia, Czechoslovakia, Cuba, the German Democratic Republic, Hungary, Laos, Mongolia, North Korea, the People's Republic of China, Poland, Romania, the Soviet Union, and Vietnam [1]. Thus, compliance with CoCom restricted a great deal of trade with potential partners.

1949	Founders: Belgium, France, UK, Italy, Luxembourg, Netherlands, U.S.
1950	First Expansion: Canada, Denmark, Norway, Portugal, FDR (West Germany)
1952	Japan
1953	Greece and Turkey (after admission to NATO)
1985	Spain
1989	Australia

Union, which had been $236 million in 1946, dropped to $2 million in 1953 [16]. The U.S. made many demands on their European allies from 1948 to 1952, but these were accepted because of the prospect of Marshall plan aid. Adler-Karlsson [15] reports that one official said, "Western Europe sold out their trade principles for good American cash." The uncertain duration of funding led to an effort to accede to U.S. policy while simultaneously sustaining trade (p. 47). As Marshall Plan aid was coming to an end, though, the U.S. Mutual Defense Assistance Act of 1951 (also known as the Battle Act) stipulated that no military, economic, or financial assistance would go to any country unless it embargoed nations that threatened the security of the U.S. The blockade was never negotiated as part of a formal treaty and relied on voluntary, multilateral cooperation. From this point forward, though, it would be enforced by the threat of the loss of U.S. economic assistance.

2.2   CoCom Expansion and Chincom

China and Japan came under the purview of CoCom in the aftermath of the Korean War. North Korea invaded South Korea in June 1950. North Korea had sided with China's communist party in its civil war, so China reciprocated, as did eventually the USSR. The war drew to a stalemate by 1951. In 1952, when Japan regained its sovereignty, Japan expressed its desire to join CoCom. Concurrently, China declared that the United States was an adversary. In addition, in April 1952 USSR launched a "Peace Offensive," inviting almost 500 people from 47 countries (including the United States) for an economic conference. These events spurred a CoCom meeting on 26 June 1952 to discuss Japan and China. The end of Korean War and Marshall Plan funding in 1953 prompted a recession in Europe, and European leaders requested an easing of export restrictions. The U.S. acquiesced, reducing the list to 200 items.

The U.S. opposed Britain, France, and Canada in admitting Japan. First, it did not want to weaken NATO, which was mostly synonymous with CoCom. Second, the U.S. wanted stricter treatment of trade in Asia, particularly on China. For its part, England wished to constrain Japan in order to control competition [17]. China was a more difficult question: would an embargo have the unintended consequence of strengthening China's ties with the USSR? Or would an alliance create an economic burden for the USSR? President Eisenhower sought an evolution of policy – the blockade should become "economic, political, and psychological" and not just a military standoff. In this, he was joined by Churchill, who believed that trade was "a weapon to penetrate the iron curtain" [17, pp. 28–29]. The compromise was that a group subordinate to CoCom, Chincom, was established. For a brief time, the committee sought stricter foreign trade barriers on China than had been in place for the East Bloc, a policy that resulted in what came to be known as the "China differential." CoCom hoped to use Japan as a "wedge" between the USSR and China [17, pp. 25–26]. The China differential foreshadowed a larger shift in policy because it was not a strategic effort, but instead targeted to influence political development [15, p. 204]. Japan would join CoCom in 1952, and the China differential was ended in 1957. The blockade had become ideological, but still it did not address computing.

2.3   Computing in the Early Years of CoCom

CoCom did not originally apply to computers. In the 1950s, the idea of a computer transformed from a mathematical device to a data-processing machine for business [18, p. 105]. In 1952, a "a spectacular publicity stunt" was arranged for ENIAC, one of the first commercial computers: it was used to predict the U.S. presidential election result using voting returns in key states [18, p. 110]. At the end of the 1950s, journalists would refer to the computer industry led by IBM and the "seven dwarfs," or companies that were attempting to enter the market (p. 117). Consequently, when CoCom was established in 1949, there was still little attention paid to computing devices.

Although computers were not part of the CoCom deliberations, technological devices were. The USSR in 1955 exploded its first hydrogen bomb and launched the Sputnik satellites at the end of 1957, the latter being a particular embarrassment especially because the U.S. space program had been beset by failures. The feedback from U.S. diplomatic posts was that this launch had caused a crisis of confidence in the ability of the capitalist approach to high-tech development. What it also showed, though, was that economic containment was not blunting Soviet technology. European leaders took these developments as a sign that the blockade was not reaching its aims, but the U.S. shifted its rationale to state that the embargo should continue "on moral and symbolic grounds" [4]. In the wake of Sputnik, the U.S. made efforts to connect the scientific community between east and west. In 1958, some results of U.S. nuclear research were published. The following year, an agreement was reached for academic visits by scientists and joint symposia [19, pp. 100–101]. CoCom countries requested and the U.S. granted a reduction of the proscribed lists in 1958. The new list of 100 items was mostly related to "a narrow band of military equipment" [12, p. 148], even though the United States continued to enforce its own embargo of a larger list of 700 items to the USSR.

As computing developed near the end of the 1950s, the U.S. estimated it was four years ahead of the Soviet Union and considered an embargo necessary to maintain that edge. The British, however, felt that computers were business machines and were exempt. From 1960 to 1961, the United States sought to convince the British that the majority of computing equipment in the USSR was used for military purposes [11, p. 137]. China, with the assistance of the USSR, had begun its own computer research program and in 1964 exploded its first nuclear bomb. In 1965, China sought to import British computers, the Electric-Leo-Marconi KDF-9, and others. The U.S. again sought to tighten restrictions at this time, and in 1966 even suggested the return of a China differential for computers [11, p. 141]. The USSR also made progress in computing in the 1950s, creating a stored program digital machine, producing small computers serially, conducting a high-level programming seminar, and building one of the first "supercomputers." These developments were contemporary with U.S. and UK achievements but independent and innovative [20]. Even if CoCom countries had a technological edge in computing, it did not seem as if it would last.

3 Relaxation of CoCom with a New Definition of Technology

After its first twenty years, CoCom went through a period of reevaluation and relaxation. The interconnectedness of world markets made it increasingly unlikely that a small group of nations could effectively control the flow of devices, resulting in a turn to technical knowledge, and the economic losses and political strife caused by the blockade could not be defended with a growing awareness that technologies are imbricated in cultural assumptions that are not easily changed. Two revisions of the U.S. laws that governed exports in 1969 and 1979 reflect a shift in the academic understanding of the relationship between technology and society. Computers were finally added to the law in 1979, creating challenges in the academic realm that would undermine the policy further.

3.1 The Politics of Technologies

In the 1960s, U.S. government funding was provided for distributed computer networks. Notably, Paul Baran went against the spirit of the technology blockade, insisting on publication of his research on communication networks that would survive a nuclear attack. His thinking was that the evidence that the U.S. military could survive a first strike would deter a Soviet attack. Instead of trying to make it available to spies, he says:

> We published it! I gave a course on it at the University of Michigan in '65. We were a hell of a lot better off if the Soviets had a better command and control system. Their command and control system was even worse than ours. [21]

Although Baran's communication network was never built, his attitude toward openness would be reflected in the leadership of ARPANet.

A U.S. Central Intelligence Agency (CIA) report in 1961 underscored the point that a blockade would be ineffective. Even an effective blockade would have "no impact" on Soviet military preparedness. Only Soviet consumers would feel the pressure [14, p. 127]. Multilateral cooperation for such a blockade would be unlikely, though, so the CIA said unilateral embargo would be "an exercise in futility" [14, p. 128]. As an alternative, the CIA determined that targeted restrictions might be effective in the short term For instance, the USSR had made a strategic decision to expand its energy production, not only for its own interests but also so that it could generate cash purchase Western technology [4]. As a result, the CIA recommended withholding large-diameter pipe in 1962–1963, resisting the USSR's westward expansion of the Druzhba oil pipeline. A Soviet pipeline, the U.S. believed, would provide immediate financial gain as well as future political power.

The U.S. stance on the pipeline project would show, however, how an economic blockade has unintended political consequences that reach beyond the opportunity cost of lost trading partners. President John F. Kennedy witnessed this during the Cuban missile crisis of October 1962. "How strong would allied support for the U.S. be in a future confrontation with the U.S.S.R. when the latter might threaten to turn off the spigot of oil?" [12, pp. 149–150]. The U.S. denied the pipe needed for the project, but Europe saw trade opportunities. The U.S. bypassed CoCom and went instead to NATO, winning a 25 November 1962 recommendation that NATO members withhold the pipe. This was only a temporary victory; NATO was advised to reverse this decision because West Germany and Britain already had contracts for the oil. The pipeline began operation in 1964. As noted by Mastanduno [14], the U.S. got its way but it came at a high cost and the pipeline was completed anyway; furthermore, allies became suspicious that U.S. had a vested interest to protect its own oil industry instead of following a symbolic policy of containment, further undermining support for the blockade.

With the 1969 moon landing having assuaged the sense of inadequacy caused by Sputnik, the U.S. decided it was time to engage further with the East Bloc. Given the general mood that embargoes would be less successful than engagement, a relaxation of CoCom took place in the ten years after the moon landing. The Export Administration Act of 1969, which dictated how the U.S. would conform to CoCom, was passed to loosen the restrictive character of the expiring 1949 and 1951 acts. The U.S. Congress sought to promote East-West trade, aware that "trying to control Soviet economic growth was now untenable" and in the end only disadvantaged U.S businesses [4]. Aware of the East Bloc's desire for high tech equipment in computers and milling, the act encouraged trade with all nations with the intent to obtain "tacit Soviet agreement to abide by the status quo in international affairs" [19, p. 101]. The new legislation sought to maintain a technological differentiation between capitalist and communist countries, but it also acknowledged that trade should not be sacrificed for national security. This placated U.S. businesses, who believed they were being kept out of East Bloc markets by the U.S.'s regulations, which were stricter than in other CoCom countries [22]. After its first twenty years, CoCom's economic embargo had been redefined as a strategic embargo

3.2   Reevaluating the Threat Posed by Equipment

In spite of the embargo, it became clear that the USSR could obtain sensitive equipment illicitly. "The incentives for firms to bypass CoCom's formal controls were great" [14 p. 181]. Often cited is a 1972 instance where the Soviets obtained precision ball bearing equipment from the Bryant Grinder Corporation in Vermont that would help them make guidance systems for nuclear missiles; Soviets conducted MIRV tests the next year, leading some analysts to state that the grinders alleviated a "critical bottleneck" [14, p. 172]. This export of 168 grinders to make anti-friction ball bearings for use in gyroscopes was justified because the equipment was also available from Japan, Switzerland, Italy, and France, not to mention that other equipment of this type had already been sold [14, 16, 23]. In 1979, the U.S. semiconductor I. I. Industries was convicted of trade violations after they mislabeled semiconductor equipment in order to facilitate its sale to the USSR in 1975 and 1976. The processing equipment was sent first to Canada, then to Switzerland, and ultimately to the USSR to hide the circumvention [16]. These were serious breaches, but a growing question was whether they provided an advantage.

The new thinking in academic definitions of technology in the 1960s was mirrored by evidence on the ground that devices, whether obtained legally or illicitly, might not positively impact a country's military advantage. The Soviet innovation in computing seen in the 1950s seemed to have stalled by the late 1960s, even though the interest in computing increased.[2] This resulted in a shift toward acquiring capitalist technology.

As noted by Goodman [20], obtaining computing devices was an unsuccessful transfer of technology not only due to CoCom but also because of what might be called cultural differences. Potential partners were unwilling to come to the USSR because the country did not have the money, expertise, or "positive working environment" to get companies or individuals to stay for years. In addition, Goodman states, the Soviets constrained technology transfer themselves through travel restrictions, subject matter prohibitions, centralized meetings control, and small-volume purchases. It was not the embargo so much as it was local policy that impeded development.[3]

The blockade was far from impervious. Beyond the direct purchase of computing technology, the USSR attempted other methods of technology transfer such as "sister plant" relationships with IBM, turnkey production facilities, licenses and joint projects, not to mention encouraging the defection of trained personnel. Weaker measures of technology transfer such as academic exchanges, plant visits, training, and conferences were also tried. However, these were not as effective as they could have been. Often the Soviets lessen the potential by "interposing" intermediaries [20, p. 123] like the KGB or foreign trade organizations, limiting feedback between the suppliers and receivers. These might allow information to pass between the nations, but they would not result in the advantages gained by their counterparts on the other side of the iron curtain who worked in different environments. Even when equipment was obtained by the USSR, it would not have an impact overall. Peters [24] calls 1 October 1970, the day when the Politburo reviewed a proposal for Soviet decentralized network for economic planning, "the day of reckoning," and notes that nothing was built in the years that followed (p. 161). The cultural differences were much more effective in limiting development.

The strength of the cultural barrier calls into question the high diplomatic cost to the U.S. of enforcing the technology embargo. The U.S. probably would have been successful in convincing its allies to join the program voluntarily, Adler-Karlsson [15]

---

[2] For an updated perspective on the supposed lack of innovation, see Kitova and Kitov, "Anatoly Kitov and Victor Glushkov," and Kitov, "Main Teleprocessing Monitors," this volume.

[3] For further insight into this difficulty, see Sikora, "Cooperating with Moscow," this volume.

noted in 1968, but instead the U.S. chose to coerce them with the threat of withholding Marshall Plan aid. Thus, the persuasive value was lost (p. 48). The outcome of the policy did not compensate for the bad feelings that came along with it, Adler-Karlsson continues. Soviet development, measured in terms of gross national product, was at most delayed after ten years of embargo. In terms of military development, the delay was about four months (p. 190–191). Both of these measurements presume there were no counter actions; assuming that to CoCom policy was fifty percent effective, the delay was more like 6 months and 2 months, Adler-Karlsson writes (p. 200). This slight gain was at the cost of lost trade as well as diplomatic conflict, even if one is not convinced that the true barrier was one of technical culture.

In parallel with the growing awareness in STS that devices reflect a constellation of historical, economic, political and ideological considerations, the experience of the 1960s led to a reform in thinking about the technological embargo. The recognition that the devices themselves were not the main issue is seen in the final report of a U.S. task force headed by the president of Texas Instruments, Fred Bucy. The so-called Bucy report [25] in 1976 called for a change in thinking. Except for military devices, the Bucy report recommended a relaxation of trade barriers. Recognizing that superiority comes from knowledge, the report recommended loosening the restrictions to devices themselves. Accordingly, techniques like cryptography were determined to be a weapon and placed under restricted access by the Arms Export Control Act of 1976.

3.3   Adding Computers to CoCom

With a new vision of technology in the West and growing demand in the East, requests for exceptions to CoCom proscriptions increased. In 1966, there were 228, with 12.7 percent (30 exception requests) coming from the U.S. By 1978, there were 1,680, with 62.5 percent (1,050 requests) of these coming from the U.S. [26]. The value of the exceptions in 1967 was $11 million, but by 1977 there were $214 million in exceptions [16]. As shown in Table 2, in 1971 computer exceptions were 23%, or $21 million; by 1977 their proportion was nearly three times as great and the value had increased eightfold. These exception requests in 1970s show that revision of CoCom was needed because, although a majority of requests involved computers, there was no agreement on what was appropriate.

The recognition that technology was more a way of doing things than it was access to physical devices came at a time when mainframe computers came under its purview. In the 1970s, a shift in sentiment about the embargo was reflected in congressional studies. The end result was a recommendation that the lists of restricted items be shortened and licensing procedures be "less onerous" in order to promote U.S. economic competitiveness [4]. The new Export Administration Act, passed in 1979, described how the U.S. would interpret and implement CoCom. A shift in the Congressional debate was palpable. One contemporary reviewer noted:

> Export restrictions employed as a foreign policy tool are rarely effective in influencing the internal or external policies of economically powerful nations like the Soviet Union, which is not dependent on U.S. exports, because such use makes it impossible for foreign leaders to change their conduct without damaging their individual or national pride [27, p. 91]

Table 2. Requests for exemptions from CoCom export restrictions for computing equipment [16].

Year	Value of computer exception requests ($ million)	Percentage of computer exceptions to total
1971	$21	23%
1972	$66	39%
1973	$80	50%
1974	$120	66%
1975	$147	64%
1976	$123	52%
1977	$168	63%

The symbolic nature of the embargo came under scrutiny from many angles. Given the recent recession, not to mention the U.S. effort to promote international trade for its business, the costs of the economic embargo were harder to justify. Additionally, the use of the embargo as a foreign policy symbol was questionable; because of their "inflexibility," once established as a symbol they cannot be removed "without sending unintended messages to other nations" [27]. Thus, the U.S. moved from a realist to a constructivist approach in this act.

In addition to demanding that foreign policy consider the significant economic cost of the embargo, the Act broadened the definition of technology as not just devices but also "information and knowhow." According to the act, training and services were just as important as prototypes and manuals. Henceforth, the knowledge or devices to produce goods, including computer software, would be proscribed. It also put supercomputers under embargo, but it left it up to the Commerce Department to set the definition and access guidelines. Finally, the act authorized the U.S. executive branch to control exports in support of foreign policy and to limit trade with countries who supported terrorism. As much as Chincom had aimed to influence politics, it had been limited to China and was relatively short lived. Now, perhaps because it was clear that the impact of the embargo on devices was minimal, the new law authorized the use of CoCom as a political tool. The Soviet invasion of Afghanistan at the end of the year led the Carter administration to suspend all CoCom licenses to the East Bloc, bringing and end to the relaxing period with respect to the USSR and its allies [28]. This gave the U.S.-led blockade against communism an opportunity to show its sense of moral superiority; it was a system not just "different from or irreconcilable with" the East Bloc, nor was it a policy centered on "self-interest," but simply one that was "morally superior" [4].

The U.S. established diplomatic relations with the People's Republic of China on 1 January 1979 and committed to support efforts to modernize the country. Although the U.S. had been imposing a national embargo against China, within a few months they became a favored trading partner. With respect to China, the new status led to new guidelines, particularly for dual-use technologies, including electronics and computers [29]. This policy had a noticeable effect on technology exchange. Under the new policy, China would be allowed to receive exports at twice the level as given to Eastern

Europe. In 1983, a new policy to allow exports of seven categories of goods included computers and computerized instruments. As result, exports to China increased eightfold in the ten years after 1979, to $1.7 billion, while trade to the USSR and Eastern Europe decreased [29]. In 1981, Burroughs Corp asked for permission to install a B-7830 a computer in 1983 in Beijing for $5.5 million. This computer, which could compute 3.5 million instructions per second, would be the most sophisticated computer in China. An earlier computer installed in 1980 for the Chinese census was capable of 1.08 million instructions per second [30]. These projects would lead to further expansion in the market. In 1985, IBM donated, at a cost of $1.7 million, 100 microcomputers (their 5550 model) to the Chinese Ministry of Education. In 1986, IBM planned to begin the joint manufacture of the 5550 with a Chinese company. Hewlett-Packard also agreed to provide China with one of its minicomputers [31]. China was not unique in these acquisitions, but in terms of CoCom, this new China differential reflects the political weight accorded to technology transfer.

4   Personal Computing and CoCom

The personal computer revolution began during the relaxation period. Intel began to sell its 4004 microprocessor, a "computer on a chip," in 1971 [18, p. 236]. The first microprocessor-based home computer was the 1975 Altair. Like other hobbyist products, it was sold as a kit. Apple introduced its first computer the next year. The intention of these designs was to "liberate" computers from their business uses. IBM came around in 1981 with the IBM personal computer. The personal computing revolution, which aimed to bring computing to a wider range of users, brought with it a concern that it could provide tactical superiority to belligerent countries. Even so, there was a growing awareness that access to the devices themselves would not give a country an advantage. This tension is seen in how government used CoCom to justify its actions.

4.1   Unintentional Impact on Universities

The redefinition of technology in the 1979 Export Administration Act from device to technique was protested almost immediately by universities, where politicians and bureaucrats assumed soft technology transfer occurred. In February 1981, presidents of Cornell, MIT, Cal Tech, the University of California, and Stanford wrote a letter to protest an effort to restrict access to the Very High Speed Integrated Circuit program and other actions related to the export and control of technical research. The presidents feared the that would be a situation where:

> faculty could not conduct classroom lectures when foreign students were present, engage in the exchange of information with foreign visitors, present papers or participate in discussions at symposia and conferences where foreign nationals were present, employ foreign nationals to work in their laboratories, or publish research findings in the open literature ... Restricting the free flow of information among scientists and engineers would alter fundamentally the system that produced the scientific and technological lead that the government is now trying to protect and leave us with nothing to protect in the very near future. The way to protect that lead is to

make sure that the country's best talent is encouraged to work in the relevant areas, not to try to build a wall around past discoveries. [19, pp. 137–138]

Rather than classify the research, the presidents requested only that the sensitive parts of the research be carried out in secure facilities. The Corson report [19] would later reinforce the necessity of the open research community for technical and scientific progress.

In a related September 1981 incident, the U.S. State Department official sought to enlist the aid of a professor at the University of Michigan to restrict the access of Qi Yulu, a visiting scholar interested in computer software from the People's Republic of China, from classified information. The official's rationale was "export control and national security concerns," referring vaguely to the Arms Export Control Act and the Export Administration Act. The letter stated that Qi's program of study should focus on classroom activities "with minimal involvement in applied research." Qi should have no access to "the design, construction, or maintenance data" of computers nor "to source codes or their development." Additionally, the officer requested advance notice of "any visits to any industrial or research facilities." The officer concluded, somewhat ludicrously, that in spite of all of this, "Qi should not be denied as full an academic program as possible" [19, pp. 172–175]. This request makes it clear how the principle that technology was a way of doing work was firmly established and how export control policies had assumed a broader scope as a result.

In an exchange, the UM president made it clear that the university cherished its "extensive involvement" with students and scholars from the PRC while also respecting student privacy and the importance of free inquiry as a foundation for technical research. He believed the government's request was unnecessary, because as a matter of policy the university did not conduct classified research, but also noted that "the restrictions you propose can only have a chilling effect upon the academic enterprise." He took a jab at the official, noting that the Reagan administration had promised to reduce government interference, but also questioned whether the export control regulations were applicable, calling the laws "lengthy, complex, and ambiguous" and "difficult to interpret even by those dealing daily in munitions or exports." He concluded:

we are insistent that our faculty and our students (regardless of their country of origin) be allowed to operate in their teaching and research functions … in ways consistent with our academic traditions and the applicable laws, which we believe are totally on the side of openness and do not make it appropriate for faculty to report on or control the activities of our students. [19, p. 181]

The exchange between these two officials was included as part of the Corson report and underpinned the importance of maintaining an atmosphere of free exchange among scientists from different countries on university campuses.

4.2   Reevaluating Restrictions on Computers

The USSR's invasion of Afghanistan seemed to be coupled with new communist movements in Angola and Nicaragua. Likewise, after the declaration of martial law in Poland in 1981, the administration reinstated oil and gas restrictions [22]. The USSR shot down flight KAL 007 in 1983 after it was mistaken for a spy plane, further precipitating anti-communist sentiments in the United States. The response of the Reagan administration was to revisit the contents of the lists, which had largely been ignored since the 1960s [32]. A meeting set in 1982 was politicized by the Soviet military takeover of Poland, leading Reagan to demand an end to sale of technological equipment to the Soviet Union.

At the time of these increased tensions, the ability of the Soviet Union to obtain capitalistic devices was confirmed by a Soviet spy, Vladimir Vetrov, codenamed Farewell. In an editorial printed in several newspapers on 12 January 1982, Secretary of Defense Caspar Weinberger revealed "a massive, systematic effort to get advanced technology from the West" that led to hundreds of embedded Soviet agents who stole many documents, leading to 4,000 Soviet projects based on information gained from this program. The Corson report had pointed out that 70 percent of technology acquired by the USSR had come from intelligence agencies, determining only a few times the loss came from students and universities. The spies were typically visiting researchers violating their status [33, p. 17]. The conflict between the Corson report call for academic freedom and the Reagan administration's increasingly public attacks on illicit technology transfer show how CoCom had become political theater.

In May 1982, Weinberger decried that the west had been giving the Soviets the technological "rope to hang us," citing the Bryant Grinder Corporation grinders, but said that the Reagan administration would put an end to it [34]. The following year, Weinberger would make the case that all technology transfer and even trade aids the Soviet military. Even when the technology transfer does not have military value, it permits them "to put their own engineers to work on military research and development." When other countries buy Soviet raw materials, they provide "hard currency which the Soviets can use to acquire additional Western technology" [33, p. II-30]. The administration went as far as to accuse CoCom members of selling sophisticated material to the East Bloc [35]. This increasing tension was a prelude to Reagan's call to review the CoCom lists. In a summit in Ottawa in July 1984, the reassessment of the 30-year-old lists led to 58 proposals to expand the list of embargoed goods. "Categories added included computer software, floating dry docks, robots, spacecraft, super alloys, superconductive material, and telecommunications equipment" [12, p. 151].

Energy was again the most prominent among the concerns to the U.S. The Soviets needed 25-megawatt compressor stations and 56-inch pipe that they could not produce for a pipeline project [14, 36]. The 3,000-mile Trans-Siberian Pipeline to bring natural gas from Siberia to West Germany, France, Italy, Belgium, and Ireland had been funded by German banks in 1981 in exchange for $10 billion in trade over twenty years. Even though the project was well underway, the Reagan administration felt it would make Europe dependent on Soviet energy [32]. West Germany was against the sanctions. Aside from the investment in the project, almost 7 percent of West Germany's trade was conducted with countries in Eastern Europe, and Chancellor Helmut Schmidt did not want sanctions to interfere with his effort to build relationships with East Germany [37]. The U.S., as before, worried about political leverage. The U.S. was successful in gaining stricter control of technology exports, the reason for the meeting, but a wider ban on technology exports was not supported. The gas pipeline, notably, would go forward [37]. Two days after the meeting, France sealed an agreement to purchase 8 billion cubic meters of Soviet natural gas a year for 25 years [38]. The friction caused by the U.S. demands again strained allegiances.

To some, it seemed like CoCom restrictions on personal computers were relaxed in summer 1984, a few months after Apple announced its Macintosh computer with great fanfare during Super Bowl XVIII. This was because manufacturers no longer needed exception requests for PCs. After restrictions in the wake of the lists developed to comply with the 1979 act, under pressure from the U.S. computing industry a control limit for smaller computers was set between 7 and 8 million bits per second. Although the U.S. believed that these smaller computers had military uses, it also recognized that U.S. manufacturers were losing ground to European competitors. For mainframes, the limit was raised to 48 million bits per second (it had been 32 million) [39]. For the first time, CoCom sought to protect production or development of computer systems, even proscribing equipment that could manufacture computers that were not restricted. In addition, restrictions on technology with military potential, like distributed databases, CAD, telecom equipment, and switching, were tightened [40].

The Reagan administration's new policies came at an important time for the modern Internet as well. The switch to TCP/IP on the ARPAnet was made official on 1 January 1983 and the DNS system in use today was fully functional by 1985. CSNET (started in 1983, connecting most computer science departments in the US by 1986 as well as connecting many international users) and NSFNET (backbone created in 1985), both of which were funded by the National Science Foundation and used DNS and TCP/IP protocols, ostensibly allowed many users access to high-performance computers. Connecting China or a country from the East Bloc to these networks would seem to be a violation of the demand that access to high-performance computers be restricted. At the end of this period, the Chinese would be connected to CSNET in spite of the presumption that CoCom proscribed the transfer of computer software and connections to high speed computers [41].

4.3   Increasing the Cultural Argument Against CoCom

More questioning of the cost-benefit ratio of CoCom is evident in the 1980s. Notably, Bertsch [16] writes in 1983, the detente period from 1965–1980 showed limited expansion of imports of western technology but it did not seem to make a big difference in the growth of communism. "The Soviet Union has a poor record of assimilation and diffusion of technology and Western technology will tend to have a short-term impact with fewer long-term implications than in the West" (p. 24). Bertsch counters those who say that Soviet foreign policy was antagonistic in this period to CoCom countries by saying it could have been worse. He asks critics to imagine the USSR had invaded Yugoslavia after the death of Tito, if they had entirely closed access to Berlin, or if they had made a violent response in Poland. These more heinous actions might have transpired had there been no economic interest and ties to maintain, even though either side cannot be proved. Thus, he concludes, there is more benefit to economic engagement.

This high-handed attitude led Norman Tebbit, the British trade secretary, to warn that the most persistent source of allied tension with the United States was "your claims to be able to impose your laws on people in other countries, inside their own homes and businesses" [42, p. 132]. This was a reaction to a public reminder by IBM to its UK customers that the U.S. government believed it had the right to control the diffusion of technology beyond its borders. Re-exporting technology, they believed, required permission from the U.S. Commerce Department. No one disputed, for instance, that Western chipmaking equipment contributed to Soviet electronics and, in particular, that the designs for the IBM 360 and 370 were used by the Soviets to make their own mainframe computers. The U.S. said it was "unwise" to say that the ability to purchase computers "in a shop on Trafalgar Square or 47th Street, or on the Causeway in Hong Kong" means the item should not be sold to the USSR. Nevertheless, "almost everyone else and certainly all the Europeans believe that now that the personal computer genie is out of the bottle, it is quite impossible to put it back in again" [42, p. 134].

The Corson report in 1982 had noted that the blockade was not the only factor in developing military technology. Even when the Soviet military obtained a device, the absorption of acquired technology was low due to "inhibiting tendencies." There were not incentives for military researchers to innovate, for one. Also, the organizational effort to obtain devices was large and complex, meaning that there were "inefficiencies in transferring information to those who have requested it." Finally, it noted that there were adverse effects from the way the Soviet military compartmentalized its scientists and engineers [19, p. 19]. In 1985, Goodman [20] continued the negative assessment of CoCom, focusing more on the intention of limiting access to technological devices. Goodman seeks to redefine technology as "the know-how to specify, design, build, maintain, and use a product." Technological capability comes not just having a device or information, but what one can do with it.

To illustrate this point, Goodman asks readers to think of the impact of a new journal article on an U.S. industrial or academic researcher. The researcher knows the author and saw a preprint of the article six months before it was published (thus a year ahead of Soviet a counterpart, where journals arrive six months after publication). The U.S. researcher has a relationship with the author or can easily form one by using the telephone or computer network. Additionally, the U.S. researcher can take more advantage of published research because of on-site hardware and software or the means to get it (p. 125). This context matters when the Soviets obtained a proscribed device. Once acquired, Western hardware would become a "host" for a "Sovietized" prototype (p. 126). However, Goodman points out, copiers were at a disadvantage due to the cultural difference:

> Effective development of modern hardware and software is becoming more dependent on comprehensive, sophisticated, integrated, tool environments, which include an interwoven set of computerized tools and a working environment built around those tools. (p. 127, emphasis in original)

As a result, allowing the technology into the USSR was actually more effective than an embargo, Goodman suggests. "Western technology has been a substitute for, rather than a complement to, domestic research and development" (p. 130). This is not to say that there was no innovation in the presence of Western devices, just that it was local innovation, like making East Bloc peripherals work with Sovietized copies.

Goodman asks readers to imagine what it is like to be a group of "bright and energetic" scientists who have little experience. Their government is happy with the copy effort because they get a system at an accelerated pace. However, the people who do the work do not enjoy "hacking away" at the good and bad work done by others, and they are not permitted to improve it. Moreover, they are not going to make something new if they then have to maintain it; it is easier to use the American products (p. 131). Goodman counters the Soviet boast of obtaining technology and saving time on development with the long-term detriment to innovation.

To underscore this difference, Goodman notes the difference in the source of innovation. Many industry problems find solutions based on feedback from the user community. The Soviet military is not such a community. Soviet innovators have some privileges above other workers, but their restricted communication does not mirror the user community in the U.S. or Japan (p. 133). The Soviet military is a small group and it is, understandably, risk-adverse and conservative. The U.S. military research community is larger and it is less conservative technologically (i.e., the Soviet military could never have embarked on ARPANet). Even more so, the U.S. civilian community is much bigger than the first two combined, it is robustly diverse, encompassing many types of users and applications, "and is the main prize of what may be the most singular technological competition in history between the U.S. and Japanese computer industries" (p. 133). This community's access to international colleagues for collaboration was key, Goodman says. "No computing community, including that of the US would be able to move at its current pace if it were to have its contacts with the rest of the world severely restricted" (p. 134). Thus, by 1985, one can see a forceful awareness that the goal of limiting technical development by restricting the flow of technical know-how was seen as severely limited.

Cultural episodes illustrate the growing distrust of CoCom. In 1984, Piet Beertema pretended to announce that the Soviet Union had joined USENET. The April Fool's message, allegedly from General Secretary of the Soviet Union's communist party, read "today, 840401, this is at last the Socialist Union of Soviet Republics joining the Usenet network and saying hallo to everybody" and provided connection details to Kremvax, a fictional computer in the USSR [43]. The so-called Kremvax hoax illustrates the annoyance among CoCom countries with the boundaries to communication with colleagues. The Star Trek film *The Voyage Home* illustrates this theme to a new conclusion by means of the role played by Pavel Chekov. In the 1966 television series, Chekov was a symbol of the hopes for collaboration in spite of the cold war. Twenty years later, the crew travels back to 1986 and Lt. Chekov, suspected of being a Soviet spy, is injured while being detained. The military does not stop the transfer of technology needed by the Enterprise, is not depicted as stopping the crew from accomplishing its aims, but instead puts a kindly officer in danger. These incidents illustrate the growing awareness that CoCom was a futile exercise that had negative consequences.

4.4   Diversions Weaken CoCom Credibility

Several high-profile failures of the policy underscored how the interconnectedness of trade and a lack of investment in interdiction made CoCom ineffective in battling technology transfer. Soviet agents and businesses interests worked cleverly within the regulatory framework, taking advantage of loose enforcement. These cases demonstrate the difficulty of maintaining CoCom restrictions on computing but also the challenges of seeking enforcement in a globalized production environment.

One way computing devices found their way to the USSR was through subterfuge from foreign agents. In 1983, it was revealed that a Digital Equipment Corporation VAX 11/782 was shipped from New York to South Africa and then to Hamburg, Germany. The next stop of the $1.5 million computer, which was also used by the U.S. military, would have been to be Sweden and then to the USSR, but it was seized by West German customs agents [44]. It was revealed that a KGB agent in South Africa had orchestrated the diversion [45].

Some transfer of technology resulted from legal sales. From 1977 to 1980, the Swedish firm DataSaab contracted with the USSR to upgrade the Soviet air traffic control system. The equipment was cleared because it was used for civil aviation. However, it was revealed in 1984 that Soviets obtained military technology in the upgrade – a primary radar digitizer, computerized aircraft tracking, a system programming center, training simulators, and other hardware and software – giving the civilian facility military capabilities. U.S. Commerce Secretary Malcolm Baldridge termed this a serious trade violation. The scandal ended with jail sentences, loss of export rights, and fines [23, p. 120]. This case illustrates the complexity of dual-use technology.[4]

Another scandal involving falsified export licenses entered public notice in 1987. What came to be known as the Toshiba-Kongsberg case is another earnest effort by Soviets to purchase technology legally. The scandal had its roots in 1974, when the Soviets approached the Toshiba Machine Tool Company in Japan but were rejected because of their interpretation CoCom. The Soviets then obtained nine machines from 1976 to 1979 from a French firm. Toshiba became "bitter" because of the lost sale and was more receptive when the USSR returned in 1979 [14, p. 303]. The small Japanese trading house went to a larger house to obtain grinding equipment for large ship propellers. The two arranged a deal with Toshiba Machine Company to sell four room-sized robotic devices. Both would earn a percentage of the five-year, $33 million agreement. Kongsberg Vaapenfabrtikk was a Norwegian manufacturer that supplied numerical controller units and software. Toshiba installed four 9-axis milling machines in 1983. More machines were subsequently shipped. The paperwork mislabeled the equipment, calling it a "vertical lathe" that was not on the proscribed export list [23, 46]. The software modification was sent without an export license.

The added symmetry provided by the grinders would make the propellers of Soviet submarines quieter and, as a result, harder to detect. "This was exactly the kind of technology transfer to the Soviet Union that the United States wanted to prevent" [46, p. 267]. Analysts suggested that U.S. might not recover the advantage it formerly held in anti-submarine warfare [23]. These were not items of U.S. origin, but still they violated the principles of CoCom. The result was that the Japanese government banned Toshiba from exporting to the East Bloc for one year. The U.S. Commerce department demanded both companies stop shipping sensitive equipment to third countries until it could review their export controls.

---

[4] See also Schmitt, "Socialist Life," this volume.

In addition to lax enforcement, Toshiba-Kongsberg reveals the difficulty of imposing penalties. The U.S. Congress initially called for a boycott of Toshiba, leaving Kongsberg relatively untouched. Crawford points out why this ban was unsuccessful: by 1983, the U.S. had fallen behind Japan in semiconductors, fiber optics, and robotics, as determined by the Commerce Department. Thus, the U.S. was dependent on trade; 40 percent of advanced electronic components were coming from Japan. Of the 3,000 types of chips needed for the military space program, 93 were coming from foreign companies (all but one of them being Japanese). As a result, about 10 percent of Toshiba's sales were coming from the U.S. Toshiba was supplying about one-half of the world's one-megabyte dynamic RAM chips, and the company had established many corporate alliances with U.S. firms. Had this ban been implemented, it would have imposed hardship on the U.S. The immediate impact would have been billions of lost sales, harming hundreds of companies. Apple computer said it would suffer "financially and competitively" from the ban [46, p. 270]. Not to mention, foreign firms would still have access to these banned products, putting U.S. firms at a disadvantage. Ultimately, the sanctions were weakened.

In the same year as Toshiba-Kongsberg, other cases of subterfuge were revealed. Luxembourg also interrupted a division of the French company Sogexport, Scientific Accessories, that was shipping U.S. equipment for chip etching. The U.S. suppliers seemed to be unaware that Sogexport intended to resell the equipment to the USSR. [47]. Police raided the Tokyo company Prometron Technics Ltd. because of reports they had shipped material to make nuclear reactors to East Germany. The ensuing investigation showed that Prometron had set up business arrangements around the world for Canon and a South Korea firm to ship Japanese-made equipment for advanced chip-making to East Germany via Hong Kong. The engraving devices could produce about 15,000 chips an hour and "rank among the technologies most closely controlled by western allies." In 1987 and 1988, shipments of equipment worth more than $10 million were made, but Canon maintained that it was unaware of the ultimate destination [48].

The failure of CoCom to stop the illicit diffusion of computing technology was coupled with a growing awareness of the negative effects on companies that try to follow the rules. In 1987, the National Academy of Sciences described the "de-Americanization" of world markets: the phenomenon of capitalist countries turning to non-U.S. sources or initiating their own development efforts because of CoCom complications [49, p. 12]. The loss to the U.S. economy was estimated at 188,000 jobs and $17 billion, considering lost sales to CoCom countries that found the application process cumbersome, potential sales to communist countries, loss of licenses and reduced research and development effort (p. 264). Coupled with the revelations of the loss of strategic technology that would impact military preparedness, these losses suggested that CoCom was harming U.S. companies, not the Soviet Union.

5 Ending CoCom in the Age of the Dot-Com Boom

CoCom was disbanded with the end of the cold war, suggesting that it had completed its task. Although this would seem to indicate that it had fulfilled its mission, the discussion about ending the program failed to incorporate lessons about technology and society. The rationale for ending the organization was just as rooted in determinism as had been the rationale for continuing it. News reports in the period 1991 to 1994 cast the embargo as a mission accomplished, even though the original design of CoCom was unconcerned with technology in general or computers specifically. The notion that computers and telecommunications would uniformly and inevitably transform societies lay behind the release of industries from the proscriptions, though, showing the birth of a new determinism.

5.1   Connecting Eastern Europe to Information Networks

The way the interpretation of CoCom could have inhibited the computing community was illustrated by the University of Michigan case, but also in the way connections to Eastern European countries were limited. The leaders of the European Academic Research Network (EARN) had made efforts to connect eastern countries to its network starting in 1987 in order to maintain connections with colleagues, but it was not until March 1990 that the connections were permitted.

The president of EARN described the situation in terms of the interpretation of CoCom offered by the 1983 implementation of the 1979 law. The purchase of a supercomputer, most of which came from the U.S., first required a so-called super-computer safeguard plan (SSP) that stipulated the equipment could not be used by people in CoCom proscribed countries nor could it have a "direct tie" to their networks. This was a bit perplexing in 1987, when there were many connections that did not give users direct access to the internal mechanisms of a computer, but it also raised the question about computers operating within the U.S. that were sold without SSPs: why could *they* not connect to eastern Europe?

The management of EARN met with the U.S. Department of Commerce to try resolve these issues in March 1989. EARN learned that there were two concerns. First, it was assumed that connecting a supercomputer to a CoCom country was tantamount to giving them a computer. Second, embargoed software and data could potentially be transmitted. After discussion, Commerce was willing to allow modification of the SSPs. The political changes at the end of 1989 served as an impetus, and the new stipulations were that the users must be made aware of the export rules, links should be limited to 64 kbps, electronic mail could be made freely but file transfer must be monitored, and traffic logs must be made. With this agreement, Bulgaria, Czechoslovakia, Hungary, Poland, and the USSR began making preparations to connect to EARN [50]. The choice of these countries was not random: they were the five countries that had developed industrial and educational backgrounds needed in spite of CoCom.

EARN was not the only mechanism to sponsor connections. Hungary's plans for a national network date back to the mid 1980s, and by 1989 a UUCP (USENET) connection was established to other countries while EARN and Internet connections were still proscribed [51]. However, this connection could not transform the academic environment immediately. One researcher noted that the "technique of collaboration" would require some adjustment in Hungary. The acceptable use policy, for instance, would create a lot of bureaucracy because certifying that "the behavior of our users is perfectly acceptable" could lead to an administrator stating "therefore I should control everything" [51, p. 446]. It was not just the access to the devices – the researchers also needed the support of a collaborative culture implied by USENET.

In 1990, Hungary told the World Bank that its computer science research capability was fifteen years behind the west. They blamed three factors: the lack of funding for travel, the language barrier with the international community, and technological blockade. Mandatory Russian language instruction led dissatisfaction in foreign languages in general, and as a result many Hungarian researchers spoke no international languages. Researchers were prohibited from connecting to colleagues in capitalist countries via email and the official Soviet sources of information were expensive and slow. A visitor in 1991 noted that telephone system was inadequate; there were fewer than 1 line per 100 people and the quality of the connections were so poor that data could not always be transmitted. Researchers claimed that CoCom had not affected their field, other than sometimes instituting delays in obtaining material [52]. Structural issues, as much or more than access to technology, were to blame.

Similar to the developments in the USSR and Hungary, the development of computing has already been reported for Poland, where academic research networks and a rich community of amateur computing enthusiasts grew in spite of CoCom restrictions [53].

5.2   Post–Cold War Reevaluation

Despite political rhetoric praising CoCom, contemporary scholars preferred to blame the culture of the USSR rather than the economic embargo for Soviet difficulties in developing new technology. Igor Artemiev [54] argued at length in 1991 that technology transfer to communist countries is different than in capitalist companies. In a communist system, research is funded by the state and technological innovation does not become private property. Instead, all benefits from an innovation are immediately made the property of the collective. Thus, if a company creates an innovation, there is little compensation. Innovators are required to disseminate their new idea and are only compensated for the reproduction of materials and travel expenses to do so.

The official line in the USSR was that all innovation was shared, but this does not tell the entire story. According to the 1949 Sofia principles, technology would be spread among cooperating countries. For thirty years, the USSR sent out 35,000 sets of documentation and received 17,000 from CMEA countries, supposedly saving members $20 billion for technology they would have had to purchase on the open market. Artemiev counters, "One has reason to doubt the meaningfulness of such estimates, when technology transfer is equated with mere copying and mailing of information. Technology transfer can be reduced to information dissemination only when both partners are equally developed and possess strong capabilities for the quick and effective transformation of information into productive technology" (p. 82).[5] This assessment helps to mount a counterargument the CoCom policy even if it does not represent a true success.

After the invasion of Afghanistan and martial law in Poland, Artemiev writes, it was clear that the CMEA was economically vulnerable. A new plan, the Comprehensive Program of Scientific and Technological Progress, was devised to accelerate the development of new technology and effect cooperation among member countries. This program only resulted in 25% of new technology being shared, while most needs were being met from imports from capitalist countries. This program also failed to help entrepreneurs and research institutions interact, and in fact such a vital function was discouraged. Communist states assign suppliers to consumers, making sure that industrial goods can be assembled into products. "In such an environment, there is no room for joint projects or joint ventures initiated from below" [54, p. 86]. According to Ishi, the effectiveness of trade sanctions "cannot be determined," especially the China trade embargo, but "confusion" is observed among Allies and within Washington [17, p. 30]. In other words, the failure of cooperation among the members of the group makes it difficult to assess whether or not the program was effective.

5.3   Closing CoCom: A New Determinism

The Warsaw Treaty Organization disbanded in 1989, and in the same year the Berlin Wall came down, making CoCom's days numbered. In 1990, CoCom announced that about half of the restrictions would be lifted on exports of computers, telecommunications and machine tools to Czechoslovakia, Hungary, and Poland, but nevertheless they would not have as favorable treatment because of the concern that they could forward the material to Russia. The three countries had requested this change and asserted that they could monitor the equipment and make sure it was not put to military use. The favorable arrangement was not as good as China's, though [35].

In its final days, one can see how the assumptions about what CoCom was had clearly changed. One journalist pondering the fate of CoCom in the era of glasnost characterized it this way:

> Currently, the 17-member Coordination Committee for Multilateral Controls (COCOM) restricts trade in three broad areas: military hardware, nuclear technology, and industrial or 'dual-use" equipment, such as electronic components and advanced optics that have both commercial and military applications....
> NATO military strategists have long thought of the Western technological edge as a "force multiplier" which mitigated the numerical advantage enjoyed by Warsaw Pact armies. [55, p. 21]

In 1990, then, it can be said that the attitude toward CoCom was that it was developed to compensate for the lower number of troops in North Atlantic Treaty Organization (NATO) countries as compared to the Warsaw Pact. CoCom's origin, of course, had been related to the export of metals, fuels, and foods – raw materials that could support technological innovation, but not the devices themselves. The new

---

[5] In this volume, Sikora, "Cooperating with Moscow," details Comecon transfers in more detail.

definition of military hardware, nuclear technology, and industrial equipment was more in line with the Reagan administration's export list than anything that had been "long thought of" as the "Western technological edge." This definition was much more recent, and with respect to computers, it was less than ten years old.

This attitude is also seen in the debate over the Export Administration Act reauthorization in 1990, which ultimately eliminated restrictions on all telecommunication equipment. European CoCom countries had argued that "democratic institutions require access to the tools of information gathering and dissemination. Without them, a free press, a responsive government, and an informed electorate are impossible" [56]. The Bush administration had argued that allowing fiber-optic cable to be exported to communist countries would lead to difficulties to monitor communication and that satellite and microwave communication were easier to intercept. The Europeans, for their part, were successful in arguing that CoCom was not designed to facilitate intelligence gathering but to prevent technology transfer to communist military forces.

The new guidelines in 1990 were revisited in 1991, with the result that many personal computers, commercial mainframes, peripheral equipment, and software could be exported without a license [57]. In 1993, during the Clinton administration, it was noted that Israel and Taiwan benefitted from CoCom restrictions because they were not restricted from doing business with Russia, China, and Eastern Europe, even for equipment that intended for civilians. The market for fiber-optic cable and switching equipment was "a potential gold mine": China was expected to spend $30 billion and Russia $15 billion to update telephone networks [58, p. D3]. Companies like AT&T and Sun Microsystems in the United States, Northern Telecom of Canada, Alcatel of France, and Siemens of Germany were impacted.

On 31 March 1994, the Clinton Administration announced the end of licensing requirements for much technology that might aid communist countries, including China and the members of the former Soviet Union. The decision was made in order to open what was estimated to be a $150 billion market over the following 10 years and lead to the creation of thousands of jobs [59]. The installation of the data networks that would support advanced communication, such as the Internet, represented in a break in the cold war policy. Al Gore's dream of an "information superhighway," which would later lead him to misspeak and claim to have invented the Internet, bled over into foreign policy. One form of determinism had morphed into another.

In the previous year, Clinton administration had proposed raising the limit from 250 million theoretical operations per second (MTOPs) to 500 MTOPs. The administration had received 25,000 applications for export licenses and with the new allowances the number would be cut in half (as noted above, the 1978 total had been 1,680, 62.5 percent of which had been for computers). Basic computer designs from Apple or IBM were limited for export. In 1994, the United States removed licensing requirements for civilian telecommunications equipment and computers that operate up to 1,000 million theoretical operations per second (MTOPs) to former communist countries. The Clinton administration had defined supercomputers as operating above 1,500 MTOPs [59].

CoCom was disbanded in March 1994. Its successor is the Wassenaar Arrangement on Export Controls for Conventional Arms and Dual-Use Goods, which was agreed on at the end of 1996. The experience of failed technology transfer that challenged ideologies based on determinism was not much discussed; indeed, the 1979 paradigm about preventing technology transfer still guides U.S. policy.

6 Conclusion

In spite of the fact that technological embargos seem to be tested and tried mechanisms today, the story of CoCom shows it was not necessarily the best and only way to achieve policy aims. Although politically popular, the failure of CoCom in terms of technology theory was evident nearly from the beginning.[6] The various permutations of CoCom, not to mention the high-profile failures, call into question whether the policy could ever have been effective aside from its use as political symbolism. The Soviet success in the atom bomb and Sputnik certainly showed that the earliest version of CoCom was not successful. As well, the contrasting policies of the Reagan and Clinton administrations in the last years of CoCom show how the policy was rooted more in political ideology than it was in a sound theory of technological innovation.

The story of CoCom answers certain mysteries about the history of computing, like why the management of the DNS system became a responsibility of the Department of Commerce – and may perhaps suggest why one of the first top-level domains was dot-com. Some might say that CoCom was effective in delaying the deployment of the Internet into the USSR, arguing that reverse engineering and working from published knowledge was not successful. Yet, Abbate [60] has amply demonstrated how the early culture of the ARPAnet, where research teams at different universities attempted to come together to create a network of peers, was tied to the flexible solution that took hold. This flexibility was necessary for the development of the network. The desire for a "cybernetic society" and a hierarchical reporting structure was more important for computing in the USSR, leading to what Gerovitch [61] has termed the "InterNyet." The lack of development in areas of computing that would lead a western examiner to say that the East Bloc was successful in computing has more to do with the aims and goals of the region than it does with the effectiveness of the embargo.[7]

The evidence provided by the history of computing has provided support for expectations of the situation based on the social construction of technology. A policy that suggests that a technological device landing on foreign soil will take root and unequivocally transform the economics of the receiving country, after all, is a policy based on technological determinism. From the perspective of social constructivism, one would suggest that the foreign device would have to find a place within the technological environment before it would succeed. Furthermore, devices that are designed to support one type of user environment cannot be facilely transferred to a different milieu. If anything has been convincingly shown by social constructivism, it is that users matter – and the concept of the user precedes the design of a particular device.

---

[6] In this volume, Sikora, "Cooperating with Moscow," suggests that there were in fact increased costs in technology due to CoCom, suggesting that the impact was more than symbolic.

[7] The development of the OB telemonitor shows that in the 1980s, Soviet computer science was at least the level of the west's: see Kitov, "Main Teleprocessing Monitors," this volume.

This should have led to the conclusion that the embargo of technology would largely fail in the effect it purported to achieve.

This is not to say that CoCom had no effect, however. It was certainly effective in the way it segregated the technical communities on either side of the Iron Curtain. It is impossible to say what could have happened had the sides been in closer communication, but if innovation depends on the international scientific community, then conceivably the damage to the international community that supports innovation harms both sides. The ignominy and even punishment meted upon those who sought to encourage cooperation under the Iron Curtain had a chilling effect on the international community instead of mobilizing that community to be cultural ambassadors, which could have been a more effective deterrent to hostilities.

References

1. Cupitt, R.T., Grillot, S.R.: COCOM is dead, long live COCOM: persistence and change in multilateral security institutions. Br. J. Polit. Sci. **27**(3), 361–389 (1997)
2. Wendt, A.: Social Theory of International Politics. Cambridge UP, New York (1999)
3. Baldwin, D.A.: Economic Statecraft. Princeton University Press, Princeton (1985)
4. Harris, J.M., Blackwill, R.: War by Other Means: Geoeconomics and Statecraft. Harvard University Press, Cambridge (2016)
5. Wittfogel, K.A.: Oriental Despotism: A Comparative Study of Total Power. Yale University Press, New Haven (1957)
6. Mumford, L.: Authoritarian and democratic technics. Technol. Cult. **5**(1), 1–8 (1964)
7. Ellul, J.: The Technological Society (1954, trans. 1964). Trans. by J. Wilkinson. Knopf, New York (1970)
8. Winner, L.: Autonomous Technology: Technics-Out-of-Control as a Theme in Political Thought. MIT Press, Cambridge (1977)
9. Pacey, A.: Technology in World Civilization. MIT Press, Cambridge (1990)
10. Jakhu, R., Wilson, J.: The new United States export control regime: its impact on the communications satellite industry. Ann. Air Space Law **25**, 157–181 (2000)
11. Cain, F.: Computers and the Cold War: United States restrictions on the export of computers to the Soviet Union and Communist China. J. Contemp. Hist. **40**(1), 131–147 (2005)
12. Libbey, J.K.: CoCom, Comecon, and the economic Cold War. Russ. Hist. **37**, 133–152 (2010)
13. Yasuhara, Y.: The myth of free trade: the origins of COCOM 1945–1950. Jpn. J. Am. Stud. **4**, 127–148 (1991)
14. Mastanduno, M.: Economic Containment: CoCom and the Politics of East-West Trade. Cornell UP, Ithaca (1992)
15. Adler-Karlsson, G.: Western Economic Warfare 1947–1967: A Case Study in Foreign Economic Policy. Almqvist & Wiksell, Stockholm (1968)
16. Bertsch, G.K.: East-West Strategic Trade, COCOM and the Atlantic Alliance. Atlantic Institute for International Affairs, Paris (1983)
17. Ishii, O.: China trade embargo and America's alliance management in the 1950s: the Japanese case. Hitotsubashi J. Law Polit. **20**, 23–31 (1992)
18. Campbell-Kelly, M., Aspray, W.: Computer: A History of the Information Machine Basic, New York (1996)

19. Corson, D.R.: Scientific Communication and National Security: A Report Prepared by the Panel on Scientific Communication and National Security Committee on Science, Engineering, and Public Policy. National Academy Press, Washington, D.C. (1982)
20. Goodman, S.E.: Technology transfer and the development of the Soviet computer industry. In: Trade, Technology, and Soviet-American Relations, pp. 117–140. Indiana University Press, Bloomington (1985)
21. Brand, S.: Founding Father. Wired 9.03, 1 March 2001
22. Kemme, D.M. (ed.) Technology Markets and Export Controls in the 1990s. NYU Press (1991)
23. Leitner, P.M.: Decontrolling Strategic Technology, 1990–1992: Creating the Military Threats of the 21st Century. University Press of America, New York (1995)
24. Peters, B.: How Not to Network a Nation: The Uneasy History of the Soviet Internet. MIT Press, Cambridge (2016)
25. Bucy, F.: An analysis of export control of U.S. Technology – a DOD perspective: a report of the Defense Science Board Task Force on export of U.S. Technology. Office of the Director of Defense Research and Engineering, Washington, DC (1976)
26. Kemme, D.M. (ed.): Technology Markets and Export Controls in the 1990s. NYU Press (1991)
27. Donovan, C.J.: The export administration act of 1979: refining United States export control machinery. Boston Coll. Int. Comp. Law Rev. **4**(1), 77–114 (1981)
28. Freedenberg, P.: The commercial perspective. In: Bertsch, G.K., Elliot-Grower, S. (eds.) Export Controls in Transition: Perspectives, Problems, and Prospects, pp. 27–58. Duke UP, Durham (1992)
29. Yuan, J.: The politics of the strategic triangle: the U.S., COCOM, and export controls on China, 1979–1989. J. Northeast Asian Stud. 47–79 (1995)
30. Holstein, W.J.: Burroughs Corp. announced Wednesday it has contracted to sell…" UPI Archive: Financial, 4 November 1981. Infotrac Newsstand. http://link.galegroup.com/. Accessed 13 June 2018
31. Burns, J.F.: China's Passion for the Computer. New York Times, 6 January 1985
32. Allies meet on sanctions against Moscow. UPI Archive: International, 19 January 1982. Infotrac Newsstand, http://link.galegroup.com/. Accessed 13 June 2018
33. Weinberger, C.: Annual Report to Congress, 8 February 1982. https://apps.dtic.mil/dtic/tr/fulltext/u2/a113991.pdf
34. Gelb, L.H.: Weinberger says Soviet weapons are aided by Western technology. New York Times, p. 5, 22 May 1982
35. Phillips, J.: Cocom to Ease Restrictions on Eastern Europe. UPI Archive: International, 16 February 1990. Infotrac Newsstand (1990). http://link.galegroup.com/. Accessed 13 June 2018
36. Jentleson, B.W., Matlary, J.H.: Soviet-Western energy trade: from trade controls to energy interdependence? In: Bertsch, G.K., Elliot-Grower, S. (eds.) Export Controls in Transition: Perspectives, Problems, and Prospects, pp. 203–231. Duke UP, Durham (1992)
37. "The United States and its European allies reached unanimous…" UPI Archive: International, 20 January 1982. Infotrac Newsstand. http://link.galegroup.com/. Accessed 13 June 2018
38. "France signed a 25-year agreement today with the Soviet…" UPI Archive: International, 23 January 1982. Infotrac Newsstand. http://link.galegroup.com/. Accessed 13 June 2018
39. Beardsley, T.: COCOM agreement on computers. Nature **310**, 355 (1984)
40. Wilkins, B.: U.S., allies restrict technological exports to Eastern bloc. Computerworld, p. 16, 30 July 1984

41. Leslie, C.: Flame wars on Worldnet: early constructions of the international user. In: International Histories of Invention and Innovation: IFIP Advances in Information and Communication Technology, vol. 491, pp. 122–140
42. Buchan, D.: Technology transfer to the Soviet bloc. Wash. Q. **7**(4), 130–135 (1984)
43. Schonfeld, Z.: 'KREMVAX': the strange story of the internet's first April fools' Prank. Newsweek, 1 April 2015. www.newsweek.com. Accessed 23 June 2018
44. Werner, L.M.: U.S. Has Bonn Stop Soviet-Bound Computer. New York Times, 15 November 1983: A1
45. Swedes Sieze [sic] 2d Shipment of Equipment. New York Times, 25 November 1983: A3
46. Crawford, B.: Changing export controls in an interdependent world: lessons from the Toshiba case for the 1990s. In: Bertsch, G.K., Elliot-Grower, S. (eds.) Export Controls in Transition: Perspectives, Problems, and Prospects, pp. 249–290. Duke UP, Durham (1992)
47. Greenhouse, S.: French Linked to Soviet Sale. New York Times, 17 October 1987
48. Sanger, D.: New Hints that East Bloc Got Japanese Equipment. New York Times. 30 July 1989
49. Allen, L., et al.: Balancing the National Interest: U.S. National Security Export Controls and Global Economic Competition. National Academy Press (1987)
50. Greisen, F.: EARN connections to East Europe and regulatory issues. N.-Holl. Comput. Netw. ISDN Syst. **19**, 177–180 (1990)
51. Turchanyi, G.: Networking in Hungary. Comput. Netw. ISDN Syst. **25**, 444–447 (1992)
52. Peck, S.S.: Research in post-communist Hungary. Inf. Dev. **8**(4), 204–209 (1992)
53. Leslie, C., Gryczka, P.: Ingenuity in Isolation: Poland in the international history of the internet. In: Kimppa, K., Whitehouse, D., Kuusela, T., Phahlamohlaka, J. (eds.) HCC 2014. IAICT, vol. 431, pp. 162–175. Springer, Heidelberg (2014). https://doi.org/10.1007/978-3-662-44208-1_14
54. Artemiev, I.E.: Global technology markets and security issues (73–103). In: Kemme, D.M. (ed.) Technology Markets and Export Controls in the 1990s. NYU Press (1991)
55. Hamilton, D.P.: Will glasnost wash over U.S. export controls? Science **248**(4951), 21 (1990)
56. Freedenberg, P.: COCOM in a Period of Change (MITJP 90-06). The MIT Japan Program, Cambridge (1992)
57. IDG News Service: New COCOM rules ease net exports. Network World, pp. 25, 32, 12 August 1991
58. Ramirez, A.: Move gains to liberalize U.S. high-tech exports. New York Times, p. 3, 21 September 1993
59. Friedman, T.L.: U.S. ending curbs on high-tech gear to cold war foes. New York Times, p. 1, 31 March 1994
60. Abbate, J.: Inventing the Internet. MIT Press, Cambridge (2000)
61. Gerovich, S.: InterNyet: why the Soviet Union did not build a nationwide computer network. Hist. Technol. **24**(4), 335–350 (2008)

Analog Computing

Israel Abraham Staffel: Lost Book Is Found

Timo Leipälä[1], Valery V. Shilov[2(✉)], and Sergey A. Silantiev[2]

[1] University of Turku, Turku, Finland
timo.leipala@saunalahti.fi
[2] National Research University Higher School of Economics, Moscow, Russia
{vshilov, ssilaniev}@hse.ru

Abstract. This article is devoted to the rediscovery of a document by Israel Abraham Staffel (1814–1885), a prolific Polish inventor. It is a handwritten book in Russian and Polish that provides detailed information about one of the most famous of Staffel's inventions, a 13-digit arithmometer, honored at the Great London Exhibition in 1851. The brief biography of Staffel, born into a Jewish family of meagre means who became famous in his time as an inventor, and a description of his developments are presented. Particular attention is paid to his mechanical calculating machines. In the Appendix, an English translation of the handwritten book by Staffel appears for the first time. Typical mechanical calculating machines by the end of the nineteenth century were based on Leibniz's stepped drums. Staffel's arithmometer was based on pinwheels. The content of the discovered book allows us to raise the question of the influence of Staffel's invention on the arithmometer's design. The paper, which also clarifies and complements certain facts about his life, activity and inventions, demonstrates the need for further archival research to confirm the currently accepted history of innovation.

Keywords: Calculating machines · Great London Exhibition · Israel Abraham Staffel · Pinwheel arithmometers · Stepped drum

1 Introduction

In the diaries of the famous British financier, banker, and philanthropist Sir Moses Montefiore the opening of the London exhibition, held on 1 May 1851 was described:

Sir Moses and Lady Montefiore went to the opening of the Exhibition. The building was already full on their arrival, but Lady Montefiore secured a good seat. The Queen and the Prince entered at twelve. The procession was a splendid one, and the Palace presented a magnificent scene. The ceremony passed off extremely well, without the slightest hitch, to the great delight of spectators. Sir Moses' attention was drawn to the Russian Division of the Exhibition, where an apparatus was exhibited for ascertaining the value of gold and silver coins and other metals without the use of fire or chemical analysis, also to a calculating machine for simple and compound addition, subtraction, multiplication, division, and extraction of square and cubic roots, both invented by Israel Abraham Staffel of Warsaw. Being most anxious to befriend so clever a young man, he at once invited him to his house, and after impressing upon him the necessity of raising and maintaining the standard of education in Russia and Poland among his co-religionists, made him a handsome present. [27, p. 24]

© IFIP International Federation for Information Processing 2019
Published by Springer Nature Switzerland AG 2019
C. Leslie and M. Schmitt (Eds.): HC 2018, IFIP AICT 549, pp. 229–251, 2019.
https://doi.org/10.1007/978-3-030-29160-0_12

It seems that the name and works of Israel Abraham Staffel (Fig. 1), this "clever young man" – Polish inventor and one of the pioneers of mechanical computing in Eastern Europe, are not forgotten. Indeed, his inventions are mentioned quite often in modern publications on the history of mechanical calculating machines. However, usually it is only brief mentions. His biography is still known in only the most general terms, and the descriptions of his machines are very brief and sometimes contradictory.

Izrael Abraham Sztaffel.   Podług fot. Brandla.

Fig. 1. Israel Abraham Staffel [13].

In this paper, we want to give an overview of contemporary sources and modern scholarship on the life and inventions of Staffel, to clarify and supplement some of the facts and judgments, and introduce a unique historical document, a manuscript book, written by Staffel in 1845, which was considered lost. This document, which also clarifies and complements information about his main invention, demonstrates the need for further archival research to confirm the currently accepted history of innovation.

2   Literature Review

Staffel's activity attracted the attention of contemporary Polish newspapers and magazines several times. Usually, this was due to the successful demonstration of his machines at various industrial exhibitions. Probably the first and, to our knowledge, only publication was Staffel's own article *O nowej maszynie rachunkowej z wykazaniem potrzeby mechanicznej pomocy do odbywania rachunków* [1], which appears to be unavailable. Judging by the title, Staffel proved the necessity of using mechanical machines to facilitate calculations and, perhaps, briefly described his first developments. Three more notes [2–4] were also published on the eve of the Warsaw Exhibition of 1845, where his arithmometer was demonstrated.

Several publications in English [5, 6] are associated with the London Exhibition of 1851. The Report of the exhibition jury adjoins them [7]. These publications are extremely important, because in them we find the description of one of Staffel's machines and its external appearance. Furthermore, it contains the English translation of the Report of the commission of the Academy of Sciences in St. Petersburg, which had studied this machine several years earlier. Later publications in Polish [8–12] also contain some additional information about Staffel's calculating machines. An obituary [13] is very important because it provides the main information we know today about the Staffel's biography.

Contemporary sources also include publications in London newspaper *The Jewish Chronicle* [14–18], containing information about Staffel's time in London in 1851. Strangely enough, modern authors do not even mention this trip. Therefore, most of what we know about Staffel comes from newspaper sources.

However, modern publications devoted to Staffel personally are not numerous. First of all, we should mention here the paper *From the History of Computing Devices (Based on the Archives of the USSR Academy of Sciences)* [19], which for the first time after a long break drew the attention of researchers to the inventions of Staffel in the field of computing technology. In this paper, several Russian translations of documents originally written in French related to Staffel's contacts with the Academy of Sciences in St. Petersburg were published. Very important is the work *Mechanik warszawski Abraham Izrael Staffel (1814–1885) i jego wynalazki* [20], the most detailed of those devoted to Staffel. Several review articles in German [21] and Polish [22, 23] consider Staffel's inventions among a number of works of other Polish inventors of the nineteenth century. Finally, there is the only one review paper about Staffel in Russian [24].

Thus, we see that among the sources there are no memories of contemporaries and Staffel's own works. So, the rediscovery of the document that we give in Appendix – Staffel's handwritten book – has a unique significance for the history of computing.

3   Brief Biography and Inventions

Israel Abraham Staffel was born in 1814 in Warsaw, the capital of Poland (on 1815 the Kingdom of Poland became the part of Russian Empire) to a poor Jewish family. He received his primary education in Cheder, a traditional Jewish elementary school teaching the basics of Judaism and Hebrew language. After his graduation the boy was sent to serve as an apprentice to a watchmaker. At the age of 19, Staffel got a license and opened his own watch workshop in Warsaw. Although Staffel was a conscientious and talented watchmaker, the workshop did not provide him great profit and prosperity. He always was interested in the design of mechanical calculating machines, measuring instruments and other devices.

Many of his developments were presented at national and international exhibitions, in particular, at the Great London Exhibition, and were awarded medals and monetary prizes. Besides calculating machines, among his inventions were a precious metal alloy assaying device on the basis of the Archimedes principle, ventilators, an anemometer, an automatic taximeter for cabs which was controlled automatically (it started during the getting on of passengers and stopped after their getting off), a device to prevent forging signatures, and a two-color printing press. The latter was used to print the first Polish postage stamps in 1860 and later for printing banknotes [20].

Staffel died in poverty in 1885 at the age of 70, spending all his savings on his inventions. The anonymous author of his obituary [13] wrote that Staffel was very modest; glory and recognition did not interest him. So, his death remained almost unnoticed, and few of his contemporaries guessed that the work of the man who died would gain worldwide fame.

4 Staffel's Calculating Machines

Before presenting the first of his machines to the public at the Warsaw Exhibition in 1845, Staffel had been working hard on them for more than ten years. In total, Staffel designed four different types of calculating machines. Unfortunately, we know very little about them.

The exemplar of his earliest machine is stored in the Museum of Technology in Warsaw (Fig. 2).

Fig. 2. Staffel's adder of 1842 (property of Muzeum Techniki in Warsaw, Poland).

It is held in a walnut box and has the inscription in Polish: *Arithmetical Machine Invented and Constructed by Izrael Abraham Staffel, the Watch-Maker in Warsaw, A. D. 1842*. The mechanism consists of gear wheels and allows adding and subtracting. The results of these operations (numbers to a maximum of seven digits) appear in the window. To perform these operations, one must pull forward pins in appropriate fields of the values of digits of the added numbers during adding and pull backward digits of subtrahend while subtracting. Another specific feature of this calculating machine is the ability to mutually convert zloty and ruble currencies. On the both sides of the field that displays the results of main operations, Staffel placed adequate conversion values. One side is designated for conversion from zloty into ruble currency, and the other one from ruble into zloty currency.

The most famous of his machines, a 13-digit arithmometer, was also demonstrated for the first time at the Warsaw Exhibition in 1845. A year later, it aroused great interest in the Russian Academy of Sciences and then made a sensation at the London Exhibition in 1851. We will not specially mention these events, which are described in detail in the literature [19–24]. Let us recall only that the magazine *Scientific American* named Staffel's arithmometer "the most extraordinary calculating machine, we ever heard of" [6]; that means, at the time of his invention, it was probably the best calculating machine in the world.

The only one known until recently drawing which shows the external appearance of this arithmometer (Fig. 3) was published repeatedly (see, for example, [5, 9, 20, 21]). But its internal construction has not been known.

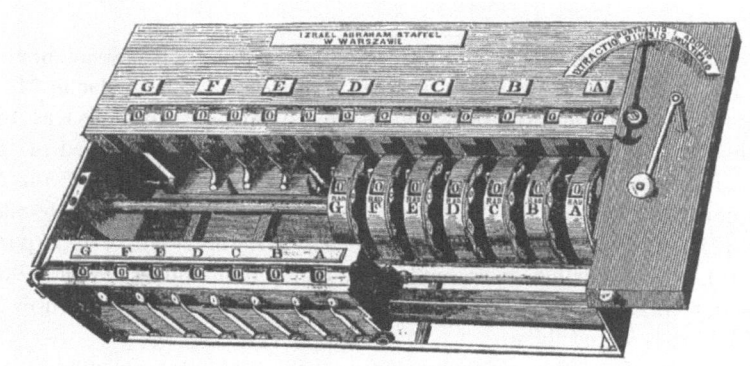

Fig. 3. Staffel's arithmometer [9].

In 1876, Staffel handed over his 13-digit arithmometer to the Physical Cabinet of the Russian Academy of Sciences in St. Petersburg [19, p. 586], but its current placement is unknown.

At the London Exhibition Staffel also presented another machine. It is only known that it performed adding and subtracting fractions with denominators 10, 12, and 15 [7]. This machine is not preserved.

Finally, around 1858, Staffel designed another seven-digit adding machine without the function of mutual converting of zloty into ruble currency (Fig. 4).

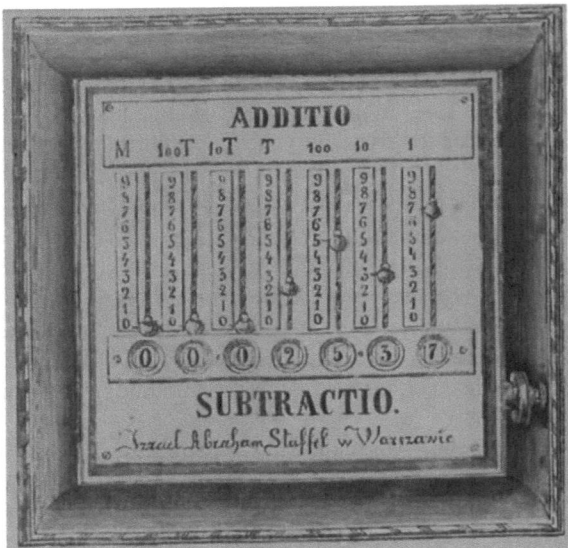

Fig. 4. Staffel's adding machine of 1858 [11].

This machine was presented and awarded at the exhibition in Warsaw in 1858. It is possible that Staffel also presented it at other exhibitions, in particular in Moscow in 1882 (see the next section). The only known exemplar of this machine was owned by the famous German firm Grimme, Natalis & Co, which was established in 1871 and produced arithmometers under the brand name "Brunsviga" from 1892 on. Staffel's machine constituted a part of the firm's rich exhibition of historical calculating machines [25]. In 1959, the firm was absorbed by Olympia Werke AG (part of the AEG group), and production of arithmometers came to an end in the late 1960s. The said collection was then delivered to the State Museum in Brunswick and now Staffel's adding machine is stored there.

We have no information about how many copies of these calculating machines Staffel made. We know that "mechanical schoty" were produced in Staffel's workshop (see Sect. 5 below). Most likely, their number (as well as other Staffel's machines) was small. In general, in the Russian Empire until the end of the 19th century the demand for calculating machines, including those designed by Russian inventors, was not very significant. This is due, among other things, to the wide utilization of *Russian schoty* in this country – a simple, cheap and reliable device for calculations [35].

Thus, till now from all Staffel's calculating machines only one exemplar each of the 1842 and the 1858 adders are preserved.

5   Supplements and Corrections

As we have already pointed out, there is very little information about the life of Staffel. Nevertheless, we can add some new facts to his biography.

It is known that he was born and spent his entire life in Warsaw. His workshop was first located on Marshalkovskaya str., 1379, and then his whole life Staffel worked in a workshop at Grzhibovskaya str., 982. However, no data is available in the literature on the volume and assortment of his workshop's production. We were able to find the following entry in the Index of the All-Russian Industrial and Art Exhibition of 1882, in which Staffel took part:

Staffel Israel. Warsaw, Grzhibovskaya str., 982
Mechanical schoty; ventilating apparatus; anemometer (wind meter); room ventilator.
Workshop, since 1835; 2 workers; annual production up to 3,000 rubles; purchase of material in Russia and abroad; marketing in Russia" [26, p. 64].

Thus, we see which of his inventions Staffel presented at this exhibition. The list of exhibits awarded with bronze medals in the section "Educational and scientific equipment" contains the line: "Staffel, Israel, in Warsaw – for ventilators and anemometers" [26, p. 352]. Probably, this was one of the last exhibitions in which Staffel participated, and one of the last awards he received. It is interesting that the Index mentions "mechanical schoty." It can be assumed that this was the 1853 adder.

We have already mentioned that authors of the works about Staffel do not note his personal presence in London during the Exhibition of 1851. At the same time, this visit is fixed in a number of sources, as Sir Montefiore's Diary, quoted above (unfortunately, this book does not contain information whether Staffel visited Sir Moses or not).

We found interesting information about Staffel also in the London newspaper *The Jewish Chronicle*, noted above. His name is cited on its pages five times. In the issue of 18 July 1851 the article from *Illustrated London News* [5] was reprinted. In one of the following issues, the newspaper describes a visit the members of the Royal family to the Russian court of the London Exhibition:

On Friday morning last, about nine o'clock, Her Majesty and His Royal Highness Prince Albert, accompanied by Princess Alice, paid a visit to the Great Exhibition. In passing through The Russian court, the royal visitors stopped for several minutes, and inspected Mr. Staffel's calculating machine (of which an illustration and full particulars appeared in our last number). Mr. Staffel, be desire of Prince Albert, worked sums in addition, subtraction, and multiplication, with which His Royal Highness expressed his gratification; and, addressing the Princess Alice, said, "Notice, this is a self-calculating machine." His Royal Highness then addressed a few remarks to Mr. Staffel on the pleasure he had experienced with respect to the calculating machine, and also of Mr. Staffel's ingenious machine for proving the value of gold and silver, and the royal party then passed on to other portions of this wonderful building. [15]

The issue of August 1 states that the inventions of Staffel caused interest in the Governor of the Bank of England, who expressed a desire to test in action the arithmometer and machine for testing the precious metals:

Mr. Staffel's Calculating Machine. – On Friday last, the Governor of the Bank of England, accompanied by another gentleman of establishment, attended the Great Exhibition, by appointment, to inspect the above work of art, as also Mr. Staffel's machine for testing the precious metals. After some time in testing the machines, the Governor desired that they might be brought to the Bank at the close of the Exhibition, for the purpose of their relative proficiency being more fully proved. [16]

We do not know if such tests were ever conducted. Here it can be noted that the mechanization of calculating operations at the Bank of that time was clearly no less urgent problem than coin testing.

In the issue of October 24, Staffel's name is mentioned among the names of other Jewish inventors awarded at the exhibition [17]. Finally, in the issue of November 21, we find a note in which the author expresses his satisfaction that the work of a talented inventor has received a monetary reward:

> Liberality of the Prince Albert. – It must be a source of great delight to our brethren, to be made acquainted with the munificent liberality of the royal consort of our beloved Queen towards a humble mechanic of the house of Israel. The liberality of his Royal Highness has been exercised in the case of J. A. Staffel, of Warsaw, the inventor of the calculating machine, etc., which was exhibited in the Russian department of the Crystal Palace, who has received from his Royal Highness a cheque for 20 *l.* as an acknowledgement of his Royal Highness's appreciation of Mr. Staffel's ingenious invention.
> Since writing the above, we are glad to hear that Baron L. Rothschild, M. P., also presented our scientific brother with a cheque for 10 *l.* as a due acknowledgment of Jewish talent. [18]

Unfortunately, the information published about Staffel and his inventions is not always free of errors. For example, there is a statement that he was awarded the highest scientific prize of Russian Empire, the Demidov prize: "Staffel was awarded a Demidov prize amounting to 1,500 rubles" [23, p. 60]. The same mistake is repeated in [28]. In fact, the commission of the Russian Academy of Sciences considered Staffel's machine worthy of the Demidov prize, but on formal grounds he was recommended to put forward his work for the prize next year. They stated on the possibility of awarding the Demidov Prize to I. Staffel in the minutes of the meeting of Physical and Mathematical Branch, November 6, 1846 St. Petersburg:

> The rescript dated October 24, No. 9570 was announced, in which the Mr. Minister of Education informs the Conference that due to the very favorable response of the Academy about the arithmetic machine of Mr. Staffel, which from the mechanical point of view deserves special attention and in practical application has the advantage over Slonimsky's machine, His Excellency considered the invention could be worthy of the Demidov Prize.
> It was decided to reply that Slonimsky's machine was awarded a prize for the principle on which it was designed and which reveals a new property of numbers proven by Slonimsky and not known so far. Whereas, Staffel's machine is distinguished only by a cleverly constructed mechanism. The latter, moreover, is so complex that, even under the most favorable conditions, its high cost will always prevent its practical use. Nevertheless, if Staffel wants to join the applicants for the nearest Demidov competition, it will be enough for him to submit his machine with a printed description, and the Academy will resolve the matter with all fairness and impartiality" [19, p. 572–573].

Even though, that never happened. Thus, Staffel did not receive the Demidov prize (3,000 rubles). He was paid 1,500 rubles from the budget of Kingdom of Poland according to an order of the Emperor.

The shortness and fragmentariness of information about calculating machines built by Staffel leads to the fact that researchers do not always correctly interpret it. For example, in the book of Ernst Martin, Staffel's arithmometer is not even mentioned; as well, the adder of 1858 is dated 1845 [29]. Incorrect information that Staffel submitted to the Russian Academy of Sciences his adder of 1842 is given also in [28]. In fact, to both the Academy and the London Exhibition Staffel presented the same machine, namely his famous 13-digit arithmometer.

6 Staffel's Innovation

As it was said above, the only work published by Staffel and known to authors is a newspaper article [1]. Unfortunately, the text remained inaccessible to us, but probably it provided some explanation of his invention. At the same time, it is known from a report (written in French) of Russian academicians Victor Bunyakovsky and Boris Jacobi that, when presenting his machine to the Academy of Sciences. Staffel accompanied it with a handwritten description in Russian and Polish (English translation of this report is given in [5], and its Russian translation in [19]). However, this handwritten description was considered lost until recently. Thus, all information known about Staffel's machine was reduced to its description [5, 19], and a published drawing [5, 9, 14].

However, a few years ago, one of the authors of the present article purchased a hand-written book in antique store.

This document is undoubtedly a description of the machine that Staffel submitted to the Russian Academy of Sciences in 1846 along with the machine itself. Its value lies not exclusively in the fact that this is the only full description of how to work with a calculating machine, but also that the drawings attached (Figs. 5 and 6) make it possible to understand its construction.

Due to this finding we for the first time got an opportunity to see the inner construction of Staffel's arithmometer that made it possible to substantiate the assumption about the influence of its design on the construction of other arithmometers of the XIX and XX centuries.

Gottfried Leibniz's Stepped Reckoner, the first arithmometer that survived to our time, had the so-called stepped drum as the main unit. The stepped drum is a cylinder on the lateral surface of which there are nine steps of different length parallel to the generatrix. Stepped drums were the basis for the design of many arithmometers in eighteenth, nineteenth, and twentieth centuries: Philipp Matthäus Hahn's calculator (1774), the first commercially available arithmometer patented in 1820 in France by Charles-Xavier Thomas de Colmar and its improved versions (Arthur Burkhardt, 1879; Samuel Tate, 1903, and others).

However, arithmometers with a different construction, in which the main unit is a wheel with variable number of teeth, or pinwheel, became widespread only at the end of the nineteenth century. It is all the more surprising that apparently already Leibniz initially intended to use pinwheel. In 1685 Leibniz wrote a manuscript describing his machine, *Machina arithmetica in qua non aditio tantum et subtractio sed et multiplicatio nullo, divisio vero paene nullo animi labore peragantur*. Its design was based on wheels with variable number of teeth, not on stepped drums [30]. Even earlier, Leibniz's manuscript contained the image of pinwheel (Fig. 7).

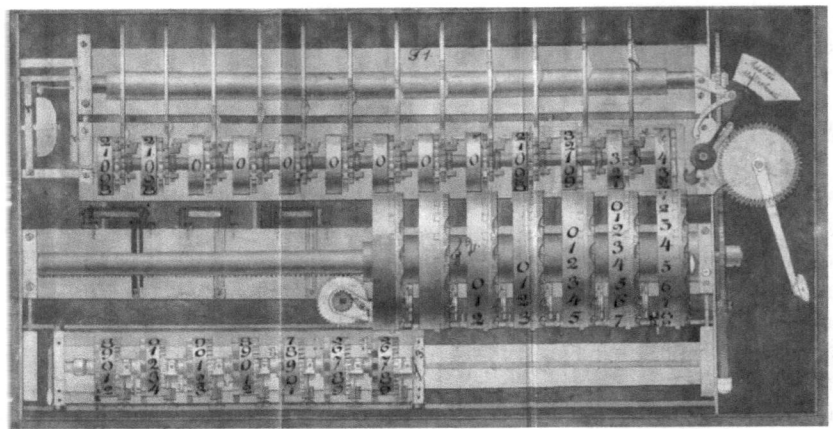

Fig. 5. Drawing from Staffel's handwritten book.

Fig. 6. Drawing from Staffel's handwritten book.

This idea of Leibniz was hardly known to other inventors, and in the next two centuries it was repeatedly rediscovered. Already in 1709 Giovanni Poleni in his arithmometer [31] used the mechanism of teeth erecting, the original version of

Fig. 7. Pinwheel (G. Leibnitz, c.1673) (from [30]).

pinwheels (see the right-hand side of Fig. 8, borrowed from Jacob Leupold's book [32]). A few years later, the Austrian mechanic Anton Braun, who was undoubtedly familiar with the Leupold's book, manufactured arithmometer also based on the use of pinwheels. The well-known inventor Dorr Felt wrote that the pinwheels were the basis for the construction of Charles Stanhope's arithmometer built in 1775 [33, p. 15].

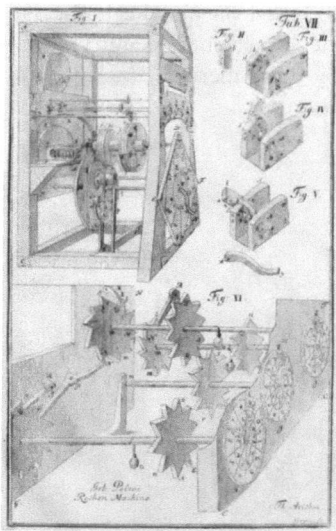

Fig. 8. Mechanism of teeth erecting (G. Poleni, 1709) (from [32])

On November 24, 1842, an emigrant from Austro-Hungarian Empire Didier Roth, who lived in Paris, received a patent on an arithmometer using pinwheels (Addition 3, No. 14535, Fig. 9, left). Then, his device was also patented in England by David Isaac Wertheimber (patent No. 9616, July 23, 1843). Soon afterward, Staffel's arithmometer appeared, in which we also see a similar unit (Fig. 9, right). Here we may note that the

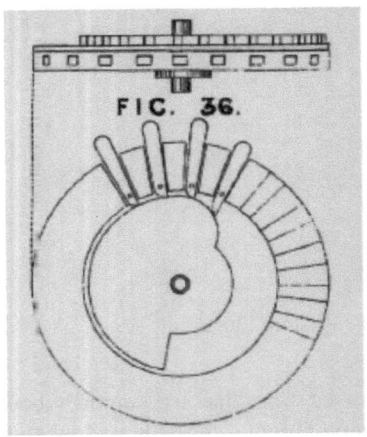
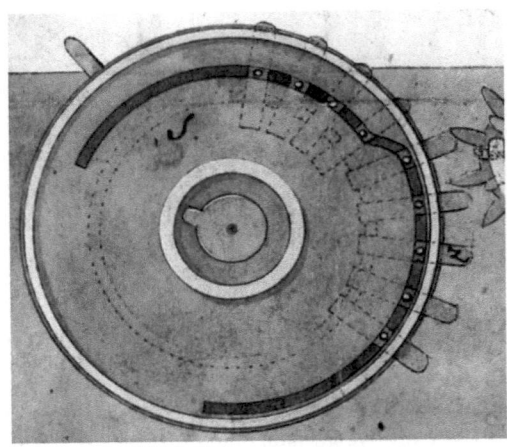

Fig. 9. Pinwheel (D. Roth, 1842, and I. Staffel, 1845).

acquaintance of Staffel with Roth patents seems extremely unlikely: the French patent was a manuscript, and the English one was published only in 1856.

However, arithmometers, based on pinwheels, began to receive wide application only from the end of the nineteenth century. On February 2, 1875 patent No. 159244 was received by the American Frank Baldwin. The pinwheel from this patent is shown in Fig. 10.

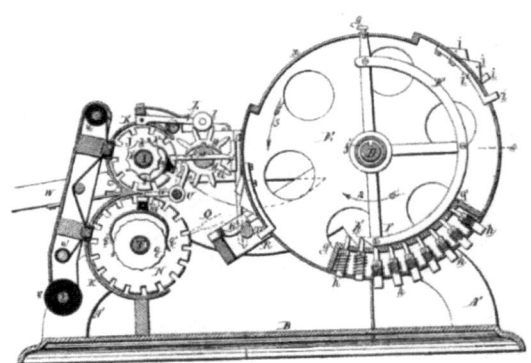

Fig. 10. Pinwheel (F. Baldwin, 1875).

A few years later, on 31 December 1879, the Russian *privilegia* (patent) No. 2329 on the arithmometer, invented by the Swedish engineer Willgodt Odhner (who lived in St. Petersburg), was given to the trading house "Königsberger & Co." The variant of pinwheel from this patent is presented in Fig. 11. Earlier, U.S. patent No. 209416 and German patent No. 7393 were granted. It is particular the design of

Odhner became the basis of most of the arithmometers produced under various trademarks throughout the world for a hundred years.

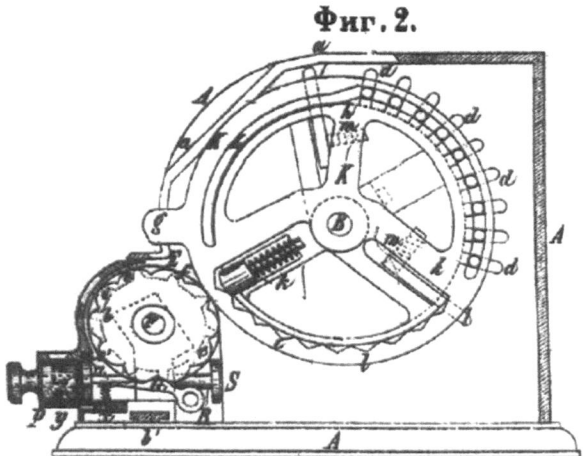

Фиг. 2.

Fig. 11. Pinwheel (W. Odhner, 1878).

In a 1919 interview, Baldwin said,

One of my 1875 models found its way to Europe, falling into the hands of a Mr. Odhner, a Sweden. He took out patents in all European countries on a machine that did not vary in any important particular from mine, and several large manufacturing companies in Europe took it up. [34]

The question of whether Odhner was acquainted with Baldwin's arithmometer is still open, although most likely Odhner have been unaware of it. But with Didier Roth's construction he could be familiar. However, one question is extremely interesting: could Odhner or Baldwin have known about the construction of Staffel's machine? Although Staffel's arithmometer was well known at the time, its drawings were never published, so Baldwin could not be familiar with the internal arrangement. At the same time, since Staffel's arithmometer in February 1876 was transferred to the Physics Department of the Academy of Sciences in St. Petersburg and became "accessible to those wishing to study it" [19, p. 586], it is possible that Odhner got acquainted with this device. Though the prototype of Odhner's first arithmometer was already finished at that time, he may have seen and studied the handwritten description of Staffel's machine before. This description (the translation of which we present in the Appendix) was available in St. Petersburg in 1846. Subsequently it was lost, but perhaps in the early 1870s it was still available.

However, regardless of whether or not Staffel's work influenced the design of the probably most commonly used arithmometers, he managed not only to offer, but also to realize, a calculating machine that received the highest appreciation of his contemporaries.

7 Conclusion

We hope the new materials presented in this paper will be an impetus to further study of the inventions of Israel Abraham Staffel and help to determine more accurately their place in the history of mechanical computing devices. We also hope that new documents related to the life and work of this remarkable inventor, who in 1851 was called the designer of the best calculating machine of all times, will be found in the archives of Poland, Russia, and England.

Appendix

The handwritten Staffel's book has 71 Russian and 57 Polish unnumbered pages plus 3 color drawings. Its cover of green color has a title in Russian, *New Calculating Machine* (Fig. 12).

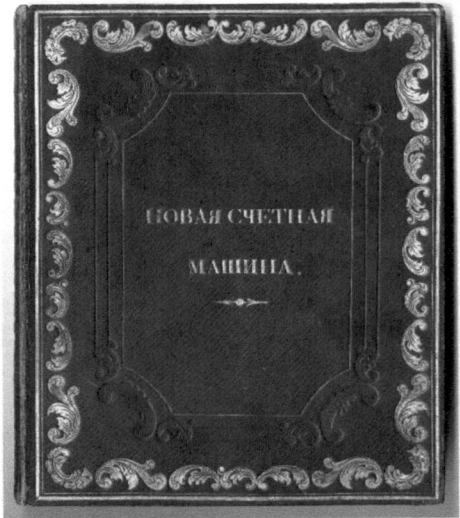

Fig. 12. Cover of Staffel's handwritten book.

The book has 71 Russian and 57 Polish unnumbered pages plus 3 color drawings. Both Russian and Polish texts are preceded by title pages (Fig. 13), on which it is written, respectively in Russian and Polish, "New Calculating Machine (Aritmetica Instrumentalis). Invented and designed I. A. Staffel. Warsaw. 1845."

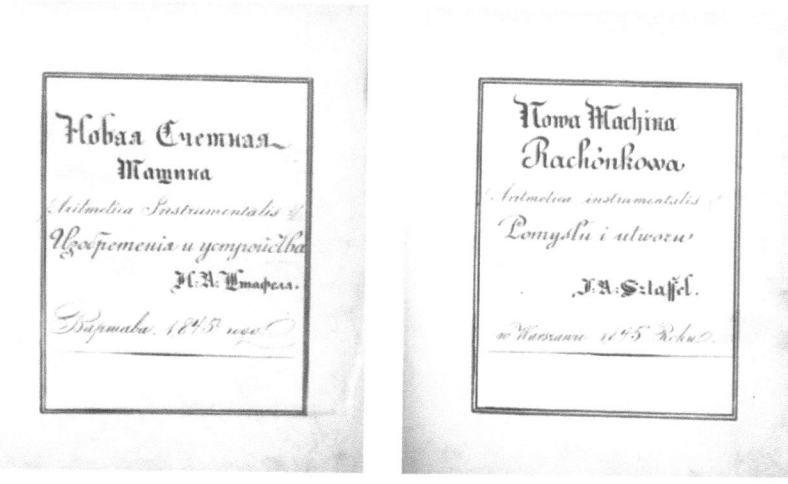

Fig. 13. Title pages of Staffel's handwritten book in Russian and Polish.

The text is written neatly, in a large legible handwriting (Figs. 14 and 15), but the Russian part contains many errors and slips of the pen. It seems the Russian language was not native for the writer, who was most likely not Staffel himself, but a professional copyist. The language of the document contains many obsolete even that time expressions and words. Sometimes it is even difficult to understand the author and we tried to interpret the text in modern English.

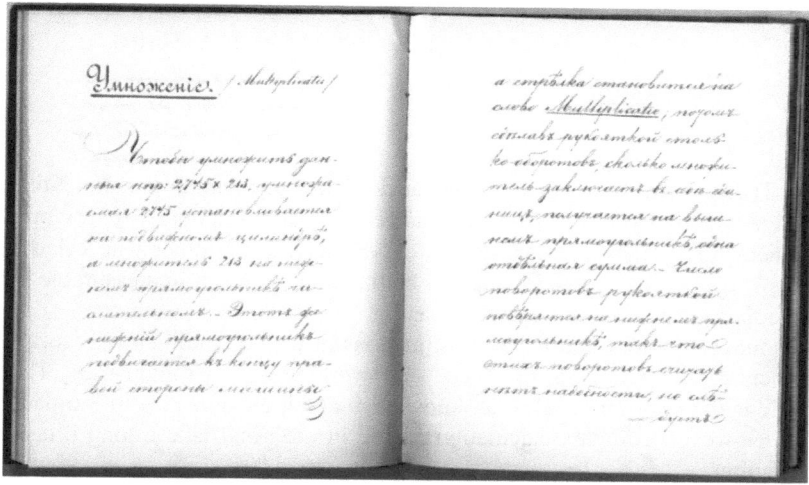

Fig. 14. Pages of Staffel's handwritten book in Russian.

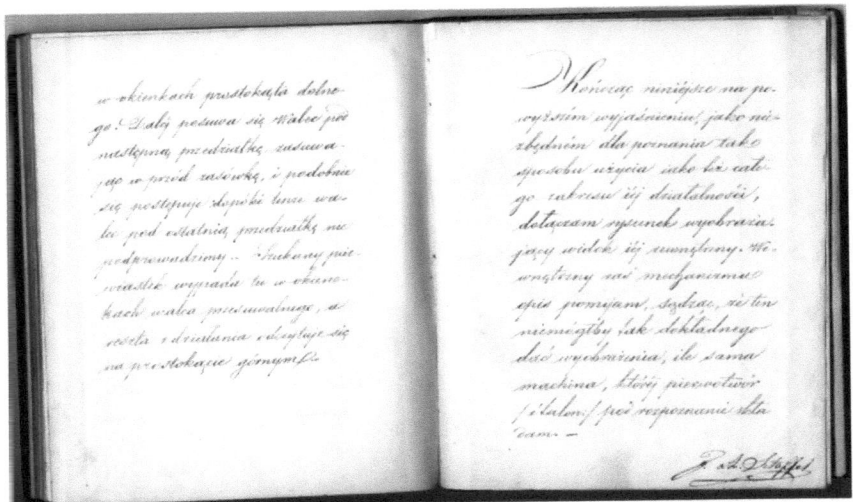

Fig. 15. Pages of Staffel's handwritten book in Polish with his autograph.

The translation of the Russian text is presented below. The number in curly brackets refers to the page number and after it is the text of the page.

New Calculating Machine
/ Aritmetica Instrumentalis /

Invented and designed

I. A. Staffel

Warsaw. 1845

{1} There is no doubt that mathematics is the most important field of human knowledge which also got the most extensive application. People of every profession use mathematics {2}, beginning with an experienced Astronomer who calculates the distances and turns of countless celestial bodies moving in an immeasurable space to the last countryman who cultivates the land.

Without calculations and without estimations, it would be difficult to work {3} for governments, farmers, artisans, traders, and workers of other industries. Therefore, arithmetic is the basis and soul of all knowledge and it alone is able to estimate all the benefits. However, complex calculations made in the mind take a long time and are very fatiguing.

We know from experience that often even simple addition, subtraction, multiplication, and division, especially of multi-digit numbers, requires mental effort and attention because a mistake in one figure often destroys the entire result. During calculation, arithmetic doubts, thinking, repetition, and rewriting are testing one action by another, but meanwhile the error that has appeared during verification could {6} stipulate the error of the main action. And what are the means for reducing this work, this mental strain? Of course, in subtraction we could replace one rule by another, in multiplication searching for a quotient is possible, in division – skipping digits of the dividend {7} or finally using logarithms. All this, however, is nothing more than the tedious check of the mental action by an equal mental action. These actions do not bring a real effective facilitation, but on the contrary, they take a person in one difficult job to another even more difficult.

{8} As for addition, there are no reductions in this case and no verification by other rules, except for a repetition of the action. So, this kind of calculation is the most dubious. Therefore, in commercial operations where significant {9} amounts are considered, or when there is a lack of time, usually two or three accountants produce the same action simultaneously.

Due to this burdensome intellectual labor, the vital necessity itself has long pointed out various means, in order to shorten the actions [10] of this kind. Among them there are certain tables known at Chancelleries and offices which facilitate calculations to a certain extent. Already among ancient Greeks, Pythagoras, the creative genius of Geometry, understanding the need to eliminate difficulties in counting, compiled a well-known multiplication table {11}, which facilitates addition. According to his example, various other calculation tables were invented later and applied to the four main rules. Those tables, however, are either very small or too large. Some do not fit to their purpose and others {12} are so inconvenient and insufficient due to their vastness that it is not possible to find the desired results conveniently and with the required speed. Scientists of different epochs and times, concerned about the public benefit and bearing in mind that all methods of training young people {13} to calculations are inseparable from mathematical principles, tried to replace them[1] with a simple mechanism in order to eliminate, or at least reduce in some way, the labor associated with written and mental counting.

Among such scientists we can mention on the first place such renowned persons as: Leibniz, Hahn, Babbazh[2], Miller (see footnote 2), and Stern, who applied significant efforts and spent large sums in the invention of machines[3] for mechanical counting.

Here I will keep silence about the inventors of different tables and {15} devices with mobile rollers because they also do not give all the desired final results, and therefore do not meet the requirements of effective mechanical calculation. Equally, I am far from a detailed investigation of machines invented by my venerable predecessors. I shall mention {16} them only to such extent as it is necessary for characterization of my own machine.

Although their devices did not achieve the desired perfection, they all do not lose their quality, though along with some shortcomings such as mechanisms {17} consisting of numerous rings, springs, and watch chains, moved by several handles. For

---

[1] The tables. [Present author's note].

[2] So is written by Staffel. [Present author's note].

[3] Leibniz 24,000 [thalers]; Babbazh 17,000 [pounds sterling]; Stern 10,000 [thalers]: and others had got appropriate expenses. [Staffel's note].

this reason, they are quite prone to breaking, tearing and any other damage that is difficult to repair. This requires great attention and caution during operation, and to work with them demands {18} studying the rules, perhaps more concerning the mechanism itself, than it is necessary for ordinary calculations. Meanwhile, only one mistake in operation destroys all labor and causes the necessity to start again; the work slows down and the machine could be damaged. At last, the obtained intermediate results {19} are often not yet completed and one needs to use a pen or chalk in order to get the final result.

Yet in my young years I felt an irresistible {20} passion for calculus and. experiencing great mental efforts in this branch of the sciences, I wanted to free myself from burdensome counting by some extraordinary means in order to be able to dedicate my mind and time to other useful sciences. This thought, once settled in my mind. {21} had grown further to the point that I finally stopped thinking only about my personal purpose. All my aspirations I turned to the general liberation of people devoted to this science from the difficult implementation of arithmetic operations. Then the time came that {22} gave me the opportunity to get acquainted with the already existing macnines, devices, and counting tables, and in the intricate complexities of their Mechanism and construction I managed to find the reasons of their shortcomings.

Having in mind completely different ideas, I avoided {23} this paved road, choosing a new direction, inventing a completely new method for mechanism.

I had been working for about 10 years on the construction of a new calculating machine while being a watchmaker, and I directed all my efforts {24} to use in it the most simplified and highly perfect mechanism. However, there is nothing more difficult than to simplify and, together with that, improve such a great thing.

Success happily was achieved due to such intense work and numerous costs {25}. I reached my deliberate goal and a machine I invented was completely built.

_t represents a rectangular parallelogram of length 18, width 9, height 4″, equipped with three cylinders of special purpose. Its advantages are as follows:

1. It consists of {26} 13-digit numbers reaching billions (see footnote 2).
2. With the help of a single handle, four main rules are produced, that is addition, subtraction, multiplication and division, and also extraction of square roots with fractions in accordance with the direction of the arrow placed on the screen. All this is very rapid {27} and without the use of a pen or chalk. The purpose of the arrow is that it facilitates the resolution of all tasks like the triple rule and others, composed from the above-mentioned arithmetic rules, by moving it from one word to another.
3. In all cases {28} where a subtrahend is bigger than a minuend, a multiplier is bigger than the sum that can be installed on the machine, or a divisor is bigger than dividend, the ringing of a small bell is heard, so all arithmetic operations can be performed on this machine even without light.
4. The mechanism of this machine is quite simple and does not require {29} mental strain for using it. It does not break down even during excessive handling and could be used for the construction of another calculating machine, more accessible for public use, although it may differ in value, type and number of digits.
5. Construction of this machine is understandable for anyone who just wants to use it, so one can learn it in half an hour and perform calculations without any difficulty. In

short, it is the first, as I know, hitherto nonexistent machine of this kind, convenient, perfect and simple.

This machine is really Automatic and similar to a practical *rakhmistr*,[4] who solves {31} tasks according to the rules of theory in a rapid and correct manner. From this point of view, it unquestionably provides a great service to the chancellery, offices, bankers, commercial houses, architects, geometers, and anyone who needs to perform calculations in a rapid and correct {32} manner. It can also be placed at home libraries and successfully used at other premises designated for mental exercises.

{33} Description of Machine and its external appearance.

The machine has the form of a rectangular parallelogram, length of 18 inches, width of 9 inches and a height of 3½ inches without a handle.

Looking from above it is visible:

a: two rectangles connected with each other at an angle.

One so-called numeral is located along the machine, having {34} on the surface thirteen openings, in which digits from 0 to 9 can be installed. Above these openings from the left to the right there are letters A, B, C, etc., but only over every second of them. These letters are needed for extracting square roots.

Another is lying in transverse to the machine direction, on which a handle is placed of 3 inches length {35} and 1–3/4 inch height, as well as the clapon[5] that fixes the turning of handle, and the arrow with the scale adjoining to it with the inscriptions of arithmetic rules. This handle is drawn from the right hand to the left when the arrow is placed on the words Additio and Multip, and from the left to the right when placed on the words Substractio, Divisio or Extractio.

{36} *b*: The cylinder lying horizontally, 6½ inches, made up of seven permanently connected circles, about 31/4 inches in cross section. These circles are designated by letters [A, B, C], etc. from right hand to left. Each circle has an opening on its surface under which it is possible to enter the digits from 0 to 9 by using balls mounted {37} on its toothed circumference. So, the cylinder, made up of seven separate circles, is fixed on the horizontal axis, with which it rotates together when the handle (mentioned in point *a*) is actuated. In addition, it can be moved along the same axis and fixed as needed with the help of a clapon.

c: Lower rectangle, {38} similar to the same upper or numeral, with the only difference that it has only seven openings, under which figures can be brought, moved by the help of lateral toothed heads. This part of Machine is movable and, just as the cylinder [*mentioned in point b*] can be fixed as needed.

{39} How to use Machine
Addition. /Additio/

Wanting to add the numbers, for example 5372 + 3845, you must first point the arrow on the word Additio. Then (assuming that there are zeros in the openings of

---

[4] Treasurer, cashier, counter in Polish. [present author's note].

[5] Staffel uses the word *clapon* (клапон) in Russian text. There is no such word in the Russian language. Probably Staffel meant *stopper* or *detent* [present author's note].

upper numeral rectangle), set the first number 5372 on the movable cylinder, and, after stopping the handle by pressing the clapon make one turn from the right hand to the left.

As a consequence, the digits (5372), set on the movable cylinder, go into the openings of upper rectangle. On the same movable cylinder another number 3845 is set and another turn of the handle is made. Then {41} in the openings of upper rectangle appears the number 9217, which is the sum of two given numbers 5372 + 3845 = 9217 which we alternately set on the movable cylinder. In the same way, we do for getting sums of other three, four, etc. {42} numbers.

Notes on the following Arithmetic Rules

1st Note. The same method of transferring the first of sums for addition from the cylinder to upper rectangle is used for subtraction and division, since the upper rectangle {43} has its application in subtraction and division as well as. For on this upper rectangle, it is necessary to set the sum more than the other in the case of subtraction, and divisible in the case of division, when producing these arithmetic operations.

2nd Note. As the movable cylinder is made up of seven separate circles only, then {44} the sum consisting of seven digits can directly be transferred to the upper rectangle. But, if there were a need to transfer the sum of eight, nine or more digits, then by transferring the first seven digits, it is necessary to move cylinder to the other end of the machine and set the digits eight, nine and eight on the eighth, ninth {45} or following openings of the upper rectangle etc. Then, making one turn with a handle, transfer these digits to the corresponding openings, which will make up with the seven previous digits the sum that we want to transfer to the upper rectangle.

{46} **Subtraction** /Substractio/

If you want to subtract amounts, e.g., 6428–5879, you must first transfer to the upper rectangle the larger number 6428 in the way described in addition. Then, set on the movable cylinder the subtrahend or smaller number 5879. Put the arrow on the word Substractio, {47} take off the handle brake, and make one turn from the left hand to the right. Then the number 549, appearing in the openings of the upper rectangle, is the result.

1st Note. If suddenly the machine user mistakenly transferred to the upper rectangle the lesser number {48} and from it wanted to subtract a larger number, than as a caution from this arithmetic improbability he would hear the sound of the bell placed inside the machine. Such an error could be conveniently corrected by moving the arrow to the word Additio and making one turn to the opposite side.

2nd Note. If it is necessary {49} to clear the openings of the upper rectangle from the digits on it and replace them by zeros, this is done evenly by subtraction. For, if you put on the movable cylinder the same numbers that are visible in the openings of the upper rectangle and, furthermore, point the {50} arrow at the word Substractio and make one turnover with the handle then the zeros appear in the upper rectangle, because the difference of two numbers is equal to zero (327 − 327 = 0).

3rd Note. If the number of the upper rectangle consists of more than seven digits, then by moving the cylinder to {51} the other end of the machine and repeating the same process as explained above, the remaining digits are also zeroed out.

{52} **Multiplication** /Multiplicatio/

To multiply the numbers, e.g. 2745×213, the multiplicand 2745 is set on the movable cylinder, and the multiplier 213 on the lower numeral rectangle. The same lower rectangle moves to the end of the right side of the machine {53} and the arrow point on the word Multiplicatio. Then making by the handle as many revolutions as the multiplier encloses the units one separate number is obtained on the upper rectangle. The number of handle turns is verified on the lower rectangle, so there is no need to count these turns. But it is necessary {54} only to pay attention to the corresponding opening of the lower rectangle, in which the numbers with each revolution are reduced by one unit and rotate until the zero appears in that opening. Then, the cylinder moves to the next digit of the multiplier and the handle rotates until {55} the zero appears in the opening of the lower rectangle, and so on.

After such a transition with the cylinder through all the multiplier digits, although not according to their arithmetic order, but only so that all the multiplier digits be reduced to zero, the sought number 584685 {56} appears on the upper numeral rectangle.

All reductions obtained by multiplying on paper could also be produced on this Machine.

{57} **Division**. /Divisio/

To produce the division, you need to transfer the dividend to the upper rectangle according to the method described in addition. Set the divisor on the movable cylinder, on the lower rectangle set the zeros. Move this rectangle to the right side {58} of the machine, and point the arrow on the word Divisio. After this, the movable cylinder is placed under the dividend, so that part of it from the left hand to the right is greater or at least equal to the divisor. Then the handle rotates until the number of the dividend, decreasing with each rotation {59}, becomes less than the number of the divisor. However, there is no need to observe this, because if you make more turns, the sound of the bell will immediately warn about that, and the error can be corrected by turning the handle to the opposite side.

{60} After that, the cylinder moves one digit further and the process continues in the same way to the last digit of the dividend. The result appears in the openings of the lower rectangle, and the remainder of the division, or fraction, appears on the upper rectangle.

General note.

Knowing the rules of the theory, {61} it is convenient to solve on the same machine all other tasks, arising from the four above described operations, such as: Arithmetic proportions, rule of three, etc., moving the arrow from one word to another as needed.

{62} **Extracting the Square Root** /Radix/

At the very beginning of the machine description and, in particular, in the paragraph under letter *a* about the numeral rectangle, it has already been said that there are letters **A**, **B**, **C**, etc., above the openings over each second of them {63} from the left to the right, needed for extracting the square roots.

Two such openings, denoted by one letter, will be called pairs, when extracting the square roots proceeding, however, according to the following:

If you want to extract the square root of any number, you need to set it on the upper rectangle {64} and set the zeros on the movable cylinder and the lower rectangle, except for the first opening from the right hand of this rectangle. Then point the arrow on the word <u>Extractio</u>, rotate the handle so that fixing clapon falls into its place. Move {65} the movable cylinder to the highest pair of the given number so that the letter of the cylinder corresponds to the letter of the given pair. In the same way, the lower rectangle is placed. Then the latch located next to the word <u>Radicis</u> moves to it, and the handle is turned until the number on the upper rectangle {66} becomes lesser or at least equal to the number in the openings of lower rectangle. After that, the cylinder moves to the next pair (sliding before the latch) and process continues in the same way with all the following pairs.

The sought root appears {67} in the openings of the movable cylinder, and the remainder is on the upper rectangle.

{68} Finishing the present description by above written explanation, necessary to learn how to use the machine and the whole range of its actions, I attach a drawing depicting the machine external appearance. As for its internal construction, I believe that the description could not give such a detailed its understanding as the machine itself, as the original exemplar (étalon), which I present.

I. A. Staffel

References

1. Sztaffel, I.A.: O nowej maszynie rachunkowej z wykazaniem potrzeby mechanicznej pomocy do odbywania rachunków. Korespondent Handlowy, Przemysłowy i Rolniczy **33**, 1 (1845)
2. Kurjer Warszawski **119**, 579–580 (1845)
3. Kurjer Warszawski **180**, 874 (1845)
4. J. Z.: Machina rachunkova wynalazku Staffla. Tygodnik Rolniczy i Przemyslowy **22**, 178–179 (1846)
5. Staffel's Calculating Machine. Exhibition Supplement to Illustrated London News **19**(518) (1851)
6. New calculating machine. Sci. Am. **6**(49), 392 (1851)
7. Calculating Machines. In: Reports by the Juries on the Subject in the Thirty Classes into which the Exhibition was divided. Class X, pp. 310–311. London (1852)
8. Alexandrowicz, B.: Machina rachunkova. Kurjer Warszawski **23**, 119 (1857)
9. Machina rachunkowa p. Izraela Abrahama Staffel z Warszawy. Tygodnik Ilustrowany **192**, 207 (1863)
10. Machiny rachunkowe w Polsce. Gazeta Warszawska **23**, 2 (1863)
11. Liczebnica mechaniczna. Tygodnik Ilustrowany **XVI**, 44 (1867)
12. Machina rachunkowa. Wędrowiec **49**, 361–362 (1882)
13. Izrael Abraham Sztaffel (Wspomnienie pośmiertne). Kłosy, XL (1041), 385–386 (1885)
14. The Jewish Chronicle, pp. 324–325, 18 July 1851
15. The Jewish Chronicle, p. 336, 25 July 1851
16. The Jewish Chronicle, p. 339, 1 August 1851

17. The Jewish Chronicle, p. 23, 24 October 1851
18. The Jewish Chronicle, p. 55, 21 November 1851
19. From the history of computing devices (based on the archives of USSR the Academy of Sciences) (Из истории вычислительных устройств (по материалам Архива АН СССР). In: Istoriko-matematicheskie issledovaniya, iss. XIV, pp. 551–586. Nauka, Moscow (1961). (in Russian)
20. Wyka, E.: Mechanik warszawski Abraham Izrael Staffel (1814–1885) i jego wynalazki. In: Opuscula Musealia, Zeszyty Naukowe Uniwersytetu Jagiellońskiego, z. 16, pp. 127–139. Kraków (2008)
21. Detlefsen, M.: Polnische Rechenmaschinenerfinder des 19. Jahrhunderts. Wissenschaft und Fortschritt **26**(2), 86–90 (1976)
22. Bondecka-Krzykowska, I.: First calculating machines in Poland. In: International Conference "History and Philosophy of Computing", HAPOC 2011. Book of Abstracts, Ghent, Belgium, pp. 24–26 (2011)
23. Bondecka-Krzykowska, I.: The beginning of mechanical computing in Poland. Stud. Log. Gramm. Rhetor. **27**(40), 45–62 (2012)
24. Brylevskaya, L.I.: The lost artifact (Утерянный экспонат). Magic of PC **4**(26), 16–17 (2000). (in Russian)
25. Brunsviga Rechenmaschinen Museum Katalog. Band 1–4
26. Index of the All-Russian Industrial and Art Exhibition in 1882 in Moscow. Moscow (1882). (in Russian)
27. Diaries of Sir Moses and Lady Montefiore: comprising their life and work as recorded in their diaries from 1812 to 1883, vol. II. Chicago (1890)
28. http://history-computer.com/MechanicalCalculators/19thCentury/Staffel.html. Accessed 11 Dece 2018
29. Martin, E.: The Calculating Machines: Their History and Development. Ed. by P.A. Kidwell, M.R. Williams, p. 60 (1992)
30. Morar, F.-S.: Reinventing machines: the transmission history of the Leibniz calculator. Br. J. Hist. Sci. **48**(1), 123–146 (2015)
31. Poleni, I.: Miscellanea. Hoc est 1. Dissertatio de barometris, & thermometris, 2. Machinae aritmeticae, ejusque usus descriptio, 3. De sectionibus conicis parallelorum in horologiis solaribus tractatus, Venetiis, apud Aloysium Pavinum (1709)
32. Leupold, J.: Theatrum Arithmetico-Geometricum. Das ist Schauplatz der Rechen und Mess-Kunst. Leipzig (1774)
33. Felt, D.E.: Mechanical Arithmetic, or the History of the Counting Machine, Chicago (1916)
34. http://www.monroe-systems.com/company_history_personal_story.asp. Accessed 11 Dec 2018
35. Shilov, V.V., Silantiev, S.A.: Russian schoty: long way to the west and back. In: Proceedings of the 2017 IEEE HISTory of ELectrotechnolgy CONference (HISTELCON), Kobe, Japan, pp. 70–75 (2017)

Mathematicians at the Scottish Café

Chris Zielinski[(✉)]

University of Winchester, Sparkford Road, Winchester SO22 4NR, UK
chris@chriszielinski.com

Abstract. Between 1935 and 1941, "The Scottish Book" – a collection of almost 200 mathematical problems – was compiled by a group of Polish mathematicians who gathered at the Scottish Cafe in the Polish (earlier Austro-Hungarian/now Ukrainian) city of Lwów (Lemberg/Lviv) (Note: In this paper, I am using the names Lemberg, Lwów and Lviv, according to whether at the time the city was a part of Austria-Hungary, Poland or either the Soviet Union or Ukraine. Some essential history: (1) When Hitler invaded Poland in September 1939, the Germans crossed the whole of the country and reached as far as Lwów in the East; (2) Then they stopped and handed over the eastern section, including Lwów, to their Soviet allies (a result of the Molotov- Ribbentrop Pact), and retreated to the present-day Polish border; (3) Between October 1939 and May 1941, Lwów was under Soviet control. (4) In June 1941, with Germany and the Soviet Union allies no longer, the Germans ousted the Soviets from Lwów and stayed until the end of the War. (5) Lwów then became a city in the Ukrainian SSR; and (6) it is now is a part of independent Ukraine.). The Scottish Café had nothing to do with Scotland. It was owned by the author's grandfather, Tomasz Zielinski. The Scottish Book and its problems survived World War II (a successor tome is being compiled and kept at the University of Wroclaw, Poland). Many members of this Lwów School of Mathematics went on to have illustrious careers and make indelible contributions to their chosen subject. This paper describes the evidence on the Scottish Book and the history of the various participants in this small but lasting component of the edifice of modern mathematics, which has been termed a "classic in mathematical thought".

Keywords: Mathematics · Lwów · Eastern Europe · Computing

1 Prologue

It was like an American Western of the 1890s – except that it was August 1937 in the far East of Poland: the door of the Café opened and a tall, dark stranger walked in. He was over six feet tall and broad shouldered. He had the slightly sad air of a gipsy. There was a pause as everyone in the Scottish Café took a covert glance, then resumed their conversations. Except for those at the long table in the back, who looked up and got to their feet. A smaller, antic young man who had entered with the colossus now stepped forward and introduced him to the group, "This is John von Neumann," he said.

Von Neumann had been in Lwów once before, ten years ago, and he wasn't a stranger to many of the older mathematicians, philosophers and dreamers who filled the Café. A long-time friend of Stanislaw Ulam's – the shorter man who had introduced

Published by Springer Nature Switzerland AG 2019
C. Leslie and M. Schmitt (Eds.): HC 2018, IFIP AICT 549, pp. 252–275, 2019.
https://doi.org/10.1007/978-3-030-29160-0_13

him – they had been taking turns. Ulam would come to teach at Harvard at von Neumann's invitation, and then spend the summers at home in Lwów. Von Neumann would come to Lwów for the occasional major conferences held in Lwów. In between his visits, von Neumann's reputation had grown. Now he was fully in the ascendant, capable of provoking awe with his incisive, original thought – but he was also good at telling jokes. The conversation grew louder.

A second undisputed genius was also sitting at the table – Stefan Banach, as tall and broad as von Neumann, and with an equally original character. But Banach was blond, and he dressed much less formally than von Neumann. They worked in similar domains – von Neumann was later to generalize and expand many of Banach's ideas – and held high opinions of each other's worth. Banach was the anchor for whole Lwów School of Mathematics which gathered at his table (Table 1).

Table 1. Members of the Lwów School of Mathematics (*denotes "leading member of the school", according to Polish Wikipedia)

Mathematician	Field and present relevance	Fate
Mieczysław Altman	Number theory (some of his divisibility algorithms are used in computer science…), cryptography and cryptanalysis, computer algorithms connections to physics! (mainly in the area of analytic regularizations in quantum theories), also data compression	1916–97 Banach's last student, starting 1939 when he escaped from Warsaw. Escaped from Lwów in 1941, studied in Soviet Union, left for the USA in 1970
Herman Auerbach*	Theory of convex bodies, Auerbach's lemma is still in constant use in areas such as C*-algebras. "Contact graphs have emerged as an important tool in the study of translative packings of convex bodies and have found numerous applications in materials science"	1903–42 He was either murdered at Bełżec extermination camp or committed suicide to avoid going there
Stefan Banach*	Banach was the founder of modern functional analysis. the entire realm of quantum field theory, with the calculations of Feynman propagators, gauge theories, scattering amplitudes and all the rest is entirely based on functional analysis. Much of the theory of probability can be considered as a branch of functional analysis. The functioning of the 4G-smartphones depends on the phones ability to quickly carry out certain transformations (DFT/IDFT) in	1892–1945. Was a lice-feeder at the Weigl Institute during the War years. Died of lung cancer in 1945, just as he was preparing to move to Krakow to teach. Buried in Lwow

(continued)

Table 1. (*continued*)

Mathematician	Field and present relevance	Fate
	certain (for example) 1024-dimensional subspaces of the space of (periodic) functions. The concept of Banach spaces is used in spacecraft and missile trajectory planning. Quantum mechanics, optimization, Sobolev Spaces and partial differential equations. The list of things named after Banach is long, and includes: Banach algebra, Banach algebra cohomology, Banach bundle (non-commutative geometry), Banach–Mazur compactum, Banach fixed-point theorem, Banach function algebra, Banach game, Banach limit, Banach manifold, Banach measure, Banach norm, Banach space, Banach–Alaoglu theorem, Banach–Mazur game, Banach–Ruziewicz problem, Banach–Steinhaus theorem, Banach–Stone theorem, Banach–Tarski paradox, Banach's matchbox problem, Hahn–Banach theorem,…	
Feliks Baranski	Differential equations	1915–2006. Assistant to Banach and a lice feeder, like Banach. Worked in Krakow University of Technology
Zygmunt Wilhelm Birnbaum*	Functional analysis, nonparametric testing and estimation, probability inequalities, survival distributions, competing risks, and reliability theory	1903–2000. Studied under Steinhaus. Worked as an actuary, before moving to US in 1937. Prof of Mathematics at U of Washington
Leon Chwistek*	Philosophy of mathematics. He applied his "doctrine of the plurality of realities" to mathematics and art. He was also a renowned avant-garde artist	1884–1944 Died near Moscow of natural causes
Max (Meier) Eidelheit*	Functional analysis, isomorphisms of rings of linear operators, automatic continuity – contributed problems to the Scottish Book. Eidelheit's theorem on separation (on separation of convex sets in normed spaces)	1910–43 murdered by Nazis. Student of Banach
Władysław Hetper*	Problem of completeness of the system of elementary semantics, a system without axioms for sentential calculus – issues in mathematical logic and philosophy	Dates unknown. Died in a Soviet camp

(*continued*)

Table 1. (*continued*)

Mathematician	Field and present relevance	Fate
Mark Kac*	Probability theory, spectral theory, theory of Fourier series, Feynman-Kac formula, statistical mechanics, number theory	1914–84 A student of Steinhaus, he moved to the US just before the War. Became a professor at Cornell, Rockefeller and USC
Stefan Kaczmarz*	Kaczmarz method which provides the basis for many modern imaging technologies, including the CAT scan; theory of orthogonal series	1895–1939 Circumstances of death not known – suspected murdered with Army officers in Katyn
Bronisław Knaster	Point-set topology. in 1922 discovered the hereditarily indecomposable continuum or pseudo-arc and of the Knaster continuum, or buckethandle continuum. He also developed the "last diminisher" procedure for fair cake cutting. Knaster–Tarski theorem, Knaster–Kuratowski fan, Knaster's condition	1893–1980. Student of Steinhaus. Like Banach, he was a lice feeder at the Weigl Institute. Became Professor in Wroclaw
Edward Kofler	Game theory, fuzzy sets, incompleteness (of information) theory, "partial information theory". His work developed further by John von Neumann	1911–2007. During the war, escaped to Kazakhstan and ran a children's home in Alma-Ata. Emigrated to Switzerland in 1969
Kazimierz Kuratowski*	Set theory and topology. His characterization of topological spaces now called Kuratowski closure axioms; he proved the Kuratowski–Zorn lemma; in graph theory, the characterization of planar graphs is now known as Kuratowski's theorem; identification of the ordered pair (x, y) {\displaystyle (x,y)}with the set $\{\{x\}, \{x, y\}\}$; {\displaystyle \{\{x\},\{x, y\}\};}; the Kuratowski finite set definition, see Kuratowski-finite; introduction of the Tarski–Kuratowski algorithm; Kuratowski's closure-complement problem; Kuratowski's free set theorem; Kuratowski convergence of subsets of metric spaces; the Kuratowski and Ryll-Nardzewski measurable selection theorem; topology: robots, finding patterns in big data sets	1896–1980. He left for Warsaw before the Scottish Book, but is nevertheless counted a member of the Lwów School

(*continued*)

Table 1. (*continued*)

Mathematician	Field and present relevance	Fate
Antoni Marian Łomnicki*	His work was in training engineers, writing popular school book s and textbooks about mathematics	1881–1941. Murdered by Nazis in Murder of Professors
Stanisław Mazur*	Geometrical methods in linear and nonlinear functional analysis, Banach algebra, summability theory, infinite games and computable functions. Known for numerous results in functional analysis. (one of his classical results says that the convex envelope of compact subset of a Banach space is again compact). The Mazur-Gelfand theorem is widely known. Mazur also collaborated closely with Orlicz obtaining results in non-linear functional analysis (polynomial operators) and in locally convex spaces	1905–81. Taught at University of Warsaw. Long-time member of Communist Party
Władysław Nikliborc*	An academic administrator and teacher, rather than an applied mathematician. Played chess with Auerbach and others at the Scottish Café	1889–1948 Faculty Dean. Moved to the Warsaw Polytechnic. Died under interrogation by Polish Public Defense authroities
Władysław Orlicz*	Orlicz spaces, non-linear functional analysis (polynomial operators) and locally convex spaces. Known for his results on orthogonal series, real functions, summability theory and functional analysis (polynomial operators, interpolation of operators and theory of modular spaces). Applications in statistics and probability	1903–1990. A lice feeder, like Banach
Mathematician	Field and present relevance	Fate
Józef Pepis*	Mathematical logic	1910–1941. Murdered by Nazis
Stanisław Ruziewicz*	Set theory and real functions	1889–1941 murdered by Nazis in Murder of Professors
Stanislaw Saks*	Theory of integrals	1897–1942 (murdered by Nazis in Warsaw)

(*continued*)

Table 1. (*continued*)

Mathematician	Field and present relevance	Fate
Juliusz Paweł Schauder*	Schauder bases, functional analysis, partial differential equations and mathematical physics. Associated with his name are the Schauder basis, Schauder fix-point theorem and the Lerey-Schauder theory of non-linear completely continuous operators (with topological methods based upon the concept of an index and with applications to partial differential equations)	1899–1943. Shot by Nazis in Lwów ghetto
Józef Schreier	Functional analysis, Group theory, combinatorics, topology. Baire–Schreier–Ulam theorem, Schreier–Ulam theorem	1909–43. Contributed to the Scottish Book. Died in an underground bunker when the Germans came – committed suicide by cyanide rather than be captured
Wacław Sierpiński	Set theory, number theory, theory of irrational numbers, theory of functions and topology – three well-known fractals named after him: the Sierpiński triangle, carpet and curve & Sierpiński numbers "In 1916, Sierpiński gave the first example of an absolutely normal number"	1882–1969. Apart from teaching in Lwów 1908–1914, he wasn't really Lwów School – he studied and taught in Warsaw
Hugo Steinhaus*	Banach-Steinhaus theorem, and many other results – although he claimed that his greatest discovery was not a mathematical formula, but Stefan Banach	1887–1972. Became Professor in Wroclaw
Ludwik Sternbach	Borelian types of linear qualities, convergence sets of linear operations. From 1929, he worked part-time as an editor for the newly established Studia Mathematica	1905–1942. Died in the Bełżec extermination camp
Włodzimierz Stożek*	Theory of integral equations, logarithmic and potential theory	1883–1941 One of those murdered by Nazis in the Murder of Professors
Stanisław Ulam*	Many results with Banach, Mazur and others in the Lwów School. In the US, participated in the Manhattan Project to develop the A-bomb, originated the Teller–Ulam design of thermonuclear weapons, discovered the concept of cellular automaton, invented the Monte Carlo method of computation, and suggested nuclear pulse propulsion. Also worked on ENIAC, "the first general purpose computer"	1909–84. Left Lwów just before WW2 broke out and spent the rest of his life in the USA. IN the US, worked at Harvard University. The Institute for Advanced Studies in Princeton and Los Alamos

(*continued*)

Table 1. (*continued*)

Mathematician	Field and present relevance	Fate
Menachem (Maniek) Wojdysławski	Important work in topology, which is still being cited and developed	1919–1942

We will later meet more of the cast at the Scottish Café in Lwów between the Wars. Almost all the others at the table also contributed important ideas – and often their names – to the study of mathematics, and to the practical applications that resulted from their equations. As technology developed, much of this work fed into the new fields that were emerging, notably computer science (Von Neumann and Ulam were involved in designing and operating the first machines constructed), probability theory, topography, number and set theory, game theory, and various allied mathematical fields.

During and after the War, about a third of the table emigrated to the US, where they became professors in new American faculties and were responsible for mathematical and technological innovations that propelled America's post-War rise as a global industrial power. Several (including Ulam and von Neumann) worked on the Manhattan Project, constructing the first atom bombs.

Another third stayed home – well, to be exact, they stayed in Poland by leaving their homes in Lwów and moving to Warsaw or Wroclaw. The whole east of Poland was taken by the Soviets, to be divided up into SSRs – Lwów and its surrounds became part of a new Ukrainian SSR, and later Ukraine.

And finally, at least a third of the mathematicians died during the War – mostly lined up against a wall and shot, some mowed down in cellars and fields, some in the extermination camps... But even they left some mathematical gems behind.

'The Book," shouted von Neumann. "Give me the Book. I have some new problems."

And a waiter was sent out to the secret place where the Scottish Book of Mathematics was kept. A simple exercise book in marbled black covers, this was laid reverently on a small table in front of von Neumann. The mathematicians grew quiet as he unscrewed the cap of his pen and began to write.

2   Introduction

This is an account of the brief flowering of a school of mathematics in Eastern Europe in the years between World War 1 and World War 2. Leading members of the school met almost every day in Lwów at the Scottish Café, where they discussed and considered and set problems in evolving mathematical topics of the day. A journal was founded and published, international connections made, congresses held. A book of problems – The Scottish Book – was initiated and kept at the Café for mathematicians to work on, solve, refute, or add to. Famous mathematicians visited, including such household names as Birkhoff, Fresnel, Lebesgue and John von Neumann.

The Scottish Book somehow survived the carnage of World War 2 and persists to this day (in Wroclaw) as the cornerstone of a "Scottish School of Mathematics", which has little to do with Scotland, but everything with a Café in a formerly Polish city now in the Ukraine.

This would be a matter of only local interest if the mathematics was not superior. In fact, it was world-class. A number of new branches of mathematics were established and their domains vastly extended over those little marble tables. Dozens of papers are still being written citing the works of those mathematicians. Many of them emigrated just before or after the War and went on to activities in technology – and were involved in work that was fundamental to the emergence of the Computer Age. Many died in the War, but live on with their names attached to an axiom, a lemma, a space or a fractal.

Thus, this short history seeks to give an entirely factual, but at the same time impressionistic, account of the mathematicians and their world at the Scottish Café, trying to put them in a social context.

The paper is based on a comprehensive reading of the growing literature on the era, on personal visits to the location, and on some family history.

Tracing the impact of all the mathematics devised during the flourishing of the Lwów School of Mathematics would be a major task beyond the scope of this paper, owing to its scale. Almost all of modern mathematics owes something to this group of mathematicians – as do fields like quantum physics, econometrics, computer science, and algorithmic number theory. Nevertheless, I will sketch out the main streams of posthumous development.

3   Brochwicz-Lewinski and the Scottish Café Building

Since the events we will relate happen in a specific and special building, it may be of interest to understand how that building came to be.

Zbigniew Brochwicz-Lewinski was 26 when he successfully completed his architectural studies at the St Petersburg School of Fine Art in 1903 [1]. A year later, when the Russo-Japanese war broke out, Lewinski escaped being drafted into the Imperial Russian Army by moving south to the Austro-Hungarian city of Lemberg.

He arrived in Lemberg as a newly-minted architect, and immediately plunged into work. He may have had family connections to Ivan Lewinsky, "The Man Who Built Lviv" [2], because, with barely enough time to catch his breath, the young architect began raking in significant architectural commissions in his new home city. Over the next decade, he was responsible for a series of imposing and decorative residential and public buildings. He ended his architectural career in Lwów with the huge Railway Administration Building, started and finished in 1914. To this day, it is considered the jewel of Lwów's 20th century architecture.

Brochwicz-Lewinski's buildings offer a clear testimony to the influences of his architectural upbringing in imperial St Petersburg, mingled with his own streak of pure fantasy. These are distinguishing features of the four-storey townhouse that housed the Scottish Café, which Brochwicz-Lewinski built for the entrepreneur Emil Weksler in 1908-9.

Throughout his life, Brochwicz-Lewinski exhibited a rare blend of the practical artist and the military man. His architectural work in Lwów effectively ended with the onset of World War I, when his military career took over in earnest. For the next thirty years, Lewinski fought in every war possible – World War I, the Polish-Ukrainian War, the Polish-Bolshevik war, and finally World War II – amassing medals and rising to ever-more-senior ranks as he went. And then, as Hitler invaded France, the pendulum swung again. In 1940, Brochwicz-Lewinski was posted to Scotland to look after army families stationed there. He liked it so much he stayed on after the war. At the age of 62, he embarked on his third career – as an artist. Not as a Sunday dauber, either: in the ten years before he died (in Glasgow, in 1951) he had achieved a reputation as one of Poland's leading 20th Century artists. A remarkable man.

Yes, Scotland. An appropriate destination for the architect who was responsible for Lwów's Scottish Café. To the city's citizens, the residential townhouse, with its two towers and swirling modernized Gothic balconies looked so much like a Scottish castle from a romantic novel, that the cafe located on its ground floor could have no other name [3]. Situated at one corner of Academic Square, 100 metres from the old University, the Café was destined to become the magnet for a mathematical revolution.

4 Tomasz Zielinski and the Scottish Café

At this point, I must declare a personal interest. My grandfather, Tomasz Zielinski, was the owner of the Scottish Café between WWI and WWII. Born in 1871 in the village of Zimna Woda just outside Lwów, Tomasz Zielinski was by all accounts a serious and dignified man. He does not offer a smile in any of the few photos of him I possess. He looks clear-eyed and alert, with an unlined face and a small, sober white moustache. Neatly suited, he walks a cane down a gravel path, with his wife, my grandmother Catherine, on his arm.

In the literature surrounding the story of the Scottish Café, Tomasz appears at various points as a concerned proprietor, anxious that his marble-topped tables were being defaced by the scribbling mathematicians who began to drift in after the various wars receded, and as the University and Polytechnic revived. But he was also sensitive to the possible significance of their academic work, causing scribbled-on tables to be stored until the perpetrators could copy the text onto paper the following day. What was almost as important was his tolerance when it came to the complex arithmetic involved in paying the bill: here he showed his heart.

At first, the mathematicians would meet Banach at the Café Roma directly across the street from the Scottish Café. But the owners there clearly ran a tighter ship than my grandfather did. They demanded payment on consumption. Offended by the lack of credit extended to him and other impecunious academics, Banach picked up his papers and crossed the road. Around 1930, thus, the Scottish Café took over as the centre of Lwów's – and for a while the world's – mathematical universe.

Tomasz Zielinski was the owner of the café and not its manager (he hired a man named Brettschneider [4] to run the place), but I can imagine him sitting there at some side table, resting his cane and watching the desultory traffic with a benevolent eye.

How the Scottish Café fell into my grandfather's hands is a mystery to me. I never met the man, but archival records show he came from a farming family, as did my grandmother. Still, in short order, he somehow acquired the capital to buy the Scottish Café, as well as a nearby 4-storey apartment building which served as the family's city residence, and a sizeable country estate including the hydrotherapy spa Marjówka on the edge of town. He owned all of these throughout the inter-war years. Wherever he got the money from, it certainly wasn't from selling cups of coffee to mathematicians.

5 *Knajpes* and the Scottish Café

When World War I ended in November 1918, Poland emerged from partition and Lwów found itself integrated into a culturally and intellectually starved nation. Peace did not come immediately, though, as Lwów played a central role in both the Polish-Ukrainian War and the Polish-Soviet War. By March 1921, hostilities finally stopped and a genuine peace arrived. This was to last 18 years until the German invasion of Poland on 1 September 1939.

Those inter-war years saw Lwów thrive. During this all-too-brief interlude, it was a multicultural city, boasting several universities and a vibrant artistic and intellectual society. *Knaijpes* flourished – the local term for Jazz Age "joints" [5]. Clubs and bars and cafés offered high life and low life depending on your tastes and wallet. There was a palpable energy and sense of iconoclasm evident. Everything must change! The Roaring 20 s were fully in operation in Lwów, with a Polish tinge, but roaring there just as much as they did everywhere else. Jazz, cabaret, painting, cinema, the dance craze, fashion – local versions of all were developed, and all levels of society were affected.

So let us walk to the corner of Academic Square and push open the doors of the Scottish Café. At that time, it occupied the whole ground floor of the building. Photos show a long wide room with an oriental carpet on the marble floor, on which some 20 tables of various sizes and shapes are scattered – a row of squarish tables by the windows, and round and larger rectangular tables elsewhere. Central towards the back, next to the billiards table, is the largest table –the "Stammtisch" for larger gatherings. This is where Banach and his mathematicians would have sat. An ornate gilt-framed mirror covers the back wall, reflecting the row of brass chandeliers hanging from the high ceiling. The walls are cream; racked along a cream waiters' side-table are cake stands topped with bunches of flowers. Each table is hemmed in by wooden art-deco chairs with S-shaped backs and solid seats. These must have been springy and comfortable, given the lengthy duration of some of the mathematical deliberations they supported – over 17 h in not a few cases, according to Ulam [6]. From the photos it seems there was adequate space for at least 50 customers at a time – but not much more.

Who were these 50? Histories of mathematics understandably focus entirely on the mathematicians. However, despite the descriptions of the Café in the memoirs I have consulted, they certainly weren't all mathematicians. What is striking, if you cast your net wider, is the amazing density and diversity of culture that filled the space. There were completely parallel universes operating in the same room, and evidently at the same time.

For example, while the mathematicians were contemplating Banach spaces at one table, speaking in sudden bursts and sketching geometric shapes on the table tops, Roman Jaworski and his friends were conducting regular sessions of the Constructivists' Club (Klub Konstrukcjonalistów) at another, and there the norm, indeed the requirement, was to orate as mellifluously as possible [7]. The Constructivists talked up a synthesis of culture, science and technical knowledge that was to appear in art, poetry and theatre. According to Radoslaw Okulicz-Kozaryn "The topics of the conversations of its members were very broad, and their philosophy, developed primarily by Roman Jaworski, included mainly aesthetic issues. Constructivism was supposed to be a way to save art in the period of multiple changes taking place in the modern world" [8]. The Constructivists Club rules demanded elegance and refinement in clothing and behaviour – quite different from the motley attire and robust behaviour of the mathematicians. There is a whole parallel story about Constructivism and the Scottish Café to write, which I will omit here.

The Café was throbbing with intelligence. Near to the mathematicians, another table united the philosophers and logicians. These were led by Kazimierz Twardowski, the founder of the Lwów-Warsaw school of logic, who used the Café as an office, writing his philosophical works here, and holding professional discussions with colleagues. Again, these were not obscure rural savants: there was the painter-philosopher Leon Chwistek; Jan Łukasiewicz, who among his other pursuits in logic invented Polish and Reverse Polish Notation, which are still being used in computer science and calculating machines; and Alfred Tarski, of whom *Philosophy Now* writes "together with Aristotle, Gottlob Frege, and Kurt Gödel, Alfred Tarski is widely regarded as one of the greatest logicians of all time – an opinion he wholeheartedly endorsed. Like Gödel, Tarski revolutionized twentieth century logic" [9]. Notable foreign guests would stop by, including American philosopher Willard Quine who visited in 1932 while on a fellowship from Harvard.

To counterbalance the intellectual heavyweights, tables were regularly occupied by the arty, noisy, chatty radio people who came to the Café to discuss and write the scripts for the Wesola Lwowska Fala (A Cheery Wave from Lwów) cabaret, a very popular programme which was beamed out twice a week throughout Poland. Journalists scribbled at the tables – including Bruno Winawer, who wrote his popular socio-scientific comedies and columns on science and literature here.

Apart from spouting mathematical and other fantasies, people played billiards or chess. The cattle traders who used to come from all over Galicia to the big Saturday market held in the square outside would sit and reflect about changing times. Although the square no longer filled up with animals, as the market had moved elsewhere, the traders still habitually came to the Scottish Café.

And there were of course lone stars sitting in the tables between these distinct groups, some of them quite special. For example, there were sightings of the pianist Artur Rubinstein, home in Lwów between world tours. The future Prime Ministers of Poland and Mongolia occasionally appeared for a coffee and a chat. Writers such as Bruno Schulz – as unique as Kafka, and a remarkable painter as well – would drop in on one of his frequent visits from nearby Drohobycz (where he was born, where he taught art at school, and where a Nazi killed him) [10]. Another was the young Stanislaw Lem, the future science fiction writer, who would come in for a warm milk and honey, just out of boyish curiosity about the famous names inside[1].

And another fascinating coincidence of careers brought into the same room Simon Wiesenthal, the future Nazi hunter, Raphael Lemkin, the originator of the term "genocide", and perhaps Hersh Lauterpacht, who established the concept of "crimes against humanity" in the legal framework. As it happens, all three were in Lwów in the summer of 1928. Wiesenthal was studying architecture at the nearby University. Lemkin had two longer spells in Lwów – in the early 20 s, when he would show up to ponder his linguistics studies and draft translations, sitting by a window, and from 1926 to 1929 when he did his law degree. He would stroll over to the Café from the University, and think the thoughts that led him to originate the word and concept of "genocide". His subsequent career was largely focused on developing the legal weapons to detect and fight genocide through legislation and the United Nations. Strange to think about Wiesenthal and Lemkin both sitting in the Café, blissfully unaware of the terrible historical that would bring them a sad renown and consume so much of their future lives.

The circumstances are different regarding the originator of "genocide" and the father of "crimes against humanity" – the two rival accusations flung at Frank, Goering, Hess, and other Nazi leaders during the Nuremberg War Crime Trials. Both of these lawyers were from Lwów. According to Philippe Sands, "Lemkin and Lauterpacht had the same teachers at law school... both of them attended the first post-War Conference of the International Law Association in Cambridge in August 1946, [and this was] the first time I could place Lauterpacht and Lemkin in the same town and building at the same time" [11]. We have no eyewitness evidence for it, but they could have rubbed shoulders in the Scottish Café in 1928...

The more one delves into the clientele, the more remarkable it seems that so many varied and irrepressible memes were spread unstoppably throughout the world from a little-known corner of Galicia, launched by the extraordinary individuals sipping a coffee or chewing a chop at my grandfather's café.

Let's take a closer look at the mathematicians.

6 Mathematicians in the Scottish Café

6.1 The Academic Scene

It is unfortunately relatively easy to situate the Lwów School of Mathematics, which developed in the ambience of the Scottish Café, in the overall history of Polish mathematics – because there is almost no history to recite. Since 1795, Poland had been partitioned between Austria, Germany and Russia. In consequence, it largely missed

---

[1] "It is worth noting that at the time when Mazur was playing the futurologist [at the Café], Staszek Lem, one of the greatest authors of Science Fiction of our century, was about ten years old and running along Brajerowska Street in shorts" - From *Brainstorm in the Scottish Café*.

the rapid development of the sciences in the 19th century. As Zelazko notes, "in the 19th century the essential effort of the nation was devoted to the humanities, since literature and poetry were necessary for supporting the idea of independence and even for the preservation of the language" [12]. Such mathematical work as was produced was written in Polish, he says, and therefore lost to the wider world.

When the partition ended with the end of World War I, a reborn Poland sprang to vivid academic life. The key drivers of this mathematical renaissance were in Warsaw and Lwów. At Warsaw University, under the impetus of Zygmunt Janiszewski, the new journal *Fundamenta Mathematicae* become the world's first specialized journal in the field of mathematics. Unfortunately, Janiszewski died precisely as issue one was being set in type.

In Lwów, the two institutions relevant to mathematics were the University and the Polytechnic. What was then called the Jan Kazimierz University was founded in 1661. In 1934/5 the University had 5,900 students in five faculties, of which 870 studied in the Mathematical-Biological Faculty. Of the larger religious groups, 64% were Roman Catholic, 21% were Jewish, and 13% were Greek-Catholic. The Polytechnic was originally established in 1816. During the interwar years, it was called Lwów Polytechnic School and then, from 1921 on, Lwów Polytechnic [13].

Both of these institutions – the University and the Polytechnic – were considered as being of equal value. Individuals seemed to move readily from one to the other, following particular teachers or ideas. As a result, it is not easy to separate the personnel and institutions. Individuals would study at one and become a teacher or Professor in the other. Students would attend lectures at either or both.

The overwhelming impression from the literature is that the Lwów students had a palpable enthusiasm for their studies. Discussions about mathematics would spill out of the lecture rooms and into the streets and cafes. Mathematical tea parties were held. Students would often visit each others homes to pursue topics of mathematical interest. Memoirs frequently refer to the febrile, passionate atmosphere surrounding this most abstruse of subjects – and not just in Lwów, but in Warsaw and Krakow as well.

One particular passionate mathematical discussion had a major impact on the creation of the Lwów School, and it took place in Kraków's Planty Park in in 1916. Stefan Banach and Otto Nikodym, both in their 20 s, were seated on a park bench discussing the Lebesgue integral, as one does on a sunny afternoon. They were passionate about it. Voices were raised. A nattily dressed military man walked by – Hugo Steinhaus, a lancer in in the Polish legion, with a doctorate in mathematics from Gottingen. He watched the two debate, stepped forward and introduced himself [14]. Both Nikodym and Banach subsequently came to Lwów to study at the Lwów Polytechnic under Steinhaus. Nikodym went on to have an illustrious career as a Professor of Mathematics in Warsaw and then in the United States of America. Stefan Banach became Stefan Banach.

6.2   Stefan Banach

Banach was a mathematical genius, although it was a while before this was recognized. His birth and early life had not been promising. His father, Stefan Greczek, was a railway official and his mother was unknown (his surname comes from a laundress,

Katarzyna Banach, who played no further role in his life). Years later, Greczek told his famous son that he had been too poor to marry his mother. Young Stefan's life was one of careful poverty. While he was still in school, he started to give lessons. He never stopped.

Whether the Lebesgue integral discussion in Planty Park was in fact a tutorial by Banach, we will never know, but an important result was that when he came to study at the Lwów Polytechnic, he had a friend in Steinhaus, who had become a Professor there. In due course, with Steinhaus' help, Banach became an Assistant and then a Professor, and eventually a Faculty Dean at the University. This was despite a lack of formal qualifications – after struggling to get a mediocre pass in his high school leaving examinations, he only completed two semesters of undergraduate studies.

But it didn't matter, because Banach was obviously special. Soon after he arrived in Lwów, Prof Steinhaus gave him a difficult problem to solve, which he did in a day, with ease. The solution was the basis of their first joint publication, and they continued to collaborate from then on, co-authoring papers, starting a mathematical journal (*Studia Mathematicase*) and writing problems into the Scottish Book. Banach married Lucy and moved along professionally. Life was good.

He was a true original. Tall, blond and blue-eyed, informal and perennially insolvent – academic salaries were a joke – it was this latter characteristic that persuaded him to abandon his earlier perch in the Café Roma and cross the road to the Scottish Café.

Banach was the centre of the Lwów School of Mathematics at the Scottish Café. He could work anywhere. Noise didn't bother him. In musical venues, his preferred working seat was next to the orchestra. His mind purred on with a famous lucidity. He loved coffee and cognac and was happy sitting in the Scottish Café, talking mathematics with almost anyone – but you had to be up for it, as he didn't suffer fools. Unlike the dapper Prof Steinhaus, Banach was informal, to the extent that he was somewhat scorned for his short-sleeved shirts, lack of a tie, and his familiar way with students – all deemed to be not professorial at all.

But it was the impact of his personality, his single-minded pursuit of ideas and solutions, that animated the Lwów School of Mathematics. Meetings were irregular at first, but then they settled into a regular, daily pattern. The Scottish Café filled with mathematicians. Banach's prize students always sat with him at the head table – Herman Auerbach, Stanislaw Mazur, and Stanislaw Ulam were always there – but many others joined in, a number of them going on to achieve international fame. There are almost 30 mathematicians associated with the Lwów School of Mathematics (see the Annex table and photos), and it is beyond the scope of this paper to provide more than summary detail regarding specific individual lives and work.

What did they talk about? According to Ulam [15]:

The main propulsion of the original research work were the areas of set theory: the basis of set theory, set topology, and then - under the influence of Banach and Steinhaus – functional analysis with applications for classical analysis. Schauder, who was a university lecturer, dealt with partial differential equations. His methods and results have become classic today ... Banach, Mazur and Schauder are the creators of the popular method of treating analysis problems using geometric methods of function spaces.

As the mathematical conversations went wider and deeper in functional analysis, set theory, topology, and probability, it became a standard procedure to formulate ideas as problems, and then to share them in what became the American "brainstorm" – developed years later as a formal technique at Los Alamos by Ulam, von Neumann and others [16].

> Sometimes their effort began with searching for a problem. Then someone on the table top drew a simple figure or wrote characters like y = f (x -t- z).... Thanks to this heuristic, original questions were often formulated or mathematical paradoxes were invented. In most cases, Banach, Ulam or Mazur came to the café with a well-defined problem.... The adventure began. The participants of the session tried to look at the issue. Their thoughts wandered freely through Banach's spaces. There were long moments of reflection, concentration and tension. They thought intuitively or analytically. ...Banach processed information instantly, like a computer, so not everyone could keep up with it. He did not like to walk around the beaten tracks, but he looked for new ways, looked for distant and surprising associations, often looked into each other's eyes, drank coffee or cognac, burned out a lot of cigarettes: they drank too much, they smoked too much, and time seemed to have stopped.

What a wonderful picture of a group think – this ruminating body of men (there were no female mathematicians in the faculty at that time), concentrated, grunting the occasional comment, absorbed in the problem. And then [16]:

> Often it happened that one of the scholars - sometimes Banach, sometimes Ulam. sometimes Mazur – experienced a revelation... Like a flash of light, there was the initial idea of a solution. If it was an interesting trail, they would write it on a table top or on napkins. Together, they experienced a feeling of joy and relief, satisfaction and pride. Then they tried to prove the claim using the deductive method. Table tops were densely covered with mathematical signs. When Banach saw that they were beginning to err, he never expressed strong opposition. Rather, he posed new questions, made gentle remarks that often allowed him to find the right path.

Apart from illustrating the method, this quotation points to the very real need for The Scottish Book.

6.3   The Scottish Book

The mathematicians came to the Scottish Café armed with soft lead pencils. With these, they attacked the marble tops of the tables, which were easy to write on and, just as important, readily erasable. One commentator explains: "The Scottish Café was organized in a Viennese style. Small tables with marble surfaces were very useful to serve as slates which they covered with numbers. This at first did not arouse the excessive joy of the owner, but after a while Zielinski got used to such 'ruination' of his property. After all, the tables were not being occupied by teenage idiots but by serious university and polytechnic professors" [16].

In the evenings, as the customers were shooed away, the tables were often wiped down and the chairs placed upside down on them so the floor could be swept as well. One can only imagine the agonized faces of the mathematicians coming back the next day to continue their theoretical work only to find it had been washed away by an industrious cleaner. Some were saved by the intercession of the owner. A partial solution was introduced. According to Urbanek [17], after one of Banach's major evening bursts of mathematical genius had vanished by the next morning, "One day

Professor Lomnicki came in….and said that if this happens again, to, please, always leave the writing on the table as it is and store the table somewhere until the next day." So the scribbled-on tables were covered with a cloth and set aside. The cleaners who came in the morning were told that such tables should not be washed, and around 11 o'clock a student would come in and transcribed the mess onto paper. This process worked, at a pinch, but it made nobody happy.

According to Ulam [18], "In 1933 or 1934, we decided to give our current wording of the problems and results of the discussion a more permanent form". Bakula describes the decision-making process as follows: "Tomasz Zieliński, the owner of the Scottish Café, came up with the idea of how to save all these theories, questions and problems so that they would not die forever. At the same time he could protect the precious marble tops that were being destroyed under the pressure of lead and water. This is how a glorious book in the history of world mathematics was born…" [19]. This origin story is refined by Rakhiel: "Indelible pencils spoilt marble tables, and the owner of the cafe complained about it to Banach's wife Lucy" [20]. So Lucy (some say Banach) went out and bought a thick, lined exercise book with a marbled cover for Polish zloty 2.50 (a few cents) – in Soviet times they were called "stock books" – and brought it to the Café.

Someone (I suppose Banach, because it was his notebook and he set the first problem) scrawled "Ksienga Szkockza" (*The Scottish Book*) on the front page. Thereafter pages were filled in with a problem on the left-hand page and its eventual solution (if there ever was one – quite a number of problems remain unsolved today) on the right. The names of the problem setter and solver were entered, as was the date. Small prizes were offered for solutions: a bottle of wine, five beers, a live goose – the goose was handed over by Mazur in 1972 when Per Enfilo of Sweden provided a negative solutions for problem 153. Although the prizes suggest a certain levity, adding problems to the book was not an impromptu act. As Ulam wrote, "Most of the questions proposed were supposed to have had considerable attention devoted to them before an 'official' inclusion into the 'Book' was considered" [18]. This accounts for its persisting relevance and durability [21].

Although there are 193 numbered problems in the book, in fact there were a few more. Some were unnumbered, and some were presented as second or third parts to previous problems while in fact being completely new. Duda counts a total of 198 problems in all [22]. Some thirty mathematicians were among the authors –contributors in the first few years included Banach, Mazur, Ulam and Orlicz leading the field, with Schreier, Auerbach and Steinhaus also prominent. Schauder, Ruziewicz, Lomnicki and Kuratowski round off the first few years. Later contributors include such prominent foreign visitors as John von Neumann from the United States, and Cyril Offord, the first Professor of Mathematics at the London School of Economics.

Opinions vary about who looked after the Book in the Café, and where it was hidden when not in use. Suggestions about the guardian include the headwaiter "who, upon demand, would bring it out of some secure hiding place, leave it at the table, and after the guests departed, return it to its secret location" [18]. Ulam's version is that "This notebook was stored in the Cafe and the waiter brought it on demand. We wrote in the problem and the waiter ceremoniously took it back to the place where it was hidden" [23]. Hugo Steinhaus claims that the Scottish Book was not kept by the cloakroom attendant, nor by a waiter or the owner, but by another paid member of staff [24], but Bogdan Mis insists the book was "stored in a cloakroom and provided to mathematicians on request: anyone could post a solution to a problem" [25]. And when the cafe was closed, the Book was given to the owner, Tomasz Zielinski" who "treated it very carefully. Evidently, he understood its historical value." [23].

As the years went by, the mathematicians in the Scottish Café continued to perform their mental acrobatics and enter the fruits of their thoughts and discussions into the book. The left-hand pages filled with questions and many right-hand pages offered answers. A substantive analysis of the book and its numerous authors has been done thoroughly in the referenced literature.

So the book proved to be not only good for Mr Zielinski's marble tables, but for the field of mathematics. Results from this work have infiltrated much of modern mathematics, and the book still has an absolute value as a repository and source of unsolved problems.

7   The Beginning and the End of Everything

7.1   The End of the Scottish Book and Scottish Café

In 1939, a couple of weeks before World War II started, Mazur told Ulam that "if the city is bombed, I will put all the manuscripts and the Scottish Book into a case and bury it somewhere". The suggested location was to be "near the goal post of a football field outside the city" [18]. It is uncertain that this ever happened. In effect, World War II broke out on 1 September 1939, and by 17 September, the German Blitzkrieg had swept over the whole of Poland from West to East and right up to a hill at the borders of Lwów. The Germans sat on this hill with their artillery, taking pot-shots at city landmarks, but mercifully for only a few days. The German-Soviet Non-aggression Pact (or Molotov-Ribbentrop Pact), which had been signed the previous month, took effect, and the Soviets rolled into Lwów, relieving the Germans of their task, on 22 September 1939. They stayed there until July 1941.

Problems kept being added to the Scottish Book during the Soviet occupation. Ulam notes that "some Russian mathematicians must have visited the town; they left several problems (and prizes for their solutions)." [18] So the Café continued to operate under the Soviets. The last entry, no 193, was dated 31 May 1941 – a problem set by Prof Hugo Steinhaus about the distribution of matches in a box.

This was the point at which the Soviet/German Pact broke down. Hitler marched his forces into Soviet-controlled territory on 22 June 1941 and Operation Barbarossa reached Lwów on 30 June 1941. Anticipating the arrival of the Germans, it seems likely that Tomasz Zielinski closed the Scottish Café on 31 May. The inscriptions in the Scottish Book ceased after that, and both the Book and Café were inactive throughout the German occupation.

The closing of the Café on the last day of May suggests an orderly management of the accounts, with one months' notice given to everyone – mathematicians, philosophers, constructivists and waiters. The Scottish Book, with Steinhaus's last problem in it, would have been picked up by Tomasz Zielinski. Stefan Banach was in Kiev for a conference when the Germans marched into Lwów, so he gave it to Lucy Banach, who kept it for the rest of the War.

In the Café, the chairs would have been placed upside down on the tables, with dustsheets draped over the legs. Time to take a final look, sigh and lock the doors. My grandfather and grandmother set off on their final train journey towards Warsaw. Somewhere along the line – probably at the border between Soviet-occupied Poland and German-occupied Poland – the Germans brought all the passengers out onto a platform and separated the men from the women: "Women to left. Men to the right." My grandmother was travelled on to Warsaw alone. Tomasz Zielinski was never seen again.

7.2 Murders and Other Deaths

There were of course many, many murders committed in the immediate aftermath of the German invasion of Lwów – the entire Jewish population was massacred, Poles and Ukrainians died in their hundreds of thousands. Equally, many people managed to escape, either by fleeing the territory or hiding, usually with someone's help. No doubt some also saved themselves by making unholy pacts with the invaders.

Zelazko considers that during World War II "Poland lost about 50% of its mathematicians by death or emigration" [26]. This percentage is so high only because just before the war, by great good fortune, a number of mathematicians emigrated – these included Kac, Tarski and Ulam.

The table summarizes the fates of the Lwów mathematicians. A few key concluding biographies are summarized in the next few pages.

Banach. The Banachs stayed on in Lwów after the Germans came in June 1941. Like many other academics (including his fellow Café mathematician Feliks Bararski and the poet Zbigniew Herbert), Banach avoided arrest and deportation to a concentration camp by accepting employment as a lice feeder at the Rudolf Weigl Typhus Research Institute [27]. Weigl, a Polish parasitologist, had developed the first vaccine against typhus, made from lice fed on human blood. It was the only effective vaccine available, and the Germans wanted a supply for their soldiers. The blood was harvested by strapping lice in cages to the thighs of "volunteers" like Banach who had been vaccinated against the disease. In their cages, throughout the day, the lice grew fat on the blood they sucked from the volunteers' thighs. In the evening, the lice cages were unstrapped and the lice were crushed into a paste. Volunteers were given extra food rations and guaranteed certain immunities – for example passes which warned people that the bearer was potentially a lethal parasitological threat. Banach survived the war – but only just. A compulsive non-stop smoker, he died of lung cancer in August 1945 and is buried in Lwów.

The Murder of the Lwów Professors. A total of 45 professors at the University and Polytechnic of Lwów were executed by a German *Einsatzkommado* unit after the city was captured on June 30, 38 of them on the night of 4 July 1941 in the Wulka Hills above the city. Among the Lwów mathematicians were Antoni Łomnicki, Włodzimierz Stożek ad his two sons, Kazimierz Vetulani, and Kasper Weigel and his son.

Steinhaus. [28] On 4 July 1941, a couple of German SS troopers came to interrogate Steinhaus at his home. They accused him of being an NKVD agent, asked him where his wife and daughter were, and they beat him. They searched the house for gold, coffee and soap. Finding a box containing bars of soap, they told the Professor to bring it to their lodging in the villa next door the following morning. And then, miraculously, they left. Steinhaus needed no further warning. The same afternoon, when his wife and daughter returned, they packed two suitcases and left the family home through the garden, over the fence and across a neighbour's plot. He spent most of the rest of the War in Rudne near Lwów, just down the road from Zimna Woda, where my grandfather's family lived. After the War, Steinhaus joined the mathematics department at Wroclaw University. He died din 1972.

Ulam. Stanislaw Ulam had what was probably the most spectacular career of all the doyens of the Scottish Café after Lwów. Having started lecturing at Harvard before the War at the invitation of John von Neumann, he only spent his summers in Lwów. As a result, he had the very good fortune to return (with his brother) to the US two weeks before the War started. Through his collaboration with von Neumann, he was absorbed into the Los Alamos Institute at the start of the Manhattan Project to build the US atomic bomb. Subsequently, working with Edward Teller, he helped design the hydrogen bomb. Ulam was undoubtedly brilliant and multi-faceted. He was one of the relatively few "pure" mathematicians who was also able to function – and function brilliantly – in the applied world of physics. Everything he did seemed to spark a mathematical connection. For example, his invention of the Monte Carlo method occurred after a bout of illness left him playing patience in bed. Among Ulam's other practical achievements are developments leading to the first computers. It was Ulam who brought the Scottish Book of Mathematics to international public attention, by translating it and circulating photocopies of his translation widely until it went the equivalent of viral in 1957. Ulam was frequently asked about the ethics of his atom bomb research. His reply was always that, as a rule, Pandora's Box should never be opened, but once someone had opened it, you needed to be sure that ethically trustworthy scientists continued the work. He died in the US in 1984.

Mazur. Stanislaw Mazur escaped Lwów and worked at the University of Warsaw from 1948 until his death in 1981. He had been a loyal member of the Communist Party in the 1930s, which protected him and enabled him to rise in academic politics. Throughout his life he continued producing important mathematical results. He died in Warsaw in 1981.

8   A New Start

8.1   The Old Scottish Book, Wroclaw and the New Scottish Book

The Germans stayed until the Soviets ousted them again on 27 July 1944 and the Ukrainian SSR was constituted. A Ukrainization process was applied throughout the SSR. Lucy Banach was compulsorily repatriated to Wroclaw in 1946, after the death of her husband. She travelled with her son, and with the Scottish Book in her luggage.

Lucy died in 1957. The Book is now in the possession of her son Dr Stefan Banach Jr. Bogdan Mis reports [29] a sighting:

> After a while, Dr Banach brought out a large reel-to-reel tape box and from it extracted a neat, old-fashioned notebook, with a "marbled" effect cover. Even before it opened, I was already speechless with shock, guessing what it was. Yes! It was the famous Scottish Book, perhaps the greatest relic of Polish mathematicians, known throughout the world, which many thought was lost! The Scottish Book - a collection of problems and solutions to these problems, the results of a circle of brilliant Lwów mathematicians, with Stefan Banach, the father of my interlocutor, at the helm. The Scottish Book, surrounded by a legend today, mentioned in a thousand anecdotes, priceless!
> With due respect, we turned the slightly yellowed pages of the book, noting the handwriting of the most famous mathematicians today: Alexandrov, Sobolev, Schauder, Mazur, Kuratowski, von Neumann and many others. And among them – the sprawling handwriting of Stefan Banach, one of the greatest mathematical phenomena of our time, and yet one of the most interesting people of our country, the holder of a resume so rich and complex, which few scholars can boast.

After World War II, many of the surviving mathematicians from Lwów continued their work at the University of Wroclaw, including Prof Hugo Steinhaus. It was E. Marczewski's decision to revive the tradition of the Scottish book by initiating The New Scottish Book. The first problems in the new Scottish Book were entered by Prof Steinhaus at the beginning of July 1946, a symbolic act, as he also added the last problem in the old Book.

The new Book is in the Library of Mathematics Faculty of Wrocław University. Problems can be tackled on MathOverFlow (https://mathoverflow.net/users/105651/lviv-scottish-book). A working version of the original Book is here: http://www.math.lviv.ua/szkocka/view.php.

A copy of the original book stayed with Stanislaw Ulam who had it translated into English and began circulating photocopies to key readers. This sparked interest and gave rise to what has been called "The Scottish School of Mathematics" (to the bemusement of the citizens of Glasgow and Inverness). An international conference was held in Denton Texas in 1979.

9   Conclusions

This paper is a contribution to the History of Computing in Eastern Europe, and yet it focuses on a group of mathematicians and their conversations in a Café in the years up to 1942. How does this relate to a history of computing? There are two main devices for tying the narrative together.

The first relates to the practical applications of the mathematics in subsequent years. Now, most (but not all – Ulam was a notable exception) mathematicians are notoriously irritable when faced with the question, "what practical use does this have?" They see it as a question coming from another frame of reference. For them, the objective of great pure mathematics is to find perfect solutions to mathematical problems. Most of the mathematicians sitting at that table were simply not interested in how one might apply one of their insights to building a better bridge or improving the taste of coffee. The key thing was to make beautiful and unassailable mathematics.

The fact is, of course, that much of their beautiful mathematics has embedded itself inextricably in the computer age. To quote Ulam again [18]:

> *In a conversation in the coffee house, Mazur proposed the first examples of infinite mathematical games. I remember also (it must have been sometime in 1929 or 1930), that he raised the question of the existence of automata which would be able to replicate themselves, given a supply of some inert material. We discussed this very abstractly, and some of the thoughts which we never recorded were actually precursors of theories like that of von Neumann's on abstract automata. We speculated frequently about the possibility of building computers which could perform exploratory numerical operations and even formal algebraical work.*

But conversation is speech and ideas are ideas. More practically, Ulam and von Neumann were part of the team that developed the first general-purpose electronic computer, the ENIAC, and participated in a review of results from these calculations. Ulam later worked on further prototype models. That's as direct a link as you can have.

Here are some examples of other practical applications of Lwów mathematics, in no particular order:

- Banach spaces are used in spacecraft and missile trajectory planning
- Vector spaces enable 4G-smartphones to quickly carry out certain transformations (DFT/IDFT) in certain (for example) 1024-dimensional subspaces of the space of (periodic) functions
- The Hahn-Banach theorem applied to the Black-Scholes equation, an important computer algorithm in calculating arbitrage values
- Banach was the founder of modern functional analysis – the entire realm of quantum field theory (analytic regularizations in quantum theories), with the calculations of Feynman propagators, gauge theories, scattering amplitudes and all the rest is entirely based on functional analysis
- Much of the theory of probability can be considered as a branch of functional analysis and almost all current work descends from the Lwów School
- Auerbach's lemma and his work on convex bodies are applied in materials science and in packaging
- Game theory and the Monte Carlo method (Ulam's contributions) appear in a wide range of computer and business applications
- Number theory devised in Lwów is being used in cryptography and cryptanalysis, and in data compression algorithms
- The Kaczmarz method provides the basis for many modern imaging technologies, including the CAT scan....

I am sure there are many other examples to be found of practical applications.

It is also worth mentioning that the study of mathematics is riddled with the names of these Polish mathematicians – there are over 20 mathematical ideas with Banach's name attached, such as the Banach space, Banach bundle, Banach algebra, and so on. Auerbach, Kuratowski, Mazur, Orlicz and Schauder are not far behind in numbers of mathematical terms and concepts attached to their names. Sierpinski names three fractals for us – a triangle, carpet and curve. The Lwów School will endure for quite a while yet. All of their names are part of the continuing discourse. Papers citing their works keep being published by the thousands.

Finally, in this attempt to conclude, it may be worth reflecting how this happened. What were the factors that led to the sudden outburst of mathematics, logic and philosophy, law and literature, in Lwów during the inter-War years? Was it something in the water?

As my paper indicates, the long stifling of Polish intellectual contribution to the rapid scientific and technological development between 1795 and 1918, the prohibition on using the Polish language seemed to have a pressure-cooker effect. The minute the repression was lifted, the ideas began to flow.

This urge to let ideas flow was strongly abetted by the spirit of post-War iconoclasm, which operated on a number of levels. Youth, tired of the constrictions and dangers of war, brought in the Jazz Age, and with it a more democratic and egalitarian air, and with adventures in all the arts. From Europe, there were the more radical first cultural explosions of Dadaism and Surrealism, Kafka's works were trickling in from Prague, while there had been a complete bloody revolution in Russia. This was certainly the time when people felt the ability and the need to think radically, and it gave rise to such extraordinary bursts of creativity as the Lwów School of Mathematics.

Epilogue: The Scottish Café Today
In a sense, the Scottish Café itself also presents a spectacular story of escape, and has its own colourful career. Somehow, like the rest of Lwów/Lviv, Brochwicz-Lewinski's building looks untouched by bombs or bullets. Without seemingly turning a hair, it has weathered hot and cold wars and national and supra-national revolutions.

Since World War II, the Café has suffered the indignity of becoming a bank, and subsequently it went completely under cover for a few years as the Desertniy (Desert) Bar. However, in 2014 it reopened as the Scottish Café again, now part of the ground floor of the Atlas Hotel, an elegant boutique establishment, which occupies the rest of the building.

Visitors to the Café who express an interest are shown a facsimile copy of the Scottish Book, brought out of some hiding place by a manager or waiter, just as it would have been proffered during the 1930s. The tables are small and square, as they used to be, but they no longer have marble tops: you have to scribble your mathematics on a napkin or tap your tablet.

Given the present-day hotel's need for a reception area, the Café no longer occupies the whole ground level. It is small, cosy and new. However the floors – which are laid in white marble veined with black, and set in a herringbone pattern with a dotted line of marble rectangles along the edges – is the original floor. You can admire it while imagining the footsteps of your favourite illustrious mathematician walking across it in his – and its – heyday.

So I will leave you with thoughts of Banach standing there tall and blond, greeting the swarthy von Neumann, with Mazur and Ulam spinning mathematical spells or telling jokes beside him, Steinhaus eloquent and dapper in a frock coat, Auerbach rising from a game of chess in someone's dirty hat, Chwistek tapping across the floor in mismatched shoes....

...while I observe my grandfather, decorative cane in hand, in a light suit and with a somewhat severe expression, strolling across to my table to say hello.

References

1. Except as otherwise indicated this section is based on https://pl.wikipedia.org/wiki/Zbigniew_Brochwicz-Lewi%C5%84ski. Accessed 18 Nov 2018
2. http://www.lvivtoday.com.ua/lviv-personality/4169. Accessed 18 Nov 2018
3. The historical description of the building and plot section is derived from the Lviv Interactive entry ID: 2210. http://www.lvivcenter.org/en/lia/objects/pr-shevchenka-27/. Accessed 18 Nov 2018
4. Urbanek, M.: Genialni: Lwówska szkoła matematyczna. Iskry, Warsaw. ISBN: 978-8324403813 EAN: 9788324403813, p. 27 (2014)
5. Bakula, B.: Świat naukowo-artystyczny lwowskiej "knajpy" lat 30. (17 August 2004) eurozine.com. http://www.eurozine.com/swiat-naukowo-artystyczny-lwowskiej-knajpy-lat-30/. Accessed 18 Nov 2018
6. Ulam, S.M.: Adventures of a Mathematician, p. 33. University of California Press, Oakland (1991). ISBN 0-520-07154-9
7. Section derived from. https://pl.wikipedia.org/wiki/Klub_Konstrukcjonalist%C3%B3w. Accessed 20 Nov 2018
8. Okulicz-Kozaryn, R.: Gest pięknoducha: Roman Jaworski i jego estetyka brzydoty. Instytut Badań Literackich PAN. Wydaw., Warsaw. ISBN 83-89348-09-8, p. 158 (2003)
9. https://philosophynow.org/issues/111/Alfred_Tarski_1901–1983. Accessed 21 Nov 2018
10. Ficowski, J.: Regions of the Great Heresy: Bruno Schulz – A Biographical Portrait. Norton & Co, New York (2003). ISBN 978-0-393-32547-8
11. Sands, P.: East West Street, p. 464. Weidenfeld and Nicolson, London (2016)
12. Zelazko, W.: A short history of Polish mathematics. Mathematical Institute, Polish Academy of Sciences, Warsaw, p. 1 (2017). https://www.researchgate.net/publication/228701193_A_short_history_of_Polish_mathematics. Accessed 20 Nov 2018
13. https://en.wikipedia.org/wiki/University_of_Lviv. Accessed 21 Nov 2018
14. Steinhaus, H: Stefan Banach. Studia Mathematica, Seria Specjalna, Z. I., pp. 7–15 (1963)
15. Ulam, S.: Annals of the Polish mathematical society series II: Wiadomosci matematyczne / Messiah Announcements XII, pp. 49–58 (1969)
16. Jakimowicz, E., Miranowicz, A.: A w Szkockiej: Burze w Muzgu (Brainstorm in the Scottish Café) (2017)
17. Urbanek, M.: Genialni: Lwowska szkola matematyczna./Wydawnictwo Iskru, Warsaw, p. 111 (2014)
18. Ulam, S.M.: Adventures of a Mathematician. op cit, p. 32
19. Bakula, B.: Comparison as evidence. Polish-Ukrainian cultural, literary and historical relations 1890–1999. Wyd. Naukowe UAM, Poznań, pp. 207–219 (2001)
20. Rakhiel, Y.: Scottish Book: Lviv's mathematical relic – About the role of Ukrainian scientists in the formation of new mathematics, 1 April 2010. http://day.kyiv.ua/en/article/society/scottish-book-lvivs-mathematical-relic. Accessed 17 Aug 2018
21. Thanks to Stan Ulam, the entire book was translated and published in English as The Scottish Book: Mathematics from the Scottish Café, Ed by Mauldin, R.D., Birkhäuser, Boston. ISBN 3-7643-3045-7 (1981)
22. Duda, R.: Lwówska szkoła matematyczna, 2nd edn. Uniwersytet Wrocławski, Wroclaw (2014). ISBN: 978-83-229-3211-7. (Also available in English as Duda, R. Pearls from a Lost City: The Lvov School of Mathematics. (translated from Polish by Daniel Davies). American Mathematical Society, Providence, USA. ISBN 978-1470410766) (2014)
23. Rakhiel, Y.: Scottish Book: Lviv's Mathematical Relic – About the Role of Ukrainian Scientists in the Formation of New Mathematics. op cit

24. Steinhaus, H.: Stefan Banach. op cit
25. Miś, B.: Opowieści Księgi Szkockiej (Tales of the Scottish Book). Perspectives No. 12, pp. 17–19 (1969)
26. Zelazko, W.: A short history of Polish mathematics. Mathematical Institute, Polish Academy of Sciences, Warsaw (2017)
27. Lice feeding. https://en.wikipedia.org/wiki/Feeder_of_lice. Accessed 22 Nov 2018
28. Section adapted from Rakhiel, Y.: Scottish Book: Lviv's mathematical relic – About the role of Ukrainian scientists in the formation of new mathematics. op cit
29. Miś, B.: Opowieści Księgi Szkockiej (Tales of the Scottish Book). op cit

Background Literature

1. Bylczynska, M.: Pamietnik Galicjanki (1914-17) Mnemosyne No 1 Ed. Maciej Dęboróg-Bylczyński. Oficyna Wydawnicza Zakładu Aktywności Zawodowej im. Jana Pawła II, Branice, Warsaw. ISBN 978-83-62319-04-6 (2012)
2. Kaluza, R.: Through a Reporter's Eyes: The life of Stefan Banach. Springer, Boston (1995)
3. Kuratowski, K.: Pól wieku matematyki polskiej, 1920–1970. Biblioteka wiedzy współczesnej, Omega, Warsaw (1973) (Also available in English as Kuratowski, K. A Half Century of Polish Mathematics – Remembrances and Reflections. Pergamon Press, Oxford. ISBN-10: 0080230466 ISBN-13: 978-0080230467 (1980))
4. Mekarski, S.: Lwów: Karta z Dziejów Polski. Naklada Kola Lwówian, London (1962)
5. Okulicz-Kozaryn, R.: The gesture of the great-hearted man: Roman Jaworski and his aesthetics of ugliness. Institute of Literary Research of the Polish Academy of Sciences, Warsaw, ISBN 83-89348-09-8 (2003)
6. Schleyen, K.: Lwówskie Gawedy. Gryf, London (1967)
7. Stefan Banach: Remarkable Life, Brilliant Mathematics. In: Jakimowicz, E., Mirancwicz, A. (ed.) American Mathematical Society, 3 edn. ISBN-10: 8373264515, 185 p. (2011)
8. Szałajko, K.: Research Notebooks AGH IM. S. Staszica. Opuscula Mathematica 1522(13), 45–54 (1993)
9. Szolginia,.W.: Zycie miasta, vol 5. Wysoki Zamek, Wrocław (1994)
10. Wasylewski, S.: Lwów. R, 173 p. Wegner Publishers, Poznan (1935)

Public History

Discovering Eastern Europe PCs by Hacking Them … Today

Stefano Bodrato, Fabrizio Caruso, and Giovanni A. Cignoni[✉]

Progetto HMR, Pisa, Italy
{stefano.bodrato, fabrizio.caruso,
giovanni.cignoni}@progettohmr.it

Abstract. A rich array of personal computers was developed in Eastern Europe during the later years of the Cold War. Because computer science would not be the same without personal computers, these devices deserve greater attention in the history of computing. The story in the West, the so-called PC revolution, started in the late 1970s: it was rooted in hobbyist and do-it-yourself clubs and brought the discipline closer to many people. A revolution took place also on the other side of the Iron Curtain: it happened a few years later, yet in a comparable way. Faced with an embargo that limited the availability of the first western PCs, Eastern Europe companies and hobbyists innovated on their own, providing the users with a number of home and personal computers. Today, the scenario of personal computing has completely changed; however, the computers of the 1980s are still objects of fascination for a number of retrocomputing fans who still enjoy using, programming and hacking the old *8-bits*. Yesterday's hobbyists have become today's retrocomputing enthusiasts: they provide an important window into these Eastern Europe PCs, which otherwise would have been forgotten.

In this article we give an overview on about fifty Eastern Europe PCs from the late 1970s to the 1980s. A few were clones of Western PCs, others shared some hardware and were compatible, others used significant portions of the firmware. Besides the preservation of old hardware and software, the retrocomputing community is engaged in the development of emulators and cross-compilers. Such tools can be useful for historical investigation based on reverse engineering. For example, we used one of them to investigate the originality of the BASIC interpreters loaded in the ROMs of Eastern Europe PCs.

Keywords: 8-bit computers · Emulators · Hacking ·
Retrocomputing communities · Software development tools

1 Introduction

The diffusion of home and personal computers has brought information technology and computer science closer to many people. Actually, it has changed the computer industry by orienting it toward the consumer market. Today, personal computing is perceived as a set of devices – from smartphones to videogame consoles – made just to be used. The average customer of personal IT is hardly interested in programming.

© IFIP International Federation for Information Processing 2019
Published by Springer Nature Switzerland AG 2019
C. Leslie and M. Schmitt (Eds.): HC 2018, IFIP AICT 549, pp. 279–294, 2019.
https://doi.org/10.1007/978-3-030-29160-0_14

At the beginning, it was different. Programming, even hacking, was a common activity among the owners of the first PCs. It was so in the West, but also in the East. In the West, hobbyists and clubs like the well-known "Homebrew Computer Club" were determinant in the beginning and in the initial rise of the PC industry [1]. During the following years, hacking groups [2] emerged and often competed against each other to prove who was the most skilled programmer. In Eastern Europe, the computer hobbyist movement developed later, only a few years indeed, yet a significant delay. Western computers were impossible to obtain and the availability of the few Eastern-made models was very limited. Even though, this kind of hacking attitude existed [3].

Nowadays, the meaning of the hacking attitude has shifted and hackers have been institutionalized. Meanwhile, the term itself mutated its original, positive, meaning into an evil one. However, one place where hackers remain active is inside the communities of retrocomputing enthusiasts – in fact, some of them actually never stopped: they were hackers back in the 1980s.

Besides preserving old pieces of hardware and software for the purpose of using them as in the past, these present-day hackers also enjoy programming their machines. Moreover, to ease their coding activities they develop new tools like emulators and cross-compilers able to run on modern PCs to generate binaries for vintage computers. Writing a program using the screen editor of the *Commodore 64* is fun, it is even an immersive way to revive the spirit of the era. Nevertheless, working on a modern PC using a full-featured editor and a cross-compiler, and then testing the result on an emulator running in a side window, is far more productive.

In this paper, we highlight the continuity between yesterday's hobbyists and today's retrocomputing enthusiasts. Focusing on a particular subset of 8-bit machines – the Eastern Europe PCs – we show how the retrocomputing community is playing an important role as unofficial, but valuable, repository of knowledge about old technologies. Moreover, the tools the community is developing and maintaining are useful to dig inside the old machines and discover relevant facts about their history, like measuring the similarities between different systems and giving better meanings to words like "compatible," "copy," "clone" – which in the particular context of Eastern Europe PCs have some relevance.

The paper is organized as follows: Sect. 2 provides a list of the computers that were produced in Eastern Europe in the late 1970s and early 1980s; we do not go into technical details, but rather we try to provide an organized and representative map of the fascinating Eastern Europe PCs galaxy. Sections 3 and 4 describe some modern development tools for 8-bit computers, focusing in particular on those that make it possible, today, to enjoy programming/hacking old East Europe 8-bit computers. Section 5 provides an example of using such tools to prove or disprove the originality of some of the computers produced in Eastern Europe.

2   A Diverse Galaxy

In the West, the beginning of the PC era was characterized by a plethora of attempts. Many of the first commercial PCs had very limited success and short lives: *Radio Electronics Mk8, Sphere 1, Sol-20, ISC Compucolor 8001*, just to cite some. Better luck had the *MOS Technology KIM-1*, from which originated the *Commodore PET* series, and the *Apple-1*, which started the well-known success story. While all of these PCs were based on a little set of microprocessors (*MOS Technology 6502*, *Zilog Z80*, *Intel 80xx*, *Motorola 6800*), no real standard was in place. Some of the early proposals were a bit more popular, like the *Altair 8800*: its *S-100 Bus* had limited success as a compatibility layer. The *CP/M* as an operating system had success only among 8-bit business computers. More successful models like the *Commodore PETs*, the *Apple][*, the *Tandy TRS-80* were "standard" only because of their good numbers on the market. In 1981 the introduction of the *IBM PC* eventually gave a de facto standard for the PC world while the home segment, for few years more, was still dominated by Commodore and Sinclair with a significative – at least as standard attempt – presence of the *MSX Consortium*.

The Eastern Europe scenario was not on par with the large variety of machines that in the late 1970s and early 1980s were available in the West. Nor was possible to replicate the selling results of the West. This was mainly caused by the CoCom [4] embargo, which made it hard to sell Western technologies to the Soviet Bloc. However, a remarkable diversity existed: the embargo did not stop Eastern Europe countries from designing their own computers as well as cloning Western computers by all sorts of reverse-engineering techniques [3].

In the following section we list those models for which it is possible to speak of "production". There were also handmade projects built in very few exemplars, but these are beyond our survey.

Many Eastern PCs were clones of Western popular machines (e.g., the ZX Spectrum, the Apple][, the TRS-80) as well as less common ones, some even built under license. The iconic Commodore 64 is remarkable for its absence. The probable reason was its use of custom chips (the VIC-II and the SID), which were hard/expensive to clone.

Some Western products were also marketed in Eastern Europe countries and a few computers that sold poorly in the West had some luck in the East (e.g., the *Commodore 16* and *116* in Hungary or the British *Sord M5* in Czechoslovakia), but these were Western computers and are therefore outside of our survey.

2.1   The Map

In the Appendix, we summarize a "map" of 8-bit personal computers that were produced in Eastern Europe. The map does not aim for a technical comparison and details are limited to the essential. It focuses on the models that can be considered PCs, excluding, for example, borderline products such as learning boards (e.g., *Poly-computer 880*, *PMI-80*) or computerized chessboards (e.g., *Schachcomputer-SC2*)

The table is grouped by categories. The choice of categories is obviously subjective, yet it helps to have a presentation order. We propose four categories: do-it-yourself projects, home computers (generally targeted to entertainment and education), personal computers (targeted to business), and clones. Inside each category, the order is chronological with respect to the date of first introduction.

As a last note, we have to remark that, despite the definitions, few home computers were actually used in Eastern Europe homes. For most of the 1980s, given the high costs and demand by industries and educational institutions, computers were not easy to buy for personal use.

2.2 Insights and Stories

A detailed narration of the events related to the development of personal computers in Eastern Europe is beyond the objectives of this paper. In the following, we collect just some of the most relevant facts.

The Microprocessors. The PCs produced in Eastern Europe countries were usually based on CPUs that were equivalent to the most common Western CPUs. Eastern chips were made either from copies of the original die masks or by reverse engineering the chips. One notable case was the *K1801* series, which was able to run binary code compiled for the DEC PDP-11, but did not have a correspondent Western chip and had to be mounted on specific circuit boards. The following summarizes the facts about the CPU families present in our map.

- *K580*, Soviet Union, since 1979 → Intel 8080
- *K1801*, Soviet Union, since 1980 → DEC PDP-11 binary compatible
- *U880*, German Democratic Republic, since 1980 → Zilog Z80
- *MHB8080*, Czechoslovakia, since early 1980s → Intel 8080
- *MMN80*, Romania, since late 1980s → Zilog Z80
- *CM688*, Bulgaria, since early 1980s → Intel 8086
- *KP1810*, Soviet Union, since 1982 → Intel 8086

In few cases Eastern PCs were mounting chips made outside the Iron Curtain, like the *CDP182* that was made by RCA or the *UM6502* that was a 6502-equivalent made by UMC in Taiwan. Other PCs based on "original" CPUs probably used second-source chips, maybe coming from the South East Asia were Western brands were starting to outsource their production.

Technologies and components were sometimes shared among different countries of the Eastern Bloc under Comecon agreements. Comecon (Council for Mutual Economic Assistance) was an economic organization under the leadership of the Soviet Union.

Soviet Union. During the Khrushchev era, until the mid-sixties, computer production had been identified as strategic and sustained through government policies. However, in the 1970s the competition among different government departments led to the lack of standards and to a wider gap with the West. At this point, the Soviet government decided to abandon the development of original computer designs and instead tolerate the pirating of Western systems.

The computer hobby movement emerged in the Soviet Union during the early 1980s. In 1978–79, G. Zelenko, V. Panov and S. Popov at the Moscow Institute of Electronic Engineering built a computer prototype based on the new *KR580IK80* microprocessor and named it *Micro-80*. Eventually, the schematics were published in *Radio* magazine becoming the first Soviet do-it-yourself computer. The project was successful and later led to the development of another DIY successful computer: the *Radio-86RK* [5].

The *Agat* started as an educational project commissioned by the USSR Ministry of Radio. It was inspired and compatible with the Apple][, but it was not exactly a clone. The first version in 1983 suffered from reliability problems and was discontinued. The *Agat-7* and *Agat-9* models were mass produced and were often used in schools.

Piracy was common and copies of Western applications were widespread. In July 1984, the CoCom embargo was partially lifted on common desktop and microcomputers. This made it possible for the Soviet Union to purchase thousands of Western computers in 1985.

During Perestroika, a program to expand computer literacy in Soviet schools was started in 1985 [7]. A common computer in schools was the *Elektronika BK-0010* which, while being a home/educational computer, was inspired by the PDP-11 architecture. In 1987, as part of an educational program, it was followed by the *Elektronika MS-0511*, which was still PDP-11 compatible and featured enhanced graphics. In 1987, the *Vector-06C* was also released; still aimed at education, it had similar capabilities to the *MS-0511*, but was based on an 8080/Z80 architecture. Clones of the Sinclair Spectrum computers were common and many hobbyists built their own versions. It is impossible to track all versions because many assembled and modified them in different ways. The *Pentagon* [8] and *ZS Scorpion* [9] models were common. Both were clones of the Spectrum 128 k. The Pentagon, designed by Vladimir Drozdov in 1989 and manufactured by amateurs all over the Soviet Union, was the most common model. In 1994 the ZS Scorpion was released and manufactured by Zonov and Co. While less common, the ZS Scorpion was a more accurate clone.

In 1987, the Law on Cooperatives allowed independent worker-owned cooperatives to operate in the Soviet Union. As a consequence, there was a proliferation of small companies selling hardware and software. Moreover, during the late Perestroika years, Western technology embargoes were relaxed further, leading to decline of local production in favor of the adoption of Western systems such as IBM-compatible PCs.

German Democratic Republic. Commercial East German home computers were manufactured by VEB Mikroelektronik and by VEB Robotron. In particular, the KC "Klein-computer" [10, 11] home computers were built by VEB Mikroelektronik and later by VEB Robotron. This resulted in a conflict between the two companies [12]. The KC home computers were based on the U880 CPU. They were mostly used in schools. For personal reports on Robotron from its former employees see [10] and [13]

From a technical point of view, the Robotron home computers can be divided into four series, not compatible among them. The *KC 85/1* (originally *Z9001*) and *KC 87* models were produced from 1984 until 1989 by VEB Robotron-Meßelektronik "Otto Schön" in Dresden. The *KC 85/2* (originally *HC900*), *KC 85/3*, *KC 85/4*, were produced from 1984 until 1989 by VEB Mikroelektronik "Wilhelm Pieck" in Mühlhausen. The *Z 1013*, presented in 1984, was produced from 1985 and sold as a kit by VEB Robotron in Riesa. The *A5105*, also known as *BIC* (for "Bildungscomputer," i.e., educational computer), was produced from 1989 until 1990 by Robotron in Dresden.

In 1984 VEB Büromaschinenwerk Sömmerda developed the PC1715 and PC1715 W computers and presented them to the public. Serial numbers span the years 1985-1989. They used the UA880 processor RAM and were meant primarily as office PCs [14].

Robotron produced also educational boards with a limited built-in display, for instance, the *Polycomputer 880*, introduced in 1983. At the very end of the GDR, Robotron produced and sold in small quantities the *KC Compact*, an *Amstrad CPC* clone close to the Amstrad *CPC 6128* and *664* models.

Romania. In Romania, both Western clones and original computers were created in the 1980s [15]. In many cases they were designed by Adrian Petrescu from the Politehnica University of Bucharest. The most notable original computer was the *aMic*, designed by Petrescu, in 1982 and later produced at Fabrica de Memorii in Timişoara until 1984. It was used in research, education and in the industry.

From 1985 to 1994, Romania produced mostly the *HC* family of computers (*HC 85, HC 85 +, HC 88, HC 90, HC 91* and *HC 2000*). They were all clones of the Sinclair ZX Spectrum, originally designed by Adrian Petrescu and later redesigned for mass production by ICE Felix, a brand which was already selling the *Felix PC* (1985–1990), an IBM-compatible, as well as other lines of micro and mini computers, including a line inspired by the *IBM/360*.

Poland. During the 1980s, Poland produced primarily clones of Western computers [15] *Meritum I* and *II* were released in 1983 and 1985, respectively, by Mera-Elzab, a brand originally specialized in cash registers. They were clones of the *Tandy TRS-80*. The *800 Junior* (1986) and the *804 Junior PC* (1990) were ZX Spectrum clones primarily intended for education and they were produced by the Elwro plant for schools.

Bulgaria. Most of the home computers produced in Bulgaria were manufactured in the city of Pravetz and so a number of different models were named Pravetz. For the most part they were clones of the Apple][; the first one was named IMKO-1 and was released as early as 1979. The 8D was instead a clone of the British Tangerine Oric. ZOT had already produced computers of the ES EVM series (Soviet clones of the IBM/360) under a Comecon agreement. In the 1980s IZOT produced the IZOT 1030, based on East German-made U880, and later several IBM PC and PC/XT clones.

Yugoslavia. Yugoslavia was not a member of the Warsaw Pact and therefore was less affected by the CoCom blockade on technology imports. A notable home computer was the Yugoslav *Galaksija* [16], built in 1983 by Vojislav Antonic, whose schematics were published as a DIY project in a special issue of the *SAM* popular science magazine. It is estimated that at least 8,000 people bought the kit to build this computer, but others may have bought the required chips separately. It was also adopted by many schools.

Less successful computers that were built in Yugoslavia were the *Lola 8*, *Pecom 32* and *64*, *Galeb*, *Orao*, *Ivel Ultra* and *Ivel Z3*.

Czechoslovakia. The main producer of computers in Czechoslovakia was Tesla (for "Technika Slaboprouda," or low-voltage technology). As a major electronics factory, Tesla was involved in building computers since the late 1960s. For a detailed and personal account on the Czechoslovakian home computers, refer to [17].

In the 1970s, Eduard and Tomáš Smutný designed the industrial computer *JPR-12*, based on the Israeli *Elbit* version of the PDP-11 and pushed it into production by Tesla.

Some years later they made the *JPR-1*, a simple 8-bit computer based on the Intel 8080. The complete schematics of these computers were later (1983) published in the hobby magazine *Amatérské Rádio*. A Z80-based and CP/M-compatible version was also released. In 1985, the U880-based *Ondra* was introduced.

Other Tesla computers were designed by Roman Kišš. The *PMI-80* single board computer was used in schools. The *PMD-85* series was very popular in Slovakia due its graphics capabilities. The PMD had some clones (*MAŤO, Zbro-jováček, Didaktik Alfa/Beta*) that were built mainly for schools. In the Czech region the *IQ-151*, built by ZPA, was common in schools. Didaktik Skalica also built the *Didaktik Game* (1987), *Didaktik M* (1991) and *Didaktik Kompakt* (1992), which were ZX Spectrum-clones.

Some Western computers were available through the state-run Tuzex shops. In addition to the most common and known computer models (ZX Spectrum, *Atari 800 XL, Sharp MZ800*), the *Sord M5* developed quite a rich hobbyist scene.

Hungary. Hungary produced both Western clones as well as original home computers. In the early 1980s, the Budapesti Radiotechnikai Gyar (Radiotechnical Factory of Budapest) produced the *BRG ABC-80*; it was a re-branded Swedish *Luxor ABC-80* built under an official license and meant for schools. From 1983, Híradástechnika Szövetkezet built the *HT-1080Z* and the *HT-2080Z* computers, which were rebranded versions of the Honk Kong–made EACA *VideoGenie I* computers, which, for their part, were an evolution of the TRS-80 Model I. In 1986 Videoton built the *TV Computer*, which was derived from the British *Enterprise* computer and was used in schools.

From 1984, Microkey manufactured the *Primo A* and *B* [18] as an original project which, unfortunately, suffered from poor assembly and a inferior keyboard. The *HomeLab-2* was an original Hungarian design by József & Endre Lukács. It was also marketed under the name *Aircomp-16*. The successor *HomeLab-3* was sold in kit form.

3 Emulation to Keep Old Hardware Alive

All the different systems presented above are rare nowadays and inaccessible. Some completely died-out. To keep them alive, emulation is one solution. By emulators here we mean any program that can reproduce the behavior of a given system at a specified interface level. We are interested in the machine-language level (excluding, for instance, simple BASIC-level compatibility). In practice, the effects of the instructions are reproduced exactly. In other words, it should not be possible to write a program able to detect that it is running on a machine different from the original. Emulators can be based on different approaches to hardware modelling and simulation; they may for instance replicate the hardware at very low level (e.g., discrete logic). For the historian however, the most relevant fact is the ability to run legacy 8-bit binaries and (re) discover how software ran decades ago.

As far as Eastern Europe computers are concerned, for most cases, the best choice is the well-known "universal" *MAME* emulator [19]. Although originally targeted to be a multiple arcade machine emulator, it has, over time, become a generic emulation platform well suited for many PC architectures. The code used to emulate some common hardware components is shared by different systems. This results in a huge base library that is constantly updated to support new systems – a valuable starting point in the emulation of less-known systems like the Eastern Europe computers.

Moreover, MAME is not meant for retro-gamers: the project's goal is accurate emulation of systems with no extra frills such as net-play, ROM hacks, improved graphics, and so on. They are actually forbidden as part of the rules governing the community of MAME developers.

MAME provides emulation for the East German Robotron KC series, the Yugoslav Galaksija, the Bulgarian Pravetz 8D, the Hungarian Primo series and many more. For the Galaksija, there is no usable alternative because the other existing emulators (e.g., *GalaxyWin* [20]) are no longer maintained.

For a few specific Eastern Europe systems there are dedicated emulators that, currently, may be more accurate than MAME. For the Robotron KC series and nearly all other East German home computers from the 1980s, a good alternative is *JKCEMU* [21], which is a specialized multi-system emulator for East German computers. For the Pravetz 8D there is *Oricutron* [22], which is an emulator for the full Oric series, clones included. Concerning the Sinclair Spectrum clones, many good Spectrum emulators support them. A notable example is the *Fuse* emulator [23], which supports both the Soviet Pentagon and ZS Scorpion clones.

4 Other Tools for Hacking and Discovering

The scenario of personal and home computers made in Eastern Europe was quite rich. A likewise rich community of retrocomputing enthusiasts is playing an important role as an unofficial, but valuable, repository of knowledge about the memory and the technologies of such machines. Moreover, the community is developing and maintaining tools to continue programming the old Eastern Europe PCs. As a testimony to the continuity between yesterday's hobbyists and today's retrocomputing enthusiasts, we propose a brief survey of the development tools for Eastern Europe computers that are currently available and actively maintained.

The most widespread and, among the retrocomputing developers, most appreciated development tools are the ANSI C cross-compilers and cross-assemblers. The prefix "cross" means that the compiler/assembler does not run on the system for which it is generating the binary code. Compilers and assemblers have old 8-bit systems as targets but run on modern computers.

Today's cross-assemblers can be used within modern integrated development environments for those who still want to code in the Assembly language for maximum efficiency; or just on principle: out of nostalgia or to exhibit skill. Assembly is, in practice, a human-readable form of machine language. Therefore, it is portable, at best, only across computers with the same architecture.

On the other hand, C is a universal language; yet it is very efficient. C was used extensively by old PC programmers that had to make the best possible use of every byte of memory and of every processor clock cycle. Thanks to modern compiler optimization algorithms and to the power of today PCs, cross-compilation produces by far better code than compiling through original compilers running on the old 8-bit systems: carefully written C code can today be almost as fast as manually written Assembly code.

Among larger projects, the currently most active are *CC65* [24], for the systems based on the MOS 6502 microprocessor, and *Z88DK* [25], for those based on the Zilog Z80. A project that supports many modern 8-bit CPUs, as well as a few legacy CPUs, is the retargetable cross-compiler *SDCC* [26]. Some projects have a very long history; both *Small-C* [27] and *ACK* [28], for instance, were born as native 8-bit compilers and assemblers in the early 1980s.

4.1 The Z88DK Development Kit

The Z88DK kit was, in the beginning, an evolution of the Small-C compiler (*SCCZ80*) in its variant for the Z80 CPU. The project started in 1998 to support the *Cambridge Z88*. The portable computer was released ten years before (by one of the many companies founded by Clive Sinclair) yet had a community of enthusiastic users. The first releases of Z88DK were very appreciated as well as the first experimental port to the ZX Spectrum. Many supported the development with feedbacks and contributions.

Over time, the software architecture of the project has evolved toward greater flexibility. Currently Z88DK supports development in both C and Assembly for about 80 PC architectures based on the Z80 and its close relatives. Recently, the inclusion of SDCC as a second compiler required relevant changes on the assembler, a global revision of the libraries and the adaption of many other elements like the compiler front-end and the optimizer. Beyond the technical details, the integration of SDCC is a demonstration of the maturity of the project and of the ability to collaborate with other groups of developers.

Despite being a Small-C descendant, Z88DK compilers (SCCZ80 and SDCC) are mostly ANSI compliant and include features that were not present in the original Small-C such as function pointers and floating-point arithmetic. Z88DK provides cross-target libraries: i.e., routines that can be used with the very same interface to build binaries for different systems. A developer may compile its code for different systems without any modification. Compared to other similar projects such as CC65, Z88DK is by far the largest in terms of supported targets, development activity and library support.

4.2 The CC65 Development Kit

CC65 is a complete cross development package for 6502-based systems. It includes a macro assembler, a C compiler and several other tools. It is based on a C compiler that, in the early 1990s was adapted for the Atari 8-bit computers by John R. Dunning. The original C compiler in CC65 is a Small-C descendant, but without most of Small C shortcomings: CC65's compiler is mostly ANSI compliant; it still lacks an implementation of floating-point arithmetic, but it supports function pointers.

CC65, as Z88DK, provides cross-target libraries that can be used by different systems. However, CC65 is a smaller project than Z88DK in terms of number of supported targets, development activity and library support.

4.3   Other Actively Maintained 8-Bit Cross-Compilers

Small Device C Compiler (SDCC) is a retargetable cross-compiler which supports a multitude of legacy and modern 8-bit architectures, including the Z80. Unlike CC65 and Z88DK, SDCC provides very basic and generic C libraries that can be used on all its targets. This means that SDCC routines cannot invoke ROM routines. A modified and optimized version of SDCC is part of the Z88DK development kit.

CMOC [29] is, currently, the only actively maintained compiler for systems based on the Motorola 6809 CPU. It is developed by Pierre Sarrazin and features a very limited library for input and output.

Amsterdam Compiler Kit (ACK) is a retargetable cross-compiler suite and tool-chain written by Ceriel Jacobs and Andrew Tanenbaum, author of *Minix* [30], which originally used ACK as its native tool-chain. It currently supports various 8-, 16- and 32-bit architectures including the Intel 8080.

4.4   Developing for All the 8-Bit Systems Through Abstractions

All the cross-compilers mentioned above provide a common library and allow writing "universal" code across one architecture, i.e., the same code can be compiled for different systems within the same CPU family.

CrossLib [31] extends this concept: it is a universal 8-bit library that, heavily exploiting the C preprocessor, provides a hardware abstraction layer across all 8-bit systems: computers, consoles, handhelds, pocket calculators, etc. Code using only CrossLib for input/output can be compiled by different development kits like Z88DK, CC65, CMOC, etc. to produce binaries for nearly any 8-bit system.

The action game *Cross Chase* is an example to demonstrate CrossLib. It is written in ANSI C with CrossLib. Basically, it can be compiled, without any code modification, for nearly all 8-bit architectures of the 1980s, including many Eastern Europe computers such as the Robotron series and the Galaksija.

CrossLib and CrossChase prove the maturity of the above compilers in terms of both ANSI compliance and efficiency. They also demonstrate the technical level reached by the communities behind the development tools that enable us to keep old systems alive.

5   Proving the Originality of Some Eastern Europe PCs

The tools described above testify to the creativity and the longevity of the hobbyist movements born around the first PCs. They are still active as international retrocomputing communities. Moreover, thanks to the deep knowledge of the systems gained in the development of such tools and to the hacking techniques they support, it is possible to discover new insights to the history of the original systems. For instance, the origins of the BASIC interpreters loaded in the PC ROMs or shipped as external cartridges, cassettes and disks can be shown. Tracing such relationships may hint to a different level of technological connections within the Eastern Bloc and the West.

5.1 BASCK, the BASIC Check Tool

Among the Z88DK tools, *BASCK* is a utility to support library development. The main use of BASCK is to detect the entry points for BASIC and other firmware routines in computer ROMs. If entry points of common routines are known, then they can be made available through a C library allowing the user's code to call them. Maybe ROM routines are not the best on the performance side, yet relying on them may save memory e and coding effort. The main reason for writing the BASCK tool was that documentation on ROM routines was scant and information could be only partially retrieved by disassembling the ROM. As of 2018, the BASCK tool is capable of detecting common ROM or disk routines for multiple Sinclair, Microsoft and HuBasic variants for both the Z80 and 6502 architectures. BASCK is also capable of finding equivalent routines that share the same core logic.

5.2 How BASCK Identifies Routines

BASCK uses sets of *Sinclair*, *Microsoft* and *HuBasic* patterns. The patterns are "hard-coded" in the BASCK sources. From this point of view, BASCK is less flexible than other approaches and tools [32] that search for generic partial matches; however, it drastically reduces the chance of false positives.

BASCK scans ROM files and searches for multiple patterns of the portions of the code that call the ROM routines. If it finds one of these patterns, it extracts the address from parameters of calling instructions such as CALL, JP, JR.

BASCK is not meant to tell whether two systems are similar, yet it can be used to detect with high accuracy portions of code that are derived from multiple variants of either Sinclair, Microsoft or HuBasic firmware.

Other methods may be used to test the originality of Eastern Europe PCs. For instance, a common test is to check at start-up whether the command "?A" produces "0" as result, i.e., whether "?" is an alias of "PRINT" and variables (e.g., "A") are initialized to "0." Because these are both peculiar features of Microsoft BASIC, a positive test is considered a clue of a Microsoft BASIC clone. However, on a strict logic, it is only an indication of a Microsoft compatible BASIC, and in fact, late HuBasic ROMs behave like Microsoft BASIC in this respect. The findings obtained by BASCK are more accurate because they depend on the actual implementation of the binary code instead of its external behavior.

5.3 BASCK Discoveries

We used BASCK to detect whether one specific BASIC interpreter from Eastern Europe was derived from either Microsoft BASIC, Sinclair BASIC or HuBasic. Using BASCK on multiple Eastern Europe systems, we found, as expected, that most systems either cloned the Microsoft BASIC or the Sinclair BASIC.

However, there are two very notable exceptions: the East German Robotron Z 1013 and the Hungarian HomeLab-2 (Aircomp 16). These systems seem to use original BASIC implementations. Moreover, we can confirm that the Yugoslav Galaksija uses original code even though its BASIC implementation started as a heavily modified version of Microsoft Level 1 BASIC. The only code from Microsoft Level 1 BASIC left on the Galaksija ROMs are the parser and some floating point routines.

On the other hand, BASCK gives a different result for the Hungarian Primo: we suspect that it uses a derivative of the Microsoft BASIC and not an independent BASIC developed by SZTAKI (Szamitastechnikai Kutato Intezet, Computer Technology Research Institute) as generally claimed (see for instance [28]).

6 Conclusions

In this paper we have described the remarkable and maybe unexpected diversity of the galaxy of 8-bit Eastern Europe PCs. We have also shown how today's enthusiasts have built modern development tools for these computers.

These tools allow us to easily write code for these computers for educational, recreational and historical purposes. By using these new tools – by coding, experimenting, disassembling and hacking the old 8-bit computers – it is possible to preserve them for future generations of historians and to discover some of the secrets of these machines. These may hint to bigger technological relationships within the Eastern Bloc and to the West hard to obtain from the archives.

Furthermore, through hacking of old systems, knowledge is preserved about the work of people who were active in the 1980s and, sometimes, are still active in the retrocomputing "scenes" of today. Among the many, we want to thank Henrich Raduska for his historical account on the Czechoslovakian 8-bit computers.

Appendix: A List of 8-Bit Personal Computers Produced in Eastern Europe

Model	CPU	RAM (KiB)	Year	Notes
1. Do-It-Yourself Projects				
Micro-80	K580	64	1982	Soviet Union Published by the *Radio* electronics magazine
Galaksija	Z80	2–54	1983	Yugoslavia Published as a special issue by the SAM science magazine
HomeLab III	Z80	64	1983	Hungary Sold as a kit
Irisha	K580	4–16	1985	Soviet Union Intended as educational computer
Specialist	K580	32–48	1985	Soviet Union Published by the *Modelist-Constructor* magazine

(continued)

(*continued*)

Model	CPU	RAM (KiB)	Year	Notes
86RK	K580	16–32	1986	Soviet Union Successor of Micro-80. Also industrially produced as *Microsha, Krista, Electronica*
Orion 128	K580	128	1990	Soviet Union Published by the *Radio electronic* magazine Industrially produced in Livny
2. Home Computers				
JPR-1 (SAPI-1)	i8080A	1	1980	Czechoslovakia Produced by Tesla
Galeb, Orao	6502	9–64	1981	Yugoslavia Produced by PEL Varaždin
aMIC	Z80	16–48	1982	Romania Produced by Fabrica de Memorii
HomeLab II	Z80	64	1982	Hungary Produced by *Personal Agroelektronikai GT* as Aircomp 16
Electronica BK0010	K1801	32	1984	Soviet Union Developed under the Electronica brand by the NPO research centre. PDP-11 compatible
C 85/1 (Z 9001), KC87	U880		1984	German Democratic Republic Produced by VEB Robotron
KC 85/2 (HC900), /3, /4	U880	16–64	1984	German Democratic Republic Produced by VEB Mikroelektronik
Primo A-32, A-48, A-64, B-32, B-48, B-64	U880	16-48	1984	Hungary Produced by Microkey
Z1013	U880	1–64	1984	German Democratic Republic Produced by VEB Robotron
Ondra	U880	64	1985	Czechoslovakia Produced by Tesla
PMD 85, 85-2, 85-2A, 85-3	MHB8080	48	1985	Czechoslovakia Produced by Tesla
IQ 151	MHB8080	32–64	1985	Czechoslovakia Produced by ZPA Nový Bor
Lola 8	i8085	16	1985	Yugoslavia Produced by the IvoLola Ribar Institute in Belgrad

(*continued*)

(continued)

Model	CPU	RAM (KiB)	Year	Notes
Peccm 32, 64	CDP1802	32	1985	Yugoslavia Produced by EI Niš
Elektronika MS-0511	K1801 (2 ×)	64	1987	Soviet Union Part of the Electronics MS 0202 set of educational facilities PDP-11 compatible
A5105	U880	64–128	1988	German Democratic Republic Produced by VEB Robotron
3. Personal Computers				
Agat-4, -7, -8, -9	UM6502	64–256	1983	Soviet Union Largely inspired by Apple][. Later models were more successful and mass produced
IZOT 1030	i8086	256-1 Mb	1985	Bulgaria
Juku E5101	K580	64	1988	Soviet Union Educational for schools
4.1 Clones (miscellanea)				
ABC-80	Z80	16–32	1981	Hungary Clone of Luxor ABC-80. Built under license
Meritum I, II	U880	16–64	1983	Poland Clones of Tandy TRS-80
HT-1080Z, HT2080Z	Z80	16–48	1983	Hungary Clones of EACA VideoGenie. Built under license. Tandy TRS-80 compatible
Pravetz 8D	6502	16–48	1985	Bulgaria Clone of Tangerine Oric Atmos
TV-Computer	Z80	32–64	1986	Hungary Clone of Enterprise. Built under license
KC Compact	U880	64	1989	German Democratic Republic Clone of the Amstrad CPC
4.2 Apple][Clones				
Pravetz IMKO-1, Pravetz 82 (IMKO-2), 8 M, 8A, 8E, 8C	6502	48–1080	1979	Bulgaria
Ivel Ultra, Z3	6502	64	1984	Yugoslavia Produced by Ivaim Electronika

(continued)

(continued)

Model	CPU	RAM (KiB)	Year	Notes
4.3 ZX Spectrum Clones				
HC 85, HC 85+, HC 88, HC 90, HC 91, HC 2000	MMN80	64	1985	Romania Produced by ICE Felix
Elwro 800 Junior, 804 Junior PC	U880	64	1986	Poland Produced by Elwro for schools
Didaktik Gama, M, Kompakt	U880	48–64	1987	Czechoslovakia Produced by Didaktik Skalica
Pentagon	Z80	48–1024	1989	Soviet Union Design by Vladimir Drozdov. Manufactured by amateurs
ZS Scorpion	Z80	256–1024	1994	Soviet Union Manufactured by Zonov and Co
4.4 IBM PC Clones				
Pravetz 16, 16E, 16ES, 16T	i8086/88	256–512	1984	Bulgaria
Felix PC	i8086/88	256–640	1985	Romania Produced by ICE Felix
IZOT 1036C	CM688	128–640	1985	Bulgaria
ES PEVM	KP1810	128–512	1986	Soviet Union Designed by Research Institute of Electronic Computer Machines in Minsk
Iskra 1030	KP1810	640	1989	Soviet Union Designed by Elektronmash in Leningrad
Poisk	KP1810	128	1991	Soviet Union Designed by Elektronmash in Kiev (not exactly a PC clone)

References

1. Levy, S.: Hackers: Heroes of the Computer Revolution. Anchor Press/Doubleday, New York (1984)
2. Alberts, G., Oldenziel, R. (eds.): Hacking Europe – From Computer Cultures to Demoscenes. Springer-Verlag, London (2014). https://doi.org/10.1007/978-1-4471-5493-8
3. Stachniak, Z.: Red Clones: The Soviet Computer Hobby Movement of the 1980s. IEEE Ann. Hist. Comput. **37**(1), 12–23 (2015)
4. Lewis, R.C.: COCOM: an international attempt to control technology. Def. Inst. Secur. Assist. Manag. J. (Fall, 1990)

5. Gorshkov, D., Zelenko, G., Ozerov, Y., Popov, S.: Personal radio ham's computer Radio-85RK. Radio (4), 24 (1986)
6. Leslie, C., Gryczka, P.: Ingenuity in isolation: Poland in the international history of the internet. In: Kimppa, K., Whitehouse, D., Kuusela, T., Phahlamohlaka, J. (eds.) HCC 2014. IAICT, vol. 431, pp. 162–175. Springer, Heidelberg (2014). https://doi.org/10.1007/978-3-662-44208-1_14
7. Tatarchenko, K.: How programmable calculators and a Sci-Fi story brought soviet teens into the digital age. In: IEEE Spectrum (2018). https://spectrum.ieee.org/tech-history/silicon-revolution/how-programmable-calculators-and-a-scifi-story-brought-soviet-teens-into-the-digital-age. Accessed July 2019
8. Pentagon. http://speccy.info/Pentagon. Accessed July 2019
9. Scorpion. http://speccy.info/Scorpion. Accessed July 2019
10. Robotron. http://robotron.foerderverein-tsd.de. Accessed July 2019
11. KC-Club. http://www.kcclub.de. Accessed July 2019
12. Föltgen, S.: Resume: Hands-on Retrocomputing, Bochum Freiburg: Projektverlag 2016 (Computerarchäologie 1), pp. 184–187 (2016)
13. Merkel, G.: VEB Kombinat Robotron – Ein Kombinat des Ministeriums für Elektrotechnik und Elektronik der DDR, Arbeitsgruppe Industriegeschichte des Stadtarchivs Dresden, Dresden
14. Die Geschichte der Computertechnik der DDR. http://www.robotrontechnik.de. Accessed July 2019
15. The Home Computer Museum. http://www.homecomputer.de/pages/f_easteurope.html. Accessed July 2019
16. Galaksija. https://web.archive.org/web/20090504112705/, http://www.paralax.rs/pr83.htm. Accessed July 2019
17. Malý, M.: Home computers behind the iron curtain. http://hackaday.com/2014/12/15/. Accessed July 2019
18. Primo. http://primo.homeserver.hu/. Accessed July 2019
19. MAMEDev.org. http://www.mamedev.org. Accessed July 2019
20. GalaxyWin. http://emulator.galaksija.org. Accessed July 2019
21. JKCEMU Emulator. http://www.jens-mueller.org/jkcemu/. Accessed July 2019
22. Oricutron Emulator. https://github.com/pete-gordon/oricutron. Accessed July 2019
23. FUSE Emulator. http://fuse-emulator.sourceforge.net/. Accessed July 2019
24. CC65 A Freeware C Compiler for 6502 Based Systems (GitHub repository). http://github.com/cc65/cc65. Accessed July 2019
25. Z88DK: The Development Kit for over Fifty Z80 Machines (GitHub repository). https://github.com/z88dk/z88dk. Accessed July 2019
26. SDCC – Small Device C Compiler (Sourceforge repository). http://sdcc.sourceforge.net. Accessed July 2019
27. Cain, R.: A Small C compiler for the 8080s. Dr. Dobb's J. (45), May 1980
28. Tanenbaum, A.S., van Staveren, H., Keizer, E.G., Stevenson, J.W.: A practical tool kit for making portable compilers. Commun. ACM 26(9), 654–660 (1983)
29. CMOC. https://perso.b2b2c.ca/~sarrazip/dev/cmoc.html. Accessed July 2019
30. Tanenbaum, A.: https://www.minix3.org/. Accessed July 2019
31. Caruso, F.: Cross chase: a massively 8-bit multi-system game. Call A.P.P.L.E. 28(1) (2018)
32. Manber, U.: Finding similar files in a large file system. In: Proceedings of the USENIX Winter 1994 Technical Conference on USENIX Winter 1994 Technical Conference (1994)

Twentieth Anniversary of the Russian Virtual Museum of Computing and Information Technology History

Vladimir A. Kitov$^{(\boxtimes)}$ and Edward M. Proydakov

Plekhanov Russian University of Economics,
Stremyanny per., 36, Moscow, Russia
vladimir.kitov@mail.ru

Abstract. In 2018, the Russian Virtual Computer Museum (RVCM, www. computer-museum.ru), created on the Internet by Edward Proydakov, celebrated its twentieth anniversary. Over the past two decades of its existence, the RVCM (also VCM) has taken its rightful place in the historical section of the Russian and the world's Internet. The popularity of RVCM in the worldwide **Internet** space is ensured by its English-language version, functioning in parallel with its Russian-language version and providing accessibility for foreign guests. Every day, various sections of the RVCM are visited on an average by two thousand people. A large collection of books, documents and articles related to computer science subjects is stored in digitized form in RVCM. Currently, RVCM on the history of Soviet computers and computer science is the largest computer museum in the world. This article reveals the very existence of RVCM and its main features to the computer community. On the one hand, the advantages of RVCM compared to other computer museums on the Internet are shown. Analysis of its content is done in the article, and some shortcomings of the RVCM are identified and ways to improve its structure are outlined.

Keywords: Computer museum · History of information technologies · History of software development · History of management information systems · Russian Virtual Computer Museum (RVCM)

1 Introduction

In the second half of the twentieth century, electronic computers of the industrially advanced countries were mainly implemented for solving military-oriented mathematical problems, connected with the development of new weapons and command organization of various armed forces branches. Creation of computer-based information retrieval and data storage systems for making optimized managing decisions became the subject of special scientific research interest at numerous centers both in the USSR and in the USA with its NATO partners. Quite naturally, numerous theoretical and applied works aimed at the computer software and technical complex improvement were strictly classified. Most of that development was assigned the status of high secrecy [1–4].

© IFIP International Federation for Information Processing 2019
Published by Springer Nature Switzerland AG 2019
C. Leslie and M. Schmitt (Eds.): HC 2018, IFIP AICT 549, pp. 295–303, 2019.
https://doi.org/10.1007/978-3-030-29160-0_15

The history of the development of Soviet computers and their usage in solving problems of "atom and rocket shield" creation, which provided the Soviet Union military parity with the United States, is very rich. It is clear that the current publication of numerous, formerly classified materials and documents related to the development of Soviet military computers and computer systems could not take place in earlier years. As soon as the formerly classified, secret documents are openly published, they immediately become a research subject for historians of information and computer technologies. One should equally mention the damages caused to the archives of scientific centers and industrial computer enterprises in the 1990s during the changing of the national economy to capitalist development and, connected with that, transformations of the state-owned companies and enterprises. Those processes resulted in total destruction of many historical artifacts, which otherwise could have found proper places in RVCM.

That is why our researchers and historians often have to perform time- and power-consuming work (sometimes almost detective work) for restoring some of many successful computer projects of the USSR time.

The Virtual Computer Museum (www.computer.museum.ru – BKM in Russian) occupies unique place among dozens of Russian computer museums, both real and virtual.

2   First Steps of the RVCM

The first proposal for organizing the RVCM was made on 30 September 1997, when Edward Proydakov, the chief editor of Russian weekly *PCWeek-RE,* published his article "Let's Create a Museum" [5]. Proydakov described the necessity of collecting "traces of outgoing computer generations" and, therefore, of founding a special Russian Virtual Computer Museum (RVCM). The first efforts were made in 1998. However, as there were not many volunteers to immediately join the project, the main work had to be done by the author of the idea himself (nothing unusual). Therefore, establishing the RVCM Council (see Fig. 1) was the first important thing to do. Finally, a number of famous Soviet computer designers supported the idea and entered the council. Dr. V. V. Przhijalkovskiy, the first chairman of the Council, and his deputy, Dr. E. N. Filinov, initiated and headed the work on defining the structure of RVCM and preparing the first materials on computer families. Numerous biographies of outstanding scientists and designers have been written for special "Hall of Fame" section. As the volume of accumulated materials was growing, the number of RVCM structural sub-divisions was growing proportionally.

Fig. 1. RVCM logo.

For a couple of years during the museum's establishing period, sponsor support was provided by the Moscow branch of Microsoft Corporation (general manager Olga Dergunova). After Microsoft, the museum was sponsored one by one by Russian companies IBS, 1C, and RTSoft, but there were also long periods when Proydakov invested personal funds into the development of the museum. Financial assistance to the museum in conducting conferences and publishing works was rendered by the Russian Foundation for Basic Research (RFBR - state scientific foundation).

2.1 RVCM's Structure

The RVCM structure consists of three large blocks, which in their turn are sub-divided into appropriate smaller parts. The museum's materials in Russian language form the first block and its sub-divisions (www.computer-museum.ru). The second block consists of the English language sections (articles and other materials) (http://www.computer-museum.ru/english/index.php).

The third block, "Service Keys," is the line in the upper right corner of the screen. It is used both in the Russian and English RVCM parts.

Collection and systematization of historical materials on the Soviet (and Russian) computers, informatics and related subjects is the primary goal of museum's activity. Therefore, it is only natural that currently it contains much more documents and articles in the Russian language than in English.

2.2 RVCM Section in Russian

As the structure of Russian part of the museum is much different from the section containing English materials, we will describe it in more detail.

The main page of the RVCM's Russian part visually displays three parallel information columns. The left one shows references on important information blocks: "On Our Museum," "History of National Computer Engineering," "History of Electro-communications," "Hall of Fame," "History of the Soviet Electronic Components," "Documents and Publications," "Computer Press and Books," "English-Russian Dictionary." Each of these sections in its turn consists of numerous subdivisions. Each information block, in both columns (right and left), has its own link, "All Subjects," connecting user with each of the seventeen basic sub-divisions of the Russian part.

Visitors of the site can find information about the RVCM Council members, contact addresses, and information for museum's partners in the information block "About Our Museum."

The section "History of National Computer Engineering" presents the development of the Soviet computers. It consists of eight following large sub-divisions: "The Computers in Alphabetical Order" (with information about 330 Soviet computers), "The First Computers," "The Specialized Military-Purpose Computers," "The Control Computers," "The Universal Computers," "The Analog Computers," "History of Semiconductor Producing Industry," and "Systems and Complexes." The sub-division "The Computers in Alphabetical Order" contains the full list of computers. Each name of a computer in this list is linked to the description of corresponding computer. This sub-division contains big volume of information and is permanently extended. A big general overview of the history of Soviet home computers was added in 2017.

The sub-section "The First Computers" presents the first Soviet electron tube computers; such as the projects initiated and supervised by the computer pioneers, outstanding scientists I. S. Bruk (computers "M-1," "M-2," "M-3"), S. A. Lebedev (computers "MESM" and "BESM" family), B. I. Rameev and Y. Y. Bazilevskiy (the first Soviet serial computer "Strela"); also electron-tube computers "TsEM-1" and "TsEM-2," designed at the Kurchatov Institute of Atomic Energy.

The sub-division "Specialized Military-Purpose Computers" contains detailed descriptions of special computers used in the Soviet antiaircraft and anti-missile defense systems; naval computers used on battleships, on-board computers of air forces, computers for strategic missile forces, military space systems, etc. This sub-section is completed with a list of Soviet military computers.

The section "Control Computers" presents information on the computers and computation complexes for management of industrial enterprises and control of industrial technological processes, produced during the period of 1960–1980s. Control computers and computing complexes in automatic process control systems were directly connected to various industrial automation means (such as: sensors, regulators, operation units, etc.). This part stores information about the following control computers: UM-1, M-6000/M-7000, SM1, SM2, SM 1210 (designed at the Scientific Research Institute of Controlling Machinery in the town of Severodonetsk); computer MN-1 NH (designed at Leningrad enterprise "Design Bureau №2); computer "Dnepr" (designed at the Kiev Institute of Cybernetics); computers M7, M-400, SM3, SM4, SM 1420, SM 1800 (designed at the Moscow Institute of Electronic Control Machines – MIECM/ИНЭУМ); control computers designed at the Moscow Scientific Research Institute of Electro-mechanics.

The section "Universal Computers" deals with large information cluster on widely implemented computer families "BESM," large computer family "URAL," numerous computers of the "ES Computers" series (Soviet-East European analogue of IBM computers - IBM/360; IBM/370), Armenian computers "Aragats," "Razdan," "Nairi"; unique ternary computers "Setun'''; Ukrainian computers "Kiev," "Promin'," "MIR"; supercomputer family "Elbrus"; space/military computers "Vesna" and "Sneg"; big Byelorussian computer series "Minsk," and many others.

The subdivision "Analog Computers" (AC) provides essential and meaningful information on analog computers. Their industrial implementation did not need "impressive" resources but provided high performance at comparatively low costs. Characteristic features of those devices were simplicity of synchronization with various real devices and instruments, simple adjustments and readjustments for solving different problems and convenient interaction with users. Analog computers designed by computer pioneers S. A. Lebedev, I. S. Bruk, L. I. Gutenmakher and some others were famous, popular and widely implemented in the USSR.

The last RVCM subdivisions are the "History of Semiconductor Producing Industry Development" and the "Systems and Complexes." The latter contains, not yet fulfilling, information about the large-scale Soviet projects: "ЕГСВЦ/EGSVTs," "ОГАС/OGAS," "Выборы/Elections," "Самсон/Samson," and others. The narration begins with description of some of the USSR first automatic management systems at industrial enterprises "Lvov" and "Kuntsevo." This part is to be essentially extended with new documents and articles.

The RVCM section "Hall of Fame," alongside with the "History of the National Computing," is one of its most important and largest sections. The "Hall of Fame," in its turn, consists of two subsections, "Soviet/Russian Scientists and Engineers" and the "Foreign Scientists and Engineers," which contain biographic articles about 140 Soviet scientists, and also such world-famous persons as A. Turing, K. Zuse, V. Bush, S. McKinley, N. Wirth, R. Hamming, S. Jobs and others.

The RVCM has also three important sections: "History of the Soviet Electronic Components Basis," "Documents and Publications," "Books and Computer Press." There is also "Big English-Russian (on-line) Dictionary of Informational Technologies and Computing" composed by E. M. Proydakov and L. A. Teplitsky.

The middle column of the RVCM site contains complete collection of news on IT history, important dates and jubilees, information about projects and actions related to computer history, etc.

The right column on the RVCM's site contains sections: "Computations in Pre-computer Era," "History of Foreign Computing," "History of Software Development," "Technologies," "Calendar of Events," "History of Computer Games," "Computer Museums in the Internet," "Archive of News," and "Guest Book."

2.3   RVCM Sections in English

The main English site of RVCM consists of three columns: "Sections," "News," and "Persons and Articles."

The column on the right contains sections, "Hall of Fame," "Articles," and "RVCM News Archive." The section "Hall of Fame" presents sixty translated articles about the most famous Soviet computer scientists. The right column, "Articles," contains information about more than thirty types of Soviet computers and computing systems ("Radon," "Diana system," "Argon," and others) and information on the programming languages development and implementation history. There are also some articles on the first radio-communication technologies.

The RVCM's visitors can access subsections containing articles and descriptions, in English language, about the structures, systems of instructions, inner organization of RAM and ROM and about practical usage fields of widely popular computers "STRELA," "BESM," "Ural," "Minsk," "M-20," "Razdan," and some others.

The third subdivision in the right column of the English site is the "RVCM News archive," which stores all news statements published in RVCM since 2000 until the present day.

3   How RVCM Differs from Other Museums

Of course, there are a number of other, quite informative, virtual computer museums in the world. The basic advantages of the RVCM, which make it different from other museums, are the following:

- RVCM possesses one of the world's largest electronic storage of USSR computer history materials. It has the first Soviet articles, books, descriptions of IT projects, numerous veterans' memoirs, etc.
- A special section containing rich and detailed collection of materials about on-board and mobile computers (primarily military ones).
- RVCM regularly organizes international conferences and seminars on Soviet computers and software development history.
- The history of the Soviet communication systems and technologies is actively studied and displayed by the RVCM.
- Much attention is paid to analog computers and computing systems, as well as to the Soviet scientific and research institutes and industrial organizations that made that computer development a reality.

The RVCM exposition also displays the history of the national microelectronics and communication means. This is one of the museum's biggest parts and the famous expert on electrical communications P. P. Chachin heads the work on its processing. In reality, this sub-division is a sort of "museum within museum." It contains sections on: "Cable Communications," "Radio Communications," "TV and Broadcasting," "Special Communication Technologies," "Consumer Electronic Appliances," "Networks and Communication Lines," "Components and Technologies." There are also parts such as "Calendar of Events," "Companies and Enterprises," "Russian Industry of Communication Means," "Public Organizations and Associations," "Educational Institutions," "Museums of Communications," Internet links, etc. This part even has its own "Hall of Fame" with biographies of the outstanding scientists, designers and prominent administrators of this branch. The Museum's Council itself is a notable feature of the RVCM. It consists mainly of the scientists who are the Soviet computer pioneers and of some other experts. They regularly conduct workshops and other meetings; provide the RVCM with their personal (as well as other) scientific, engineering and historical materials, and also perform strict control of all museum content's value and authenticity.

4 Scientific Forums Organized by RVCM's Council

RVCM's Council, together with the Russian Polytechnic Museum, several leading universities, the Russian Foundation for Basic Research (RFBR), and number of some other scientific centers, regularly organizes the Russian national and also international conferences dedicated to the history of computers and software complexes, which were created and practically implemented in the USSR, Russian Federation and the former USSR republics.

They are SORUCOM-2006 in Petrozavodsk (RF, rep. Karelia), SORUCOM-2011 (Novgorod, RF), SORUCOM-2014 in Kazan (RF, Tatarstan) and SORUCOM-2017 (Zelenograd/Moscow area/). The conferences are sponsored by the state fund RFBR and some companies from the Russian IT-sector.

In 2011 the RVCM published a book *Proceedings of the Virtual Computer Museum. History of the National Control Computers (1955–1987).*

Running the historical documentation archive and its systematization (by authors, subjects and topics) is one of important fields of the RVCM's activity. Numerous books, scientific and other reports, theses and proceedings of various computer conferences, relevant directives of the Soviet government and many others, which could be characterized as belonging to "computers" and "information science" fields, should be digitalized. All of them are placed in appropriate storage in RVCM. That is why, each month the group of enthusiasts (volunteers) thoroughly makes scanning of new and often restores, very rare and unique, documents, articles, monographs and textbooks. RVCM support the activity concerning systematization of the first computer books both of Soviet [6] and foreign [7].

Currently, RVCM lays 10 to 15 archival publications a month on its site (for public access). The members of its Council are proud to admit that more than 3000 historical documents and articles (both archival and written specially for the RVCM) are already placed and stored in the museum's structure.

Its electronic library already contains more than 150 scientific and educational books on information technologies (published during 1950–1960s), which are hard to find in other sources.

5   Users of the RVCM

According to the statistics that are made upon the museum's visits counters' data, between one and two thousand individuals from different countries (mostly countries of the former USSR, Israel, Germany, USA, Canada, etc.) work daily with RVCM's materials, entering its sites via links provided by search engines (up to 80% of visitors). As the museum was filled with materials, the number of visitors increased steadily. Currently, the museum is visited daily by 1,500 to 2,500 unique guests. The amount of the visitors naturally depends on current season of year or educational period at schools and universities. Thus, it drastically increases at the time of semester projects preparation by university students, as the RVCM is recommended by the Russian educational organizations as an auxiliary information resource for informatics studies.

Therefore, students are forming one of the RVCM's basic user groups. Nevertheless, it is equally interesting for IT and computing experts. The veterans of computing, scientists, programmers, computer designers and other people whose professional activity was – or is – connected with computer development demonstrate particular interest to the museum's publications.

6   Perspectives, Limitations, and Difficulties of RVCM

RVCM contains a huge volume of information and is permanently extended. For example, the big general overview of the history of Soviet home computers was added in 2017. The creation on the basis of computers of information retrieval systems and the storage of a multitude of data for making optimal management decisions have been the subject of research by scientists both in the USSR and in Western countries. The development and use of automated management information systems (MIS) in the

Soviet Union is clearly not sufficiently studied and not systematized both in the historical works of Russian and foreign authors. Therefore, one of the most important directions of RVCM development is the creation of a separate section "Management Information Systems." This is very important not only for the history of Soviet computers, but also for the history of all Soviet science, because in the 1960s and 1970s in the Soviet Union, according to various estimates, about eight hundred thousand specialists in various fields worked on the creation and use of management information systems for various purposes and levels of use: economists, analysts, project managers, algorithms, programmers, employee data entry services, electronics engineers, computer operators, etc. In the USSR, at that time, a whole independent industry was created and operated – the MIS industry. The study of this industry is relevant in our time because many ideas, projects and scientific publications of those years are the primary sources for the creation of modern digital information technologies. The analysis of RVCM documents on the theory of Soviet MIS, as well as practical issues of their use, is an independent scientific research. First of all, in the new section of the RVCM it is necessary to collect and systematize projects and documents on the Soviet MIS, as well as to establish the chronology of their appearance in the USSR. The history of the Soviet MIS is little studied and is a historical "white spot." To highlight the large-scale and so far little-studied layer of the history of Soviet science – the history of the Soviet MIS industry – is the primary task of RVCM. Also, the specific step of improving RVCM is the creation in its structure of a separate section "History of Cybernetics."

Unfortunately, until now the RVCM site did not have its own servers and had to rent hosting services from a hosting provider. Therefore, the limited disc/storage space available for the RVCM is the biggest technical bottleneck in its work. Of course, the 10 Gbyte is insufficient volume for an on-line collection like this: it drastically cuts possibilities of multimedia usage, as well as of storage of video and audio-materials.

Due to the current secrecy still, RVCM has no access to the documents on military and on-board computers and software for them. The range of the museum's activity is also limited with shortage of financial resources. For that reason, some materials and work, which should be paid for, remain inaccessible; RVCM relies mainly upon the free assistance of some scientists and volunteers.

7 Conclusions

The RVCM Council in its monthly meetings constantly try to improve the structure of the museum to make it as interesting and convenient for visitors as possible. It should be noted that all their work is carried out only on a voluntary basis. Work on this article highlighted a number of necessary upgrades of RVCM. One of the most important of these is the substantial update of the "Calendar of Events." It is necessary to include in it a number of historical documents on defense and military informatics, which recently appeared in open publications. It is necessary to create a section "History of Management Information Systems (MIS)." It is necessary to create a section "History of Cybernetics." This is not a difficult task because most documents and other historical papers about world and Soviet cybernetics have already been published. They need only to be systematized. It is advisable to introduce an additional section on scientific organizations and enterprises at which system and application software was produced. The USSR and Russia, undoubtedly, can be proud of the huge number of original world-class applied computer programs. In this regard, the section "Application Software" existing in the RVSM requires significant expansion. The RVCM Council would be grateful to everyone who is interested in scientific and cultural cooperation with it.

References

1. Proydakov, E.M.: Stranitsy istorii otechestvennykh IT (Страницы истории отечественных ИТ). vol. 1–4, 1st edn. Alpina Publisher, Moscow (2014–2017)
2. Kitov, V.A.: Prezident akademii nauk SSSR M. V. Keldysh. 100 let so dnya rozhdeniya (Президент академии наук СССР М.В.Келдыш. 100 лет со дня рождения). The electronic book on the website of the Presidium of the RAS in the section "Электронные коллекции – Президенты Академии наук", Moscow (2012). http://www.ras.ru/keldysh/about.aspx. Accessed 02 Apr 2019
3. Revich, Y.V., et al.: Istoriya informatsionnykh tekhnologiy v SSSR. Znamenityye proyekty: komp'yutery, svyaz', mikroelekronika (История информационных технологий в СССР. Знаменитые проекты: компьютеры, связь, микроэлекроника), 1st edn. Knima, Moscow (2016)
4. Kitov, V.A.: Vydayushchayasya rol' pervoy sovetskoy seriynoy EVM « Strela » v dele ukrepleniya oboronosposobnosti strany (Выдающаяся роль первой советской серийной ЭВМ « Стрела » в деле укрепления обороноспособности страны). Annual Scientific Conference 2013, S. I. Vavilov Institute of the History of Natural Science and Technology, vol. 2, pp. 351–353. LENAND, Moscow (2013)
5. Proydakov, E.M.: Davayte sozdadim muzey (Давайте создадим музей). In: "PC Week", Moscow 38 (1997). www.pcweek.ru/themes/detail.php?ID=43652. Accessed 21 Mar 2019
6. Kitov, V.A., Prokhorov, S.P.: Pervyye sovetskiye publikatsii po kibernetike, programmirovaniyu, komp'yuteram i ikh primeneniyam (Первые советские публикации по кибернетике, программированию, компьютерам и их применениям). Annual Scientific Conference, S. I. Vavilov Institute of the History of Natural Science and Technology, vol. 2, pp. 778–781. RT Soft, Moscow (2012)
7. Bau, O., Kitov V.A., Shilov V.V.: Pervyye sovetskiye knigi po EVM v Kitaye (Первые советские книги по ЭВМ в Китае). Annual Scientific Conference 2013, S. I Vavilov Institute of the History of Natural Science and Technology, vol. 2, pp. 349–351. LENAND, Moscow (2013)

ICT History Study as Corporate Philanthropy in Latvia

Inara Opmane[✉] and Rihards Balodis

Institute of Mathematics and Computer Science, University of Latvia,
Raina Bulv29, Riga 1459, Latvia
imcs@lumii.lv

Abstract. There are two ICT museums in Latvia: the Riga Technical University Telecommunications Museum and the Computing Museum of the Institute of Mathematics and Computer Science of the University of Latvia. Historical studies can be carried out at museums, institutes and universities, and professional communities. The type of history study funding can also vary. The article describes the possibilities for financing of computer museums. A comparison of museum metrics in the United Kingdom, Germany, the Netherlands and Latvia, Lithuania, and Estonia is subject to discussion. This comparison outlines the possible future museum reforms in the Baltic States. The authors review the public and private funding of museum operations. Philanthropy plays an increasing role in museum operation. Currently in Latvia, museums indirectly receive public government funding from the State Joint Stock Companies or municipalities. Private museums, corporate sponsorship and wide corporate philanthropy are the upcoming wave. ICT history studies are carried out by retired academics and authoritative engineers as volunteers. Such volunteering is the main part of developed philanthropy in Latvia. Universities play an important role in ICT history research that can be considered as one particular corporate philanthropy.

Keywords: ICT history · Philanthropy · Sponsorship · Technology museum

1 Scope of the Study

A historical study can be broadly defined: education, the application of the mind to knowledge acquisition, research, examination and analysis of historical facts, reflection of technology in society. Researchers are introducing various sources for the conduct of historical studies – archival documents, statistical data, parts of equipment, software packages, computer collections, item exhibits, images, stories, analysis and ways they can be used to interpret and represent the past.

We look at history study within the corporate frame of the information and telecommunication industry (ICT), but in some cases we shall also analyze such closely related topics as natural science and technology history museums or general museums in the country. ICT museums are explored as part of the museum's systems. This approach allows gaining wider public information in order to analyze the facts about museums.

© IFIP International Federation for Information Processing 2019
Published by Springer Nature Switzerland AG 2019
C. Leslie and M. Schmitt (Eds.): HC 2018, IFIP AICT 549, pp. 304–316, 2019.
https://doi.org/10.1007/978-3-030-29160-0_16

In order to ensure the study of ICT history, we analyze various opportunities in Latvia. The most prominent institution for the study of history is the museum, but the operation of museums cannot be supported by the visitors' contributions alone.

Often the work of ICT history studies is carried out by volunteer researchers in research institutions. For many academic employees, history studies are a hobby. Therefore, ICT history study is often linked to technology and science research, often as an ICT historical department in a museum or a university. More or less deliberate and targeted ICT history study work is possible in various institutional forms. Three different forms of the history study organization are identified:

- Preliminary study of history – a particular study undertaken before a larger long-term targeted history study activity. Preliminary study is often a byproduct of actions undertaken for other purposes.
- ICT history studied primarily as a hobby and employee volunteer work.
- The study of ICT history, supported by a stable philanthropic funding system institutionalized at the museum.

Public information about computer museums in Europe [1–16] is analyzed. Investigative data is collected from public data sources within the wider museum community, not just computer museums [17–27], because such statistics are much broader and more accurate. Authors pay special attention to the funding of the operations of the museums. The objective of the authors is to collate data on the financing of museums in Europe and Latvia (in some positions – Lithuania, Estonia), compare that data and draw some conclusions about implementation of museum policies, financial issues and perspectives of development of computer, technology and science museums in Latvia.

The authors' study is based on analytical reviews done by other institutions at the national level (Ministry of Culture, State Administration of Museums, Association of Latvian Museums [18–21]), on the transnational level data sources (OECD, ENROP, EGMUS, CAF [17, 22–26]), and other analytical papers [27–32].

Another aspect relates to the involvement of staff in the ICT history study. The study of ICT history by volunteers (often undertaken by retired academic staff and engineers) is widespread in Latvia. Such activities are carried out at the universities, the Latvian Academy of Sciences and public institutions related to historical research. The authors, being part of the ICT History study volunteers, based their findings on academic work experience. The author's publications of ICT History in Latvia are presented [33–39].

2 Computer Museums (Museums) in Europe and Latvia

Let us explain the list of internationally renowned computer museums in Europe [1–16]. Computer museums are diverse in various aspects: size of the museum, whether the museum is a legal body or a substructure of a larger museum or university, whether computer exhibits are running in the museum, or whether the museum operates as a technological or science exhibit museum. Computer museums are often specialized in PC, games, and media.

Computer museums are changing. Museums can combine their public service missions with market-based strategies and the creative economy with web-based access to museum exhibits.[1] Museums showcase the latest scientific advances to attract visitors.

Museums can be categorized, for example, as in the Latvian Museums Act or the EGMUS classification [17, 19, 27]. It is more appropriate for us to examine statistics in relation to the full range of museums, not just computer museums. We compile information about computer museums in our data collection. Considering the peculiarities of each museum, we have identified the approximate number of computer museums in European countries according to our data collection.

This approximate information shows that the majority of Europe computer museums is located in the United Kingdom, Germany, and the Netherlands (in parentheses we indicate that the minimum number of computer museums in the country; this number is our evaluation point too): United Kingdom (11), Germany (10), the Netherlands (7), Sweden (3), Italy (3), at least two computer museums are in Denmark, France, Switzerland, Spain, Poland, Finland, one computer museum is in Belgium, Croatia, Ireland, Slovenia. Compare this data, for example, with the United States (23), Canada (4), Latvia (2). In Latvia, we have the Communications Museum at the Riga Technical University and the Computer Museum at the Institute of Mathematics and Computer Science of the University of Latvia [33, 39].

The origins of establishing computer museums stem from universities (Kiel, Cambridge), well-known companies (UNISYS, Nixdorf Siemens), widely used computer components (IBM, Burroughs, Apple, Atari, Commodore), museums established by ICT communities (German Engineering Association, Leibniz Association) or the idea of establishing develops from a philanthropic support of wealthy interested individuals.

The Law on Museums classifies Latvian museums according to their type of ownership: state-funded or local-authority museums. All other museums that have not received funding from the state budget or local authorities in accordance with the Museum Law are private museums and are managed by legal entities. The network of private museums is multifaceted and spacious; they are funded by founders of the museums who are legal entities or private individuals.

For comparison, we have prepared Table 1 showing the museum metrics in Latvia, Lithuania, Estonia in comparison with UK, Germany and the Netherlands as the countries where computer museums are the most popular.

Table 1 is prepared on the basis of the EGMUS data source [17]. Data in Table 1 should be considered rough and outlines trends since EGMUS data is available in different years, not all countries have submitted data to EGMUS, and the semantics of the data submitted may vary.

From the date of Table 1 we can conclude that the museum's metrics in Latvia and Lithuania are approximately similar, Estonia is slightly different. In Latvia there are fewer private museums as in the United Kingdom, Germany and the Netherlands.

---

[1] For example, take a look at the web museums list in Germany: http://museen.computerarchiv-muenchen.de.

Table 1. Museum metrics in the UK, Germany, the Netherlands, Latvia, Estonia, Lithuania.

	2012	2016				
	UK	Germany	The Netherlands	Latvia	Estonia	Lithuania
Number of museums	1,712	6,712	694	151	246	103
State-owned museums	58 3.3%	431 6.4%	61 8.8%	41 27.15%	78 31.7%	19 18.4%
Regional-owned museums	581 33.5%	2,585 38.5%	–	95 62.9%	86 35%	54 52.4%
Other public-owned museums	83 4.8%	441 6.6%	–	10 6.6%	–	22 21.3%
Private-owned museums	910 53%	2,995 44.6%	633 91.2%	5 3.3%	82 33.3%	8 7.8%
Museums per 100.000 inhabitants	2.75	8.17	4.10	7.6	18.7	–
Public expenditure per 100,000 inhabitants	–	–	3,021,358	1,634,004	3,321,156	–
	Highest: Luxembourg 8,069,000 EUR; lowest: Slovakia 195,101 EUR. Latvia, according to EGMUS data, is in third-lowest position before Slovakia and Bulgaria					
Science and technology museums	–	–	158 22.7%	–	22 8.9%	–
	Highest: Belgium 35.8%; lowest; Sweden 7.6%; average: 20%					
Public subsidies income	–	–	49.5%	80.8%	58.1%	–

Latvia has a high level of state subsidy income, despite the fact that public expenditure per 100 000 inhabitants in Latvia is lower compared to other European countries.

National sources [20, 21] have insignificant differences in museum data, which explains the different semantics of these data. According to these data, currently there are 220 museums in Latvia and 18% of the total number consists of science and technology museums.

For comparison, data is collected on nine technology museums in Latvia (see Table 2) and compared with the largest Science Centre in the Baltic States (Estonia). AHHAA is an internationally recognized partner in several organizations in Estonia. Table 2 includes museums that are well-known in the community and are accredited in the museum register.

Table 2. Well-known in the community technology museums in Latvia.

Museum	Sponsorship		Philanthropy		Income
Riga Motor Museum[a]	CSDD	Road transport	CSDD	Society	CSDD > 5 partners
LR History Museum[b]	LR	Railway	LR	Society	LR
Museum for history of medicine[c]	Legal body	Health sector	No reward	Society	The Ministry, >13 supporters
Anatomy Museum[d]	RSU (Health)	RSU	RSU	RSU	RSU
Kurzeme Demo centre[e]	Ventspils High Technology Park	Municipality	Municipality	Society	Philanthropy, >8 companies
Jaunmokas technology museum[f]	Legal body	Forests community	Reward to LSF	LSF	LSF
Museum of Natural History[g]	Legal body	Society	No reward	Society	The Ministry, >14 sponsors
Museum of Science and Technology[h]	IMCS UL	IMCS UL	Week reward to UL	IMCS UL	UL, IMCS UL
Telecommunications museum[i]	RTU	RTU	Week reward to RTU	RTU	RTU contribution
AHHAA[j]	Tartu University (TU)	TU	Week reward to TU	TU	Philanthropy, >12 supporters

[a]Historic Vehicle exposition with multimedia solutions, highlighting the museum's collections and unique exhibits.
[b]Dedicated to the history of the railway and its development in Latvia, subdivision of the LR.
[c]Direct administration institution under the Ministry of Health.
[d]Learning about historical anatomical preparations but also a premises for varied social, educational and cultural activities.
[e]Science and technology museum. Interactive center that offers active, entertaining, educational and interesting adventures, united with Tartu AHHA in a single network.
[f]Jaunmokas Palace museum established by Joint Stock Company "Latvia's State Forests."
[g]Largest and one of the oldest complex museums of natural history and sciences in the Baltic States.
[h]Alliance of: Latvia History Museum; Zoology Museum; Geology Museum; Computing Museum, [37]; Botanical Museum; Pedagogy Museum; F. Cander Space Exploration Museum; Human Pathology Museum; Chemical History Museum.
[i]Now mainly a radio museum.
[j]Science Centre AHHAA, Tartu, Estonia.

In Table 2, data show that in most cases a large industrial company (usually a state-owned enterprise) finances the history museum. In addition to this form of museum funding, there is support from the public sector and sponsorship. In the case of Latvia, we can rarely speak of philanthropy (altruism).

3 Various Philanthropy Funding for Museum Operations

It is not possible to support an historical study from museum visitors' contributions (money earned by the museum) alone, which ranges from 3 to 15 euro per visitor; for this purpose, historical institutions and historical collections attract funds, projects, and donations. Museums have a permanent strategy how they can combine their public service missions with market-based strategies.

Policy makers in U.S. museums recognize that in earlier times, museums were supported by three periods of museum funding:

1. *Philanthropic period*, characterized by the exclusive support of wealthy individuals.
2. *Transitional period*, in which increasingly professional management increased revenues.
3. *Funding phase*, in which institutions such as corporations and foundations picked up the work previously ascribed to wealthy philanthropists and amplified the pressure toward populism and large-scale exhibitions [28].

Regardless of the diversity of the situation, it can be estimated that there are at least three shares to the funding of a museum: the government (state) budget (20–25%), private (35%), and earned (25%) [17]. Public funding is determined by politicians or community leaders. They earn a share of the museums themselves, but part of private funding is publicly exposed.

The public part covers direct financial support (subsidies, awards and grants, as well as lottery funds provided by central and lower government levels); state indirect financial support (tax expense); private financial support from non-profit organizations, business organizations, and individual donations. Museums require donations from citizens and corporations. The ENROP 2017 study shows that households are the main source of philanthropic contributions (53%), followed by corporations (25%), foundations (19%) and lotteries (3%) [25].

As can be seen in Table 3, in Latvia, the World Giving Index and the population's charity culture are low. The situation is ameliorated with volunteering. Donations in Latvia most typically reach organizations whose public benefit status allows companies and individuals to receive tax rebates [27]. Individual donations for various charity campaigns are popular, either with a donation phone call or a supermarket cash register with special donation boxes. There are extremely few foundations created by individuals. The public benefit status in Latvia can be granted in nine areas. The following areas overlap with the classification of public benefit activity fields provided by The European Research Network on Philanthropy (ERNOP): education (ICT History study projects), health, culture (ICT History study projects), environment and social welfare (ICT History study projects). Religion and international assistance included by ERNOP but are missing in Latvia.

There are different requirements for philanthropy, charity, donations, sponsorship, cash contributions to different countries, in particular for various tax obligations. The situation assessment in Latvia is given in Table 4.

The financing of a historical study meets the corporate social responsibility from commercial sector and public authorities. Typically, funding is as follows: private

Table 3. Data from the World Giving Index published by the Charities Aid foundation (2011).

	UK	Germany	The Netherlands	Latvia	Estonia	Lithuania
People giving money to charities	73%	49%	77%	16%	12%	4%
People volunteering time for an organization in the last month	29%	28%	39%	18%	15%	6%
People who have helped a stranger in the last month	58%	56%	46%	34%	37%	33%
World giving index score (average)	53%	44%	54%	23%	21%	14%

Table 4. Assessment of charity in Latvia.

	Philanthropy	Donation	Sponsorship
Type of supporter	Private persons, funds	Private persons, companies	Companies
Support motives	Altruism	Altruism, tax rebates	Supports the motive with the ability to achieve their goals
Cooperation with the supported	Partly	No	Yes
Spor	Very rare	Rare	Dominant
Culture	Dominant	Often	Often
Social area, ecology	Often	Dominant	Rare
Media	No	No	Dominant
Political parties	No	Dominant	No
NGC	Often	Dominant	No
Design maker	Private companies	Financial system	Company board

foundation (includes corporate foundation), public foundation (government related foundation), community foundation, fundraising foundation. philanthropy (corporate philanthropy) and sponsorship (corporate sponsorship) are different. We will analyze four distinctions [39]:

1. Corporate sponsorship is a mutual business proposition that offers value in exchange for money. Corporations get a return on their "investment," enhance their profile, associate their brand with a cause, and or attract customers who support that cause.

2. Corporate sponsorship can be managed by most any department within a corporation including: sales, marketing, training and development, etc.
3. Corporate philanthropy is motivated by altruism and supports a socially beneficial cause without financial or material reward to the corporation.
4. Corporate philanthropy is often managed by an internal community relations team or a corporate foundation. The corporation aims to enhance its image and promote goodwill with stakeholders and the community.

The wealthy Latvian state joint-stock company funds are allocated to cultural, sports and educational projects, either managed by the companies themselves as separate projects or by entering into contractual relations with cultural, sports and charitable organizations that organize open tenders to beneficiaries. According to the classical understanding, these funds cannot be called philanthropic foundations.

The first priority of a commercial company is economic considerations, which means profitable business, followed by obligations arising from the performance of legal duties, including taxes and other statutory requirements. If the company has met these essential requirements, this may apply to Corporate Social Responsibility, including sponsorship and philanthropy. Obligations of philanthropists are duties that go beyond what is simply needed or considered by the company to be correct. They try to benefit from the community, for example by donating services to community organizations, engaging in projects to support the environment or donate money to charities.

Latvian practice shows that companies start with sponsoring political organizations and individual NGOs, donations for sports and art, and only the next wave is wider philanthropy. Various forms are used to transfer funds for Corporate Social Responsibility and voluntary help, usually in cash, for those who need it: philanthropy, charity, donations, sponsorship and contribution.

There is no strict borderline between sponsorship and philanthropy. The main difference is that there is no direct reward to the donator. Usually the money donor wants direct or indirect benefits, and we are most often talking about sponsorship.

If there are more sponsors, then it is less possible to pinpoint the benefits to the money lender. In our classification in Latvia, if the number of sponsors is more than 6, then we believe that the goals of the philanthropists are fulfilled.

4 Preliminary ICT History Study Activities in Latvia

We talk very often about history – in everyday life and in events, in various corporate documents. Innovative project proposals often start with a historic background. In corporate events we remember historical facts. We find historical facts in the staff CVs.

In the short term, we usually talk about history. It is an unconscious, indirect gathering and analysis of ICT historical facts. A historical study is another side effect for someone else's purpose. The history study closely reflects science and research activities. Typical historical facts are remembered at scientific and public organization conferences. Let us take a look at organizational events in Latvia, where historical facts are discussed and analyzed indirectly.

a. The University of Latvia organizes Programmer's Days since 1998, and since 2000, students have been awarded the Ada Lovelace and Charles Babbage Prize.
b. In 1990, the Latvian Radio Electronics and Communications Engineers Foundation established the J. Linter Prize. But on 20 December 1993, Lattelekom, LMT, and Tele2 founded the J. Linter Foundation. In 18 years, 423 specialists of the electronic communications industry received J. Linter awards. The purpose of the prize is to stimulate the contribution of individuals and groups of individuals to the comprehensive development of the Latvian radio and electronic communications industry.
c. Recognition, which can be acquired only once in a lifetime, was founded in 2000, named after Professor Eizens Āriņš, the founder of computer science in Latvia.

Corporations (Lattelecom, Latvian Mobile Operators LMT, Tele2) hold annual professional conferences – Technology Days – to talk about future innovative technologies and history before and discuss the annual success of the corporation and the state.

5 ICT History Study as Volunteering (as a Hobby)

Why are Latvian (Eastern Europa) ICT museums and ICT development history important internationally?

a. Since the 1990s, Latvia has rapidly changed its economic system to a market economy. The subject of the ICT history study is how the economic restructuring reflects to following changes in the technology platform.
b. In the late 1960s, the Union of Soviet Socialist Republic brand of computers were replaced by development of mass production of the ES EVM (United System Electronic Computing Machines), which is a cloned prototype of the IBM computers.[2] At the beginning of the 1990s, the technology platform was changed back to the original Western products. Which conclusions could be received from that?
c. What can we say about ICT convergence in both economic systems?

Nowadays, historical study had engaged corporations retired academics and authoritative engineers. However, such a historical study model in the long term is exposed to high risk of being discontinued.

The following activities in Latvia are mainly based on volunteer's work (no salaries or tiny salaries for involved employees); all these activities are characterized by a minor annual budget. A similar situation in the ICT history study is found in the universities and historical studies supported by associations:

• Baltic Association of the History and Philosophy of Science (Conferences & Seminars, The journal *Acta Baltica Historiae et Philosophiae Scientiarum*, publishing articles of the history and philosophy of natural and social sciences), from the Latvian branch of Association of History of Science;
• Latvian Association of History of Medicine;
• Baltic Association of Historians of Pedagogy.

---

[2] See Kitov, "Main Teleprocessing Monitors," this volume.

Authors are volunteers too, and their competence in ICT Historical Study is presented in publications, for instance"

a. Computing Museum of Institute of Mathematics and Computer Science University of Latvia (IMCS UL). The museum has 7,372 exhibits. In 2017, there were 239 visitors per year. IMCS Computers and IT museum was established 1984. Historical documents, computer parts and photos are collected in the museum. History of computer use in IMCS UL to the middle of the 1990s and the transformation from computing center to research institution. History of collaboration with Nordic Countries that provided political, scientific and technological support [33].

b. IMCS UL and three socio-technological waves of IT (from 1959). The first wave – the formation of industrial computer production in Russia (1960–1970). These were the first original computers of the Soviet production of the BESM series and Minsk. The second wave is the production of the EC EVM computers cloned from IBM's developments (1970–1990). The third wave (last) – the use of personal computers, the rapid development of the Internet, the globalization of IT. For Latvia, this wave was accompanied by significant social changes by integration into the European Union [34].

c. History of Data Centre Development. Publication describes the history of data center development. In the beginning of the computer era, computers were installed in computing centers because all computing centers have specific requirements according to which their operation is intended for [35].

d. Way of Internet development in Eastern Europe. Collection of Untraditionally Developed Academic IT Services and development of Internet in Eastern Europe. Deep and radical social reforms of the last century's nineties in many Eastern European countries caused changes in Information Technology's (IT) field. Compared to the international practice, academic services were developed in Eastern Europe in an untraditional way, which provided positive technological changes [36].

e. Accounting System for Computing Resources Usage – History and Development in Latvia. Introduction of accounting system for computing resources usage mainly has two goals: optimizing operating systems performance and billing tracking as well as invoicing customers for use of computing services. This problem becomes obvious with the introduction of time-sharing systems. In the era of personal computers, the accounting problem disappeared, but now due to the development of cloud computing it has renewed. The paper proposes to discuss the accounting systems for different computing resources – virtual machines, high-performance computing and data storage, accounting for use of different applications and development today [37].

f. The Convergence of Telecommunications and Information Technologies – Historical View in Latvia. The article identifies the main cornerstones in the history of ICT convergence process in Latvia. The technological basis for convergence is the transition from analog to digital communication and processing of all incoming information in digital computer devices. The authors of the article analyze the transformation of the higher education in industry sector and structural changes of company's employees in the process of convergence. The analysis of the transformation in education programs is carried out on the basis of the Association for

Computing Machinery (ACM) Curricula Recommendations in different times and different disciplines. Concept of computing and communication convergence has many years of history – as strategic concept it started about 1977 and yet has many definitions. The idea behind convergence concept is mostly related to convergence between computing and telecommunication common technologies, services and service provider's business models. In this academic position paper some less significant obstacles of influence-reflection of convergence to legislation system, higher education programs and industry labor market are discussed [38, 39].

6   Conclusion

Preliminary ICT History Study activities are performed by state institutions or professional associations, mainly engaging retired scholars or highly skilled engineers in historical research and analytics. Today, the main business case for ICT (science, technology) historical study in Latvia is based on volunteers (possibly, the same is true throughout Eastern Europe). Utility sectors (such as the Ministry of Environmental Protection and Regional Development, the Ministry of Transport, The Ministers for Agriculture) ensure the maintenance of museums directly or through the State Joint Stock Companies. A more stable ICT historical study business model is based on sponsorship or the next phase of Corporate Social Responsibility – Philanthropy. Today, Corporate Social Responsibility is related to sponsorship for political parties, NGOs (for example, ICT professional associations support over 100 corporations), sports, art, but the authors believe that support of the Museum (ICT History Study) is expected only at the next level.

Acknowledgement. The publication has been supported by European Regional Development Fund within the project No. 1.1.1.5/18/I/016 University of Latvia and Institutes in the European Research Area – Excellence, Activity, Mobility and Capacity.

References

1. Heinz Nixdorf Museums Forum Homepage. https://www.hnf.de/start.html. Accessed 16 Aug 2018
2. Unisys Computer Museum Belgium Homepage. http://www.unisys.be/aboutus/about-unisys-belgium. Accessed 16 Aug 2018
3. Deutsches Museum in München Homepage. https://www.deutsches-museum.de. Accessed 16 Aug 2018
4. Computermuseum der FH Kiel Homepage. http://www.fh-kiel.de/index.php?id=186. Accessed 16 Aug 2018
5. Oldenburger Computer-Museum Homepage. http://www.computermuseum-oldenburg.de. Accessed 16 Aug 2018
6. Computer spielemuseum Berlin Homepage. http://www.computerspielemuseum.de. Accessed 16 Aug 2018
7. Technisches Museum in Wien Homepage. http://www.technischesmuseum.at. Accessed 16 Aug 2018

8. ENTER Museum Switzerland Homepage. http://www.enter-online.ch/index.php?id= taetigkeit. Accessed 16 Aug 2018
9. The Centre for Computing History Cambridge Homepage. http://www.computinghistory. org.uk. Accessed 16 Aug 2018
10. The National Museum of Computing, Bedfordshire Homepage. http://www.tnmoc.org. Accessed 16 Aug 2018
11. Musee de l'Informatique in Paris Homepage. http://www.eutouring.com/musee. Accessed 16 Aug 2018
12. Danish Museum of Science and Technology Homepage. http://tekniskmuseum.dk. Accessed 16 Aug 2018
13. Swedish Computer Museum Homepage. http://www.datamuseet.se/english. Accessed 16 Aug 2018
14. Dansk Datahistorisk Forening Homepage. www.datamuseum.dk. Accessed 16 Aug 2018
15. The Computer History Museum California Homepage. http://www.computerhistory.org. Accessed 16 Aug 2018
16. The Russian Virtual Computer Museum Homepage. http://www.computer-museum.ru/ english/. Accessed 16 Aug 2018
17. EGMUS - The European Group on Museum Statistics Homepage. http://www.egmus.eu/. Accessed 16 Aug 2018
18. Latvia. Ministry of Culture Homepage. www.km.gov.lv. Accessed 16 Aug 2018
19. Latvia. State Authority on Museums Homepage. http://www.km.gov.lv/en/ministry/depend. html#mus. Accessed 16 Aug 2018
20. Latvian Museum Association Homepage. http://www.muzeji.lv. Accessed 16 Aug 2018
21. Cultural map portal. Homepage. http://www.kulturaskarte.lv/lv/muzeji. Accessed 16 Aug 2018
22. OECD Homepage: Public and Private Social Expenditure by country. http://www.oecd.org. Accessed 16 Aug 2018
23. The OECD Centre on Philanthropy Homepage. Data and Analysis for development. www. oecd.org/development/philanthropy-centre. Accessed 16 Aug 2018
24. Giving in Europe country reports Hompage. http://ernop.eu/giving-in-europe-launched-at-spring-of-philanthropy. Accessed 16 Aug 2018
25. The European Research Network on Philanthropy (ERNOP) Hompage. http://ernop.eu. Accessed 16 Aug 2018
26. Charities Aid Foundation Homepage. https://www.cafonline.org. Accessed 16 Aug 2018
27. State of Giving Research in Republic of Latvia (2016). https://www.lu.lv/fileadmin/user_ upload/lu_portal/projekti/lu_fonds/Velos_atbalstit/GivingLatvia_Report_2013_20160811. pdf. Accessed 16 Aug 2018
28. Kwatinetz, M.: The Bull & the Ballot Box: Art Museum Economic Strategies https:// penniur.upenn.edu/uploads/media/Bull%20and%20the%20Ballot%20Box%20Art% 20Museum%20Economic%20Strategies.pdf. Accessed 14 Nov 2018
29. Alexander, V.D.: From philanthropy to funding: the effects of corporate and public support on American art museums. Poetics **24**(2–4), 87–129 (1996)
30. An overview of philanthropy in Europe. Observatoire de la Fondation de France, CERPhi (2015)
31. Financing the Arts and Culture in the European Union, Directorate General Internal Policies of the Union European Parliament IP/B/CULT/ST/2005_104, 30 November 2006
32. Kundzina-Zvejniece, L.: Corporate philanthropy in Latvia. https://www.lu.lv/fileadmin/user_ upload/lu_portal/projekti/lu_fonds/kapec-ziedot/KundzinaZvejniece_ CorporativeFoundations_Latvia.pdf. Accessed 16 Aug 2018

33. Balodis, R., Borzovs, J., Opmane, I., Skuja, A., Ziemele, E.: Research directions profile in the computing museum of the Institute of Mathematics and Computer Science, University of Latvia (IMCS). In: Impagliazzo, J., Lundin, P., Wangler, B. (eds.) HiNC 2010. IAICT, vol. 350, pp. 453–461. Springer, Heidelberg (2011). https://doi.org/10.1007/978-3-642-23315-9_51
34. Balodis, R., Opmane, I.: Institute of Mathematics and Computer Science, University of Latvia, and three socio-technological waves of IT. In: Materials of the Second International Conference on the Development of Computer Technology and its Software in Russia and the Former Soviet Union (SoRuCom 2011), pp. 36–40
35. Balodis, R., Opmane, I.: History of data centre development. In: Tatnall, A. (ed.) Reflections on the History of Computing. IAICT, vol. 387, pp. 180–203. Springer, Heidelberg (2012). https://doi.org/10.1007/978-3-642-33899-1_13
36. Balodis, R., Opmane, I.: Collection of untraditionally developed academic IT services. World Acad. Sci. Eng. Technol. Int. J. Humanit. Soc. Sci. 7(2), 350–354 (2013)
37. Balodis, R., Opmane, I.: Accounting system for computing resources usage - history and development. In: Computer Technology in Russia and in the Former Soviet Union, Selected Papers 2017, Zelenograd, Russia, pp. 179–182. IEEE Computer Society (2018)
38. Balodis, R., Opmane, I.: The convergence of telecommunications and information technologies - historical view in Latvia. In: Computer Technology in Russia and in the Former Soviet Union, SoRuCom 2017, Selected Papers, Zelenograd, Russia, pp. 183–190. IEEE Computer Society (2018)
39. Opmane, R., Balodis, I.: Computing and communication convergence reflection to legislation system and higher education programs. In: The 8th International Conference on ICT Convergence, IEEExplore 2017, 18–20 October 2017, pp. 184–189 (2017)

The Engineering Heritage of Bashir Rameev at the Polytechnic Museum: Honoring the 100th Anniversary of His Birth

Marina Smolevitskaya$^{(\boxtimes)}$

Computer Collection Curator, Polytechnic Museum, Moscow, Russia
msmolevitskaya@yandex.ru

Abstract. Bashir Iskandarovich Rameev fulfilled one of the main roles in the informatization of Russia as the developer of Ural computer. In English publications, information about him and his contribution to science is practically absent. Nevertheless, he left a valuable legacy in the form of his developments of the family of universal automatic digital computing machines "Ural" with advanced software. The engineering heritage of B. I. Rameev is kept at the Polytechnic Museum in Moscow. The tube automatic digital machine "Ural-1" takes a special place in the computer collection at the Museum. The personal documentary collection of B. I. Rameev is voluminous and unique in its content. The documents of his collection reflect the entire history of the creation and development of domestic electronic computing machines. Among these documents the project "Automatic Digital Computing Machine" of I. S. Brook and B. I. Rameev and patent No 10475 (USSR author's certificate) on 4 December 1948 are preserved. This patent was the first officially registered invention in the field of electronic digital computers in the USSR. On the suggestion of the Polytechnic Museum, 4 of December 1948 is considered (not yet officially) to be the birthday of Russian informatics. It is impossible to overestimate the contribution of B. I. Rameev to domestic electronic computing equipment. His name should be preserved in the history of Russia.

Keywords: B. I. Rameev · URAL · Electronic digital computing machine · Museum · Archive

1 Introduction

In the Soviet Union, the engineer and chief designer of the computer family "Ural" B. I. Rameev together with scientists such as academicians S. A. Lebedev and V. M. Glushkov, corresponding members A. A. Lyapunov and I. S. Brook stood at the origins of the creation of domestic electronic computers. The merits of Lebedev, Glushkov and Lyapunov were recognized by the international scientific community. They received the rank "Computer Pioneer" from the IEEE Computer Society. These scientists created their computers in the system of academic science; they themselves took part in international conferences. Therefore, their names are better known abroad. For example, only the computers of Academician Lebedev are mentioned in the dissertation of Peter Wolcott "Soviet advanced technology: The case of high-performance

© IFIP International Federation for Information Processing 2019
Published by Springer Nature Switzerland AG 2019
C. Leslie and M. Schmitt (Eds.): HC 2018, IFIP AICT 549, pp. 317–341, 2019.
https://doi.org/10.1007/978-3-030-29160-0_17

computing" [1]. Furthermore, Wolcott only mentions the *Institute of Precision Mechanics and Computer Technology* in Moscow and the *Computer Center of the Siberian Department of the USSR Academy of Sciences/Institute of Informatics Systems* in Novosibirsk as organizations that developed computers in the Soviet Union. In parallel with Lebedev, the work on the creation of the very first computers was carried out at *the Laboratory of Electrosystems of the Energy Institute of the Academy of Sciences of the USSR*, headed by I. S. Brook, and in the *Special Design Bureau SDB-245*, formed at the *Moscow Plant of* Counting - *Analytical Machines*. Rameev first worked with Brook, and then together Yu. Bazilevskiy in SDB-245.

Likewise, almost nothing is known about Brook's computers and the computers developed in SDB-245 in the international literature. Alex Bochannek, a researcher of the *Computer History Museum in California*, showed in his paper [2] that information about general computing work done in the Soviet Union was available in unclassified environments. The merits of Brook and Rameev in this area are almost unknown abroad, while they are not less significant. Rameev is one of the founders of electronic computers in the Soviet Union. The merits of Rameev in the field of creating digital computers are recognized by all domestic scientific schools unconditionally. Representatives of various organizations that created computers in the Soviet Union regularly meet in the *Virtual Computer Museum* [3] and all they agreed that Rameev's contribution to domestic electronic computing was significant.

An attempt to present Rameev's contribution to the creation of computers in Eastern Europe is done in this article. The collections of the *Polytechnic Museum* can serve as sources for further research by historians of computer technology [4–6].

As known, at the turn of the 1950s the development of the first electronic computers was conducted in the USA, England, Germany and France. Since the machines were developed mainly for military purposes, the publications on them were very terse. Most machines were built on electromechanical relays, not electronic tubes. Rameev received his knowledge of electronics working at the Institute of Electronics No 108, and also he was fond of radio amateurs. Once he heard the BBC broadcasts that the electronic computer ENIAC was produced in the USA [7], interest in this new technology led Rameev to correspond with academy member I. Brook. Brook was interested in computing and was engaged in the development of analog computers already before the second World War. He was happy to find such an able assistant. In May 1948, Rameev received a position as computer engineer in the *Laboratory of Electrical Systems* at the *Power Engineering Institute of USSR Academy of Sciences.*

In the collection of Polytechnic Museum in Moscow, electronic digital computing machines of domestic production from the 1950s to 1990s are presented together with the developments of leading scientific schools, research institutes and plants, that created them. This collection is the only one in the whole territory of the former Soviet Union. All the exhibits that make up the collection are unique: from the operative memory device on the cathode-ray tubes of the first domestic serial computer "Strela" to the onboard computer complex "Argon-16," which controlled flights of space vehicles. The tube computer "Ural-1" is given a special place in the collection (Fig. 1). Its chief constructor was B. I. Rameev (Fig. 2).

On the suggestion of the Polytechnic Museum, 4 December 1948 is considered to be the birthday of Russian informatics. Although in Russia this holiday is not yet

Fig. 1. The Small Automatic Universal Electronic Computer "Ural-1" at the Polytechnic Museum, 2014

Fig. 2. A photo of Bashir Rameev of the 1950s (left) and one of his last pictures, December 1993 (right). Polytechnic *Museum, Personal Documentary Collection of B. Rameev No 221.*

official, it is noted by all those who are related to computer science. This date on December 4 was chosen not accidentally. In August 1948, Corresponding Member of the *USSR Academy of Sciences for the Department of Technical Sciences* I. S. Brook, along with his collaborator, the young engineer B. Rameev, presented the project "Automatic Digital Computing Machine." The Flowchart of the projected Automatic

Digital Computing Machine and Rameev's manuscripts are shown in Figs. 3 and 4. In October of the same year, they presented detailed proposals on the organization of the laboratory for the development and construction of such computer in the *USSR Academy of Sciences*. On the 4th of December 1948, I. S. Brook and B. Rameev

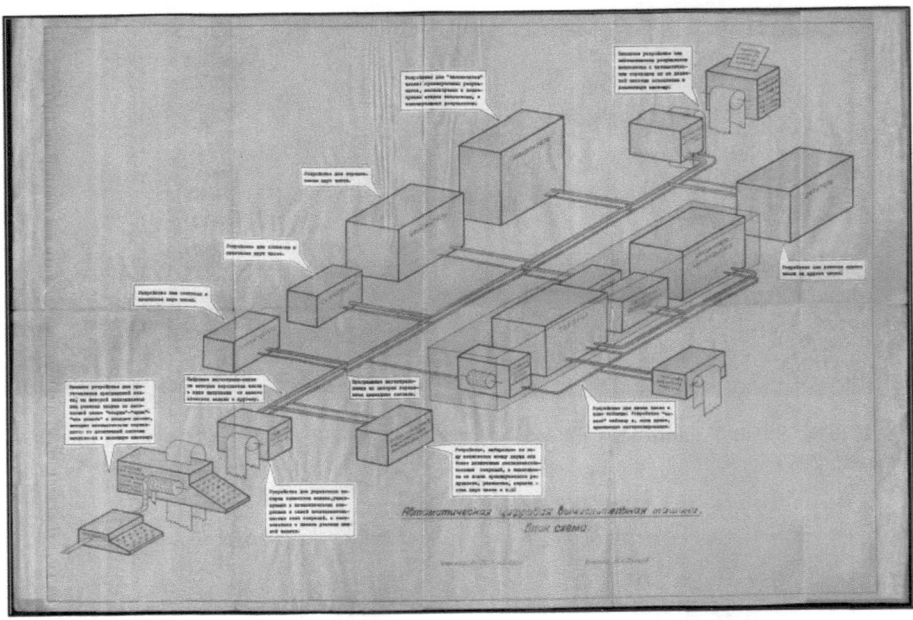

Fig. 3. The Flowchart for the Project of the Automatic Digital Computing Machine. *Polytechnic Museum, Personal Documentary Collection of B. Rameev No 221.*

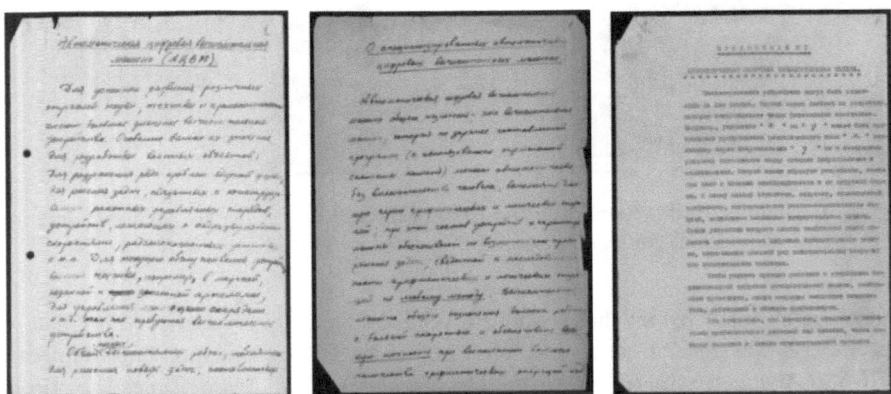

Fig. 4. The manuscripts of Rameev. *Polytechnic Museum, Personal Documentary Collection of B. Rameev No 221.*

received patent No 10475 (USSR author's certificate) (Fig. 5). It was the first officially registered invention in the field of electronic digital computers in the USSR. All these documents are preserved in the documentary collection of B. Rameev at the *Polytechnic Museum.*

2   B. Rameev's Engineering Heritage

The primary source of B. Rameev's biography and the description of his contribution to electronic computer technics is B. N. Malinovsky's book *The History of Computer Science in Persons,* published in 1995 [7]. The chapter "The son of an epoch" of this book was written by Malinovsky in many respects thanks to the materials that Rameev himself gave him. Later, there were memories about Rameev of other people who knew and worked with him. Margarita Badrutdinova, director of the museum of the Kazan's Electronic Computers Plant, not only carried out scientific research on the roots of Bashir Iskandarovich Rameev concerning his father and grandfather, but also compiled a list of his inventions (given in Appendix 5.1) [8, 9].

Rameev's companion on the "Ural" family of computers, Gennady Smirnov, made a unique contribution to the description, study and preservation of Rameev's legacy. He wrote several books about the school of construction of Rameev [10, 11] and compiled a bibliographic index *The Computer "Ural" in the World of Publications and Documents 1945–1972* [12].

The biography of Rameev in English is given in [13, 14]. Also, according to Rameev's biography and his heritage in the Polytechnic Museum in Moscow, one can trace the entire history of the development of electronic computers in the Soviet Union. Almost all his conscious life since 1948 he created electronic computers, and he one of the pioneers was in this area. Rameev was an active developer of the very first computers in the Soviet Union: the first serial domestic computer "Strela" and the Small automatic digital computer "Ural-1."

2.1   The First Domestic Serial Electronic Computer, "Strela"

In 1950, another computer research and design center was established in Moscow. It was called *Special Engineering Bureau 245* (SDB-245). This center was empowered by joining it the *Moscow Plant of Counting-Analytical Machines* that had been founded for commercial production of calculating machinery, both mechanical and electrome-chanical. Rameev was recommended to head one of its new laboratories [7]. He had been demobilized on the personal request of P. I. Parshin – the *USSR minister of machinery and instrumentation.* Although military authorities reacted with consent, Parshin had to provide a guarantee of his personal responsibility for Rameev's further actions. Computer development in the USSR was and remained a secret matter for a long time. Rameev submitted a draft project of a computer which integrated some ideas of his earlier work with Brook. It was confirmed by the SDB-245 technical council and taken as basis for new electronic computer "Strela" – the first soviet computer produced in series, in total seven machines. Rameev was deputy construction-general of the whole project. He headed the construction of its central arithmetic unit and magnetic drum storage. He also persuaded designers to use electron valves, not slow electro-magnetic relays. Rameev proposed a symmetrical trigger on a 6H8S tube as the main element of the "Strela." This device served as the main universal element for building typical computer "Strela" devices - registers, adders, decoders and others.

In 1953, the experimental model of "Strela" was tested by a state commission and recommended for serial production. In fact, the seven computers were not absolutely identical because some corrections were always implemented in each following piece after testing the previous one. They were placed in the *Applied Mathematics Institute of USSR Science Academy (USSR SA)*, the *Computing Center of USSR SA* and computer centers of some ministries. They were used mainly in tasks related to nuclear power and space research. In 1954 Rameev and other collaborators of "Strela" team were awarded the USSR State Bounty. The exposition of Polytechnic Museum devoted to B. I. Rameev, Yu. Ya. Bazilevskiyi, SDB-245 and the Electronic Computer "Strela" are shown in Fig. 6.

In 1955, Rameev moved to Penza with a group of talented young specialists from *SDB-245*. In Penza, Rameev became chief engineer of the Penza branch of *SDB-245*, and then deputy director for research at the *Penza Scientific Research Institute of Controlling Computing Machines*, later called *Research Institute of Mathematical Machines*. In Penza, Rameev created his own computer science school. Many leading computer designers began their activity in the Penza school: V. V. Przhialkovsky, V. Ya. Pikhtin and others from the Minsk branch like V. V. Rezanov Severodonetsk [11]. There, he worked on the construction of the The Small Automatic Universal Electronic Computer "Ural-1".

2.2   The Small Automatic Universal Electronic Computer "Ural-1"

In the years 1930–1940, USA, Great Britain, France and Germany imposed restrictions on the supply of a number of goods on the Soviet Union. In 1949, the Coordinating Committee on Multilateral Export Control (CoCom) was established by these countries to impose an embargo on the supply of goods to Comecon countries. So the development of the first computers was carried out in isolation from the developments that were carried out in western countries, that actually established a regime of secrecy for the exchange of scientific and technical information.[1] According to Academician S. Lebedev, the available foreign publications that were received in those years in the USSR were of an "advertising nature." It should be recognized that, unfortunately, later foreign publications to many Soviet specialists remained unknown. In addition, the publications of Soviet specialists were very rare. The exchange of experience occurred with the US was mainly at the level of personal meetings and visits to enterprises [10]. In October 1955, in Darmstadt (Germany) S. Lebedev and Yu. Ya. Bazilevsky presented BESM-1 as the fastest computer in Europe with RAM consisting of potentialoscopes, special cathode ray tubes. Furthermore, they presented on the Small Automatic Universal Computing Machine "Ural-1" and on mastering the serial

---

[1] See Leslie, "From CoCom to Dot-com," and Schmidt, "Socialist Life of a U.S. Army Computer," this volume.

production which had already begun [15] (see Appendix 5.1 for a technical description of the Ural-1 computer). In 1956, Rameev presented the report "Universal Automatic Digital Computer of the type Ural" at the conference "Ways of Development of Soviet Computing Engineering" [16] in Moscow. This was the first scientific conference in the Soviet Union on this subject.

One of the first samples of the "Ural-1" computer was used mainly for training specialists at the Computing Center of the USSR Sciences Academy. Since 1957, these machines have been supplied to computer centers, research institutions, military schools and other organizations. At the same time, the Computing Center of the Baikonur Cosmodrome was created on the basis of the Ural-1 computer.

By the early 1960s, "the Ural-1" computer was the most widespread machine in the USSR; it was operated in 128 cities. More than 30 machines operated abroad in 25 countries: in the GDR, Bulgaria, Hungary, Czechoslovakia, Norway, Turkey, England, Egypt and many more. Differently from bigger machines and chiefly used by large computer centers, Ural-1 was the first computer to be widely implemented by relatively small enterprises [10].

Despite the very low speed of 100 operations per second, especially by today's standards, the research and training institutes of the country were lining up behind this machine. For many years, the "Urals" had become the main "labor force" in our computer centers. It also became a "primary school" for numerous constructors, mathematicians-programmers and maintenance specialists.

"Ural-1" was followed by universal computers with the same electron valves-based circuitry, mainly used for civil purposes: "Ural-2" (1959), "Ural-3," "Ural-4" (1961) with ferrite cores RAM and extended ROM on magnetic drums (8 × 8K words) and magnetic tapes (12 × 260K words). Besides universal computers, "Ural" Rameev produced several special machines: "Weather" for meteorological calculations, "Granite" for probability characteristics of the experimental data arrays, "Crystal" for crystal structure X-ray analysis, a special computer for (geographic) bearings defined from radio detection data, etc.

In 1968, Rameev moved to Moscow and went to work at the *Scientific-Research Center of Electronic Computer Technology* to engage in a promising project: the Unified Computer System. He negotiated with the English firm ICL on scientific and technical cooperation in the field of computer production. Documents on cooperation between the *State Committee of the USSR on Science and Technology*, the *Ministry of Radio Industry of the USSR* and the English firm ICL are indicating this. They are presented in the documentary collection of Rameev in the *Polytechnic Museum* [17]. Also, in this collection there are documents on Soviet-American cooperation 1972–1974 in the field of computer application in management within the framework of the *Meetings between the Governments of the USSR and the USA on cooperation in the field of science and technology*. These are work plans and reports of a mixed Soviet-American group. Rameev also took an active part in the discussion of the problem of copying IBM-360 machines. The minutes of the meetings concerning the copying of the IBM 360 machines from December of 1969 testify to the intensive discussions held.

Rameev did not agree on the decision of the country's leadership on copying IBM-360 machines. Notwithstanding, he went to work for the *State Committee on Science and Technology of the USSR* [7]. Here he conducted the large scientific and orgarizational work on the formation of the all-Union scientific and technical programs for the creation of computer hardware and software. He coordinated the construction of systems for the automation of scientific research and design work, as well as for the introduction of automated control systems into practice. Furthermore, he contributed to the creation of the State Fund for Algorithms and Programs.

Fig. 5. Author's certificates of B. Rameev. *Polytechnic Museum, Personal Documentary Collection of B. Rameev* No *221.*

Since 1971, Rameev worked in the *Main Administration of Computer Technology and Control Systems of the State Committee on Science and Technology of the USSR.* He was the deputy head of the department. The *Main Department of Computer Engineering and Control Systems* had become an organization which coordinated and organized interdisciplinary complex scientific research and experimental development in the field of improvement in the national economy. They were in charge of building an extensive system of computer facilities by organizing automated management systems for planning and processing information for various purposes and creating a state network of computer centers, united by communication channels. His next 20 years were busy with coordination and implementation of national computer design projects and the estimation of their technical level and efficiency. He was also in charge of planning the scientific development programs and cooperating with the *State Collection (Library) of Computer Algorithms and Programs.* Only the absence of a diploma on graduation did not allow him to run for a full membership in the *Academy of Sciences,* of which he would have deserved to be a member.

Rameev came from the family of the largest gold miners in Russia. Bashir's grandfather was a famous Tatar poet. His father was repressed and perished in labor camps during Stalinist purges. Bashir Rameev, who by that time was a sophomore at the *Moscow Power Engineering Institute,* was named the son of an "enemy of the people" and was expelled from the institute [7]. Many years later, in 1962, forty-four-year-old Bashir Rameev was awarded the academic degree of Doctor of Technical

Sciences without defending his dissertation. Positive recommendations were given by academicians S. A. Lebedev, A. I. Berg and *Corresponding Member of the USSR Academy of Sciences* I. S. Brook [7].

In 2018, Rameev would have turned 100 years old, but there are specialists still alive who remember him very warmly, both as an outstanding scientist and as an extremely modest and talented person. They remember his kind eyes and smile, but at the same time remember his intransigence if he were convinced of anything. They remember his ability to gently convince, but firmly to achieve the ideal performance of all the necessary work. The many specialists who worked with Rameev note his attention to detail and the broadest technical intuition, the basis of which was the deep knowledge from different fields of technics. His commitment to unification, which is considered the cornerstone of effective mass production, showed a high level of computer construction. Rameev's name was often absent in the list of venerable speakers at various conferences, but this did not in the least interfere with his authority and popularity of the Penza scientific school he was leading. This holds true also thanks to the enormous creative work invested by him and his team in the development and production of universal computers.

In 2015, a technological park in the sphere of high technologies was named after Rameev to commemorate him. Technopark "Rameev" is an association of legally independent small and medium-sized innovative enterprises in Penza. The purpose of the technopark is to create favorable conditions for the development of small and medium-sized enterprises engaged in the development and implementation of innovative projects.

3   Exhibits and Documentary Collection of B. I. Rameev at the Polytechnic Museum

3.1   "Ural-1"

To date from the hundreds of UDSSR first-generation tube computers, only a single one has survived in full equipment – at the Polytechnic Museum. In 1967, the Voronezh State University gave the Small Automatic Universal Computing Machine "Ural-1" to the Polytechnic Museum (Fig. 1). Of course, the museum exhibitions in which the device is turned on and demonstrated how it worked cause the greatest interest of museum visitors. All of the authentic parts of the "Ural-1" computer are almost impossible to restore, but the processor and the RAM can be implemented on modern microchips. When studying the state of the "Ural-1" computer, it turned out that the control panel and the display panel are still working and can be used to demonstrate the operation of this machine. In 2007, two students developed the demonstration complex based on the Small Universal Automatic Electronic Computer "Ural-1" in the Polytechnic Museum. This complex along with authentic machine parts includes a number of additional blocks implemented on programmable logic microchips. This demonstration complex fully supports the command system of the computer "Ural-1" and with its help it is possible to solve any problems which were possible to solve on the original machine. The bit grids and the ways of representing numbers and operations on numbers correspond completely to the real "Ural-1" computer.

The created demonstration complex includes:

1. Power supply system of the "Ural-1" computer.
2. The control panel of the "Ural-1" computer.
3. The display panel of the "Ural-1" computer.
4. The processor, which is the full functional analog of the "Ural-1" computer processor and implemented on the Field Programmable Gate Array (FPGA) chip XC3S200-4FT256C from "Xilinx".
5. The operative memory simulating the operation of a magnetic drum of the "Ural-1" computer, implemented on an asynchronous memory chip IS61LV25616AL-10T, manufactured by ISSI.

Fig. 6. The exposition devoted to B. Rameev, Yu. Bazilevskiyi, SDB-245 and the Electronic Computer "Strela" in Polytechnic Museum, 2014.

6. The device for long-term data storage simulating the operation of a tape and/or magnetic tape drive, implemented on the microchip M25P16, manufactured by "ST Microelectronics".

In order to fully interface authentic devices of the "Ural-1" computer and devices simulating the operation of the processor, operative and long-term memory the following devices were additionally developed:

7. The block of interrogation of the section of buttons and toggles of the control panel, and also the block of interrogation of keyboard sections of the control panel, realized on microchips ИР22 and ИД7.
8. The output unit implemented on the registers ИР 27, ИД 3 and ИД 7 decoders, as well as the buffer elements HCF4050BE.
9. The optoelectronic isolation block, implemented on optotriacs (triode for alternating current) MOC3041, manufactured by "Motorola".

The operation of the "Ural-1" computer was demonstrated to all categories of museum visitors until the closure of the main building of the Polytechnic Museum for major overhaul in 2014. The following mathematical problems were proposed for solving: demonstration of binary number system, demonstration of counting and displaying numbers in Gray code, demonstration of addition of small integer binary numbers, demonstration of operations of subtraction and multiplication based on addition operation, game "Guess Number," game "Tic-Tac-Toe," demonstration of the normalization of fractional numbers with a fixed point and obtaining floating-point numbers. The language of the intermediate presentation of the Ural-1 computer programs, called UASM'07 (Ural Assembler), was specially developed for this demonstration complex. An automatic translator of this language in the machine codes has also been developed.

3.2 Documentary Collection

The exhibits of the collection "Electronic digital computing machines' of the Polytechnic Museum were complemented and supplemented by a documentary in printed and pictorial materials [4–6]. From 1989, the museum implemented the program "History of Engineering Thought in Russia". One of its goals was the creation of a database on the heritage of outstanding Russian scientists. The results of this program were reflected in the series of publications "Problems of Cultural Heritage in the Field of Engineering".

Within the framework of this program, items related to the biography, scientific and official activities of the computer creators in the Soviet Union and Russia were collected and continue to be collected. An important component of the documentary collection is the personal documentary collections of the founders of domestic computer technics.

We opened fourteen personal documentary collections on "Domestic Science and Engineering Schools in the Field of Computing and Informatics." The Polytechnic museum holds documentary collections of academician S. A. Lebedev, academician V. M. Glushkov, corresponding member of the USSR Academy of Sciences I. S. Brook, his disciples – M. A. Kartsev and N. Ya. Matyuhin, talented creator Rameev and Yu. Ya. Bazilevskiyi, the developer of the only ternary computer in the world, N. P. Brusentsov, mathematician S. N. Mergelyan, organizer and leader of the first in our country hydraulic analogies laboratory V. S. Lukyanova, Director of the Moscow Factory Accounting Machines V. S. Petrov, founders of the national school of cybernetics A. A. Lyapunov and A. I. Kitov and academician V. S. Burtsev.

Among the above-mentioned collections, the personal collection of B. Rameev is the most voluminous and unique in its content. The documents of this collection reflected the entire history of the creation and development of domestic electronic computers. Rameev was not only the constructor of a number of domestic computers, but for more than 20 years he was engaged in coordinating the development and application of domestic computers, assessing their technical level and efficiency, the formation of scientific and technical programs, and the creation of the State Collection for Algorithms and Programs. In 1971, B. Rameev moved to the *Main Department of Computer Technology and Control Systems* of the *USSR State Committee for Science and Technology*. Because Rameev became deputy head of this department, documents related to the state policy of the development of computer technics are presented from the 1960s to the early 1990s.

In 1994, the activity of the researchers of the Polytechnic Museum on the acquisition of the Rameev personal documentary collection was timed to coincide with the anniversary date - the 40th anniversary of his basic development of the "Ural-1" computer. Rameev personally took part in the selection of documentary materials from his archive. For him, the manuscripts of academicians S. A. Lebedev or A. I. Berg and the office notes of the Penza period were equally important. Probably, due to his accuracy, discipline and careful attitude to the "memory" of the documentary, Rameev managed to keep a rich archive – both in terms of importance and volume of documents. Unfortunately, for health reasons, Rameev was unable to complete the work begun. However, the firm decision to keep the archive exactly where his first and most important brainchild, "Ural-1," is located, has found understanding and support of Rameev's relatives. Until 1998, the wife of the scientist, Vera Ivanovna Rameeva, continued to work with the museum. For four years, from 1994 to 1998, 438 items of storage were transferred, and the number of sheets of the documentary collection totals about tenthousand.

In 1999, after systematization and scientific processing, the personal collection of B. Rameev was opened at the Polytechnic Museum [17]. It included items of clothing stock – the student's briefcase, the logarithmic ruler, the folder for papers, the Badge of Honored Inventor of the Russian Soviet Federated Socialist Republic, the Medal of the Exhibition of Achievements of the National Economy, etc. The most valuable items are the badge of the USSR State Prize and the Order of the Labor Red Banner.

The first textbooks on electronic digital machines by A. I Kitov and programming by V. N. Bondarenko, I. T. Plotnikov and P. P. Polozov were included in the collection of printed publications. They mainly document operational experience of "Ural" series computers and the development of their software. Also, famous domestic scientists and designers M. A. Kartsev, N. P. Brusentsov, and others are among the authors of the books of the Rameev's collection. The most unique printed publications include the materials of the conference "Ways of the Development of Mathematical Engineering and Instrument Making" (1956) and the abstracts of the reports of the Vth All-Union meeting of users of the "Ural" computers (1966). The individual books have the stamp with the inscription "From the books of B. I. Rameev". The publications with the dedications from authors and users of the "Ural" computers are of great interest. They testify the wide scientific, business and friendly contacts between specialists (Fig. 7).

For an unknown reason, Rameev handed over a small part of his documents about himself to the *State Museum of Political History of Russia* in St. Petersburg. In the collections of this museum items like: a leaflet of a candidate for deputy of the Penza Regional Industrial Council of Workers' Deputies (1963), a membership card of the All-Union Society of Inventors (1935), Rameev's letter to chief of the Office for Inventions and Discoveries of the USSR Council of Ministers with a request for the resumption and revision of the case of a high-speed digital computer for the integration of differential equations (1950), and some others are stored.

Throughout his professional life, Rameev actively communicated with the leading developers of electronic computers in the Soviet Union. In particular, Rameev worked with Academician A. P. Ershov [18] on software issues. The archive of this scientist is stored in the *Institute of Informatics Systems of the Siberian Branch of the Russian Academy of Sciences* [19]. It contained documents on the AutoCode project for a number of "Ural" computers, a single programming language for the "Ural" family of computers; on the draft technical specification of the software systems of the Unified Computer System "Ryad-3"; documents related to the work of the *Interdepartmental Scientific and Technical Commission on Software of the State Committee of the Council of Ministers of the USSR on Science and Technology*; documents on the reception of the delegation from the United States and so on.

Rameev's documentary archive, together with pictorial sources, was collected and formed personally by scientist throughout his creative work. The main custodian of the sources of Rameev's creative heritage in Russia is the Polytechnic Museum [17]. A brief description of his personal documental fund is given in the Appendix. Rameev's granddaughter Anna Belkina-Tentler was doing a cartoon about him and published an article entitled "System Preferences: Animated Documentary about B. I. Rameev" [20]

4   Conclusion

Bashir Rameev fulfilled one of the key roles in the creation of domestic electronic computers and in the computerization of the Soviet Union. He left valuable legacy in the form of his developments of the family of universal automatic machines "Ural," a whole computer family with advanced software.

The main features of the new generation of computers embodied in the new series of "Ural," briefly boil down to the following. The machines of different capacities must be constructive, schematic and software compatible with each other. They should have a flexible block structure and a wide range of devices with a standard connection method, which allows selecting the computers package most suitable for a particular application and maintain the machine parameters in the process of operation at the level of changing customer needs and new device developments.

The exceptional merit of Rameev was the creation in the USSR not of individual computers, but of a whole family of computers compatible with software, the production of which he put on an industrial basis. Later, the institute created by Rameev in Penza was the "forge of cadres" for many institutes of computer technology in a number of cities of the Soviet Union. At the *Main Administration of Computer Technology and Control Systems of the State Committee on Science and Technology of the USSR* he was in charge of building an extensive system of computer facilities by organizing automated management systems for planning and processing information for various purposes and creating a state network of computer centers, united by communication channels. It is impossible to overestimate the contribution of Rameev to domestic electronic computing equipment. His name should be preserved in the history of Russia.

5 Appendix

5.1 Rameev's Inventions

1935	Rameev constructed the radio-controlled model of an armored train that moved along rails, shot a cannon, created a smoke screen. He presented it at a contest in Moscow. At the age of 17, he became a member of the All-Union Society of Inventors
1940–41	Rameev proposed the method for detecting darkened objects from an airplane by infrared radiation passing through the curtained windows. He also invented a relay device for turning on loudspeakers in case of an air alarm
1945–46	Rameev invented the device for accelerating charged particles (USSR author's certificate No. 74398)
1948–49	Together with I. S. Brook, Rameev submitted more than 50 patents for inventions of various Automatic Digital Computing Machines, part of which were issued USSR author's certificates. He proposed the project of the "Electronic Digital Analyzer" (USSR author's certificate No. 15153)
1948	Together with I. S. Brook, Rameev received the first USSR author's certificate No. 10475 from 4.12.1948 on the Automatic Digital Computing Machine
1950	Rameev developed a draft design electronic computer "Strela"
1949–54	Rameev participated in the development of the first domestic serial electronic computer "Strela" in SDB-245 (Special Engineering Bureau)
1951	Rameev began to give lectures on digital computer technology to the fifth-year students of the Moscow Institute of Mechanics
1953	Rameev chose a key method for developing small universal digital machines for engineering calculations: unification of circuit, constructive and technological solutions. The symmetrical trigger on a 6H8S tube, tested as the main element of the "Strela," became the basis for all new machines. Rameev made new decisions on the construction of panels, frames-corpuses, on the power supply and cooling systems of machines and others decisions [7–9]
1954	A team of developers, including B. Rameev, received the State Bounty for the first domestic serial electronic computer "Strela"

(continued)

(*continued*)

1955–68	In Penza under the leadership of B. I. Rameev, universal electronic computers "Ural-1-4," (1955–1961), specialized machines "Weather," "Crystal," "Granite," M-17, M-27, M-30, M-46, M-56 (1954–1961) and universal computers "Ural - 11, 14, 16" (1964–1969) were developed. The main characteristics of the universal electronic computers "Ural" and the number of machines produced by year are given in Appendices 5.1 and 5.2
1963	For the first time in the USSR, Rameev proposed the principle of building computers and computer systems in the form of a number of software and information compatible machines. They were of various performance and completeness, built on the single element base with standardly connected peripheral devices. This principle was implemented in the models "Ural - 11, 14, 16" and the digital computers of subsequent generations
1965–68	He participated in the creation of systems for collective use and computer networks, as well as in the creation of automatized control system (ACS): "Bank", "Stroitel", "Lotus"
1968	Rameev suggested creating a number of software and constructively compatible computers based on the architecture of the System 4 family of the English firm ICL (International Computers Limited)
1971–94	Rameev was engaged in assessing the technical level of domestic digital computers, the formation of scientific and technic computerization programs in Russia and the creation of the State Collection for Algorithms and Programs

5.2   Main Characteristics of Universal Electronic Computers "Ural"

With an occupied area of about 70 m^2, the Ural-1 machine contained more than 838 electron tubes, consumed about 7 kW of power and was able to perform 100 operations per second: addition, subtraction, transition and multiplication. The division operation was performed four times slower. The operative memory was realized on a magnetic drum. Its capacity was 1024 machine words or about 4.5 kB. A punched tape drive and a magnetic tape drive were used for data input and output of programs and data. The usual medium at that time was punched tape. An engineering control panel was used to control the machine. The machine printed the solution of a problem on a narrow strip of paper. A detailed technical description of the Small Universal Automatic Electronic Computer "Ural-1" can be found on the Virtual Computer Museum website [21].

	Ural-1	Ural-2	Ural-3-4
Components	Electron valve circuits and diode-resistor gates		
Arithmetic	One-address binary arithmetic with a fixed and floating point		
Performance	100 op/sec	5 000–6 000 op/sec	5 000–10,000 op/sec

(*continued*)

(continued)

	Ural-1	Ural-2	Ural-3-4
Memory	RAM: magnetic drum (1024 36-bit codes), magnetic tape storage ROM; punched tape storage	RAM: ferrite core memory (2048 40-36-bit codes), sampling time – 30 μs ROM: magnetic tape and magnetic drum storage	RAM: ferrite core memory (2048 40-36-bit codes), sampling time – 15 μs ROM: magnetic tape and 8 magnetic drum storage
Peripherals	Perforated film tape unit, printer	Perforated film tape unit, printer	Perforated card unit, alphanumeric printer, telegraph tape unit
Software	Testing programs and control tasks		

	Ural-11 (6 modifications)	Ural-14 (some modifications)	Ural-16
Components	Unified complex of logical components "URAL-10" - semiconductor circuits-modules		
Arithmetic	One-address binary and decimal arithmetic with a fixed point		One-address binary arithmetic with a fixed and floating point
Performance range for various tasks	14,000–50,000 o/sec	2 900–45,000 o/sec	30,000–80,000 o/sec
Memory	RAM: ferrite core memory (4096–16384 24-bit codes); ROM: magnetic tape and magnetic drum storage	RAM: ferrite core memory (8192–65536 24-bit codes); ROM: magnetic tape and magnetic drum storage	RAM: ferrite core memory (8192–65536 48-bit codes); ROM: magnetic tape and magnetic drum storage
Peripherals	Devices for preparation of punched cards, tapes and their control, devices for reading punched cards and tapes, devices for printing, device for converting continuous quantities into discrete, magnetic drum and tape, communication channels, sensors of continuous quantities, printing devices and recorders		
Software	Special translator from ALGAMS language to ARMU (Automatic-code Row (line) of URAL computers), testing, library and debugging programs for the ARMU language		

5.3   Issuance of Universal Electronic Computers "Ural"

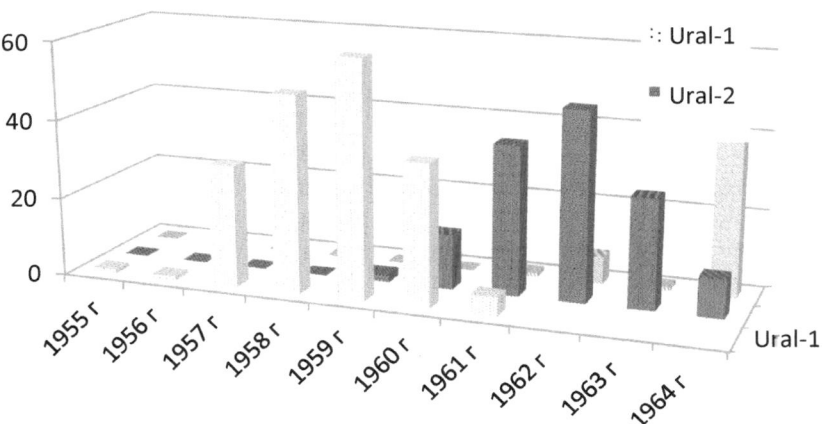

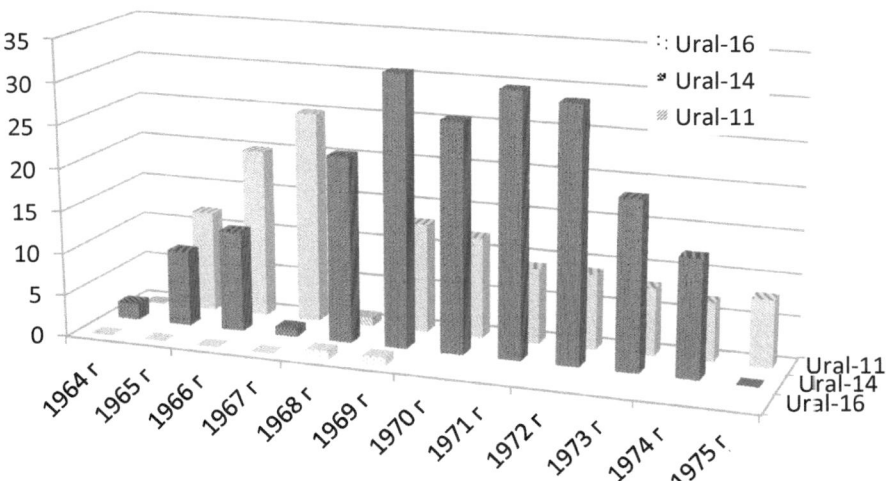

5.4   The Rameev Documentary and Visual Materials Collection in the Polytechnic Museum

The Rameev documentary and visual materials collection (numbers on the Polytechnic Museum Book of receipts: No. 27108/115-438), after studying and systematizing, was divided into the following sections:

I. Rameev Biographical Materials

- I.1. Documents on education (1933–1963 years, No. 27108/115-128): certificates from the place of study, test books, certificates, etc. The documents of school years are unique: the account card about academic achievement, the school certificate, the characteristic. One of the valuable documents is the Diploma of Doctor of Science MTH No. 000627.
- I.2. Service certificates and badges (1951–1991 years, No 27108/129-141): the certificate of a lecturer, the certificate of the deputy of the Penza Regional Council of Working People's Deputies; the certificates of the Chief Engineer of the Scientific Research Institute of Control Computers, the Deputy Head of the State Committee for Radio Electronics, the Deputy Chairman of the Scientific and Technical Council of the USSR State Committee for Computer Science and Informatics, etc.
- I.3. The characteristics and the references from the place of work, the documents for conferring the title "Honored Inventor of the Russian Soviet Federated Socialist Republic (RSFSR)," for the degree of Doctor of Technical Sciences, documents for nomination to corresponding members of the USSR Academy of Sciences, for the receipt of the certificate of the participant in the war (1951–1991 years, No. 27108/142-148) - letters of application, lists of inventions and scientific papers, certificates of scientific activity, comments, testimonials, etc. The manuscripts and autographs of academicians S. A. Lebedeva, M. V. Keldysh, A. I. Berg, Corr. I. S. Brook, D. Sc. A. A. Lyapunov are of great interest.
- I.4. The work book, the personal pensioner's book, the autobiographies, the questionnaires, the achievement list, the service record, the visiting card (1939–1986 years, No. 27108/149-156) - the documents those written by B. I. Rameev are the most valuable.

Fig. 7. The books on programming for the "Ural" computers. *Polytechnic Museum, Personal Documentary Collection of B. Rameev No 221.*

- I.5. Certificates, award documents, lists of awards (1938–1994 years, No 27108/157-170) – the certificates of awarding medals of the Exhibition of Achievements of the National Economy, diploma of awarding the USSR State Prize laureate, order book of The Labor Red Banner, the certificate of Honored Inventor of the Russian Soviet Federated Socialist Republic (Fig. 8), the application to the Commemorative Medal in honor of the successful completion of the "Intercosmos" program, the certificate of the Honorary Citizen of New Orleans (USA). The history of obtaining the title "Honorary Citizen of New Orleans" by Rameev would have been clarified.

Fig. 8. The certificate of Rameev "Honored Inventor of the RSFSR" of the Supreme Soviet Presidium of the RSFSR. *Polytechnic Museum, Personal Documentary Collection of B. Rameev No 221.*

- I.6. The materials of anniversaries (1968–1988 years, No 27108/171-182) – the congratulatory addresses in honor of 50-, 60- and 70-year anniversaries from the leading institutes and enterprises of the industry. The congratulations on the 50th anniversary of the 111 employees of the Department No. 5 of the Penza Research Institute of Mathematical Machines with their autographs (the calculation and printing on the "Ural-14" computer) is the most original.
- I.7. Other documents (1947–1988, No. 27108/183-189): references, applications, medical insurance, etc. The note by Academician A. I. Berg with recommendations, what medicines you need to have with you is of interest.

II. Creative Materials

- II.1. Monographs, articles, texts of speeches (1946–1991 years, No. 27108/190-215). Among the above documents it is necessary, first of all, to single out the project "Automatic digital computer," carried out in conjunction with I. S. Brook, as well as "Project considerations for the organization of a special design bureau for the development and construction of the Automatic Digital Computing Machine. The Advance project of the family of Ural-type automatic digital computers ("Ural-11," "Ural-12," "Ural-13," "Ural-14," "Ural-15") in five parts and the "Ural project - 25" are of unconditional interest. These documents reflected the genius of B. Rameev, as the general designer of computers.
- II.2. The descriptions of Rameev's inventions (1947 – 195 years, No. 27108/216-218) – the mostly manuscripts, with author's diagrams and drawings, with autographs.
- II.3. Documents on inventive activity (1940–1949 years, No 27108/219-230) – the acts, the conclusions, the letters of the Department for Inventions and Discoveries with descriptions of inventions, expert opinions; there are manuscripts and autographs on 11 inventions.
- II.4. The applications for the receipt of USSR author's certificate (1957–1958 years, № 27108/231) – the materials on 7 inventions.
- II.5. Author's certificates, certificates of registration of inventions (1941–1963 years, No. 27108/232-233) - 23 copyright certificates of B. Rameev (on "Automatic Digital Computing Machine," separate devices, blocks, nodes, etc.) and 5 certificates of registration of inventions ("Ural-1," "Ural-2," "Kristall" computers, etc.).
- II.6. The materials on the computer series "Ural" (1956–1973 years, No. 27108/234-259) – the documents related to the development, production and practical use of a computer series "Ural," the comparative author's analysis of the computers "Ural" with foreign similar computers, the prospects for the development of the "Ural-25" computer. The acts of interdepartmental testing of computer software systems for Ural-14 and Ural-16 computers and Ural-14 and Ural-16 machines (1970–1971), calculations for the Ural-14 computer the forecast of the game of hockey players in the world championships and Europe (1973) are of interest.
- II.7. Reviews and reviews B. Rameev on the work of other persons (1962–1965 years, No. 27108/260).
- II.8. Working drawings (1948, No. 27108/261-262) – The flowchart of the "Automatic Digital Computing Machine" is unique. It is author's drawing.
- II.9. Notebooks, working scientific diaries (1955–1989, No. 27108/263-309) - contain manuscripts related to official and scientific activities, information on cooperation with International Computer Limited, entries in English, sketches of diagrams, drawings and so on.

III. Materials of Official, Pedagogical, Scientific and Public Activities

- III.1. Disposal documents, plans, schedules, memos, working certificates, etc. (1952–1980 years, No. 27108/310-338) are concerned with the official activities of B. Rameev, beginning with the post of head of the Laboratory No. 31 SDB-245

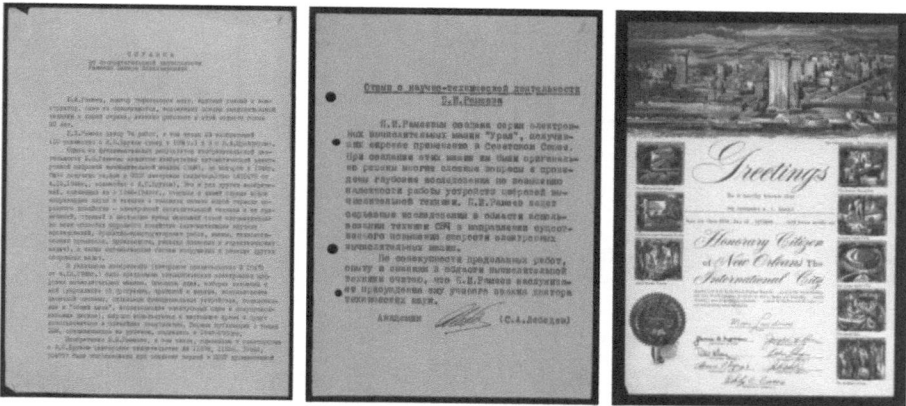

Fig. 9. The documents from Rameev's collection at *Polytechnic Museum, No 221.*

(Moscow) to the Chief Engineer of the Research Institute of Mathematical Machines (Penza), with autographs of B. Rameev, Y. Ya. Bazilevskiyi, M. A. Lesechko and other persons (Fig. 9).

- III.2. Materials on the creation of the Unified Computer System (UCS) and the problem of copying IBM-360 (1968–1993, No. 27108/339-348) - documents (draft decisions, minutes of meetings, certificates, etc.) with comments and notes of B. Rameev. The Minutes of Meetings Concerning the Copy of IBM 360 Machines dated December 4, 1969 and December 18, 1969, written down by B. Rameev, as well as the Terms of Reference for the development of hardware and software for the UCS (manuscript V. K. Levin with a note of B. Rameev from 15.02.93 after his stroke) are of interest.
- III.3. Materials on the cooperation of the State Committee of the USSR Council of Ministers for Science and Technology with the Ministry of Radio Industry of the USSR and the English firm International Computers Limited (ICL) (1969–1970 years, No. 27108/349-350) - protocols of meetings, policy directives, cooperation agreement, working translations, etc.
- III.4. Materials on Soviet-American cooperation in the use of computers in management (1972–1974 years, No. 27108/351) - work plan and report on the activities of the Joint Soviet-American Working Group.
- III.5. Materials on the creation and development of the computer such as Iskra-226 (1981, No. 27108/352) - the protocol of the technical meeting, letters, computer distribution plan, reference.
- III.6. Materials on the concepts "Informatization of society" and "Development of personal computers" (1987–1989, No. 27108/373-386) - regulations, resolutions and minutes of the sessions of the USSR State Committee on Computer Science, reports of the Interbranch Science and Technology Complex "Personal computers."

Fig. 10. The friendly cartoon on the occasion of awarding Rameev the title of Doctor of Technical Sciences, with poems. The black and white drawing: Rameev in school years. *Polytechnic Museum, Personal Documentary Collection of B. Rameev No 221.*

- III.7. Materials transmitted by B. I. Rameyev for work (1958–1992, No. 27108/361-373), - instructions, recommendations, suggestions, concepts, solutions, photocopies of documents, express information, references, reports, articles by G. I. Marchuk and other persons.

- III.8. Pedagogical activity (1951–1953, No 27108/381-385) - programs of lectures, abstracts, exam cards on the course "Automatic computing devices of discrete action" in Moscow Institute of Physics and Technology (mostly manuscript).

IV. Correspondence

Correspondence is systematized according to the following headings: letters to B. I. Rameev (1957–1967, No. 27108/386-394), letters from B.I. Rameev (1951–1966, No. 27108/395-399), correspondence between the responsible persons related to Rameev (1953–1985, No. 27108/400–404). There are letters of official and creative nature, among the correspondents of Academician V. M. Glushkov and N. P. Fedorenko, Professor N. Panin, and others, as well as the Glavtochmash enterprise, Numbered plant 732-a, The Plant of Counting and Analytical Machines, SDB-245, and others. The letter from Numbered plant M-5539 with the report on use of "Ural- 11" and "Ural-14" under the program "Soyuz-Apollo" and "Rainbow" is interest of particular.

V. Fine Materials

Pencil black and white and color drawings:

- B. Rameev in the school years (1930–1935) (Fig. 10).
- Friendly cartoon and congratulations on the occasion of awarding Rameev the title of Doctor of Technical Sciences with poems (1963) (Fig. 10).

Black-and-white photographs are included (1930–1987 years, No. 27108/405–434):

- B. Rameev for adjusting the Ural-1 computer, at the meeting of the Council for Mutual Economic Assistance (CMEA), in the Mission Control Center, in the staff of the State Committee for Computing Engineering, portraits of different years (1952–1997).
- The team of developers of the computer "Strela" (1955).
- Portraits of the staff of the Penza Research Institute of Mathematical Machines, the creators of the "Ural" series computer (1970 year).
- General view of the computer series "Ural" (1955–1978), etc.

VI. Materials Collected by the Collection Maker

Booklets, books, documents, etc., concerning memorable facts and events in the life of Rameev are included (1951–1982 years, No. 27108/435-437):

- The jubilee collection for the 100th anniversary of the New York Times (in English).
- The flight program of the "Soyuz T-6" spacecraft (June 24, 1982), etc.

VII. Materials of Other Persons

The album of poems with the dedication inscribed by the author - an employee of the Penza Research Institute of Mathematical Machines V. I. Burkov, who for many years worked together with B. Rameev and participated in the development of a series of computers "Ural" (1979 year, № 27108/438).

References

1. Wolcott, P.: Soviet advanced technology: the case of high-performance computing". Dissertation, The University of Arizona (1993). https://repository.arizona.edu/handle/10150/136298. Accessed 31 Jan 2019
2. Bochannek, A.: What did the Americans know? A review of select periodicals. In: Материалы второй Международной конференции Развитие вычислительной техники и ее программного обеспечения в России и странах бывшего СССР, SoRuCom Великий Новгород (2011). http://www.computer-museum.ru/document/sorucom2011_0.htm. Accessed 31 Jan 2019
3. Eduard Proydakov's project. http://www.computer-museum.ru. Accessed 31 Jan 2019
4. Smolevitskaya, M.: The Informatics and Computer Technologies Heritage in Russia. http://tcc.proceedings.com/36614webtoc.pdf
5. Smolevitskaya, M.: The computers' collection at the polytechnic museum. In: Tatnall, A., Blyth, T., Johnson, R. (eds.) HC 2013. IAICT, vol. 416, pp. 53–63. Springer, Heidelberg (2013). https://doi.org/10.1007/978-3-642-41650-7_5
6. Smolevitskaya, M.: The personal documentary funds of the computer technology founders at the polytechnic museum. In: Kimppa, K., Whitehouse, D., Kuusela, T., Phahlamohlaka, J. (eds.) HCC 2014. IAICT, vol. 431, pp. 203–213. Springer, Heidelberg (2014). https://doi.org/10.1007/978-3-662-44208-1_17
7. Малиновский Б.Н. История вычислительной техники в лицах. – Киев: фирма « КИТ, ПТОО « А.С.К., 1995, с. 233–289. Malinovskiy, B.N.: History of Computers in Persons, pp. 233–289. KIT, Kiev (1995)
8. Бадрутдинова М.: «История жизни замечательных людей России—Башира Искандаровича Рамеева, его отца и деда. Badrutdinova, M.S.: The life history of Russia remarkable people - Bashir Iskandarovich Rameev, his father and his grandfather." http://www.computer-museum.ru/galglory/rameev_hist.htm
9. Бадрутдинова М.:. « Разработки Б.И.Рамеева. Badrutdinova, M.S.: Developments of B. I Rameev. http://www.computer-museum.ru/galglory/rameev_5.htm
10. Смирнов, Г.: Семейство ЭВМ « Урал » . Страницы истории разработок.АО « НПП « Рубин Пенза.186 (2005)
11. Смирнов Г.: Рамеевская школа конструирования ЭВМ. История разработок в фотографиях. 1948–1972." Пенза, авторское издание, 252 (2009)
12. ЭВМ « Урал » в мире публикаций и документов 1945–1972. Библиографический указатель. http://www.computer-museum.ru/books/ural_biblio/1948.htm
13. http://www.computer-museum.ru/english/galglory_en/rameev.htm
14. Trogemann, G., Nitussov, A., Ernst, W. (eds.): Computing in Russia: The History of Computer Devices and Information Technology Revealed, pp. 143–158. Vieweg & Sohn Verlagsgesellsschaft mbH, Braunschweig (2001)
15. Bazilevskui, I.I.: The universal electronic digital machine (URAL) for engineering research. J. ACM (JACM) 4(4), 511–519 (1957)
16. Рамеев Б.: Универсальная автоматическая цифровая вычислительная машина типа "Урал" In: Пути развития советского машиностроения. http://www.computer-museum.ru/document/prog1956.htm
17. Polytechnic Museum, Personal Documentary Collection of B. I. Rameev No 221

18. http://ershov.iis.nsk.su/en/prj
19. http://ershov.iis.nsk.su
20. Belkina-Tentler, A.: System preferences: animated documentary about B.I. Rameev. In: Материалы второй Международной конференции Развитие вычислительной техники и ее программного обеспечения в России и странах бывшего СССР, SoRuCom. Великий Новгород (2011). http://www.computer-museum.ru/document/sorucom2011_0.htm
21. Urnev, I.: Electronic digital computer "Ural-1. http://www.computer-museum.ru/english/ural_1.php

Author Index